DIALOGUES
IN JUDAISM

ALSO BY RABBI WILLIAM BERKOWITZ

Conversation With

Let Us Reason Together

Heritage and Hope

Ten Vital Jewish Issues

Study Guide and Syllabus
    for Ten Vital Jewish Issues

I Believe: The Faith of a Jew

DIALOGUES

IN JUDAISM

Jewish Dilemmas
Defined, Debated, and Explored

EDITED BY

William Berkowitz

JASON ARONSON INC.

Northvale, New Jersey
London

Production Editor: *Adelle Krauser*
Editorial Director: *Muriel Jorgensen*
Interior Designer: *Ernie Haim*

This book was set in 10 point Palatino
by Alpha Graphics of Pittsfield, New Hampshire,
and printed and bound by Haddon Craftsmen of
Scranton, Pennsylvania.

Library of Congress Cataloging-in-Publication Data

Dialogues in Judaism: Jewish dilemmas defined, debated, and
explored / edited by William Berkowitz.
    p. cm.
  Includes index.
  ISBN 0-87668-654-4
  1. Judaism—20th century. 2. Judaism—United States. 3. Jews—
United States—Civilization. 4. Holocaust, Jewish (1939–1945)—
Influence. 5. Israel. I. Berkowitz, William.
BM42.J46 1991
296′.09′04—dc20   91-8732

Manufactured in the United States of America. Jason Aronson
Inc. offers books and cassettes. For information and catalog write
to Jason Aronson Inc., 230 Livingston Street, Northvale, New
Jersey 07647.

To Herbert Tenzer

This book is dedicated with great esteem to a man whose life has been the embodiment of the Jewish values that are the unique contribution of our people to civilization. In a career spanning sixty years, Herbert Tenzer has been involved in the fields of government, law, business, philanthropy, and education. In every instance, his concern for people has been the keynote of his activity, rooted in religiosity and built on the cornerstone of family and faith.

The son of an immigrant family, Herbert Tenzer as a boy at the turn of the century learned the lesson of *tzedakah* from his father, who kept a supply of pennies in his cash register for people poorer than himself. An organization that Herbert Tenzer founded, Rescue Children, Inc., saved 2,200 orphans after World War II. One of the earliest supporters of Yeshiva University as well as one of its greatest benefactors, he was a major force in the development of that institution into a world-renowned center of comprehensive learning. At the same time, he was among the American Jewish leaders who took a primary role in galvanizing Jewry to strengthen and support the Jewish State.

As a Member of Congress, Herbert Tenzer was the model of what a Congressman should be: he served his constituency and enacted legislation to enhance the quality of life of the American people.

In all, some fifty organizations, both Jewish and non-Jewish, have benefited over the years from Herbert Tenzer's interest in the welfare of his fellow man. Indeed, the dedication of a book to a person of such great accomplishments is a small tribute. It does, in fact, pay more honor to the author and the book than to the man to whom it is dedicated. Nonetheless, this dedication is a heartfelt token of the admiration and affection felt by the author for a man who stands as a giant in American Jewish life.

✄ Contents

Preface   xiii

Acknowledgment   xix

PART I   Judaism: Dimensions of Practice

Introduction   3

1.   The Judaism of Tomorrow   5

Rabbi David I. Golovensky
The Orthodox Tradition: The former president of
the New York Board of Rabbis gives telling arguments for the maintenance of Jewish Orthodoxy.

Rabbi Edward E. Klein
Reform Response to Today: One direction taken by
Judaism in the past 100 years is charted by a noted
Reform rabbi.

Rabbi William Berkowitz
The Conservative Approach: "Conservative" is a
means of conserving Jewish concepts, according to
the moderator of the Dialogue Series.

2. Reconstructionism   *27*

Rabbi Mordecai Menachem Kaplan
"Organic Judaism" is seen as a melding of Jewish
norms and 20th-century American communal concerns, by the founder of the Reconstructionist movement and the Society for the Advancement of Judaism.

3. Luminary for the Centuries   *47*

Rabbi Adin Steinsaltz
Jewish renewal is seen through the eyes of a modern
scholar who has given a new focus to age-old pages
of Talmud, mysticism, and myriad aspects of Jewish
spirituality.

4. The Joy of Judaism   *63*

Rabbi Zalman Schachter-Shalomi
A Chasid in modern garb shares a modern view of
the movement that swept European Jewry in the last
century.

5. The Scholarship of Religion   *85*

Dr. Joseph L. Blau
The place of an ancient religious tradition in the
modern world poses questions that are discussed by
a professor of religion at Columbia University who
has achieved an outstanding reputation as a scholar,
teacher, author, and speaker.

PART II   Different Jews, Different Views

Introduction   *105*

6. Religion and Psychiatry   *107*

Dr. Mortimer Ostow
A nationally prominent practicing psychoanalyst,
Visiting Professor Emeritus and former chairman of

the Department of Pastoral Psychiatry at the Jewish
Theological Seminary, sees the two disciplines but-
tressing each other.

7.   Humorist with a Serious Side   *129*

Sam Levenson
The American Jewish family, which gave the comedian so much material to make us smile, provides
food for thought as he tells of growing up in a Jewish
household and contrasts life in his boyhood days
with the world we know today.

8.   Champion of Pluralism   *145*

Professor Horace M. Kallen
Jews today successfully straddle two cultures, ac-
cording to the founder of the New School for Social
Research, a philosopher who was the colleague of
George Santayana, William James, and Charles A.
Beard.

9.   Beyond the Jewish Façade   *167*

Dr. Nahum Goldmann
The face that our people presents to the world is
discussed by an Israeli statesman, former president
of the World Zionist Organization and of the World
Jewish Congress.

10.   A Great Novelist   *187*

Isaac Bashevis Singer
The only Yiddish writer ever to receive the Nobel
Prize for Literature discusses his background, ideas,
and feelings.

11.   The Glorious Jewish Past   *205*

Max I. Dimont
The historian whose best-selling book, *Jews, God and
History*, did much to lift American Jews from their

post-Holocaust depression describes how we can use history in considering world events.

PART III   Six Million Were Murdered. . . .

Introduction   *229*

12. Nazis Face Justice   *231*

Judge Michael A. Musmanno
The American jurist who presided at the trial of the most infamous of Hitler's henchmen recounts some lessons learned from the case of Adolf Eichmann.

13. Intrepid and Selfless People   *249*

Marie Syrkin
The rescue of Jews from the Nazis through the efforts of the small Jewish community in pre-state Palestine is recounted by a world-renowned author.

14. The World Watched, Uncaring   *269*

Arthur Morse
The author of *While Six Million Died*, a distinguished writer who documented the Holocaust period, discusses how the free world's indifference to the fate of doomed Jews contributed greatly to the tragedy.

15. Seeker after Justice   *295*

Elie Wiesel
Kol Yisrael Aravim Zeh baZeh is the message of this Holocaust survivor, author, lecturer, Andrew Mellon Professor in the Humanities at Boston University, world traveler, recipient of the Nobel Peace Prize, and spokesman on behalf of all who suffered in the Nazi terror.

16. Averting a Second Holocaust   *317*

Professor Emil L. Fackenheim
A scholar who himself escaped the terror one step ahead of the Nazis analyzes factors that made possible the unique genocide of the World War II period,

and speaks of memories that today hold Jews together against another such catastrophe.

PART IV   Israel: Crossroads of the World

Introduction   *339*

17.   Self-Silenced Leader   *341*

Menachem Begin
The leader of the underground in pre-state Palestine,
who rose to become Prime Minister of Israel and
then retired in seclusion, gives his views on his nation and the world.

18.   Jerusalem, Capital of the World   *361*

Teddy Kollek
The challenges of leading a city that has a special
place in the hearts of all religions are described by a
creative social planner who is the perennial Mayor of
Jerusalem.

19.   Serving a Nation under Constant Stress   *379*

Ariel Sharon
Israel and the Diaspora are two sides of the coin to
this great modern leader, a founder of the State and
a former cabinet minister, who sees Israel as a "project of the whole Jewish people," in which the problems of politics, defense, *aliyah*, and *yeridah* are all
intertwined.

20.   Jewish Interdependence   *393*

Avraham Harman
A witty and perceptive view of life, law, and religion
here and there is provided by Israel's former ambassador to the United States, who went on to serve the
Hebrew University in Jerusalem as its president and
now its chancellor.

PART V   The Next 4,000 Years

Introduction   *415*

21. A Cure for Pessimism   417

Dr. Cecil Roth
What Jewish history can teach us is expounded by a
foremost educator and historian who has authored
600 articles and books, was a professor at Bar-Ilan
University, and was editor-in-chief of *The Encyclopaedia Judaica.*

22. All Humanity on Trial   437

Dr. Henry Kissinger
The former U.S. Secretary of State, who as a child
was a refugee from Germany and went on to be
named Nobel Laureate for Peace, presents the world
view for the future.

23. Judaism in the Year 2090   463

Dr. Sol Liptzin
The Honorary President of the Jewish Book Council
and long-time faculty member of the City College of
New York, he made *aliyah* in 1962 and became a
visiting professor at The Hebrew University.

C. Bezalel Sherman
Labor Zionist theoretician and noted sociologist, he is
a well-known author and lecturer. These two prominent Jews take a short leap forward in Jewish history
and consider the Jewish place "among the nations."

24. Shall Jews Missionize?   487

Rabbi David Max Eichhorn
The former director of Field Operations of the Jewish
Welfare Board Commission on Jewish Chaplaincy, he
was an Army Chaplain during World War II.

Rabbi Immanuel Jakobovits
The Chief Rabbi of Great Britain is the former Chief
Rabbi of Ireland and was also the Rabbi of New York's
Fifth Avenue Synagogue. These two prominent rabbis
recall that Judaism historically sought converts and
discuss the implications of a new Jewish stance on the
matter.

Index   509

❧ Preface

Returning home from a lecture I had arranged, my wife and I were discussing the evening's program. The guest speaker was a noted personality and an authority in his field; the subject dealt with current concerns. Yet for forty-five minutes the lecture had been boring, uninspired, and full of digressions. Then, after the speaker finished his formal presentation, I began the question-and-answer period and it was as though someone had flipped a switch. The mood changed in an instant. The audience stopped being passive and fidgety. The speaker himself—no longer tied to his text—seemed to come alive. We had forty-five minutes of spirited give-and-take.

When we arrived home, my wife posed a pair of questions: "Why do people have to wait for forty-five minutes until you come to the best part of the evening? And what would happen if you were to forego the formal part of the program and devote the whole ninety minutes exclusively to questions and answers?"

Thus was born the idea of a dialogue as a form of adult education. It evolved into a format based on carefully planned interviews that were based on a series of probing questions, eliciting the kinds of answers that enlighten, edify, and inspire audiences.

Now this format was unique for its time and place. When I introduced it to the speaker's platform some forty years ago, the Socratic method of teaching was unknown in popular programming. Even television, then in its earlier days and seeking innovative ideas, did not explore this kind of communication.

What the Dialogue did for the audience was to transform each listener from a passive object who was talked *to*, into an active participant in the program. The idea gained enormous popularity over the ensuing years, and Dialogues are now heard from every platform.

As I honed and refined the format, I learned a number of fundamental truths. The Dialogue is deceptively simple, but its success depends on several important factors.

First, as important as the answers given by the "expert" are the questions posed by the moderator. Therefore, a great deal of preparation must precede the actual Dialogue. The interviewer must be able to probe the expertise of the guest, and even to lead the speaker into relevant areas beyond his or her specialty.

Research and more research is the *sine qua non*. What factors in the background of our guest has led him or her to pursue this field? What published material has he or she recently produced on the subject? What opinions has he or she expressed in print? What have other authorities in the field had to say on the subject? On the speaker? What questions—based on all of this information—would members of the audience want to ask the speaker if they were sitting together over coffee?

Moreover, whenever I have been engaged in research, one question has always been paramount to me: What exactly do forty centuries of Jewish tradition have to offer to Jews living in the twentieth century? How do the colorings of Jewish culture ultimately affect the patterns of Jewish lives in today's America and today's world?

With all of this I have remained mindful of Socrates' definition of Dialogue: "The object of our discussion is not that my words may triumph over yours, or that yours may gain victory over mine, but that between us we may discover the perfect truth."

I have continually reminded myself that through my probing I wanted to discover the attitudes of the particular guest toward the important questions of the day, as well as the biographical factors that shaped these attitudes . . . and thus his or her career.

Actually, statements in response to penetrating questions are valuable on two counts. First, they make for interesting listening. After all, these are people who make headlines, who are the community's leaders, who shape opinions and set trends. Second, such statements can offer a guide for all of us when we wonder at times about which course to take and what the consequences of our decisions might be.

One additional characteristic of the Dialogue method is vital. It tends to dissolve the invisible curtain that normally separates speaker from audience. Through carefully planned questioning I have sought to elicit the kinds of information that the listener himself might want to obtain if he could talk personally with the person on the platform.

Another factor enters the equation. Basically, these national and international figures are not too different from the rest of us. They are parents, neighbors, everyday Jews. The listener gains some insight into how the speakers feel about issues that all of us face, why they hold the opinions they do, and how their experiences color their views of the yesterday, today, and tomorrow of the world. In listening, we are helped to reach our own conclusions about questions that may perplex us. Our own conclusions may be diametrically opposite to those held by the speaker of the moment—but we encourage the speaker to reveal his or her conclusions through a give-and-take process in which we have been a real part.

Over the past forty years of Dialogue, the persons I invited to share my platform—and there have been hundreds of them—have had a variety of backgrounds. They have come from the fields of art, politics, organizational life, science, philosophy, education, and entertainment. They have represented all shades of Jewish belief, from strict Orthodoxy to pure secularism, and several of them were not Jewish. But they have all had one thing in common—a firm commitment to the basic values of Judaism, which they have applied to the conduct of their daily affairs.

Because of my great respect for their status as independent thinkers, each guest has heard my questions for the first time when I posed them during a Dialogue. There was neither a previous briefing nor a rehearsal. As a result, the responses reflect a quality of frankness and honesty that would have been lost had there been any other format.

There has also resulted a sense of spontaneity that enhances, I believe, the communication between speaker and listener. I am always uneasy with the term *Moderator*, which is the only label I can put on my role in the Dialogues. Essentially, I am the *Listener*—and I am also the *voice* of the audience, speaking for the person in the sixteenth row right.

In the four decades during which I have been conducting the program, my contact with the prominent men and women who have agreed to share my platform has been truly gratifying. Most rewarding, however, has been the fact that they, in common with the audiences, found the experience stimulating and instructive. Some confessed to me that at first they had misgivings about the method. It required that they leave the security of prepared text and planned agenda, to venture out in an uncharted sea where any issue might be brought into the discussion, any question asked. It is a tribute to both the quality of the speakers and the intrinsic value of the method that a frequent comment after a Dialogue was, "I never experienced anything like this . . . I never felt such electricity in the air . . . I never sensed such rapport with each listener!"

I had another significant conversation with my wife about the Dialogue programs well after they had been underway for some time. She had initially prodded me into changing the lecture format into the Dialogues; now she advanced another suggestion. She proposed that the interviews be tape-recorded so that one day I might put them into permanent form. Thus was born the idea of the Dialogue Books. There have already been five published volumes of these transcripts, containing many arresting insights into each speaker's work and experience. Taken together, they make up a rich and varied mosaic of the finest of modern thought. These volumes reveal a range and depth that—along with the speakers' absolute commitment to Jewish and humanist ideals and values—sets the collection apart from the ordinary anthology and makes these books important contemporary documents.

All five books are now out of print, but the kernels of thought that distinguish them are not lost. The present volume is a distillation of interesting and significant contributions from some of the many prominent personalities who spoke before our audiences. Readers of this volume may notice certain informalities of expression in these Dialogues that reflect the spoken form in which they originally occurred. These include variations in the Hebrew and Yiddish transliterations, which may be based on Sephardic and/or Modern Hebrew, Ashkenazic Hebrew and/or Yiddish, generally reflecting the different backgrounds and orientations of the speakers.

Reviewing the individual interviews preliminary to editing them for this book, I was struck by the way the material fell into distinctive categories of thought and inquiry. They seemed to suggest to me, almost spontaneously, the framework for a very comprehensive thematic presentation.

Also rewarding to me was the discovery that each Dialogue stood the test of time very well. Many of them might have been held just yesterday. Despite certain changes that have occurred in the world since some of these words were spoken, and certain changes in the lives and the roles of some of the speakers—even the death of some of them in the intervening years—these Dialogues retain a remarkable freshness and a striking relevance to the issues of the present day. I daresay that the reader, upon concluding this volume, will have a deeper insight into contemporary affairs, with particular emphasis on Jewish learning and thought, Jewish contributions to the contemporary world, and possibilities for modern Judaism.

On reflection, this volume suggests that the term *adult Jewish education* may be a misnomer. It sets learning for adults aside as some special kind of activity, to be called up at specific times for specific purposes. I do not accept this. It is axiomatic that we never stop learning as long as we live. It is true that, as we mature, certain techniques are more appropriate, certain subjects have greater meaning, certain values deserve greater stress. But I have always held that education for adults is the continuation of a process that begins at birth, and that becomes shaped in the course of time by special consideration for the needs and desires of people living in an adult workaday world, facing adult problems and looking for adult answers.

I hope that this book will fill, in part, these needs and desires of Jews living in twentieth-century America.

Although there are no final answers to the Jewish problems and issues discussed here, the clarification of the two sides (or more!) of every question can only enlarge an understanding of the subject. The discussions in this anthology will help define issues that concern us as modern Jews. Hopefully they will contribute to deeper knowledge and perhaps a new commitment to the Jewish people, to the Torah, and to God.

WILLIAM BERKOWITZ
New York City
Sivan 5751
May 1991

❧ Acknowledgment

More often than not, a book is the result of the efforts of a number of people. The author or the editor credited on the jacket may be a single name, but a book is the fruition of all who helped make publication possible. Therefore, I would like to acknowledge those who contributed to this work.

The Dialogue Series was, from its inception, a family adventure. My wife, Florence, was intimately involved across the years with every aspect of the program. Her suggestions helped to structure my pioneering efforts in the field of education and furrowed new paths for others to follow.

My middle child, Adena, in addition to other responsibilities involving the planning and promotion of each series, was given the task of picking up the guests at their hotels, escorting them to my study, and ensuring their safe return after the conclusion of the evening. She welcomed them most effectively and quickly put them at ease while briefing them about the format of the Dialogues. Having escorted the brilliant, famous, and powerful from all parts of the world, she recently remarked that she ought to write her own book, entitled *Men I Have Picked Up*.

My younger daughter, Leah, was given a very unique task. It happened that one of the elders of the community developed the habit of dropping in at my study each week half an hour before the arrival of the guest speaker. With the details of the program on my mind, I could not stop to chat with him, but neither could I insult him by ignoring him. Leah, recognizing my dilemma, contrived to be in my study when he arrived each week and acted as hostess to him. Her conversation delighted him, and she helped maintain my privacy when I needed it most. Of course, Leah was also deeply involved in the planning and promotion of the annual series.

However, the greatest burden fell to my son, Perry. He remained by my side from the moment that the guest accepted my invitation until the conclusion of the visit. His brilliance and scholarship, and his grasp of a myriad of subjects, were of inestimable help in the research necessary to each program. His help and attention to detail made me aware, as the Dialogues grew to national and international prominence, that one cannot do it all alone; I needed a competent, wise, and able associate, and Perry was that.

The moderator of a series of programs such as the Dialogues becomes very closely involved with the material over the years—so much so that a fresh and objective perspective becomes necessary. In preparing material for a new volume, one must make many decisions: what to include and what to omit, how to hone down a prolix conceptualization, how to best present the material, and how to project most effectively the impact of the material. While in the final analysis these decisions must be those of the author, the help of a good editor or editors is critical in maintaining objectivity and perspective. In this respect, I have been blessed with the help of several outstanding and very talented individuals. First, there is Mr. Philip Hochstein, who was for many years the editorial director of the Newhouse Publications. In later years he was publisher and editor of the *Jewish Week* in New York and Washington. This journal was welcomed in thousands of Jewish homes every week, and the quality of its news coverage, editorials, and columns made it a valued addition to Jewish life. I turned to this veteran journalist and seasoned editor for his help and experienced eye. He extended his hand, and he treated the project as a labor of love. I am exceedingly grateful to him not only for the part he played in bringing this volume to the light of day, but also for his friendship through the years. He is a wise and truly wonderful human being.

Second is Julian Jablin, a friend who has shared my delights and labors with these volumes for more than thirty years. I met him when I began to collect the material for *I Believe: The Faith of a Jew*, my first book of Dialogues. He was always there to advise, and he readily shared his journalistic background, his experience in public relations with the Jewish Welfare Board in New York and later with the Jewish Federation in Chicago, and his continued personal interest and involvement in

Jewish communal life. I am grateful for his assistance, and also for the manner in which he provided it—with composure, good humor, and a rare perceptiveness. I cherish his abiding friendship.

And one person whose contributions have been inestimable has requested anonymity, but I must express my deep thanks to him—a dear friend, an unusual and gifted teacher. I take pleasure in knowing that, as he reads these words, at least he will know to whom I refer. His wisdom, direction, guidance, and support have been extended to me without stint. He encouraged my efforts in the field of education as well as in other areas and provided the strongest motivation for continuing when my will began to flag. I will always treasure what he brought to my life.

I also want to thank my beloved friend Charles E. Smith for his inestimable help in initiating this project. He is a special kind of person in Jewish communal life. A man of this generation, he understands his connection with the traditional past of our people, and at the same time he feels his responsibility to the shaping of the future. He has translated the Jewish values of *tzedakah* and social justice from abstract concepts into positive action. The privilege of knowing him has been one of the great rewards of living and working in our community.

I must acknowledge with deep gratitude all of the many participants in these Dialogues. Most of them, thank God, are still with us. Knowing them and interviewing them has been a special privilege. As for those who have gone to the great beyond, I recall with fond memories my association with them. May their words and thoughts as recorded in these pages serve as testimony to their commitment to the enhancement of both Jewish life and the world at large.

Finally I must thank God, Who has sustained me to carry on this noble enterprise. His beneficence has given me determination, strength, and the understanding that each of us has been placed on earth to help Him complete the work of creation in our own special ways.

PART I

Judaism: Dimensions of Practice

ॐ Introduction

No era in the past 4,000 years of Jewish creativity has presented the Jewish people with greater challenges than the past two centuries—challenges to their religion, challenges to their philosophies, challenges to their very way of life.

The breakdown of the protective ghetto and the advent of the Industrial Revolution, occurring almost simultaneously with the Jewish Enlightenment, changed the whole character of Jewish experience. Adjustments to modern living, although often painful, were essential.

Most apparent, perhaps, have been the new directions in religious philosophy and practice taken by Jewish thinkers. As Jews entered the modern world, Jewish leaders were forced to reformulate their concepts of Judaism. Mid-nineteenth century Germany was indeed the locus of new, creative Jewish ideas. The great theologian, historian, and thinker Abraham Geiger, who laid the intellectual foundation of Reform Judaism, came from that milieu. The same era saw Zechariah Frankel shape the positive historical school, which was the forerunner of Conservative Judaism. Samson Raphael Hirsch, their contemporary, held fast to the traditional concept of God's revelation of the Torah on Sinai and won individuals and communities to modern Orthodoxy.

Echoes of these ideas resound in the America of the 1990s. Admittedly, most Jews who today affiliate with congregations have little understanding of—and perhaps little concern for—the philosophies that underlie the movements represented by their synagogues. Proximity to their homes, some vague sentiment about their parents' beliefs, the affiliations of friends, even the fee structure of the religious school, are often the determinants.

Yet there are stirrings of change. More and more young people are members of Orthodox synagogues, seriously challenging the image of the bearded patriarch with his voluminous *tallit*. In Reform temples it is the young, again,

3

who are demanding both a return to some traditional forms of observance and an explanation of what such observances mean. Conservative Jews are examining the roots of their own belief to evaluate their own place in the spectrum of Jewish thought.

A religious coming of age is in progress among American Jews. Our people want to know why they are Jews, how they can express their Jewish yearnings, and what distinguishes their practice from that of their neighbors. Some of their questions may never be definitively answered, but the speakers who follow do offer some guides for the perplexed.

Rabbi David I. Golovensky,

Rabbi Edward E. Klein,

and Rabbi William Berkowitz

1. ❧ The Judaism of Tomorrow

Rabbi Edward E. Klein

Rabbi David I. Golovensky

Rabbi William Berkowitz

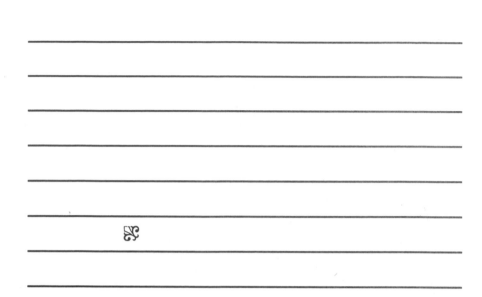

BERKOWITZ: We are going to discuss a truly fascinating subject—the Judaism of tomorrow, Orthodox, Conservative, and Reform. My own task is a twofold one. I am to serve as the moderator and to ask the questions that you would want to ask; on the other hand, I will also present the Conservative point of view.

No era in 4,000 years of Jewish creativity has presented the Jew with greater challenges than the last two centuries—challenges to his religion, challenges to his philosophies, challenges to his way of life; for the period of enlightenment, the period of emancipation, and the period of industrial revolution changed the whole character of Jewish experience, making periods of adjustment to modern living and the modern environment inevitable. All of us are familiar with Jewish history and all of us know, for example, that in the Middle Ages when Jews spoke to other Jews they would say, "*di velt zogt*," which means "the world says." Which world? Their world. The world of the ghetto, for it was the only world that they knew. And though they suffered persecution and though they lived in a ghetto, these factors served as positive forces for Jewish survival.

But then the forces of conservatism began to break down as Jews entered the modern world—the French Revolution, the modern period—and all this made for a great need for adjustment and for new thinking and new ways. And so Jewish leaders were forced to formulate anew their concept of Judaism. Consider Germany, where there was a great thinker, historian, and theologian, Abraham Geiger, who was the founder, we might say, of Reform Judaism. Consider this same Germany, where there was Zechariah Frankel, who was the founder of the positive historical school of Judaism, the forerunner of Conservative

7

Judaism. Consider the same Germany of modern Orthodoxy and its great leading exponent, Samson Raphael Hirsch.

The first attempts at reformulating a concept of Judaism in Germany at this time were piecemeal. It was only in America, where state and church are separated and where religion is free, that new approaches to Judaism flourished and developed. We certainly know that in America during these past years we have displayed and witnessed a sudden upsurge of what we might call religious revival—or at least a resurgence of interest in religion. This was brought about by Hitlerism and, more positively, because in the ashes of German Jewry the State of Israel was reborn. Sociologists point out that ties to national ancestry are gradually becoming weaker and weaker. And in America, the individual will be able to retain his group identity, not by virtue of the fact that he came from Poland, Russia, Rumania, or Ireland, but through his religion, for America is beginning to recognize religious group identification—the Catholic group, the Jewish group, and the Protestant group, among many others. Increasingly, the distinctive mark of our identification in this land is becoming our religion and the synagogue.

The fact is that a vast number of the Jews who have joined synagogues, whether they be in suburban or metropolitan areas, who seem to have become religious-minded, have little understanding of the fundamental nature of the concepts that distinguish their groups, whether Orthodox, Conservative, or Reform. A popular definition, for example, once described the three groups: if a Jew lived in New York on the East Side, he was an Orthodox Jew; if he lived on Riverside Drive, he was a Conservative Jew; if he lived on Fifth Avenue, he was a Reform Jew. Today that joke is outmoded. On Fifth Avenue you find one of the most Orthodox of synagogues. In the area of Riverside Drive, you find not only Conservative but Reform and even Chasidic synagogues. So all kinds of Jews live all over. Many Jews today join a particular synagogue, not because they are convinced that they believe in Conservative Judaism, or Reform, or Orthodox, but rather because of the social status provided by that particular synagogue.

This lack of understanding, this lack of appreciation, is revealed not only in the synagogue but in the Jew's everyday religious life, for if you were to ask thinking, sensitive, cultured Jews what basic philosophies identify today's Jewish religious life—Conservative, Orthodox, and Reform—how many could answer? If you were to ask these same thinking members the real meaning of the synagogue to which they belong, or the significance of the ideology that they profess in terms of Judaism for the twentieth century, how many would have an answer?

American Jewry, we believe, has come of age and should be able to answer these questions. It should seek to understand the fundamental distinctions among the philosophies. It is in this spirit, in the effort toward helping this understanding, that we present this discussion.

Naturally, the three discussants represent three schools of thought and have three different backgrounds. But we are going to try to be as objective as possible and to present facts. Our intention is not to engage in debate. Rather, we are engaged in a symposium about a great people, about a great way of life—the Jewish way of life.

Dr. David Golovensky has been the Rabbi of Beth El Synagogue in New Rochelle, and the president of the New York Board of Rabbis, the largest rabbinic body in the world. He has traveled to many parts of the world on governmental and Jewish missions. A noted lecturer and author, he has long been an outstanding exponent of Orthodox Jewish thinking.

Rabbi Edward E. Klein has been Rabbi of the Stephen Wise Free Synagogue in New York City, and an educator who has done pioneering work in Jewish education and youth leadership. He has been widely known for his community activities for many years and for his participation in a network of Jewish and non-Jewish organizations.

In discussing the Judaism of tomorrow—Orthodox, Conservative, and Reform—we will follow this procedure: I have prepared a group of questions that I have not shown to Rabbis Golovensky and Klein. They do have a general understanding of the nature of the discussion, however. I will ask each to discuss the question, and in this way they will provide a cross-section of the differences in the points of view, and perhaps a deeper understanding of the three groups.

To open, I ask Rabbi Golovensky first for a brief history of Orthodox Judaism from its earliest beginnings. I ask this in the spirit of Hillel, that of standing on one foot, because I am sure that to fully answer this kind of question could take the entire evening.

■ GOLOVENSKY: When you speak about the history of Orthodoxy, you speak about the history of Judaism, because actually this tripartite division of Judaism into Orthodox, Conservative, and Reform is purely and peculiarly an American creation. Orthodoxy is called that because there are other movements known as Conservatism and Reform. Orthodoxy represents the authentic Jewish tradition going back all the way to Sinai. That is what we believe. That is how we feel. Torah-true Judaism is just that. It represents that thread of authentic Jewish life and Jewish belief that takes us all through the ages. America is one of the few countries in which this tripartite division exists. Eastern Europe did not have it. In other parts of the world they still do not have it. America, for a variety of reasons, has divided Judaism into these three groups. And there are other groups, and there are groups within groups.

What are the fundamental postulates of Torah-true Judaism? First, that the Torah is *min ha-shamayim*, that the Torah is "the revealed word of God." This is fundamental. This is basic. This is the point of departure upon which there can be no question. Second, we believe that Judaism is not a response to the needs of people, but that it is the response to the commands of God. . . . And it is not only the Bible, the Torah itself, that has divine sanction, but also the Talmud and all of the commentary in the authentic Jewish tradition that has been added through the ages.

The Torah is not static. It develops, but it develops according to the pattern and the formula of the Halachah. And that which God gives, or gave, cannot be changed or compromised. The will of God cannot be compromised because of the few, nor because of the many. We believe that compromise does not strengthen but rather weakens. One compromise inevitably introduces another and leads to a third.

You remember the story of the man who willed his home to a charity with the provisos that he would live in it during the rest of his life, that he would pay for the minor repairs, and that the major repairs would be handled by the beneficiary. After a few years a friend of his asked how the arrangement had worked out. The donor said, "Wonderful. I didn't have to pay for a single repair, because when the minor repairs came along, I waited until they became major." So too with compromise; you may start with a minor compromise, but the minor leads to a major. We believe that the more complex life becomes—and it is becoming more and more complex all the time—the more we need the disciplines of religion. We often hear the expression *"Shver tzu zein a Yid,"* for while the Torah way of life is not always convenient, it is always rewarding. Do you know who really complains about Judaism being tough and hard, who complains that the Orthodox Sabbath service is long? It is usually the man who comes to services very, very rarely, and when he does, drops in at 10:15 and would like to leave by 10:30. But the Jew who comes on time and *davens* rarely complains that the service is too long. Do you know who really complains about the restraints and rigidities of Torah-true Judaism? Not those who really observe them, and therefore come to love them and live by them, but those who look from without and those who violate and ignore them.

BERKOWITZ: Dr. Golovensky has made certain statements, postulated certain ideas on Orthodoxy. We are going to elaborate on a number of these, but first we will ask Rabbi Klein to give an opening statement on Reform Judaism.

■ **KLEIN:** I agree with Rabbi Berkowitz in many respects. I agree with him in reiterating that this is not a debate. *Kol Yisrael chaverim*: all Israelites are brothers—Reform, Conservative, Orthodox. The Judaism of the future, I think, will be as the Judaism of today—Reform, Conservative, Orthodox. One of the wonderful things about the Jewish people is the pluralism in Jewish life. I am not one who laments the lack of a unanimity among the Jews. We need unity, but God forbid that we ever have unanimity. We do agree on the basic things. There are schools of Jewish thought today as there have always been schools of Jewish thought, and the great genius of our people is that we are not intellectually monolithic. The Talmud is a record of disputes, of discussions. *Elu V'elu Divre Elohim Chayim*. These are the words of the ever-living God, and the Talmud records the minority views as it records the majority view.

I agree with Rabbi Berkowitz in still another point. Unfortunately, too few Jews today understand the differences in ideology. Perhaps fortunately, most Jews join a synagogue because they like the synagogue, whether it be an Orthodox synagogue, a Conservative synagogue, or a Reform synagogue, or because they may live around the corner.

I was officiating at a very fancy wedding at the Waldorf Astoria Hotel in New York. The bride's mother, all a-twitter just before the ceremony, said, "Rabbi, please, not too Orthodox, not too Reform, just mediocre." Of course, to her, Orthodoxy meant a *kipah* and an all-Hebrew service. Reform meant no hats, no Hebrew. I would not say that Conservatism meant mediocre, but I tried to oblige with a hat and with English and a little Hebrew. I think it was the type of ceremony she liked.

This story is illustrative of the fact that too few of us really understand the differences and the similarities in ideologies.

One more story, and then I will continue, because this underscores one of my points. The other day I was walking on the street and I met a local undertaker who happens to be more than a little Orthodox. He told me, "You know, one of my clients recently asked me to recommend someone for an unveiling, a rabbi who isn't so religious, so I recommended you."

I maintain that I am as religious as Dave Golovensky. I maintain that Reform Jews are as religious as Conservative Jews, as Orthodox Jews, as Reconstructionist Jews. There are basic differences, however, in the interpretations of the role of ritual and the role of ceremony. My gifted friend Rabbi Golovensky said that the history of Orthodoxy is coterminous with the history of Judaism. Reform Judaism similarly goes back—looks back—to the beginnings of our faith for its inspiration. It finds that throughout the history of Judaism there has been adaptation to changed conditions. When the prophets emphasized the moral law; when Micah pointed out the three things God requires of us—to do justly, to love mercy, and to walk humbly; when Isaiah said, "When you make your sacrifices, I, God, will look away; only feed the hungry, help the fatherless, and plead for the widow"; they were not rejecting the ceremonial, but adding an ethical emphasis to Judaism and rejecting the emphasis on sacrifices. This made a basic change.

In the time of Jesus we had parties in Judaism as we have interpretations of Judaism today. We had the Sadducees; we had the Pharisees; we had the Essenes; we had the Rabbis, the authors of the Talmud, who liberalized our faith, who made it possible for Judaism to survive. We are learning a great deal these days about the Essenes, the authors of the Dead Sea Scrolls. We have had Maimonists, who favored the interpretation of the Rambam, and we have had anti-Maimonists. We have had Chasidim, we have had Mitnagdim. When Philo Judaeus, the great Greek rabbi of whom it has been said, "Either Philo platonizes or Plato philonizes," wrote his great work adjusting Judaism and Platonism, he was adapting without compromising, keeping Judaism viable in his day.

When Maimonides did something similar vis-à-vis the philosophy of Aristotle, he was accommodating Judaism to changed conditions. And when the great Orthodox leader

Nachman Krochmal wrote his great book, *Moreh Nevuche Hazman* (Guide for the Perplexed of Our Day), merging the basic insights of Judaism with some of the teachings of Hegel, he too was engaging in the principle of accommodation. I think this is basically what Reform stands for: accommodation, but not of the theology. I think it will emerge from this discussion that Rabbi Berkowitz, Rabbi Golovensky, and I believe in God the same way. We believe in prayer the same way, and we believe in immortality, I think, in pretty much the same way. Our interpretations differ solely in regard to ritual and ceremony.

A Reform Jew says merely this: the basic insights of Judaism are eternally valid, but the ritual law is sometimes the outgrowth of historical needs in particular times, in particular climes. When the needs change, when the times change, then the ritual, the ceremony, must be adapted to changed conditions. This became apparent, as Rabbi Berkowitz reminded us, right after the French Revolution, when the ghetto walls fell and the Jew became a free and equal citizen of the lands in which he lived. In Germany a group of Jewish laymen began to introduce certain changes in the ceremony and the ritual. They abbreviated some of the prayers and introduced some prayers in German. They introduced a confirmation service on Shavuot—a ceremony, incidentally, which is uniquely Reform and which Conservative Judaism has borrowed. And, then, in the middle of the nineteenth century, the rabbis stepped in. I repeat, the laymen—the laity— *introduced* the changes. Reform had a grassroots origin. Just as the laymen introduced some changes to keep Judaism viable under changed conditions, the rabbis stepped in to keep it Jewish. They measured every change by two norms: the needs of the present and the teachings of the past

In a series of synods, or rabbinical conferences, in the middle of the nineteenth century in Germany, a number of resolutions were passed. A number of decisions were made that adjusted the ritual, the ceremony, to the changed needs of a new age.

For example, at a time when women were coming into their own, it was decided that family pews should be introduced. The rabbis looked back into the teachings of the past: They found that in Chapter 8 of the book of Nehemiah, when the

Torah was read, it was before the men and women assembled; they reasoned that Miriam danced before the Lord; and they read in Chapter 31 of the book of Proverbs, "Who can find a woman of valor, for her price is far above rubies." So they decided that men and women might sit together and pray together.

Then, at a time when more and more people spoke German, they wanted the language of the land introduced into the synagogue. They went back to a talmudic principle that says that the *Shema* might be recited in any language that is understood. So they recited prayers in the vernacular, never really eliminating Hebrew because this was a basic bond. Of course, like many reforming movements, they went too far. As a result, Conservative Judaism was founded by Zechariah Frankel, who, incidentally, was one of the early Reformers and who left one of the synods I mentioned to found the school of positive historical Judaism.

It was, as Rabbi Berkowitz reminded us, in America that Reform has had its greatest growth because of the experimentalism, the pragmatism, the separation of church and state, the nonconformist tradition (if that is not a contradiction of terms) that made possible the growth of this uniquely liberal interpretation of Jewish life.

Permit me to recapitulate: Reform merely applies the principle of change evident in Jewish life from the very beginning; Reform Judaism is Judaism with the emphasis on an evolving ritual and ceremonial practice.

BERKOWITZ: I am here to present the Conservative point of view, in distinction to the Orthodox and to the Reform. As I said, I am present in a twofold role, representing a point of view and acting as moderator. Let me say that our movement, the Conservative movement, has been described by many people as neither *milchik* nor *fleyshik*. Our movement has been termed a *pareve* movement—endeavoring to be all things to all people. We are said to want a tepid Orthodoxy and a timid Reform, a movement requiring loyalty to tradition and yet permitting departure from tradition in our synagogue ritual. We speak of the sanctity of the Torah and the mitzvot, and yet we permit free discussion on such basic subjects as *Torah min ha-shamayim* and the need of the further development of our Jewish law.

In fact, as you know, the weapon of Jewish humor has been leveled against us. Let me just cite an example. What, they ask, is the difference between a Conservative, a Reform, and an Orthodox Jew? One answer is that a Reform Jew never wears the *yarmulke*, the Conservative Jew always keeps one in his pocket, and the Orthodox wears it on his head. Another is that the Reform Jew does not observe Rosh Hashanah one day, while the Conservative does not observe Rosh Hashanah both days.

Of course, this is humor. But people have criticized the Conservative movement and the fact that we are a movement based on negation. History teaches us that movements and philosophies are pragmatic in character, rather than carefully planned and executed ideologies. In other words, while we know what we *do not* want, we also know what we *do* want. We do know that a movement must grow out of a people, must grow out of their needs, in order to be healthy and fruitful. And so, the first postulate that Conservative Judaism has taken upon itself has been the refusal to be defined, to become sectarian, to avoid conciseness, to place upon itself rigid dogma—the straightjacket of dogma in a generation that is undergoing a transvaluation of ideas.

Therefore, if we refuse to be defined, in what do we believe? I believe that the definition can be given both in the negative and in the positive, for our movement seeks to negate the prevailing concepts held by the camps to the right and the camps to the left. In Germany, Zechariah Frankel was the founder of the positive historical school of Judaism, the forerunner of Conservative Judaism. This philosophy was carried out in America by such men as Sabato Morais, Isaac Leeser, and Solomon Schechter. Some of these men first joined the Reform movement but later severed this relationship.

We remember, also, the start of Conservative Judaism in the 1840s, the founding of the Jewish Theological Seminary in 1886, and its fullest fruition about 1902 when the great Solomon Schechter, of blessed memory, came to America.

Conservative Judaism, as a movement in America, revolted against Orthodoxy, which to Conservatives had become incompatible with the American way of life. The waves of Jewish immigration coming to this country brought the philosophy and the ways of a foreign land. Judaism became foreign—a foreign burden, shall we say—to the youngsters of these parents, and they sought to lay aside this way of life at the first opportunity.

Conservative Judaism also arose as a protest against the iconoclastic tendencies of *radical reform*. Conservatism formed a united front against the Reform Pittsburgh Platform of 1885, which repudiated some Jewish traditions, emphasized the prophetic ideals of the Bible, took the genesis of modern Judaism from the French Revolution, and accentuated the universalistic overtones of the prophets. The radical reformers reduced the authority of the Talmud. They made Judaism invisible in the home. Their misdirected patriotism led them to remove Zion from the prayer book. They went so far as to tamper with the Jewish calendar, maintaining that on Sunday, instead of on *Shabbat*, one should say, "*Mizmor Shir l'yom Hashabbat.*" In reaction to the idea that the Torah was an inert tradition or that it was an anachronistic, outmoded way of life, Conservative Judaism appeared on the American scene. It rejected the negatives of Reform.

Many people, as I said, claim, "Well, we deny, but we also affirm; we reject, but we also accept." What is it that we affirm? What is it that we include? What is the movement's position today? What is its positive character? What are its dominant formulations and contributions? Conservative Judaism feels that Orthodoxy was and is today a static civilization. We feel that it has been frozen since the sixteenth century, when the *Shulchan Aruch* was codified by Joseph Karo. Our thesis is that Jewish law has been and is an evolving process and that it has always been dynamic in its growth and in its development. The greatness, the sustenance, the maintenance, and the prevailing effect of Judaism has been dependent for 4,000 years on the fact that it has adjusted itself to the changing demands upon the life of the Jew.

We can quote examples: we started with biblical law and from biblical law came to mishnaic law. From mishnaic law to talmudic law. Then came hundreds of years of *responsa* literature in which rabbis, sages, and scholars, with the sanctity of the Torah as their basis, reinterpreted Jewish law in terms of their times. Orthodoxy, we believe, has remained at the level of the sixteenth century and at the exact code of law as expounded by Joseph Karo. Because of this, we feel that Judaism, and specifically Conservative Judaism, has to recreate in our day and age the concept that ours is a *Torat Chayim*, a living Torah. Within the framework of Halachah, change is permissible and necessary. While we recognize the authority of our tradition, our movement recognizes the need for a synthesis between the demand of law and the demand of life. Our school of thought holds that the living law is more than that which is found in the code. It is the end result of the requirements of the law as well as the collective conscience of the Jews who live under this law. This is what is implied in Dr. Schechter's famous phrase "Catholic Israel." The law grows through a democratic process, and the people of Israel determine which elements of Judaism are vital and which are obsolete.

This does not mean that we should destroy Jewish law. Reform found difficulties inherent in Jewish law under minority conditions and proceeded to abrogate the authority of the law. Orthodoxy officially maintains the structure unchanged. Conservative Judaism, as its name implies, does seek to conserve the tradition, to keep it and maintain it. Yet it also takes steps to restore the flexibility of adjustment, the inner vitality and capacity for growth, that traditional Judaism manifested in all the eras and stages of its growth and development.

That is my statement on Conservative Judaism. Now, in my role as moderator, I would like to ask a few questions of each panelist and through these questions perhaps illustrate some differences in our philosophy.

Rabbi Klein, the strength of Reform Judaism has been that it was the first attempt to stem the flowing tide of people away from Judaism. People in the era after the French Revolution and in the nineteenth century were leaving Judaism and turning to Christianity. Reform sought to stop that. Kaufmann Kohler, the great Reform leader, said something very profound: "While Orthodox rabbis wrapped themselves in prayer shawls weeping over the neglect of the Law, Reform infused new life into the dry bones of Israel and awakened new enthusiasm for the ancient faith in the young." But tell me, Rabbi Klein, did Reform Judaism not aim mostly at esthetic regeneration rather than doctrinal readjustment? Did Reform Judaism not lose all of its vision and thus create the great weakness that marked the Reform movement, limiting Judaism to universal teachings and ethical precepts? Did it not give up the Law and advance the argument that it sought to preserve the essence of Judaism? I quote Solomon Schechter, who told about the person who would give up a part and if necessary the whole of the Constitution to preserve the remainder. Did not Reform Judaism do exactly that?

■ KLEIN: No. Reform Judaism merely amended the Constitution. It gave liberal Jews, modern Jews, a new bill of rights. I differ from Rabbi Berkowitz in this regard. After the French Revolution, it was quite possible for Orthodox Jews to live as Orthodox Jews. There were some who chose to live that way and could and did. There were others, by the same token, who could not live in what they felt was a spiritual ghetto. They learned the teachings of general culture. They attended colleges and universities. They discovered cultures almost as great as Hebrew culture, and they had to adjust to this. These were the pioneers and, as I said before, pioneers often go too far. They had no objections to Jewish teachings about God, about prayer, about immortality. I maintain that these are eternally valid. And I, a Reform rabbi, am much more conservative than some of my Conservative colleagues in my attitude toward some of these theological principles. The Reformers' objection was to a ritual that they felt was no longer practicable, and so they estheticized it, they beautified it, they abbreviated it, or they translated it. They introduced an organ to beautify the service. These early Reformers also introduced a weekly sermon, an innovation of Reform that my Orthodox colleagues and my Conservative colleagues have since emulated. Of course, there were Jews long before who had done that. A great reformer, Leopold Zunz, in his magnificent work on the history of the Jewish sermon, indicated that sermons had been preached in the days of the Temple in Alexandria in Egypt and even in the days of the second Temple. Yes, these were superficial changes. But they gave rise to a certain dynamism in our movement that has made it possible to go in the direction of eliminating or adapting rituals, or, as the need arises—as we feel the need has arisen in our day—to reaccept some of the ancient rituals and reinterpret them.

As a movement, and as any reforming movement is at risk of doing, it went a bit too far. In some cases it threw out the baby with the bath water, but it has brought back much that is of value. And it is not a reckless or arbitrary process. Reform has constantly analyzed. Rabbi Berkowitz mentioned *responsa*. We have Reform *responsa*. In other words, these questions are asked of the rabbis, the great group of rabbis in the Central Conference of American Rabbis: Does this ritual still show significance, does it have meaning? Does this ritual still have beauty? Is this ritual an essential bond of Jew to Jew? And if it satisfies these three criteria, then we maintain the ritual. If not, then it must be readapted or perhaps eliminated.

On the matter of nationalism and universalism: Reform, as has been said, developed in the middle of the nineteenth century in the age of utopian idealism. If the Messiah was not already here, he was at least around the corner, in the opinion of these people. Had not the Jew been made a free and equal citizen? Tomorrow, the Messiah would be here. So they believed that we should not be sequestered or segregated, in a tiny land on the rim of the Mediterranean. They were what Herzl called *"Nein Sagers"*: "no-sayers" to Zionism. This was a big mistake.

But when it became apparent that the dream of Zion, *Chibat Zion*, was intrinsic to Judaism and necessary for the survival of the Jewish people, Reform, again true to its inner dynamism, its strength within, its ability to adjust or adapt, gave some of its greatest leaders to the Zionist movement, leaders such as Stephen Samuel Wise, Abba Hillel Silver, and Barnett Brickner.

BERKOWITZ: When you mentioned the Messiah, Rabbi Klein, I was reminded of the classic story of the husband who had a wonderful job at $100 a week and who came home and said to his wife, "My dear, I've just given up my job."

She looked at him with surprise. "Given up your job? Why so?"

"I took on another job."

"Are you getting more money?"

"No," he said. "In fact, I am getting less."

"Getting less? What are you getting?"

"I'm getting $25 a week."

"You gave up $100 a week for $25 a week? What are you doing?"

"Well, I've been delegated by the town to stand on top of a mountain to watch for the Messiah to come."

"What kind of *saichel* is that?" his wife asked him.

He answered, "Well for one thing, it certainly will be a steady job."

I think we have a steady job along that line, but before I turn to Rabbi Golovensky, I would like to ask this: Would you not say that a Judaism that has replaced the law of the Torah with the law of the Prophets has surrendered that which is the power of its faith? You speak of readapting Jewish law. But let us take, as a case in point, constitutional law. The greatness of the Constitution of the United States is the fact that this is the central document interpreted and reinterpreted in terms of constitutional law. Hence the greatness of the Constitution, hence its adaptability, hence the greatness of law. But if you alienate the Halachah, the Law, is it not a case of each individual making Sabbath for himself?

■ KLEIN: We have not eliminated Halachah. We have not eliminated law. Every halachah is measured in terms of its applicability to our day. We refuse to say that Halachah is binding in changed times and changed conditions. Do we observe *Shabbat*? Yes. Do we observe the holidays? Yes. Is our prayer book, the *Union Prayer Book*, based on the traditional framework? Yes. Is the *Machzor* based on the traditional *Machzor*? The answer is yes, by all means, in each case.

BERKOWITZ: What is the authority for your law?

■ KLEIN: The authorities are the Jewish people and the leading teachers of each individual age. Reform Judaism holds that revelation is not limited to a certain point in history. It was limited neither to Sinai nor to the rabbis of the Talmud. Revelation is a process apprehended by the inspired and knowledgeable leaders in every age.

■ GOLOVENSKY: Now you gentlemen keep on fighting it out. You know, I'm enjoying this. I have been in the deep freeze since the sixteenth century. Now we are in the twentieth century.

BERKOWITZ: We are going to thaw you out now, Rabbi Golovensky. I feel, and the school of thought that I represent feels, that, just as Reform went to one extreme, Orthodoxy has gone to the other extreme; this is its weakness. Halachah has become a static concept rather than dynamic. The word "Halachah" comes from the Hebrew word *haloch*, which means "to go"; and in going you move forward. How do you react to the statement that Halachah, in terms of Orthodoxy, is static, that Orthodoxy has congealed Jewish law rather than developed and made it a meaningful process for the twentieth century?

■ GOLOVENSKY: Judaism is a way of life in the twentieth century in America and all over the world. It is based upon the truth that the Bible is the word of God, and that loyalty to the Torah and to the tradition that came down to us leads to a beautiful, fruitful, and rewarding life. When you speak about how much Halachah you give up and how much you retain and whether the Reform retains Halachah on *Shabbat* and *Yom Tov*, I do not know. That is a little confusing to me. Whether you retain a little more Halachah according to the Conservative point of view, or a little less according to the Reform, makes me wonder what the formula is and how much should be kept and how much not kept, how much restored and how much ignored. Orthodoxy knows this: that Judaism is a thread through the ages, whether it be in America or any other part of the world. We live a Torah-true life. We are as modern as anybody else in the twentieth century. We are as progressive as anybody else. The Jewish religion is addressed not to those things that change with the current of time, things that go out of style or come into style. Judaism is addressed to the eternal needs of man. It is addressed through the eternal word of God, and there is no going backwards, no going forward. We are always in step with God and with the Torah. Those who live that way of life, those who are disciplined to the Torah, those who adhere to the sanctities of Judaism find it in complete harmony with all other aspects of life, whether it be in America with its freedom or in other countries. We are addressing ourselves as Torah-true Jews to the word of God and to the mission of Judaism, which is ever dynamic, ever living, ever beautiful, and ever creative. And finally, I will say this, if you do not mind another bit of humor. An embezzler who had taken $300,000 was asked by the District Attorney what he had done with all the money. The man said, "I'll tell you what happened. I spent a lot of money on wine and liquor. I spent a lot of other money on horses and gambling. And the rest of it I squandered foolishly."

I want to tell you how much of the Halachah we can keep and what is in conformity with the spirit of the age. We know this: the true *Shabbat*, the beautiful Sabbath and the dietary laws; the way we observe the *Yom Tov*, the *Shulchan Aruch*, the tradition—keeping the car in the garage, keeping the radio silenced, having the family sit together and enjoy each other's company at least one day in the week, going to the synagogue together, coming home, having a discussion of Judaism at the table, living this type of life in New York, in Hollywood, or in any part of the world today—is as modern and as beautiful as it ever was to those who live it!

BERKOWITZ:　The fact that each of us is so very emphatic in his point of view makes Rabbi Klein and myself equally as traditional as Rabbi Golovensky. The Bible says about the light on the altar, *"Aish Tamid Tukad al Hamizbaiach,"* "An eternal fire should always burn on the altar." In the Rabbis' comment on that particular verse, they said, *"Ha-esh hayitah m'tukedet Bo,"* "The fire was not only on the altar but was also in those who served and administered the altar." So each of us is naturally inspired and inflamed with the enthusiasm of our point of view and our philosophy.

I am going to ask a few direct questions, and I would like each of us to answer each question. The first question is, Do you think a Sanhedrin is possible in Israel, and if such a Sanhedrin were organized, would it be the answer to the question of Jewish law and Jewish problems for Reform Jews?

 ■ KLEIN:　No. I hate to be the "no" man here, but I do not think that the reconstitution of the Sanhedrin would be the answer for Reform Jews or for Judaism itself. I return to what I said at the very beginning. I think the pluralism of Jewish life, the presence in Judaism of Orthodoxy, Conservatism, and Reform, permits its development—cross-fertilization, if you will. I hope there will always be an Orthodoxy. I say this in public. I know there will always be a Reform and a Conservatism. I think the friendly tension between the latter two will enable Judaism to go forward effectively, creatively, and fruitfully into tomorrow.

BERKOWITZ: Would Reform Jewish life in America feel obliged to heed the points of view or the decisions arrived at by a constituted body in the State of Israel known as the Sanhedrin?

■ **KLEIN:** That depends pretty much on who constitutes this Sanhedrin. If it is the present Orthodox group within the State of Israel, then I would say absolutely no, because this is a group that refuses to recognize my rabbinical status, yours, or Israel Goldstein's. This group believes in the merger of church and state rather than in the separation of church and state that to me is the essence of democracy and the Judaism of the future.

BERKOWITZ: Rabbi Golovensky, do you feel that the Sanhedrin would be the answer to the revival of Jewish law and Jewish life, not only in Israel but throughout the Diaspora?

■ **GOLOVENSKY:** Frankly, I do not think I am competent to answer that question. I certainly would love to see the day when a competent body recognized by all Torah-true Jews would assemble and perhaps give some direction to the Torah way of life. I would like to see it. I am sure others would like to see it. I do not know whether that will be possible. But I want to say this in connection with what our colleague, Rabbi Klein, said about the Orthodoxy in the State of Israel. There are many things that American Jews can export with great profit to Israel. We can export money. We can export a great deal of advice, scientific people, and others to help Israel. One thing I do not think we need export to Israel is the American brand of Judaism. Let Judaism develop in Israel the way Judaism has developed in every country. I say this just as I would say that I would resent any group in Russia or in Poland trying to export their brand of Judaism to America while remaining in Russia and Poland. If people want to go to

Israel, live there, practice religion, and get into the spirit and culture of the people of that country, that is something else. But those of us who have studied sociology and history know that certain things are not exportable. Among those things that are not exportable, and I do not think that people here should try to export it, is the way that religion should be conducted in Israel.

Now, as far as the Sanhedrin is concerned, I do not feel, as I said, that I am competent to answer. However, I would certainly love to see a Sanhedrin assemble, one that would win the support of the Torah-true Jews and of the leaders of all the world, and perhaps give certain direction to the future of Jewish life according to Torah and Halachah.

BERKOWITZ: I would like to comment on this question that I asked of my colleagues. I fully agree with Rabbi Golovensky that Israel does not need imported Judaism, but I believe that world Jewry is in great need of exported Judaism. I believe that what Rabbi Golovensky and Rabbi Klein touched upon, the concept of *"Kol Yisrael arevim ze bazeh"*—"We are all responsible for one another"—conforms with Maimonides' understanding and concept of the Sanhedrin, about which the statement was made: "Because of the land, the spirit, and its association, it is out of Zion that the law shall come forth, and out of Jerusalem, the Word of God." My feeling is that if the State of Israel and its religious leadership could come to the understanding that not only Israel but Diaspora Jewry should be involved, that if the Sanhedrin were the reflection of the thinking of the Israeli *and* of the world rabbinate, and that if Israel and the Diaspora were to unite and formulate its composition, then a Sanhedrin could produce a rightful contribution toward making Jewish law far more viable and far more acceptable to many of our people who flounder among several ideologies and points of view. And now, Rabbi Klein, what are the challenges facing Reform Judaism?

■ KLEIN: I would say that the challenges of Reform Judaism are the challenges of Judaism in general. We are all faced with two basic problems: not only must we keep religion applicable to the age in which we live, but we must also apply basic insights to the reconstitution of society, for one of the fundamental ideals of our faith is the reformation, the reform, the regeneration of the world. We pray in the *Aleinu* prayer that *L'taken Olam b'Malchut Shaddai*, that we may be able to refashion the world in the image of God's kingdom. I think all of us are faced with the problem of seeking in this age of nuclear fission to build a world of spiritual fusion, a world that will be one, as God's name is One. This means that Judaism has a vital role to play because in the insights of our prophets are contained the basic insights that will build tomorrow's world, if there is to be a world of tomorrow. Each of us in our attitudes may differ about rituals, ceremonies, and Halachah. These, I think, are incidental. The main point is that Judaism must make its basic contribution to the building of tomorrow's world. I think there will be Orthodoxy, and there will be a Liberalism. I predict—I am neither a prophet nor a son of a prophet, as Amos said—but I predict that as Conservative Judaism, through one of its wings, Reconstructionism, veers toward the left, and as Reform Judaism, in consonance with the mood of our day, reintroduces more rituals, there will tend to be a merging of these two forces. I think there will be a Liberal wing of Judaism and there will be a Conservative or Orthodox wing of Judaism. There must always be this type of tension as there is in political life. And I think that Judaism, storming the future, can help to build a brave new world. I would like to repeat something I said before. We are not, any of us, wrong. We are all of us right.

BERKOWITZ: Rabbi Golovensky, what do you think are the modern challenges, adjustments, and issues facing Orthodox Judaism in terms of the future?

■ GOLOVENSKY: I would say that one very crucial and central problem that is facing Torah-true Judaism is Jewish education. If our Jewish people were educated thoroughly enough with a sound understanding of the meaning of Torah, of the richness of our tradition, if they knew Hebrew in the original and could read the Torah and other beautiful and sacred books, I think, I believe, I feel convinced, that the future would belong, certainly to a larger extent than in the present or the past, to Torah-true Judaism. We have, thank God, in the past decade or so built over 200 yeshivahs, universities, and medical schools. If I could hope that there would be 2,000 or 20,000 such institutions where our people would know

Judaism from within, from the Torah, and would come into the synagogue and be able to understand the Hebrew and glory in its poetry, I think the problem of Torah-true Judaism would be largely solved, both for the present and for the future.

BERKOWITZ: From the Conservative point of view I would like to say that Maimonides said that the greatness of Judaism has been the golden mean, it has been the middle of the road. Conservative Judaism has taken the middle of the road. The Rabbis have rightfully said that the Torah can be compared to two paths, the path of fire and the path of snow. The path, or road, of fire is Orthodoxy, and the road of snow is Reform. Conservative Jews walk in the middle. I believe that Conservative Judaism today, in terms of its philosophy and in terms of its thinking, in terms of its attitude toward Jewish law, should take a more aggressive stand on the particular point of interpreting and reinterpreting Jewish law within the framework of Halachah in order to better make it a *Torat Chayim*. With regard to the future, let me say this concerning the unification of Judaism in America. The greatness of a democracy is its cultural pluralism, and the greatness of Judaism has always been, as Rabbi Klein said, its various opinions. There can be and always should be unity in diversity. I believe, as we look to the Judaism of tomorrow, whether it be Orthodox, Conservative, or Reform, that there should be this unity within diversity. I think, Rabbi Klein, that a Reform rabbi was correct when he said that Reform's danger is emptiness, Orthodoxy's is blindness, and Conservatism's is something of both. So we have to prevent both the blindness and the emptiness of Jewish life, and the only way we can do this, as Rabbi Golovensky said, is through greater knowledge, through greater understanding, and through communication. A communication that means an understanding and a dialogue with the community, an appreciation of one another's thoughts.

We are faced, moreover, with the necessity of clarifying and organizing our own views toward the realization of a common goal, one that is based on a consensus upon which we all stand, *Am Yisrael Chai*, the people of Israel live. Conservative, Orthodox, and Reform, long may they live.

2. ❧ Reconstructionism

Rabbi Mordecai Menachem Kaplan

W.B.:* Some years ago, when I was still a rabbinical student, I was privileged to speak at a dinner that celebrated the seventieth birthday of our distinguished guest, Dr. Mordecai M. Kaplan. I would like to repeat part of what I said then about one of the great thinkers and philosophers of our age:

> Tonight I stand before you representing one link in a chain of students that goes back to the year 1910, bringing greetings to our beloved professor on behalf of the present student body of the rabbinical school, those of us who have had the rare privilege of sitting at his feet. You may ask, What is it that makes Dr. Kaplan so revered by his students? My answer is that there are three crowns of distinction that we, his students, always associate with Professor Kaplan. The first is the crown of teacher. As a teacher, he has no equal. Dr. Kaplan brings freshness, vigor, and vitality to his subject matter. He approaches it not only with intellectual honesty but also with love and devotion. And it is this love and devotion to our heritage that he radiates and inspires in all of us.
>
> His second crown of distinction is that of guide. Many of us attended his classes unconcerned and unknowing about existing problems, satisfied with our childhood and adolescent notions, complacent in our views of long standing. It was Dr. Kaplan who awakened us to the problems of our times, challenged us and, at times, provoked us. In a word, he made us think.

*The words of the moderator in these Dialogues, Rabbi William Berkowitz, will be preceded by the initials W.B. throughout this volume.

And finally, the third crown of distinction is the crown of friend. He has not only been a *nueh doreish* but also a *nueh m'kayem.* His personality, his character, his warmth, his saintliness, his respect for the opinions of others, and his love for his fellow human beings endeared him to all of us. As a result, we came to him not only with theological problems but also with personal ones. We found him ever patient in listening to our views, ever ready to give unstintingly of his knowledge and experience.

Although this speech was delivered a good many years ago, I still feel these sentiments deeply today, and I know that you share them with me. Let me introduce Professor Mordecai M. Kaplan.

> ■ KAPLAN: Thank you, Rabbi Berkowitz. I certainly appreciate what you said. In fact, my appreciation is as great as your exaggeration.

W.B.: In a book titled *Moments of Personal Discovery,* in which leading men and women from all walks of life recall turning points in their lives, Professor Kaplan is one of the contributors. I would like to read his opening statement to you:

"I share with my colleagues in this symposium the reluctance to be vocally autobiographical. One indulges in such autobiography as a rule only on birthday anniversaries. To overcome that reluctance, I have had to make use of a lesson taught to me in my late teens by a teacher whom my father engaged for the purpose of dispelling my doubts concerning the Mosaic authorship of the Pentateuch. That teacher was an ardent follower of Chasidism as well as a philosopher. I once asked him, How could Moses have written the verse in Numbers that reads 'And Moses was the humblest of all men on the face of the earth'? His answer was that the saintliness of Moses enabled him to achieve such self-detachment as to be capable of speaking about himself as though he were somebody else. That answer did not satisfy me as to the question of Moses' authorship of the Pentateuch, but it taught me a lesson in the art of self-detachment. When a person has to speak or to write about himself, he should do so as though he were speaking or writing about somebody else."

In this spirit of self-detachment, could you share with us some of the great moments of personal discovery in your life?

> ■ KAPLAN: Well, let's begin at the beginning. The beginning was a little over eight decades ago, and as you know, having learned to think of time according to the theories of Einstein, 1881 was 800 years ago. So many changes have taken place since then that it is very difficult to try to compress in a few

minutes almost eight centuries of experience. In any event, I was not born in this country. I was born in Lithuania. Before I try to describe any specific moments or outstanding experiences, I would like to think of myself in the terms in which I have just been reminded, to see myself objectively throughout the years. I find that I can best describe myself in terms identified by the well-known sociologist David Riesman, as characteristic of human nature. He speaks of people being "directed" differently. Some are "other-directed"—that is, directed by their contemporaries. Others are directed by tradition. And a limited number of people are really "innerdirected."

If I may speak of myself objectively, I would say that I am all three: tradition-directed, other-directed, and inner-directed. Being inner-directed has made me a Reconstructionist. Of that I shall speak later. Being other-directed means that my parents made me what I am. I was not born in the great era of the "beatniks," and I did not think that rebelling against parents was the required duty of the adolescent.

My father, who was an itinerant scholar rabbi and a student-colleague of the late Rabbi Yitzhak Reines, the organizer of the Mizrachi movement, told the following story of what happened when I was born: I was born on a Friday night. Since it was forbidden to record anything on the Sabbath, my father stopped the pendulum of the pendulum clock. It was then seven minutes before midnight. When he reported this to Rabbi Reines, the rabbi remarked, "You evidently expect your son to be a Maimonides." The fact is that my father did expect me to be a Maimonides. On the other hand, my mother expected me to be nothing less than the Chief Rabbi of Great Britain. With those ideas in their minds, I was being stuffed with as much Jewish learning as I could digest. By the time I was 7 I had already studied Chumash and Rashi. I recall having received from my father a present of a five-volume set of these books, which he had brought with him from his travels and which stimulated me in my study of Chumash.

I remember having seen him very few times during the first seven years of my life because he was an itinerant, semiascetic scholar who traveled from one yeshivah to another.

He was the head of one of them for a time. The first memory
that I have of his presence was when I sat on his knee and he
had me make the alphabet out of matches that were on the
table. When I succeeded in guessing the right letters, I was
presented with a leaden bird whistle that he had bought in
Vilna. The second present was a set of the Pentateuch.

If you want to know anything about the kind of background of a youngster of the type that I am describing, read
Life Is with People. It describes Jewish life in what is known as
the *shtetl*. I remember very many things, but of course this is
not the time to speak about them. When I was 7, we migrated
from where we had lived. Father went one way and my
mother, my sister, and I another way. Father went directly to
New York, and my mother, my sister and I went to Paris,
where my mother had two brothers. We went there—we
were parked, really, in Paris—until Father could establish
himself in New York. He did so after a year, becoming associated with the only chief rabbi in American Jewish life, the
late Rabbi Jacob Joseph. Father became one of his three associates known as *dayanim*, whose function it was to answer
questions of Halachah, and to arbitrate in case of litigation. I
was sent to the first all-day school, the Yeshiva Aitz Chayim,
which later developed into the Yeshiva University. I am
therefore one of the oldest alumni of the Yeshiva University.

In addition, my parents also got me a rebbe, a private tutor,
to teach me Bible and the Hebrew language and grammar. At
first he would come from 8:00 until 10:00 in the evening. I
would fall asleep in the middle of the lesson, so my parents
had him come instead from 6:00 until 8:00 in the morning.
The parts that I best remember of the Bible are in a little
Berlin edition with small type. I still use that edition instead
of a Concordance, because in it I can easily locate passages
that I look for. This teacher taught me so well that the
knowledge I acquired out of the Bible then has remained
with me even until today.

I entered public school at the age of 10½. When I was in the
third grade of P.S. 2, a fellow pupil absented himself one day
from class. When he returned, I heard him explain to the
teacher the reason for his absence. He said he had taken an
examination in a seminary, where he would study for the

rabbinate. After class I asked him to come to my home and tell my parents all about the seminary. He did, and, as a result, I entered the seminary at the age of 12½. I was admitted as a student of its preparatory class. That was in December 1893. Already then, the inner-directed forces in me asserted themselves. I criticized the seminary, then known as the Jewish Theological Seminary of New York, housed at 736 Lexington Avenue, for having such low standards of admission. I had been studying Talmud in its most advanced and difficult sections, and the then-dean of the seminary examined me only in the reading of the Commentary by Rashi. At that time I did not know English well enough to use it in translating the text, so I used Yiddish. When I came home I complained of the low standard of admission to the seminary. I have been criticizing the seminary ever since.

Please remember, the seminary is not the only institution I criticize. I find fault with virtually every type of school, academy, or synagogue. That is my business in life. That is where I act out my inner-directed convictions. What is wrong with Judaism has its source at the institutions that train rabbis, teachers, and social workers. They are trained to become keepers of the past, but they are not trained as midwives of the future. That is why I became a Reconstructionist.

It was my good fortune that one of the great Jewish exegetes of the Bible, whom the late Professor Israel Davidson described in an article in *The American Hebrew* as a modern Rashi, was a steady visitor at my parents' home during my teens. I refer to Arnold B. Ehrlich. As a young man he had studied abroad under the famous scholar Delitzsch. Having himself become a great biblical scholar, he decided at the age of 50 to write a new commentary on the Bible, in Hebrew. The reason he became a steady visitor at my parents' home was that he would come to consult Father concerning the use of Hebrew idioms in the Talmud, which might throw light on the Hebrew in the Bible. While staying at our house, he would impart to me not only his new rendering of the biblical text, but also his own ideas concerning the many problems of authorship and historicity in the biblical narratives. He thus shook my belief in tradition.

W.B.: I would like to turn now from Kaplan the man, to Kaplan the philosopher, the thinker, the founder of the Reconstructionist movement. Fundamentally, Reconstructionism views Judaism as three-dimensional. The three dimensions are Israel, God, and Torah. To put it in other words, Judaism's peoplehood, religion, and culture. Let us begin with the meaning of Reconstructionism. Why planned Reconstruction? Cannot that which has kept the Jewish people alive for more than 2,000 years of dispersal be depended upon to continue Jewish survival? Also, since Judaism in the past progressed through a process of unconscious evolution, why need we today plan its reconstruction?

■ KAPLAN: Let me answer your questions in the order in which you state them. The first question refers to the Jewish people. In the Bible, the Jewish people are referred to as the "House of Israel," which actually means the household, or the family, of Israel. For the present, however, let us take the term "House of Israel" literally, as referring to a huge edifice that houses the entire Jewish people who live in it like one great family, united by a sense of a common blood-and-spirit kinship. That House of Israel has existed for more than 3,000 years. Whatever changes took place in the inner life of the Jewish people were so gradual that they were hardly recognized by the occupants of that House. Suddenly, about 200 years ago, the earth under that House began to quake. Before long a tidal wave followed the earthquakes, rendering the House unsafe to live in. More and more of the inhabitants of the House of Israel have been leaving it. Enough, however, so loved their ancient home that they have decided to keep it in constant repair. Instead, however, of agreeing on a uniform plan of repair for the House of Israel, we have our four Jewish denominations, each with a plan of its own.

What I refer to, metaphorically, as the earthquake that shook up the House of Israel, literally took the form of desegregation of the Jewish people. Throughout the centuries, after the destruction of the Second Commonwealth, wherever Jews lived in dispersion they lived in a state of segregation from the rest of the population. That enabled them to maintain their own traditional way of life and their own sense of a common national destiny. Beginning with the last decade or two of the eighteenth century, when Jews began to be granted civil rights and to be integrated into the general population, they lost that solidarity that was essential to the awareness of their Jewish identity, their common way of life, and their sense of common destiny. Hence the problem of Jewish survival, which is still with us. In referring metaphorically to the tidal wave that soon thereafter struck the House of Israel, I had in mind the particular development that at the same time took place in Western civilization: the Enlightenment. That Enlightenment has been a standing challenge since then, both to Christianity and to Judaism. Jews no sooner began to be integrated into the general population than their Judaism began to disintegrate under the influence of the Enlightenment.

This answers the question of why the Jewish tradition, which managed to survive unimpaired up to the nineteenth century, is no longer adequate for our spiritual needs today. As a result of the political and economic desegregation of Jews, they came under the influence of the Enlightenment, with its challenge to all that they had regarded as their mission: to promulgate the divinely revealed truth.

To revert to the metaphor of the earthquake and the tidal wave, is it any wonder that so many of our Jewish people are leaving the House of Israel? To put it literally, Jews are trying to escape Jewish life. They no longer experience a sense of security, either physical or spiritual, in the House of Israel. However, we Jews have always had our saving remnant who have remained loyal to the Jewish people, and have sought to keep it and Judaism alive, despite hardship and danger.

The first organized attempt to enable the Jewish people to meet the challenge of desegregation and enlightenment was the Reform movement. It attempted, so to speak, to render the House of Israel habitable. The Reform leaders suggested that the House of Israel should be repaired to look like a church. "We will make Judaism livable," they said.

The Neo-Orthodox opposed the Reform idea. They thought that all that had to be done was merely to fix the cracks in the wall and in the ceiling and put in new windows for the light of modern knowledge to stream in, but to make sure that the House retained its original appearance.

Along came the Conservative movement. Its leaders agreed, on the whole, with the Neo-Orthodox but suggested changes in the size, number, and arrangement of the rooms within the House.

Then what happened? Along came the founder of Reconstructionism and said, "Now listen, friends, if you want our Jews to live in the House, go down to the basement and take a look at the condition of its foundation. See what has happened to it as a result of the earthquake—desegregation—and of the tidal wave—Enlightenment. Before you plan any changes in the house itself, make sure that its foundation is strong enough to withstand possible further earthquakes and tidal waves."

W.B.: I think that it would be appropriate to ask you to establish this premise: What is the foundation?

■ KAPLAN: I have tried to study the foundation. As you said in introducing the subject, the foundation is knowing what it means to be a Jew and what Judaism is. An outstanding leader of the Conservative movement not too long ago published an article in a prominent national magazine on the subject "What is a Jew?" He answered that question by saying that a Jew is a person who always asks himself, "What am I?" Is it any wonder that soon thereafter another prominent national magazine published an article entitled "The Vanishing American Jew"? These are the inevitable consequences of the fact that none of the four Jewish denominations or establishments has so far produced a normative image of an American Jew or has given us an idea of what an American Jew ought to be.

What does the Reform denomination say? It says that the Jews are only a church, a religious community. Jews are no longer a nation; they no longer have any connection or claim on *Eretz Yisrael* (the Land of Israel). We are a religious community, it says, dedicated to the belief that there is only one God and that all men are brothers. This is called ethical monotheism. This means that we have a mission from God, that we are a divinely chosen religious community, the only authentic religious community committed to the purpose of missionizing the world with the great truth of ethical monotheism. How?

By preaching it from the pulpit to empty synagogues. That in essence is the Reform version of Judaism.

The Neo-Orthodox maintain that nothing that happens in the world about us entitles us to change our divinely appointed status as God's chosen nation or to resort to political means to reclaim our ancient homeland. As a home for the homeless Jews, yes, but not as a political state with Jews as a political nation. Only the coming of the long-awaited Messiah can restore us as a nation in *Eretz Yisrael*. It was this version of our Jewish destiny that impelled the Neo-Orthodox organization known as Agudas Yisrael to combat the Zionist movement.

The Conservative denomination is inclined, like the Reform denomination, to take seriously the historical approach to Jewish tradition. Schechter's quip about higher criticism being higher anti-Semitism is passé. That, of course, implies a break with the traditional belief that is proclaimed by Conservative congregations whenever the open Torah scroll is raised. According to that proclamation, the Pentateuch was dictated by God to Moses, who transmitted it to Israel. On the other hand, Conservatism's conception of Jewish law, or Halachah, is virtually Orthodox. Evidently, Conservatism does not make a fetish of consistency. The leading scholars in the Conservative movement are of one mind with the leading scholars of the Reform movement with regard to the Jewish past, and with the leading scholars of the Orthodox movement with regard to the Jewish present. Conservatism has given us two new words, "Orthoproxy" and "Conservadox."

W.B.: Reconstructionism, on the other hand, has been described as "abstract, intellectual, and lacking in emotion." Can it then appeal to the ordinary person?

■ KAPLAN: What is wrong with being intellectual? Do you think that there are so few Jewish intellectuals that we can afford to disregard them? Let me quote to you statistics about Jewish intellectuals. The percentage of Jewish high school students who go on to college is much higher than that of non-Jewish students. On the average, only 24 percent of the non-Jewish youth goes to college, while 75 percent of Jewish youth attend college.

The magazine *Commentary* occasionally presents studies of Jewish intellectuals, from the standpoint of their concern with Jewish life. For the most part their studies reveal a shocking degree of escapism from Jewish life, of alienation from Jewish religion, and disinterest in the fate of the Jewish people. How many Jewish members of college faculties really care to be identified as Jews? How many of them evince the least interest in the Hillel Foundations at the colleges? You can well imagine what effect as examples they have on the Jewish student body. So what is wrong in trying to win the Jewish intellectuals for Judaism? Is it not a fact that people look to the intellectuals for guidance with regard to cultural values and spiritual standards? Win the intellectuals to an interest in Jewish life, and the rest will follow.

On the other hand, to charge Reconstructionism with being abstract and unemotional is to misunderstand and misrepresent it. Since its purpose is to get Jews to experience the reality of God, to love the Jewish people, and to become involved in its destiny, how could it possibly expect to achieve these objectives without appealing to the deepest and most sacred human feelings? It is to the credit of Reconstructionism that it attempts to achieve those objectives without appealing to the kind of mysticism that nowadays can be self-induced by the drug LSD.

W.B.: Why do so many intellectuals who have lost all interest in religion speak disparagingly of attempts to revise or reinterpret traditional religion and express a preference for the "good old religion" they so long ago abandoned?

■ KAPLAN: This is perfectly natural. Don't you see what happens when they refer to the old religion as the only authentic religion, to an Orthodox service that uses only Hebrew as the only authentic kind of religious worship? That gives them an excuse for not having anything to do with religion. If they could say that the old religion was not authentic, then they would be expected to explain what to them would be authentic religion, and they would have to become involved in the whole problem. By maintaining that only the good old religion is authentic religion, they imply that it is so because it is authoritarian, because it precludes doubt and questioning, because it is based on supernaturalism, all of which is, of course, contrary to their own outlook on life. Such authentic religion is not for them. The intellectual recognizes that there are those who still believe in supernaturalism, who still think that only the past is the source of spiritual truth, and who believe in it sincerely, and that such people are to be respected. But as far as he himself is concerned, he cannot be expected to accept such outlived religion.

w.b.: Reconstructionist literature states that living in two civilizations simultaneously is without precedent. Did not the Jews of Babylonia, of the Greek and Roman worlds, of medieval Spain, also live in two civilizations at the same time? Why is our situation so different?

■ KAPLAN: Let me restate what I said at the very beginning, when I tried to answer the question of why we need Reconstructionism. I then made use of a simile to describe our present situation. I compared it to a house that is struck by an earthquake and a tidal wave. The change in Jewish life from segregation to desegregation makes it impossible for the Jewish people to retain its old structural form. In ancient times, Jews who lived in Alexandria, in Rome, and in Moslem Spain lived apart from the native civilization; they were not integrated into those civilizations. Only a marginal Jew, and now and then an intellectual Jew, came in contact with the native civilization. As a rule, he would begin to question the value of Judaism. It was for such Jews that Maimonides wrote his *Guide for the Perplexed*.

Now, however, most Jews are perplexed. That is because we form an integral part of non-Jewish civilizations. The question is, How is it possible for a nation that had led a segregated existence and maintained a full civilization of its own in exile to retain that civilization after becoming an integral part of other nations and their cultures? In premodern times, Jews were never confronted by a problem of that kind. As a rule, they always lived their own way of life within some pale or ghetto set apart for them.

Nowadays, however, we Jews are immersed in the civilizations of the countries that accept us as equals. We have to share the economic, the political, and the cultural interests of those countries. That is our duty as loyal citizens. How shall we do that while at the same time retaining our Jewish corporate individuality? That is the kind of paradoxical problem described in the Talmud as a case of breaking a jug that contains wine without spilling the wine. That calls for a special kind of ingenuity. Living in two civilizations is not easy, but it can be achieved.

Fortunately, the Jewish people's will to live is such that they can find the necessary ways and means of solving the problem of living in two civilizations. In our time, the key to the solution of that problem is Zionism. Zionism has created a Jewish state where Jewish civilization is destined to develop normally as the civilization of the Jewish majority in the State of Israel. That Jewish majority, to be identified as Zion, is bound to function in the spirit envisioned by the prophet Isaiah. Said he: "For from Zion shall go forth the Torah, and the word of the Eternal from Jerusalem." The Jewish majority in the Land of Israel will hold together the Jewish communities in the Diaspora, as the hub of a wheel holds its spokes connecting the hub with the rim, the rim in this case symbolizing the historic Jewish civilization.

The Reconstructionist movement has been urging American Jews to organize themselves into the kind of organic communities that would function as spokes connected with Zion, the hub of Jewish civilization. These American Jewish communities would transmit the creative cultural and spiritual development in the State of Israel to the Jews of America in such form as to, on the one hand, integrate the universal Jewish values into American civilization, and on the other hand, assimilate the ethical and spiritual values of American democracy.

In the meantime, however, Reconstructionism could not allow the present disintegration of Jewish life to proceed as a result of the interfaith marriages that are thinning out our ranks. Long before Reconstructionism identified itself as a new movement in Jewish life, it devised a Jewish social institution that might stem the growth of interfaith marriages.

The rise of synagogue centers and Jewish community centers throughout the United States and Canada during the second decade of this century was due to the sociological approach to American Jewish life that was the first contribution of Reconstructionism to American Judaism.

An objective description of Reconstructionism would describe its beginning with my joining the faculty of the Jewish Theological Seminary in June 1909. Educationally, it began to function forthwith as a reinterpretation of our Biblical tradition. Beginning with my public agitation for creating opportunities for Jews to develop their own Jewish social life through synagogue and communal centers in April 1915, Reconstructionism has contributed to the communal aspect of American Jewish life.

I owe much of my sociological approach to the problem of living in two civilizations to my association with two Jews who have done most to lay the foundations of a future for American Jewish life. Judah L. Magnes did that in the community, and Samson Benderly did that educationally. Magnes tried to establish an organic type of Jewish community. Benderly contributed the idea that Jewish education was the responsibility not only of parents or of congregations to which the parents belonged but of the entire Jewish community. The *kehillah* was an attempt to stimulate the Jews to organize themselves as a community, as a community that would be in its very structure a link in the chain of communities throughout the world, organic Jewish communities, all of which would constitute the *reconstituted* Jewish people.

Why do I say "reconstituted" Jewish people, instead of just "Jewish people"? As a Reconstructionist, I have discovered that our life as Jews is a kind of "as if" existence—"as if" we were an existing, functioning people. Actually, we are a disbanded people, a veteran people, that, like a veteran army, parades one or two days a year. We are not engaged in living a Jewish life. We delude ourselves. The Reconstructionist movement asks us to stop deluding ourselves. In an authoritative work, *The Jews—Their History, Culture, and Religion*, we are told that we do not know who we are or what we are. People have some notion of the meaning of the basic terms *Orthodox*,

Reform, Conservative, and *secularist,* but no notion of what exactly the term *Jews* means. All because there is today no generally recognized Jewish people with some kind of constitution, whether written or unwritten, to unite them. Belonging to a congregation, paying dues to the Federation of Philanthropic Institutions, even being a Zionist, does not convey what constitutes being a Jew with a consciousness of belonging to a Jewish people. Under those conditions it is impossible to formulate an effective and meaningful system of Jewish education, since to be a genuine education it ought to integrate the child into a living, functioning, cohesive, stable, disciplined Jewish people. To have all Jews throughout the world reconstitute themselves openly before all the world on the basis of a new constitution, which would define the duties and responsibilities of the different Jewish communities in Israel and in the Diaspora, is, according to Reconstructionism, the first priority in all efforts to forestall the vanishing of the Jewish people.

W.B.: The Reconstructionist movement has been severely criticized because the idea of a "chosen people" has been removed. Is this idea untenable? Why has it been eliminated from the *brachah* when we get the *aliyah*? Why has it been eliminated from the Kiddush?

■ **KAPLAN:** If we really believe that we are a chosen people, then we believe that God, of course, has chosen us. To believe this we must have evidence of the fact that God actually Himself dictated those statements in the Bible, in which Israel is spoken of as having been chosen by God, and that it was not done merely by some great prophet or visionary who was sure he was inspired by God. To believe this is to believe in the reality of supernaturalism, to believe that reality as a whole exists on two levels, the natural level and the supernatural level. The natural level is subject to natural law, the laws of human nature and the laws of physical nature. However, from what we know of human experience, nothing within natural law is known to be the source of the belief that the Jews are God's chosen people.

Inasmuch as our purpose is to reach those Jews who can no longer think of reality as existing on two levels, natural and supernatural, we cannot use the term *chosen people* without contradicting their entire world outlook. If our purpose is to emphasize the uniqueness of the Jewish people as having arrived at a more authentic conception of God, a conception of God as manifesting Himself in human behavior that is based on equity and justice, we do in fact do so by thanking God "for having brought us nigh unto Him." That, it seems to me, is a more understandable and acceptable idea of our uniqueness as a people, insofar as we have, by our conception of God, pointed toward what must be of primary concern to men and nations if man is to achieve self-fulfillment.

W.B.: If the purpose of Judaism is to enable the Jew to fulfill himself as a human being, can he not achieve that purpose through humanism?

■ KAPLAN: Humanism is based on the assumption that it is a mistake to validate any form of human behavior as obligatory for any other reasons than that it makes for human happiness. The self-fulfillment that Judaism would have us strive for is religious humanism, in that is transcends happiness. Self-fulfillment, which is a synonym for "salvation," is achievable through nothing less than the cosmic polarity of independence and interdependence that is characteristic of everything from the most minute to the most vast entity. That polarity in human life takes the form of responsiveness and responsibility which require for their field of action involvement in an organic society that is cohesive, stable, and disciplined. For Jews, such self-fulfillment means belonging to the Jewish people, commitment to its way of life, faith in its destiny. All that is not only humanism but religious humanism.

It is only through religious humanism that we can begin to realize the authentic function of nationhood in the shaping of human destiny. Many of us, noting the extent to which national rivalries are endangering the survival of the human race, see its only hope in cosmopolitanism. In the meantime, new nations are being born in Africa, in Asia, and in other parts of the world. So far, it is only Judaism, with its religious humanism, that has a helpful answer. Judaism as a national religious civilization proclaims to the rest of the world that nations are an indispensable means to human self-fulfillment, provided that they be tamed, controlled, and directed by responsiveness to human needs and by responsibility for helping one another individually, collectively, and internationally in meeting those needs. The message of Jewish religion is not merely ethical monotheism but ethical nationhood.

W.B.: When one walks on *Shabbat* morning, one sees many Jews flocking to synagogues. On *Shabbat* morning I heard a lady say that she was being honored with an *aliyah*. There was no question about where she was going. She was going to the Society for the Advancement of Judaism. What is, or what should be, the status of women in the synagogue?

■ KAPLAN: The place of women in the synagogue is to contribute to the life of the synagogue in the same way that men do. Women, too, should help to make the synagogue a link in the chain of the Jewish people. They, too, should be concerned with the order of priorities in the conduct of the synagogue's activities, so that the synagogue becomes a spiritually educative influence in the lives and the homes of its members, a place where parents and children can engage in the lifelong education of the conscience. In general, the failure of the American synagogue to exercise a potent influence in the life of our Jewish people is that its activities are carred on in violation of its traditional order of priorities as stated in the opening sentence of the ethical treatise in the *Mishnah Avot*. The world of the spirit rests on three things: the study of Torah, the worship of God, and engaging in the improvement of social conditions. The synagogue is not likely to adopt this program with its specific order of priorities unless women take a leading part in planning the activities of the synagogue. Men in American life, as in Western civilization generally, are preoccupied with their businesses or professions and leave it to women to take the initiative in the fostering of cultural and spiritual interests. There is no reason that Jewish women should be different from other women and shirk the cultural, spiritual, ethical, and religious responsibilities that should be theirs in the synagogue.

W.B.: What do you feel is the meaning or relevance of *kashrut* today?

■ KAPLAN: If Judaism is to mean more than a way of speaking or preaching, if it is to function as a way of life and as a religious civilization, it has to make itself felt in every Jewish home in more concrete form. That is what we mean by Judaizing the home. In rabbinic lore, the home is expected to be a family temple, and the dining room table is to be a kind of altar. *Kashrut* is a religious practice that gives the meal the character of an offering to God. Translated into the modern universe of discourse, it is like saying, we eat to live; we do not live to eat.

That interpretation of *kashrut* is a far cry from the kind of rationalizations that have been in vogue. In the main, *kashrut* is interpreted as a health precaution. That is a rather foolish reason, since non-Jews manage to be healthy without *kashrut*. The authentic reason for *kashrut* is given in the Torah, in the section of the Torah that names the animals that may be eaten and those that may not, "In order that you know yourselves as a holy people." I do not believe that we are a chosen people, but I would like us to be a holy people—a people dedicated to making the education of the conscience our chief spiritual vocation and the source of control and direction in our striving after pleasure and power.

The trouble with the philosophers and the theologians is that they regard conscience as something that one acquires by intuition. The problem is not that of having a conscience. The most dangerous fanatics are those who have a conscience, particularly when they are sure that God has given it to them, or that it is the voice of the people. Conscience has to be educated if it is to control and direct our instinctive drives for pleasure and power, and that education has to be lifelong. To be motivated, however, to engage in the lifelong study of conscience, and to obey its dictates, we have to be involved with our Jewish people and be imbued with Jewish consciousness, with the consciousness of its historical career, with its achievements and its frustrations. That is the purpose of the study of Torah, which is the holiest form of worship. For that reason, it is of primary importance to plan our Sabbath services program in such a way as to have those who attend leave the synagogue each time better informed about Judaism as an evolving religious civilization and more vigorously determined to translate it into their personal lives so as to leave the world better and happier for their having lived.

W.B.: When a reception was tendered to Dr. Kaplan on the occasion of his eightieth birthday, the program said the following:

> Among Zionist leaders, he is regarded as unrealistic for believing that Jewish life can possibly thrive in the Diaspora. Among the non-Zionists and anti-Zionists, he is accused of setting up Israel as the authoritative center of theocratic realm. Among social workers, he is considered too much of a theologian. Among theologians, he is charged with being nothing more than a sociologist. Among those who call for the integration of Jews into American life, his blueprint for the organic community seems like a plan for a new ghetto, while those who worry about assimilation cannot reconcile themselves to his insistence that Jews live in two civilizations. Those who are acquainted with his personal habits of Jewish observance confuse them with the Orthodox, while the Orthodox rail at his suggestion that ritual should be removed from the category of Halachah. Finally, he himself reports that he has been taken for a thinker among men of action, and for a man of action among thinkers. But all agree, and we join this chorus, that right or wrong, Mordecai M. Kaplan might be recognized as one of the foremost philosophers of Judaism in the twentieth century.

3. ❧ Luminary for the Centuries

Rabbi Adin Steinsaltz

W.B.: Anyone who has the privilege of meeting Adin Steinsaltz soon discovers why there is such interest in him and in his work. First, his volume of writing is simply stupendous. Anyone who has ever studied a page of Talmud understands what a tremendous undertaking it is to vocalize, punctuate, translate, and write a commentary on it, and no less in the special style of Rabbi Steinsaltz. His efforts have helped to bring about a renewed interest in Talmud in the United States, particularly as a source of Jewish religious wisdom and guidance.

Second, Rabbi Steinsaltz's work in the fields of mysticism, spirituality, and Chasidism respond to the quest in this country for that part of Judaism that, in modern times, had been ignored, and yet is now experiencing great revival.

Third and most important, Rabbi Steinsaltz has had such an impact on this generation because of who he is as a person. He is a young man, although he has the knowledge and wisdom of an old one. He understands modern society, yet he represents and transmits the insights of ancient, older societies. Jews have sought to come to grips with the correct balance of modernity and tradition, and Rabbi Steinsaltz has shared with us his own unique blend of the two.

Looking at society today, we see that some American Jews are looking for the right rebbe, for the proper spiritual guide who can offer a path for confusing and troubling times. Rabbi Steinsaltz is surely that kind of guide. His appeal is that he lives in this world, understands it, knows it, and yet in the final analysis is not really of it. Thoroughly authentic in its ways, and filled with the most ardent traditionalism, his is also a piercing intellectualism endowed with a high ethical sensitivity.

Rabbi Steinsaltz is in the forefront of the movement for Jewish renewal and a contemporary Jewish spirituality. Part of this movement is an effort to bring all kinds of Jews closer together in new ways. Rabbi Steinsaltz has been able to bridge the worlds that divide the religious and secular communities, even as he has offered provocative answers to modern-day challenges. Witness his most recent stunning achievement with the opening in Moscow of a yeshivah to train rabbis.

When one enters his presence, one senses both holiness and wisdom, and one leaves with a sense of the exceptional in the midst of the ordinary. And yet, Rabbi Steinsaltz does all that he does with *chen*, which for Jews can mean both personal charm and hidden wisdom.

American Jews tody are seeking an authentic, holistic Judaism with living role models, paradigmatic exemplars, and leaders who also express fervor. This is Adin Steinsaltz's greatness.

Rabbi Steinsaltz, I think it is fair to say that we live in a generation that is interested in the biographies of well-known individuals. And I know that all of us would be very interested to hear your own tale. For example, I'd like to begin by asking whether you were always a religious man. How did you come to achieve such width and depth of learning?

> ■ STEINSALTZ: Well, I come from a nonreligious family, and I have been educated in a strange mixed-up world—a world of nonreligious Israel—but in a very Jewish way. It is a strange combination; in my case it was a very Jewish background of people who were interested in being Jewish on the one hand but on the other hand, were perhaps entirely irreligious. From that background I had to fight my way to religion.

W.B.: In fighting your way toward religion, was there anyone who had a great impact or influence on you to find that way?

> ■ STEINSALTZ: My first teacher was my maternal uncle, who was a very exceptional person, a great man and yet very much unknown. He pushed me toward religion, not by telling me to become religious but by being very Jewish himself and by imparting the idea that if one has to make a search for soul, for meaning, and for what is behind things, then there is in Judaism much to make the search worthwhile.

W.B.: Your father, as you indicated, was not a religious individual. One day someone approached him and said to him, "You know, your son, Adin, has the greatest mind in the last 2,000 years of Jewish history." And your father replied, "Wouldn't you know it had to happen to me!" Is that a true story, or is it apocryphal?

■ STEINSALTZ: Well, I think that he rather liked it—it wasn't such a misfortune for him that I discovered the world of religion. He was proud of his ancestry. He came from a very Jewish and distinguished family, and he was very happy that somehow the line goes on.

W.B.: What is this new edition of the Talmud that you're working on, and why do you see a need for it?

■ STEINSALTZ: I became involved with the project almost unwillingly. It began with my giving lectures about Talmud. People were interested and told me that I should write those lectures down. So, in fact, what I am trying to do is something that is perhaps new in our time because our times are different. Usually the talmudist achieves his learning from teacher to pupil directly. I tried to do the same by writing. I am trying to combine what I know about Talmud and to teach it to others who I think are interested in learning.

W.B.: How large a staff do you have working with you on this project?

■ STEINSALTZ: Unluckily, I cannot afford to have too big a staff. There are ten to fifteen people who work in basic research in various fields. Then I try to combine their findings. I write the material down because I am responsible for everything that will appear there. Whether it is a mistake or something very wise, I have to be responsible for it, so I'm writing everything.

W.B.: You are also the director of the Shefa Institute of Jerusalem. What is the Shefa Institute, why did you create it, and what is its purpose?

■ STEINSALTZ: It is meant to be the beginning of a school that will educate future teachers. I have a special aim: to find first-rate people who are willing to come and teach, especially those who are to be our future leaders. We as a people have so many capacities, yet they are spent on and for the outward world or for other interests. I would like to have a body of people who would be capable of leading those who are able to become leaders, whether they are rabbis, teachers, doctors, or just plain people who have the ability to be centers of activity in Jewish life.

w.b.: I think everyone has an image of a talmudic scholar as one who sits all day before the Gemora and studies. I know that your day is probably an 18- if not 20-hour day. And yet, reading some of your biographical material, I see a man, one of the greatest talmudic minds of the twentieth century, who finds time to have hobbies. I'm curious, what are your hobbies? And do they in any way relate to your talmudic study?

■ STEINSALTZ: My first hobby is the Talmud because by profession I am, or I have to describe myself as, a defrocked mathematician. I began as a teacher of mathematics and physics. I was caught by the Talmud and I really did not want to be a talmudist, I wanted to deal with it as a hobby, but the hobby grew. I'm still in love with that hobby of mine. At the same time, I'm interested in almost everything—from detective stories to science fiction to mathematics to animals. I am also interested in people—sometimes I even like them. I am interested in good literature, even though I do not read enough of it. I prefer children's stories to most earnest literature. I am interested in science for many reasons, and sometimes in politics. Sometimes I'm also interested in football, if I have time to watch it; if not, I at least read about it in the newspapers. So I'm interested in what people are interested in, and not because I have some reason but because I am curious. I am still trying to learn, and almost everything fascinates me. So as long as there is something to learn, I like to learn more and to know more about everything.

w.b.: You have spoken to many young people. Your name evokes great awe in them. What is it that they are asking and looking for?

■ STEINSALTZ: Young people are asking more spiritually oriented questions now than they did when I was 15 or 20 years old. Young people are interested to know about themselves mainly. It's a quest for identity, a quest for self. Sometimes, by searching deeper into the ego, people can also find the Almighty there, if they search long and earnestly enough. So young people are searching within themselves, and they try to find others to help them. Sometimes they find the right people to lead them, sometimes not. But this is seemingly the search.

W.B.: Speaking of this search, do you see something significant in the recent proliferation of cults? As you assess it—young people looking for identity—are there any dangers in this kind of movement within the Jewish community?

■ **STEINSALTZ:** One of the reasons that I am so interested in the study of Talmud is because I think it is the Book that teaches our people sanity. It makes our people sane because there is an element of madness in every culture. Our people need that helping hand today, they need cultural and intellectual guideposts. One of the harshest criticisms of so many of the cults is that they are not connected with the intellect; they overemphasize heart, feeling, self-expression, and so forth, and they are not interested in the person, the personality as a whole. They lack this element of intellectual integrity. Any place where there is a lack of it, there is a danger first of all to the people involved, and also to the community.

W.B.: If I were to give this next question a title, I would call it "Judaism as a Personal Encounter." You said the following: "I don't think that the tradition by itself is sufficient. Everyone has to have a personal encounter. People can do it in many ways, but they must be personal ways." What are you saying here?

■ **STEINSALTZ:** We cannot be imitators in everything that is real. We cannot be just followers. We are demanded, and especially our people are commanded, to be a Kingdom of Priests. The point is that a priest doesn't need another priest to officiate for him. A Jew doesn't need a rabbi. A Jew needs a personal connection with the "Boss," with the Lord Himself. As a person I am demanded, and as a Jew I am demanded, to have such a connection, so I have one, and for me it's a very personal one. I have to have some kind of a meeting with the essence of my being a Jew. So I think that every one of us has at one point in his life to find out what is his or her basic connection.

w.b.: You have said that we believe that the law has at least 600,000 different paths within it for individuals to enter. There is a private gate for each of us, and we each have to find our own gate. When you spoke about religion, as you do so eloquently, this is what you said: "I rather dislike spiritual people and spiritual things. In fact, I think to make the Lord a spiritual being is to belittle Him." Now, I'm puzzled by that. What is it that you find wrong with the spiritual? And with regard to God, if He is not spiritual, then what is He?

■ STEINSALTZ: When I speak about spiritual people, I speak about those people who are always immersed in higher mysteries, those who always try to deal with things that most people understand little about. I'm trying to say something else. I don't believe that if one has to look for the Lord, one has to look to the ceiling or to the heavens. The Lord is everywhere, not just spacewise, but everywhere in every meaning of things. To speak about the Almighty as being connected with the spiritual is correct as long as we don't say that He is spiritual because He is not material. But on the other hand, I can't say that He is material because He is not spiritual. Both these terms are not adequate to describe that which is beyond all this. The Gentiles say that the Lord is on high. He's sitting in heaven. We say that He is even higher because He looks down upon heaven and earth. The Lord is so infinite that He deals with the smallest physical being— with the molecule, with a germ, with a grain of wheat—in the same way that he deals with angels, with the galaxies. He is so great that all these things are in the same way insignificant, but very significant when all of them are together.

So in a way what I'm saying is that this is Judaism. Judaism is that belief that connects the earthly and those things that are not earthly. What is really of interest is something beyond us, and we can get to it by combining the two, by not leaning too much to one side or the other.

w.b.: Two quotes lead me to questions in this same area. The great psychoanalyst Carl Jung once said that the main problem facing us is not sexual repression but spiritual repression. The great Jewish thinker Chaim Greenberg once said that when Satan wants to attack religion, he afflicts it with a yawn. Rabbi Steinsaltz, is there much today that is boring in religion, and if so, how would you overcome it?

■ STEINSALTZ: There is surely a lot that is boring. I don't have
the opportunity in Israel, but I listen here in America to
numbers of sermons delivered by rabbis, and I find that there
is a lot that is boring, at least about Judaism. However, I am
not speaking only about religion. There are lots of things
that are boring. Doing things because they have "always"
been done "that way" is boring. Listening, and not participating, is boring. And this is the danger for religion, especially in
America, where people are becoming only listeners and passive participants. The way out of boredom is to participate.
Participation doesn't mean being a member of a group that
holds brunches on Sunday mornings. Participation means
being a part of what I would call the adventure of study, the
adventure of prayer, the adventure of fulfilling any mitzvah.
Thus, the way to participate is to get more involved personally, to try as much as possible to become part of things, and
to ask every day, as once young people were asked in the
cheder, "What new thing did you find out today?" That is what
is called *Chidush-Torah*, the renewal of Torah.

I would say, therefore, that the function of a rabbi should
be to call to his community and to ask each of them, "What
new thing did you find out about being Jewish?" This is what
we have to do in order to avoid being bored. We cannot be
bored when we are participating, when we are part of the
creative. Then we are a part of the Torah.

W.B.: One last question in this area before I turn to some issues in
Israel. It fascinated me, especially in light of what has been going on in
Iran and continues to go on in Israel, when you said that you prefer
religious fanatics to nationalistic fanatics. Why? In light of your statement, how do you feel about Khomeini, the religious leader, as a
national *political* figure? [*Editor's note*: This dialogue was conducted
shortly before the Ayatollah Khomeini's demise.]

■ STEINSALTZ: Nationalism is a very terrible religion. It's religion because it is based upon mystical, nonrational reasoning, and it works as a religion. Most religions have built-in
inhibitions. A person who believes in religion knows that
there are things that are prohibited from the point of view of
religion as religion.

Nationalism doesn't have any limits. It doesn't have any

inner factors to fight it. It has no law except itself. Therefore, it is very dangerous, perhaps one of the most ruthless and cruel religions that has evolved through the ages, more cruel than any ancient religion, more cruel than any inquisition, more cruel than any burning of bodies in any other culture. This is the danger of nationalism all over the world.

I think that Khomeini and those like him are a nasty combination of religion and nationalism. This combination, when it comes together, becomes worse than anything else, because if a person feels that he is a prophet, then he can do anything in the name of the Lord. But if he is a nationalist, then he can even do contrary to what the Lord says because the nation needs it. So this combination creates a terrible basic temperament and a background upon which anything can happen. These people have all the arrogance of religion without any of its limits, and therefore they have the worst of two worlds in a most dangerous combination.

W.B.: Every day, the newspapers around the country report on settlements in Judea and Samaria. What are your feelings on the issue of the settlements?

■ STEINSALTZ: I said many years ago that I think it was a basic mistake to consider the settlements only militarily important. This is a secondary consideration; what is primary is that Jews must be allowed to live everywhere in *Eretz Yisrael*. That includes the city of Hebron. The idea that Jews have to be excluded from any place, and that otherwise we cannot make peace, is abhorrent to me.

W.B.: Let me pose several questions concerning religious life in Israel, with which you are intimately acquainted. How do you feel about pluralism in Israel? For that matter, what are your comments concerning the religious establishment and the chief rabbinate in Israel? Are they doing a good job or a bad job? And should they be part of the political system?

■ STEINSALTZ: I know that it is fashionable for certain politically minded rabbis in the Reform and Conservative movements to accuse Israel of helping only the Orthodox and undermining the non-Orthodox segment of Israeli society.

The fact that the Conservative and Reform movements are not very popular in Israel is not due to politics. The point is that if there are enough people interested in Reform and Conservative Judaism, these will become huge movements in Israel with or without government approval. If there is no large Conservative or Reform community, it is because the people in Israel somehow have the notion that if one wants to be religious, there is only one way to do it. I'm speaking now about facts and not offering my own opinion. The point is that many people in Israel have a belief in the Almighty, a belief in Judaism. They keep so many commandments connected with *Eretz Yisrael* that they don't believe that they need any special religious arrangement to do so. Pluralism is allowed. If it doesn't work out in Israel, it's not because of the government but because of the people.

Now, the chief rabbinate in Israel is something entirely different. For many reasons, it is an unsuccessful body. I once told Yitzchak Rabin, when he complained about one of the chief rabbis, that the chief rabbi is not the rabbi of our rabbis—namely, the rabbi of Orthodox Jewry. He's *your* rabbi. He's the rabbi of the secular community. You elected him, you made him a chief rabbi, and if you are not satisfied, it may be because you didn't find the right chief rabbi. In general, I think that basically we have not been successful in Israel in having great religious leaders who could influence the community and the country as a whole, and this is mainly due to political reasons.

w.b.: In speaking of the current state of Judaism, you made a very interesting observation: "I think it's true to say that kosher-centered Judaism is a new phenomenon, but I don't think that this type of Judaism can really exist for any length of time. It is a sign of something dying that has no chance of survival." Rabbi Steinsaltz, what is *kosher-centered Judaism*? Why are you so pessimistic about it?

■ STEINSALTZ: Kosher-centered Judaism is a Judaism that tries to fashion two worlds—[one of which is] a small world in which you can feel Jewish through those things that are somehow obligations. They have to be of a material nature—easy to see, easy to discuss, easy to solve—things that you can easily work at. You can work at being kosher. You can buy another pair of *tefillin*. I think that this is an unhealthy sign—being kosher is only a part of being Jewish, as anybody who has any interest in Judaism knows. It becomes some kind of sport, and people deal with this aspect because they are not interested in anything really important about Judaism. Now, I don't think that it can go on forever because, as you mentioned before, it is boring, and after some time it becomes boring even for those who participate in this sport. Second, it is just a shell, and the shell has no inner core. Therefore, I don't believe that it will survive.

W.B.: If we get out of the kitchen—and women are trying to get out of the kitchen—one of the areas that is uppermost in the minds of a lot of people is the role of women in Judaism. In the United States, in particular, this subject is receiving a great deal of attention. What are your feelings on this issue? What are your views on women rabbis or women cantors? For that matter, do women have a religious mission and a special role within Judaism?

■ STEINSALTZ: This is a big question, and what is worse, it's a sensitive one. And when questions are sensitive it means that whatever you say, somebody is offended, and nobody really listens.

But I am concerned with the halachic point of view, which, I think, is the only point of view that is really Jewish. It places many limitations on women's role and on women's participation in religious commandments. That is very clear, and I think that any major change will produce a new and debased form of Christianity. On the other hand, I would like to see Jewish women participating in things Jewish, participating because there is a lot in which to participate. Wherever there is interest on the part of Jewish women in Judaism, they will take a greater role. If a person is knowledgeable, that person, whether man or woman, will be a leader in Jewish life. If women are really interested in Jewish things, they can participate actively, not by getting what you call "rights," but by getting whatever fulfillment they can. Those who will be interested will be the center, will be where Jewish life is.

W.B.: Rabbi Steinsaltz, a prominent American leader declared that "what we Jews must do is to actively missionize the unchurched Gentiles." Should we seek converts? Secondly, do we Jews have a mission to the world?

> ■ STEINSALTZ: One of my dreams is to have a Jewish mission to Jews. If anybody really needs converting, it is surely the Jews. Nobody can be as much a *goy* as a nice Jewish boy in New York or in Israel. So I think that we very urgently need a mission among our people. We are losing them, and we need them. Now, the basic idea of Judaism is that it's a family religion, and *because* it's a family religion we don't grab people in the street and say, "Fellow, I want you to become a member of my family." I think it is useless to go out into the street and invite non-Jews into the Jewish religion. I say this because the Jewish religion is basically nothing abstract. It is the religion of the Jewish family.
>
> However, there is something else that has to be affirmed, and that is that our mission for generations was mainly to exist *as Jews*. Our way of bringing a mission to the world is by being ourselves. When we were simply Jews, when we didn't try to speak about the Jewish mission to the nations, other people learned from us in one way or another. If we are not now a spiritual influence to the world, it's because we ceased to be ourselves, because we began to imitate others. When we come back to ourselves and we become more Jewish, it will spread by itself.

W.B.:   I would like to ask two final questions. We've seen in the United States and in Israel the proliferation of *baale teshuvah* yeshivot. In your opinion, what is it that so many of these young people are looking for? And what do you think of these yeshivot?

> ■ STEINSALTZ: Our young people are looking to things spiritual, to things meaningful. Some of them, sometimes, almost by mistake, look toward Judaism. I think that most of them don't know that among those gates to inner life and to religion there is also a Jewish gate. For so many of our people this gate, I suppose from the bar mitzvah on, is closed because they think that the bar mitzvah is the occasion on which a person formally announces that he is no longer interested in being Jewish. Therefore, they make it into such a big happening. For many children this is a sign that Judaism

is not interesting, that Judaism doesn't have anything to offer. Luckily, there *are* some who find their way to Judaism. So this is the reason for the *baale teshuvah* movement in this country and in Israel. It is not yet an earnest movement because it doesn't touch the people who count. It is still a fringe movement here and in Israel. I would like to see first-rate people join the movement, people who continue growing within the Jewish framework. In many of the *baale teshuvah* yeshivot, to my great sorrow, it seems that some students are somehow cut in half. They are no longer growing as personalities because somehow they become perhaps too interested only in being Jewish, and I would like our people to be bigger, bigger as personalities. I think that the *baale teshuvah* yeshivot are not yet successful in growing this type of person. It's a pity. I hope it will change in the future, and I hope more people, and more significant people, will make this change.

W.B.: I enjoy asking this next question because it provides an interesting insight. I've asked it of many people through the years. If you could go back in history and meet any three people, who would they be and why?

■ STEINSALTZ: Well, I have just finished a series of graduate lectures about personalities in the Bible, and I found so many—too many—whom I would like to meet. It is very hard to make a choice, and let me just clarify the fact that if I am now making a choice, it is perhaps only for this minute. Perhaps in half an hour, or tomorrow, I will make another choice, not because the first ones are not interesting, but because the new choice represents a new facet of myself. I hope that I'm still growing and changing.

I would like to meet Moshe Rabenu. I would like very much to meet Rashi, perhaps because I am doing similar work—not on the same level, but at least I'm working in the same way. I would also like to meet the Baal Shem Tov because he was always for me a figure of love.

W.B.: I close with a Chasidic story that is told of the great Rabbi Levi Yitzchak of Berditchev, who was once asked, "Rebbe, we have many different tractates in the Talmud that deal with many different topics.

Why, then, are there no tractates in the Talmud on the subject of the service of God, on the subject of the service of man to God, or love of man, or on the subject of the love or fear of God?" Rabbi Levi Yitzchak responded as follows: "My students, the reason that there are no tractates on these holy subjects is that in every generation we are sent great and holy men who by their lives teach us and instruct us on these paths."

Without question, we have had the unique privilege of being exposed to a brilliant mind, a gentle, sweet, sensitive soul, and a very insightful teacher. We have had the special privilege of meeting with a great rabbi who not only translates the tractates, but is a tractate himself in his rare and unusual life, a life that is marked by extraordinary service and love of God and man. I say to Rabbi Adin Steinsaltz, may you be blessed with many, many more years to bring wisdom, learning, hope, joy, and the opening of the countless gates as you help to connect heart and mind here on earth to our God, our Father in heaven.

4. ৪ The Joy of Judaism

Rabbi Zalman Schachter-Shalomi

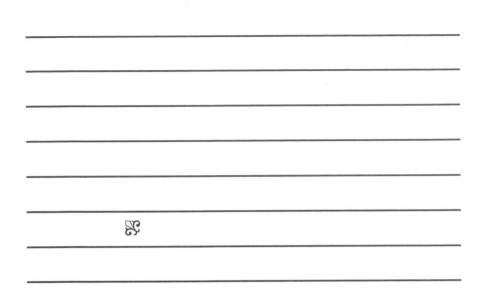

W.B.: What better way is there to begin a discussion of Chasidism than to quote a parable from Chasidic tradition?

A long time ago, a man who had been wandering through a forest for several days, not knowing the right way out, found himself at nightfall enveloped in the darkness of the woods. He was alone, frightened, and lost, and then suddenly he saw a glimmer of light in the distance. His heart grew lighter as he caught sight of a traveler carrying a lantern who was slowly approaching him.

"Well, now I shall certainly find out which is the right way out," he thought. When the two travelers neared one another, he asked the man with the lantern, "Tell me, which is the right way out of the woods? I've been roaming about in this forest for several days."

The man with the lantern said to him, "My friend, I do not know the way out, for I too have been wandering about in this forest for many days. But one thing I can tell you, do not take the way I came. That way is not the way, for it will lead you astray." He said to his fellow traveler, "Let us look for a new way together."

This is a story from a different century, from a country and a climate vastly different from ours. Nevertheless, this parable has meaning for the modern Jew. It speaks of the Jew of today with more insight and understanding than do many of the long volumes on present-day Judaism. The forest is our world of today, and the two lost travelers are the present generation of our people. Like the lost travelers, the modern Jew has not found a way out of the forest of confusion that might lead him to a clearly patterned life of Jewish living and Jewish commitment. He does not know what kind of Jew to be. He has not decided what kind of synagogue he should belong to—Orthodox, Conservative, Reform, Chasidic, or any at all. He is not certain whether he wants his children to learn Hebrew, or his wife to kindle the Sabbath candles. He has not made up his mind whether the people of Israel are really a chosen people or if the Bible is indeed the word of God. And finally, he does not know whether he should believe in prayer and in the Torah itself, with all of its Commandments.

In short, the modern Jew is lost in the forest of doubt, confusion, and consternation. The way to an acceptable and meaningful pattern of Jewish living and thinking is not clearly before him.

One of the answers to this confusion of our day and age, of finding the right road, is the answer given by Chasidism. As an ancient, powerful, and still vital force, Chasidism is part of our Jewish civilization. It not only teaches us, but, more important, it gives us a way of living. We tend to think of Judaism as traditional, unchanging, and, in a sense, unadaptable to modern life. We are continually faced with day-to-day problems that seem to force us to choose, very often against our desires or feelings, ways of living that seem contrary to our beliefs. Too often we feel that our spiritual life is out of joint with the times, or that we are not modern enough. We fail to recognize that in our dualistic society it may well be the other way around. Perhaps our religion, culture, and tradition have truths that can and should change our way of life.

It is for this reason that we have chosen to discuss a Jewish discipline about which most Jews have little real knowledge. Our guest is a traditional thinker who has adjusted in his teaching, writing, and living to our modern, atomic, satellite age. Rabbi Zalman Schachter-Shalomi is a "Lubavitcher Chasid" in modern dress, with a yeshivah education and a master's degree in psychology. For nearly forty years he has counseled men and women around the world. He has held many professional positions in religious studies in the United States and Canada, and has been a creative and highly influential spiritual guide.

I would like to begin with a broad general question: What is Chasidism? Tell us something about the origin and the history of the Chasidic movement.

■ SCHACHTER-SHALOMI: You have heard the Yiddish saying, *Eider ich gey reden vill ich zugen a por verter*—"Before I begin to speak, I would like to say a few words." One thing struck my fancy during this introduction—the name that you have given this series, the name "dialogue," two people talking to each other. Reb Mendel of Kotsk, a Chasidic master, once said, *"Az ich bin ich, vile du bist du, un du bist du vile ich bin ich, bin ich nit ich, un du bist nit du. Ober, az ich bin ich, vile ich bin ich un du bist du vile du bist du, bin ich ich, un du du, kenen mir reden."* This translates: "If I am I, because you are you, and you are you, because I am I, then I am not I, and you are not you. But if I am I because I am I, and you are you because you are you, then I am I and you are you, and we can talk"—and that is the essence of dialogue.

The other thing I want to react to before entering into this discussion was the story you quoted. It is a lovely story. There is a little sequel to that story. I do not know whether the sequel originally was there, or whether it was added later, but the sequel is this: The man asked him, "Then why are you walking around with the lantern?" And he said, "If I cannot find the way, maybe somebody will see that I have lit a lantern and he will come and find me." This is a very wonderful story with which to begin our dialogue. You have lit a lantern; you are here. We have just celebrated Rosh Hashanah, Yom Kippur, Sukkos, Simchas Torah. That is lighting the lantern. If we cannot find the way, maybe someone will find us.

Now to Chasidism. A few years ago we celebrated the two hundredth anniversary of the death of the Baal Shem Tov [the founder of the Chasidic movement]. The Baal Shem Tov was born more than 270 years ago. If you ask where and when, these are sociological questions. But if you ask *why*, that's a Chasidic question. Why was he born? Chasidism says he was born because the darkness of the *Golus*—the Exile—was lasting so long, and the Jews were so faint that they had no strength to last until the *Mashiach*, the Messiah, would come. So God took a little bit of the light of the *Mashiach* and sent it down in the person of the Baal Shem Tov to tide us over.

Where was he born? At the border between what was Russia, Austria, and Turkey in those days, in a village called Okop. There was a time when Chasidism did not have a name—it takes a while until the baby gets a name—and they were considering calling themselves *Baale Teshuvah*—Penitents. This had connotations that were too sad for the spirit of Chasidism, and so they chose a name known from before. A group of people who had lived in Germany in the thirteenth century were known as *Chasidey Ashkenaz*, the Pious of Germany, and there were some Chasidim even in the time of the Second Temple. So you see, it was natural for them to take the name Chasidism. Basically, it is a way of serving God with a greater sense of sophistication.

w.b.: One of the words often used, in fact always used, in Chasidism is *tzadik*. Tell us what is a *tzadik*, who were some of the *tzadikim*, and what was—and is—their function in the Chasidic movement.

■ SCHACHTER-SHALOMI: Joseph Albo had a saying: *"Ilu yaditiv hayitiv"*—"If I knew him, I would be he." If I could tell you what a *tzadik* truly is, I would have to be one myself. But I am not. Yet we have an interpretation of what a *tzadik* is: a *tzadik* is a person who has so fully realized the divine intent in a human being's life that he has fully gotten there already and therefore is capable of showing other people the way. In other words, he does not have to go around with the lantern any more. He knows the way, even at night. He knows where to go, what to do.

w.b.: Who are some of the *tzadikim* in the Chasidic movement?

■ SCHACHTER-SHALOMI: There was Levi Yitzchak of Berdit-chev, a good prototype of a *tzadik*, and also Reb Mordechai of Chernoble, who was the first *tzadik* to have a fine place to live, and who traveled with six horses and a *schpitz*. Chasidim would come to him for guidance. Another example is Rebbe Elimelech of Lizhensk, who, you know, was *lustig un freilach*, happy and gay, except that sometimes he was not so *freilach*; he was a very serious person.

w.b.: Would you say that the *tzadik* in Chasidism serves as some sort of intermediary between the individual and God?

■ SCHACHTER-SHALOMI: That is a lovely question. You know, one would have to put on a *tallis* and really gird one's loins for this question, because anything one might say is going to get one into trouble. If you say that Reb Elimelech teaches, for instance, that a *tzadik* is an intermediary, then this sounds Christian. If you say that a *tzadik* is merely someone who shows the way but does not get in between—this is not quite what it says. So I would just switch the metaphor and say a *tzadik* is the one who stands behind the Chasid and boosts him up.

W.B.: I recall reading some years ago that this concept of *tzadikism* was somewhat the cause of the downfall of the Chasidic movement. Would you agree with this?

■ SCHACHTER-SHALOMI: No. There is an idea that first there was the Baal Shem Tov and Chasidism was rather democratic, and then, after a while, there were some people who had the idea that there was a good business there, and because it was such a good business, started to exploit the situation. With this I disagree. Before the Baal Shem Tov and Chasidism there existed the idea of the *tzadik* being *y'sod olam*—the foundation of the world, to whom certain keys were given, and the keys were not necessarily "keys to the kingdom," but the keys to a heart to be opened, a soul to be opened. A *tzadik* has that key to open them up, so the idea of *tzadik*, *y'sod olam*, was discussed in the Zohar and in fact is even mentioned in the Gemora. The *tzadik* as a central theme is found in the literature of Reb Isaac Luria, the great Cabalist of the sixteenth century.

So you see, the *tzadik* idea was there before. Obviously, there were fellow travelers with Chasidism, people who would much rather eat *lekach* and *kugel*, drink *l'chayim* to the rebbe—not taking the obligation of coming to the rebbe to ask him questions about how to transform their lives but letting the rebbe do it. They gave him a retainer: "You're my rebbe, you protect me."

W.B.: I have a quotation: "A Chasid implies a living and continuous relationship with a rebbe. Through the rebbe there is spiritual direction, and through the *mitzvos* (good deeds) there is the acceptance of the yoke of God." Do you accept this definition of a Chasid? Do you agree with the premise that the relationship with the rebbe is basic? Especially in a democracy, where there is freedom and self-expression, do you give up your own self or your own being in going to a rebbe?

■ SCHACHTER-SHALOMI: *Yechidus* is the term that describes the audience with the rebbe. It implies that they are at one, together, alone. A Chasid comes in. He has a *kvitl*—a little note that he has written. On the *kvitl* he writes, for instance, *Lichvod k'dushas adoni moraynu v'rabaynu* ("In honor of his holiness our teacher and preacher"). This is the honorific term with which he greets the rebbe. Then he will ask the rebbe to arouse God's great mercies for the person of —— and then he mentions his own name and his mother's name, not his father's name. There are two interpretations for this. One interpretation is, *Mit a mamen is zicher, miten taten ken men kane mol nit vissen*—"The mother is a biological verity, the father is not"—and you ask God for a sure thing.

The other explanation, as Rav Nachman of Bratzlav, great-grandson of the Baal Shem Tov, would put it more politely, is, "When you come to ask God on behalf of a person, you say, 'Ribbono shel Olom' ['Lord of the World'], have *rachmones*, pity this person, have compassion on him." God may say, "He doesn't deserve it." You say, "Do it for his father's sake," and God may say, "He doesn't deserve it either." You say, "*Tu es far der mamen vus hut getrogen im unter'n hartzen far nine hadoshim lang un sie hot gehat veitigen*"—"Do it for the sake of his mother, who, for nine months, carried him under her heart and suffered pain." At this point, even God relents, for God respects mothers far more than fathers in this respect.

Then the Chasid might ask for some particular thing—for instance, "*Yiras shomayim u'briyus haguf.*" In other words, he asks the rebbe to intercede for him so that he may attain fear of heaven and health of body. Now, what does he want the rebbe to do at this point? It is a mistaken idea to say that one gives something up, one asks the rebbe to enhance one's potential. He is not saying, "I give up all my potential in becoming a Chasid." He is saying, "I have an endowment. This endowment is my physical, spiritual, mental endowment which God has given me. I cannot develop it to the fullest, and so I ask the rebbe's intercession for it."

But this is only the beginning. One then asks the rebbe for *eytzes*—counsel, advice. This is very, very important. So I do not think that the question of giving something up is on the same level as that which actually occurs when a Chasid goes to see his rebbe.

On the other hand, there is this feeling: *Az der rebbe shikt, furt men.* In other words, if the rebbe sends you to the ends of the earth, you are going to go and you are not going to ask the rebbe why. Does this not imply a reduction of one's personal freedom? Does this not imply, for instance, a giving up of one's autonomy?

w.b.:   Then is it not a matter of the rebbe making decisions for you against your own mind and your own feeling in deciding a particular activity, fact, or enterprise?

■ **SCHACHTER-SHALOMI:**   Yes and no. The rebbe often makes such decisions because he takes for granted that a person has what is called a *sefeikah*—a real doubt—that he comes with an ambivalence and he cannot decide on a question. It is not that he is saying "I want to do this. Do I have to do what you say? I would much rather do something else." If the Chasid has made up his mind as to what he really wants to do, the rebbe often says, *"Mir matern keinem nit"*—"There is no forcing a person." Obviously, this would go against a person's potential.

Let me tell you a *maisseh*, a story, to illustrate the way in which a rebbe does not force a situation.

Reb Aaron of Karlin, who was known as Reb Aaron the Great, was still a disciple of the Maggid of Mezerich, whose name was Dov Baer, the successor of the Baal Shem Tov. One day he went to him and said, "I would like to go home for *Pesach.*" The rebbe said, *"Fur gezunterheit, hob a guten veg."* He blessed him to have a good journey. As soon as Reb Aaron left, he called Reb Zushe, one of his other disciples, and said, *"Loz im nisht furen"*—"Don't permit him to go." So Reb Zushe went out and told Reb Aaron, "Don't go." Reb Aaron asked, "Why do you tell me not to go?" Reb Zushe said, "Because the rebbe *hot mir geheisen dir zogen"*—"The rebbe said I should tell you not to go." Reb Aaron protested, "But I just said good-bye to him and received his blessing." So he went back to the rebbe and said, *"Ich halt ba foren, zol ich foren?"*—"I am on my way. Shall I go?"

"For l'hayim un l'sholom, gei gezunterheit," was the reply: "Go in peace and life, go in good health."

This happened three times. Each time Reb Aaron was about to leave, the rebbe sent someone else to bring him back. Finally, Reb Aaron left and, when he arrived at home the day before Pesach, he died. The disciples were angry with the rebbe. They said, "Rebbe, if you knew what was going to happen, and if this was the reason that you wanted to keep him here, why didn't you speak up?" To which the rebbe replied, in the tradition of the Old Testament, that he saw and did not take away the choice from a person.

I think this holds true with many a rebbe and many a situation. Wherever there is limitation of freedom, the rebbe does not want to enter into it, but if the question is one of doubt, of "I really don't know," he says, "Here are the facts of the situation. Balance them either way." This is a different kind of a thing. It does not imply a pathological dependence on another person's decisions.

W.B.: What is the place of women in Chasidism?

■ SCHACHTER-SHALOMI: Now, if I could take a time machine this would be a delight, because I would take you back to *mein elter bobe*, my great-grandmother, Dvoireleh, who was married at the age of 14, and when she was 16, *hot eingeshpant dem vogen*—hitched up the horse before the cart—took some preserves that she had canned, and traveled to the rebbe. She did not travel to the same rebbe that her husband, my great-grandfather, visited because somehow the Rabbi of Belz, to whom my great-grandfather traveled, said *"Zolen di mener kumen tzu mir, zolen die veiber geyen tzu yenem"* ("Let the men come to me, let the women go to someone else"). He was more a "man's rebbe." The other one, the Samborare Rebbe, was the one who received the women, and this was very interesting. He would receive them in the court under the open sky—that is to say, that one *zol nisht zein alein mit a froi*—must not be separated from other people. It was an open view, but the women would keep a sort of *cordon sanitaire*, so that no one could overhear. This was really to be private conversation. A woman would come out with the *kvitl* and put the *kvitl* down. She did not put it in his hand, but she put it down on the table, along with the preserves, a *bissele eingemachts*, a little jam, and at this point would begin to ask the rebbe some questions about her own life, about her prayer, or ask a blessing for a child.

There is another lovely story about how the mother of Reb Hersh Elimelech, Tzvi Elimelech of Dinov, came to Reb Elimelech of Lizhensk and he rose up before the woman. The Chasidim later asked, "Why did you stand up for a woman?" He told them, "Because she carried a great *tzadik* within her, and it was for the soul of the *tzadik* that I rose." So again you see that women had access to the rebbe and there was a place for them, but not in the *beit midrash*, the study house, on the men's side.

W.B.: And what about today?

■ SCHACHTER-SHALOMI: Ah, today things are more equal. Today, women can even see the rebbe with the door closed.

I have still another story, a very interesting one. Charles Raddock wrote about the life of Chanah Ruchel, the *moyd* from Ludmir, in the *Jewish Monthly*. He described the life of a woman who was a Chasidic saint. This maid of Ludmir put on *tallis* and *tefillin* and had a *minyan* of her own. In other words, she kept ten men *davening* on the other side, and many women around her. She would even have a *Sholosh S'udos* with her women and would preach—*zogen Torah*—a "sermon on the Torah" for them. Obviously, the men did not like the situation. She did not stay too long in her ministry. After a while, she had to go to Jerusalem. A beautiful story by Agnon, "Tehillah," is a description of the life of Chanah Ruchel and her later years in the Holy Land.

So you can see that there is room for women in Chasidism. Today they even publish a magazine. I would call it "The Chasidic Woman's Home Companion." It is known as *Dos Yiddishe Heim*—"The Jewish Home." There are fine articles written by women in it. Fine poetry by women, illustrations done by them. Occasionally, a man gets a chance to say a few words there too. Half of it is in Yiddish and half in English.

W.B.: We have been speaking about many facets of Chasidism. There are certain basic premises upon which the Chasidic philosophy is built. Let us begin by discussing the role of joy in Chasidism.

■ SCHACHTER-SHALOMI: What isn't the role of joy? At this point, I have to reverse it and put it in Reb Aaron of Karlin's terms. He said: "Sadness is no sin, but what sadness can bring, no sin can bring. Joy, except on a holiday [*Yom Tov*], is no mitzvah, but what joy can bring, no mitzvah can bring. Joy is that which opens everything. It opens the mind; it opens the heart; it opens the soul. Joy is that which stems from living in God's view." You cannot be sad. *Hod v'hadar l'fanav*—"Strength and joy are in His place." From where does this strength derive? It derives from the word *shiflus*— humbleness, humility, and this seems to be a contradiction really. How can one be humble almost to the point of being nothing, and yet be joyous? Because there is a kind of happiness that comes out of not having to protect one's vulnerability, a boundless joy, because as long as joy comes from material blessings, it is a finite joy. Chasidim talk about an infinity of joy that only a poor man, a humble person, has.

W.B.: What is the importance of love in Chasidism?

■ SCHACHTER-SHALOMI: I am not a Karliner Chasid, but if you want a short definition you can do very well with the Karliner's words. Here is what he says: "To serve God with fear but without love, that is no service. The best service is when one serves God with fear and with love, because it is fear that makes a person refrain from that which he must not do." Love cannot be a one-sided situation, because love alone in *gematria* is only thirteen. How does love come to be thirteen? *Aleph* is one, *hey* is five, *bet* is two, and another *hey* is another five. But God's name, *yud hey, vov hey* is twenty-six. So when I love you and you love me, then we have twenty-six.

W.B.: What about *kavonoh*?

■ SCHACHTER-SHALOMI: Roughly translated, it means *intention*. Intentionality is one of the most important things in life. It is very, very easy to be nothing but a reflex mechanism. At one time psychology looked at people this way—stimulus and reflex. It did not even recognize that there was an organism in between modifying the reflex that resulted from the stimulus. *Kavonoh* is that which takes what the world does to a person and transforms it into a deliberate, meaningful act. In other words, if I have *kavonoh*, I fill the act that otherwise would be a reflex act, an automatic act, with intention. When a Chasid eats, he takes a *lefel*, a spoonful, and says, "For Him, for Him." You remember how *bobe* used to feed you: *A lefel farin zeiden*—"One for you and one for him," and so on. The idea is that there is no single act in life on which one cannot put a label, and the label is *L'Shem Yichud Kudsha b'rich Hu Shchintey*, "For the sake of the unification of the Holy One, blessed be He and His presence." That is, not only should He be holy up in heaven, but He should be very much present here on earth. Therefore, I do this act which I invest with this intentionality.

W.B.:   What of esthetics in Chasidism?

■ SCHACHTER-SHALOMI: Did you ever hear Chasidim discuss who is a *guter Yid*, "a good Jew"? They will say, *"A sheiner Yid, a sheiner Yid"*—"A beautiful Jew." The late Reb Moshe Pakarski, may he rest in peace, was a wonderful *neshomeh*, a wonderful soul. He used to tell a story about someone who *nebech er hot nisht kein handt, un iz blindt oif an oig*, and maybe he has even *a hoiker, ober er iz a sheiner Yid*—unfortunately, is missing a hand, is blind in one eye, and maybe even has a hunchback, but he is a beautiful Jew.

You get the idea—"a beautiful Jew." The whole esthetic sense was developed not so much along the Greek view that someone qualified through "the holiness of beauty," but rather through the "beauty of holiness." This is very important, this kind of beauty. To see a rebbe all decked out in *shtreimel un kapote, die Shechinah rut oif im*—what is the idea behind it? *Oy, azoi shein!*—Oh, how beautiful! Beauty means fitting to the situation. It is an intentional fitting to the situation. *Men darf basheinen dem Shabbos*—Sabbath has to be beautified. A few years ago in Israel, on the two hundredth anniversary of the death of the Baal Shem Tov, they had an exposition of Chasidic memorabilia. Many of them were exquisite in their beauty. How can you serve God if it is not *shein*? This is very important, the esthetic sense.

Women had to do a great deal of this. This was part of their work. *Oisneyen a paroches*, to embroider a curtain for the holy ark, and the flowers and the sequins and every soft kind of thing—that was very important.

W.B.: One of the fundamental factors in the element of joy in Chasidism is *nigun*, song.

■ **SCHACHTER-SHALOMI:** Yes. Professor Heschel coins some beautiful phrases in a book called *The Earth Is the Lord's*. He gives a number of beautiful definitions. One is a *nigun*, a tune flowing in search of its own unattainable end. I think one of our grave problems has to do with the fact that we do not sing enough. A Jew has to sing. Do you remember when a *maggid*, a preacher, came to town and began to preach in a singsong: "Once upon a time there was a king, and the king, *nebach*, had a son, and the son did not go in the proper way, and he had to send him into exile." Pretty soon there wasn't a dry eye in the house. A *nigun* is very important. Without the *nigun*, the words do not take on all the harmonies that they can take on. Now, when Chasidim sit down, they have to have a *nigun*. There are all kinds of *nigunim*. Sometimes there is a drinking song borrowed directly from Ivan next door, which says, "Don't worry fellows, as soon as we get to the end you can get all the vodka you want." Now why should Chasidim sing a song like that? *Es iz nit shein*— "It is not nice." So they sang it with a change in words: "As soon as we get to Lubavitch, we get all the Chasidism we want." This is a dancing song. Then, there is a *nigun* that is known as a *tish nigun*. A rebbe conducts a table with people sitting around it, and the rebbe begins; "Da, da doy, doy, doy, doy, doy," and the Chasidim would go, "M, m, m, m." And the *rebbe* would go: "Dai, da di da da dam," and he would begin a hymn like Reb Eleazar Askari *"Oy yedid nefesh,"* "Beloved of my soul, Merciful Father." This is a *tish nigun*. Then, there are *davening nigunim*, and among the *davening nigunim* you can find some beautiful marches. You go into an average *Galitzianer shtiebel* on *Shabbos* morning, and you will find somebody who will start "Tra, tra, tra din, ta, ta, tum, pom pom" with a march tempo that will out-Sousa Sousa, and then go on to "Praise God who is the Lord of all creation."

Today you can enjoy the *nigunim* in the privacy of your hi-fi. There are three volumes of Lubavitcher records, and you can get Chasidic music everywhere. It has become almost a by-word for cantors and music directors, when they speak of music that has a *ta'am*, they call it Chasidic.

W.B.: Are there schools of Chasidism that differ, and in what respect?

■ SCHACHTER-SHALOMI: Yes, there are differences. Often the differences seem superficial, but sometimes they go very deep. Differences that are superficial—what kind of a *shtreimel*, hat, do people wear? How long is the *kapote*, coat, supposed to be? These are superficial things. Now what are the deeper things as far as schools of thought are concerned? Some people feel that emotions, the arousal of the emotions, to be alive emotionally, is by far the more important thing. Other people feel differently, that one has to first get rid of the *yetzer hora*, the inclination for evil. There are different ideas, for instance, as to what constitutes proper study. Some Chasidim will hear only the teaching of their rebbe but will not study the literature. Others will say that one cannot really be a good Chasid unless one learns a great deal of the Chasidic literature.

W.B.: You are a Lubavitcher Chasid. What are the characteristics of Lubavitch Chasidism?

■ SCHACHTER-SHALOMI: Lubavitch Chasidism is an intellectual kind of Chasidism. It says that the arousal of emotions is not enough, that the person has to really understand, that he has to conceptualize clearly—*klor gruntig farshtein*. Only when he fully and completely conceptualizes a thing, when he understands it in all details and when he meditates on it, can he know it in its essential qualities. Only then will the emotions that he arouses not be sham emotions. And so *Chabad* stresses the intellectual life quite a bit. The rebbe will spend hours in teaching his Chasidim some of these basic concepts of Chasidism, making sure that there is going to be a good understanding, then demanding that his followers meditate and study the writings.

This is different in many other Chasidic branches. I think this is one of the things that commits me to Lubavitch because I can reach the material, I can understand the material, I can digest it, I can even, in part, disagree with it.

w.b.: What is Neo-Chasidism, and how does it differ from the original Chasidic movement?

■ SCHACHTER-SHALOMI: As an example, take Professor Buber, who may not have characterized himself as "Neo-Chasid" but who, I think, fits that description. Neo-Chasidism: if one can be a Chasid without having a rebbe, he is a Neo-Chasid. The word *rebbe* is a relationship word, as are the words *father, child, husband, wife*. One cannot be a husband without a wife. One cannot be a child if there is no mother, no father. A *rebbe* and a *Chasid*—these are relationship words.

And this is one of the basic differences that we have with Neo-Chasidism, with people who say, "I like the Chasidic flavor"—whatever that is. Chasidic does not mean jumpy melodies. Chasidic does not mean wearing a beard. . . . Chasidic does not mean these things. If someone says that he is a Neo-Chasid—that is, he wants to be a Chasid, and *daven* and celebrate *Shabbos*, and be involved—we call him a Neo-Chasid. However, we cannot agree with his point of view, because he still denies the essentiality of a rebbe, the centrality of the rebbe.

w.b.: What is your opinion of Martin Buber and his contribution to the field?

■ SCHACHTER-SHALOMI: Now, that is a different story. He is a man who has done far more than many Chasidim to put the word *Chasidism* before the general public. Many of the stories that make the rounds do so because he pulled Chasidism, as it were, out of the *shtiebel*, out of the prayer house, and put it into modern dress. He translated Chasidic tales into German, although some Chasidim were not satisfied with his translations, and I often think that the stories are twisted because of his translation. He himself admitted that he does not tell the stories quite straight. He has "Buberized" them, as it were.

But let us not say that he has made no contribution. He has made a very real and important contribution by making Chasidic ideas accessible to the general public long before any among the Chasidim were ready to do it.

If we were to ask the Union Theological Seminary who they thought was the greatest philosopher of our time, they would say Martin Buber because his contributions *mit a handt ken men ihm nisht avec machen*—cannot be dismissed with a wave of the hand. I would say that he has made a great contribution, but the contribution is not essentially to Chasidism.

W.B.: You have used Yiddish expressions quite frequently. Is this part of Chasidism or is this your own choice?

■ **SCHACHTER-SHALOMI:** When I talk to one of my students on campus, and he brings up a subject that came up in say, counseling, and I somehow have the sense that I do not want to discuss it then and there, but I want him to know that I am willing to discuss it, I slip into Yiddish. That is to say, I want to establish a sense of intimacy. I think Yiddish does this for us far more than English. This is a way in which Chasidim establish an intimacy, to say something that is *zaftig*, that is *geshmak*—a word that by itself is going to say so much more than any Webster definition of the word.

W.B.: What about the Hebrew language then, in lieu of Yiddish?

■ **SCHACHTER-SHALOMI:** If I were to say *Hitlahavut* or *Hu ish m'shulhav*, that would be a nice way of saying "He is inspired" in modern Hebrew, but it still would not be the same thing as if I were to say *Hu baal hislahavus*—"He has inspiration." Even if I were to speak to someone in Hebrew, I would use this particular term in its Yiddish pronunciation because I want him to get the full meaning of the phrase. I want him to get the full implication of the term.

Forgive me for a moment if I get to be a little technical. It is a good question and it ought to be dealt with. Korzybski, when he founded General Semantics, was very much interested in what he called "time binding." If you use the words "Liberty 1776," they would mean something else than the word "liberty" in Leviticus: "Proclaim liberty throughout the land"—so it is a different word. Korzybski always demanded that people "time bind" the word in order that it be clear. By using a Yiddish word or pronunciation, I "time bind" it, as it were, and this allows for a communication that is different than if I were to translate it or lift it out of the contextual framework in which it ought to be.

W.B.: Rabbi Schachter-Shalomi, you come to us as an exponent of the Chasidic way of life. How much of what you represent is transferable to the twentieth-century Jew? Does Chasidism have an approach to modern theology, and can you relate its psychology to a person's behavior?

■ SCHACHTER-SHALOMI: One of the important things that Chasidism has to contribute is attitude. This is even more important than its theological and psychological aspects. It has to be an attitude of real concern, what Buber and Heschel call "the attitude of ultimate concern," the significance of a person's act, the significance of a person's life. I think this is something that has to be transferred, and it is transferable. It is not a question any more of taking a *shtreimel* from Chasidism and bringing it to people. I think of people today in their search for meaning, especially students on campuses. The whole beat movement represents a search for meaning. Existentialism is a search for meaning. The question troubling people is, Am I really significant as a human being? Does my existence have any reason behind it, and is there any rationale for my being? I think that the Chasidic attitude comes to grips with such questions. Yes, it is very important. *Bei dem Riboneh Shel Olom bistu a Kenig*—"To the creator of the universe you are a king."

Then there is the question of the interpersonal relationship that Chasidism creates. A Chasid always has a *guten freind*. It is not enough to have a rebbe, you have to have a very, very close friend, and most of us do not have close friends after late adolescence. We have many acquaintances—but a friend? I wish I could tell you what the connotation of the word "friend" really is—the kind of person to whom you can tell those things that you do not dare to tell even your analyst. It has to be, therefore, a relationship of utter candor, which again is based on this ultimate-concern relationship I mentioned before.

Now coming to theology. Chasidic theology is on the one hand very flexible, and on the other hand, it is a vast thing, and, here again, it differs from what Buber does. Buber takes one idea and expands this idea, and this becomes the entire system of the philosophy. There is far more to Chasidic thinking and philosophy. It subsumes many miniature systems underneath it.

Chasidism has a doctrine of "sparks." The whole task of man is a cosmic effort of lifting up sparks of divinity that are imprisoned here below and that he has to bring back to God. I think it is an idea that has not yet fully been explored.

I am giving you just a sort of potpourri of Chasidic theology. What does it mean to say that a person has a soul? Chasidim never say, "He has a soul." They say, "He *is* a soul; he *has* a body." He *is* a soul. That is very important to them, survival after death. This is the kind of question with which theology has to deal. Here, too, Chasidism has something to say that has not been heard for a while.

Another area is the area of psychology. It is not enough to tell people what they ought to do. Chasidism does not only say, "You must do this or you must do that"; it gives you a functional way of doing what you know you ought to do.

w.b.: Rabbi Schachter-Shalomi, I know that you have worked with young people at Camp Ramah, which is one among many in the networks of camps established by the Conservative movement. You have also worked with teenagers at the Camp Institutes sponsored by the Reform movement. What motivates the Chasid to mix with Conservative Jews and Reform Jews?

■ SCHACHTER-SHALOMI: As long as there are Jews, a Chasid will not recognize the divisive definitions. It is very important that "I cover the waterfront," and the waterfront is as big as American Jewry. This means that if there is a camp such as Ramah in which a need can be filled, the need is not to make people *daven* necessarily out of an Orthodox *siddur*, but to teach them how to *daven* in their own *siddur*. It is a question of how to deal with that to which they are already committed, how to translate that into life. At Ramah we were very much concerned with the "reentry" problem, with what happens to kids when they come back from camp, back to the home congregation. Whatever skills they have acquired, whatever insights they have acquired, have to be shared with other people. One of the big problems about summer camps is that they offer a great, great experience. Then somebody asks, "So, what was it?" And the answer is, "I cannot tell it to you. You have to go there yourself." We were very much concerned about how the youngster brings his experience back to his own youth group.

W.B.:   What do you do with the children while they are in camp?

■ SCHACHTER-SHALOMI: What can one do with these kids? First of all, I had to listen. One has to listen very carefully to what they are saying, and also to what they mean when they are saying words. You have heard an expression—kids use it very often—"and all that jazz." Do you know what it really means? It really means that they are afraid of feeling. The moment that there is material with a rich feeling tone, kids do not want to quite admit that they are warm. Today you "gotta be cool," and so what they say is "and all that jazz." The kids wanted to find out what *davenen* "and all that jazz" is all about. If you listen carefully, and you are not offended by the words that they use, and if you really know that they are groping underneath the words that they are using, there is a great deal that can be done.

But naturally, it has to be done with patience. It is very difficult during a camp experience to isolate the group of kids, to sit at the *Shabbosdiker tish*, the Sabbath table, with them. If you have ever been in a camp dining room you know what happens. Yet we found a place where we could sit, sing some *zmiros*, some songs, and give them a model to take back to their homes.

There is a great deal of material that is transferable. The problem is, of course, with the person who does the transferring. Is he satisfied to transfer only part of his material, or does he have to sell all his *s'choireh*, his merchandise? Part of the mandate that we have from the rebbe is to sell as much as we can sell, and not to try to push all the *s'choireh*, because it is a buyer's market in this situation.

W.B.: What about your relationships on the campus? Our concept of the Hillel director is that of a Conservative or Reform rabbi. Yet here we have a Chasidic *rebbe*. What is your relationship with the students? [*Editor's note*: At the time of this Dialogue he was the Director of Hillel at the University of Manitoba.]

■ SCHACHTER-SHALOMI: I do not have many problems, but there are some. I do not always get to first base. Remember that the stereotypes are very, very hard to break. The same may be true of a Hillel rabbi who may come from a Reform background and who is willing to enhance any expression of Judaism among his students. There are going to be some kids who are going to feel that they cannot come to him, he is a Reform rabbi, he won't even listen to them if they have a problem about *kashrus*. There are Orthodox students who begin with a stereotype, and not a very healthy one. There is a stereotype that goes the other way too. Despite the fact that our Hillel House, since my incumbency, is the only place in Winnipeg where you can get a Reconstructionist Prayerbook—and we have enough to hold a service with—or a Union Prayerbook as well as the Silverman Prayerbook and the Birnbaum Prayerbook, it is very hard to break the stereotype once it becomes set. It takes a while until senior classmen pass the word on to junior classmen: "He's a regular guy, you can talk to him, never mind his beard," or something like that. Once this takes place, I'm at first base. Once I'm at first base, there is no problem. But until I get there, *krichen dei oygen fun kop*—"the eyes can crawl out of one's head." There are the unaffiliated students, those who do not belong to fraternities. They are always good Hillel material. Sometimes you have a fraternity that uses this as an issue: "Either Hillel or fraternity." Then a stereotype is being created, that the Hillel Director is nothing but an elongated arm of the parents reaching into the campus and saying, "You must not have a Black Mass on Friday night, drinking beer." Sometimes we may have to break the stereotype with a fraternity. How does one go about it? There is a coffee joint in every college town. Ours is called the Java Shop. I do some of my best business over espresso.

W.B.: We have had the privilege of talking not only with a very deep and spiritual Chasid, but with a man who is also very "hip," and I think that is important to the twentieth-century adult Jew and youngster alike. May I conclude with this final thought. The Hebrew alphabet has the letter *shin*, which Jewish tradition has interpreted as representing the name of God—*Shaddai*. The *shin* is on the *mezuzah* on our doorpost. It is the *shin* that is etched on the hand of the Jew wearing the *tefillin*. In a novel, Agnon tells about a Chasidic rabbi, Yudl, who, when he stood in prayer before God, lifted his hands over his head so that his two uplifted hands and his head made up the letter *shin*—all of him symbolizing the name of God. I believe that the image of this rabbi can serve as the ideal of Jewish life to which we are summoned this day, and to which we should commit ourselves—to hold up our hands for God, for Torah, and for Israel. I believe that every Jew must himself become the living embodiment of the faith he holds, the witness upon earth of the God whose name he bears. And so long as we have men who continue to lift up their hands and symbolize the letter *shin*, as does our guest, Judaism will live.

Dr. Joseph L. Blau

5. ❦ The Scholarship of Religion

Dr. Joseph L. Blau

W.B.: There is a great deal of discussion today about what is right and what is wrong with religion. We often hear that religion is behind the times, and at the same time we weigh and measure the quality and the depth of the renaissance of religious commitment we see around us. In discussions that are often not rooted in knowledge, study, or deep analysis, much of what has been said has often been superficial. Yet voices of real knowledge and understanding can often be heard above the din of opinion and polemic. Our guest has spent a lifetime of study and analysis on this subject, and his ideas about religion—its role, its past, its present, and its future—are rooted in deep and abiding scholarship.

Dr. Joseph L. Blau was professor of religion and director of graduate studies in the Department of Religion of Columbia University. He has long expounded the theme of the consonance of Jewish religion and culture with the main currents of American philosophy, and he has achieved an outstanding reputation as scholar, teacher, author, editor, and lecturer.

Dr. Blau, one of the things you have written that puzzles me is that there is a paradox in religion. What do you mean by this?

■ **BLAU:** I suppose that nowadays we are all looking for paradoxes. Someone wrote a book about thirty-five years ago called *Paradoxy: The Destiny of Modern Thought*. Paradoxy is an antithesis to orthodoxy and heterodoxy at the same time. In this particular instance it seems to me that each of us wants two things from his religion, from his commitment. The first thing that man wants is that his religion be a guide to him in his daily life. In the second half of the twentieth century, in a world that is torn and confused by any number of crosscurrents—economic, political, social, moral—he wants his religion to serve as an arrow, pointing the most direct way through these problems and difficulties. And yet at the same time each of us wants religion to give the assurance that we are living as closely as possible to the life that our ancestors lived. We want to get from religion a feeling of rootedness in the past, in the sense that everything that flowers now was originally started in seed in our ancestors—not only personal ancestors, but the ancestors of the whole group.

Wanting these two things at once, we want something that I can only describe as paradoxical. We desire at one and the same time to hold fast to a tradition and to be able to direct our life in the middle of innovations. So on the one hand we have the force of tradition that draws us to religion; on the other hand, the force of innovation. Now it is the obligation of any religion, as I have said, to change in order to meet the need for dealing with innovations in the social milieu and, at the same time, to appear to be unchanging so that it gives us that sense of being rooted in the past.

W.B.: You have written that at critical times in religious history it is especially easy to observe the relationship of these two forces, the force of tradition and the force of innovation. How do you define "critical times"? Would you illustrate what you mean? Has the Jewish people been subjected more than other people to these critical periods?

■ BLAU: Critical times would, of course, be easiest understood as times of crisis, times when the affairs of a people come to some sort of crucial need for resolution. This can happen, for example, when a nation that has its own religious traditions is overrun by another nation in wartime with a different religious tradition. This creates a crisis for the people and for their religion, and at such times the attempts to make an adjustment to a new situation are more visible than they are at times when there is no such crisis in the life of the people.

One might give illustrations of this outside the Jewish tradition. After Alexander the Great had overrun a large part of the then-known world from India through to Egypt and Ethiopia, the whole Mediterranean world went through a period of several centuries of crisis that we call the Hellenistic era. During that period, any number of new religious movements were created, some growing out of older religions and some being imported religions, but everything was in a state of upheaval, which makes that Hellenistic era one of the most exciting and interesting periods to study.

To take your second question: Since in the course of the history of the Jewish people there have been many more times when they have either been overrun or exiled, driven out of their land or have had to develop a new center of Jewish life, there have been more critical periods in the history of the Jewish religion than there have been in the history of any other religion that I know of.

We could go to the semi-legendary era and note that the first crisis was the crisis of the exodus from Egypt. This is the first crisis, at least, of which we have a significant record. And it was at that time that the God, whoever He may have been, the God of Midian or some part of the Midianite world, was adopted by the Hebrew people.

Another crisis occurred at the time of the Babylonian exile. This was apparently the point at which the first version of the Jewish religion, as we know and practice it today, was developed. Still another crisis came with the Hellenistic period itself; during Chanukah we celebrate at least one of the reactions to that crisis of Hellenization. Another crisis was the second destruction of the Temple in 70 C.E. and, shortly after that, came the need to adjust basic Jewish life to a center that was no longer in Palestine but was moved to Babylonia. Several centuries later, partly as a result of the sweeping movement of Islam, the center of Jewish life shifted from the East to the West, from Asia to Europe. The Jews were forced to live in a new cultural environment. In Spain, for example, with pressures coming at them from both sides—since the Moslems were halfway up the Iberian peninsula and the Christians were at the other half and there were Jews living in both halves—the Jews again were forced by the situation to do some radical rethinking of their religious position in order to differentiate it from both Christianity and Islam.

Still another critical period, and I think a major critical period, is the one with which we are still trying to wrestle. It started in the eighteenth century, although some of its roots go back into the seventeenth century. It started in the eighteenth century with that total shift in ways of thinking, in ways of living, that we sum up in one word: *modernity.* This problem of modernity created a crisis not only in Jewish life but in Christian life as well. Catholicism has been going through a tremendous sea of change in the last few years as a result of the decision of the Church to face this crisis of modernity. And I think this is what we have been facing since the time of Moses Mendelssohn or a little before. Now perhaps we have passed through that crisis. If that is the case, then we are in the middle of another one now. And we are in the middle of one that flows in from the change in the nature of nationalism, from a sort of cosmopolitan internationalism in the enlightened eighteenth century to the development of this romantic "blood and guts" kind of nationalism that has been so disastrous in the twentieth century.

But this began with the nineteenth century. Now, in reaction to this type of nationalism, we Jews developed our own "blood and guts" nationalism, and we took to it with a great deal of enthusiasm. We developed our own internal, fascist groups, and we approved very heartily of their activities at the same time when we were disapproving very heartily of the activities of other fascist groups. Apparently, we are still in some sort of a crisis. Whether it is the overall crisis of modernity or whether it is the specific crises of nationalism, I am not enough of an analyst to tell.

W.B.: I am curious about your reference to internal Jewish fascist groups. I'm wondering whom you have in mind, since I have no knowledge of the existence of such fascist groups.

■ BLAU: I am thinking of some of the parties that developed in the State of Israel, particularly just before its establishment as a state.

W.B.: In terms of tradition and innovation, of the outside affecting the inside and the inside trying to make changes, you have indicated in your writings that there are several ways in which Judaism has reacted and responded to the crisis through the centuries. I would like you to expand and explain these ideas. You speak of a reaction called "literalism." What is it and how did it manifest itself?

■ BLAU: Judaism is a religion with a written tradition. It claims also to have an oral tradition, but that oral tradition as we know it is also a written tradition. The written tradition becomes fixed. If it is an oral tradition, genuinely passed on by word of mouth, it can very readily change. But where it is a written tradition, its form and its content become fixed fairly early. It is obvious when someone is deviating from a written tradition.

Now, the first written tradition that we had was the tradition of the Bible itself. This tradition of the Bible was not completely accepted, not completely canonized until about the second century of the Common Era, although it had actually existed in substantially the same form some two centuries earlier than that. The Book of Daniel, supposedly next to the last of the canonic books, was written sometime around the period of the Maccabees—roughly 165 B.C.E. The Book of Esther was probably written somewhere about that time too. The other books were substantially in the form in which we now have them before the year 200 B.C.E. A literalist would say that we stand on this full text or on part of this text and we will not add to it, subtract from it, or interpret it in any way whatsoever. What it says to do we will do. What it does not say, we will not do. The Sadducee group was the manifestation of this literalist attitude toward the Scriptures at the time of the Second Temple. The Sadducees represented a largely upper-class group; they were very closely tied to the priesthood of the Temple. They seem—and this is one of the interesting features—to have used this literalism as a means of Hellenizing outside the areas covered by the biblical text. Where nothing specific was written they felt free to go along with the Hellenic influences that were rife in Palestine at that time.

The only other movement in Judaism that can be called a true literalism is the early Karaite movement, which developed in Persia and spread into the Crimea, into Turkey,

Egypt, and Palestine in the eighth, ninth, and tenth centuries and then quickly faded to a very small group. But we have had other kinds of literalism because we have an elastic tradition. Once the Mishnah had been written down, it was part of the tradition; any group that accepted the Mishnah in writing, and stopped at that point with no further interpretation, would be a literalist group.

Similarly, three centuries or so later the Talmud was written down. When a group accepted the talmudic interpretations and refused to go any further, it could be considered a literalist group. Coming to a relatively modern Eastern European Orthodoxy, until the codification of the *Shulchan Aruch*, interpretation, innovation, change, was accepted, but from that point there has been no authority to make changes. So we stand on the sixteenth-century *Shulchan Aruch*.

I will add that I think that literal acceptance, not just of Judaism but of any scriptural religion, acceptance of the letter of the law, is one of the effective ways of killing off a religion. It is a form of suicide, as far as the permanent value of the religion in meeting new situations is concerned.

W.B.: Now on the other side of the coin—the reaction and response to crisis—you speak about apostasy. What about this kind of response?

■ BLAU: I think I can be briefer about this. In every period of which we have any record, there seems to have been Jews who met the crisis by leaving Judaism, by shifting to another religion. This is apostasy. It happens today. They did it in great numbers in the Hellenistic era and in every period in between. And if I said that literalism is suicide, then obviously, completing the analogy, I must say that apostasy is murder.

W.B.: You have written: "It becomes apparent that neither literalism nor apostasy is a live option." You said a few moments ago that the best way to kill a religion is to approach it from a literal point of view. Yet my Orthodox friends certainly do not want to kill our religion. Why is it that they take a literal point of view; what is it in their literalism that will kill the religion?

■ BLAU: In my latest book I distinguish between the Orthodox and the Neo-Orthodox. I specifically mentioned East European Orthodoxy. I do not believe that we have a real and significant group of Orthodox Jews in the United States. Most of our so-called Orthodox congregations do make adaptations to the twentieth century. There are fragmentary Orthodox—really, truly Orthodox—groups in Israel. There are other groups that like to call themselves Orthodox, such as the English United Synagogue, of which Dr. Jakobovits is the Chief Rabbi. They too are a modified or, as some of them like to say, a *modern* Orthodoxy. Now a modern Orthodoxy may sound like a contradiction in terms, but really it is not. It is willing to make adaptations, to make innovations, but it throws the heaviest weight on the tradition.

At the other extreme you would have a radical reform or liberal group; this would throw the heaviest weight on innovation. The American Reform group did this in its Pittsburgh Platform of 1885, and that Pittsburgh Platform was revised in 1938 to allow more weight to the tradition. The American Reform group has, by and large, been moving in the direction of giving more weight to tradition. At the same time, the American Orthodox has been moving in the direction of a "Modern Orthodoxy" or Neo-Orthodoxy, which gives more weight to innovation. What has happened in Judaism in this country has also been happening in American politics. In recent years we have been moving closer and closer to a middle-of-the-road consensus. At the same time we are sprinkling fringe groups off at both extremes.

W.B.: What about the Conservative Jews? Where do they fit in this panorama?

■ BLAU: Actually, Conservative Jewry started in the middle of the road, a somewhat zigzag middle of the road. I once defined it—and I may have picked this up from someone else and remembered it, so I do not want to take all the credit for it—as a movement in which rabbis who are a little to the left of Orthodoxy minister to congregations that are a little to the right of Reform. There have been a few occasions in which the rabbis in the Conservative movement have been more radical than their congregations; generally, though, the rabbis have been holding to the tradition most closely, and the congregants have pressed, sometimes effectively and sometimes not so effectively, for innovations. It seems to me, and I have gone on record as saying this, that the ultimate direction of American Judaism, as it comes closer and closer to the middle-of-the-road consensus, will come close to the Conservative movement. There may still be, for political reasons, three separate groups. After all, if there are three separate groups, there are three separate sets of officers. What we are likely to have is a Conservative Reform movement, a Conservative Conservative movement, and a Conservative Orthodox movement.

W.B.: You have written: "There are other ways of adjustment, and all these ways of adjustment give some weight to both tradition and innovation and vary in techniques that are proposed for recognizing, for reconciling the claims of tradition and innovation." I would like us to consider other ways in which we could bridge these two points of view. *Rationalism* is one way. What does rationalism seek to do in terms of the Jewish religion?

■ BLAU: I use the term *rationalism* to describe a type of philosophic reconciliation of the claims of tradition and those of innovation. This implies that there is some kind of philosophic system, a system perhaps that is proposed within the particular culture in which Jews are residing at any one time. In the culture of medieval Spain the philosophy of Aristotle was interpreted by Persian writers in Arabic; we call them the Arabic philosophers. These Persian–Arabic philosophers adopted the work of Aristotle as a structure for their system of interpreting the religion of Islam. When Judaism was forced by the situation to offer a philosophic definition of its own system, the Jews of the period took the Arabic Aristotle and imposed this as a structure on Judaism. Where the two conflicted in any way, as they were inevitably bound to conflict, the devices and logical tricks of the philosopher were used to make the religion come into accord with the philosophic system. There have actually been very few times in Jewish history when in this technical sense Judaism developed a philosophic rationale. One was in Alexandria. We do not know much about it, except from the work of one man, Philo, but there were others to whom we have references and of whom we have just a few fragments.

A second time when this became necessary occurred in the Middle Ages, when both Islam and Christianity were defending themselves by the use of the philosophies of Plato and Aristotle; Judaism had to get into the act, and we developed Jewish Platonists like Yehuda Halevi and Jewish Aristotelians like Maimonides and Gersonides.

The same thing happened again in the Renaissance, but only mildly. The next time that we had a really strong development of a philosophic rationale in Judaism was in the nineteenth century, or just before the beginning of the nineteenth century, with Moses Mendelssohn. This trend was continued by people such as Abraham Geiger, Salomon Steinheim, Samson Raphael Hirsch, and Samuel Hersch. This carried over into the twentieth century with such figures as Hermann Cohen and Martin Buber. Most of this was done in Germany, and Germany, during the nineteenth century at least, was the one nation in the modern world that had the most elaborately developed position in terms of religious philosophy. Religious philosophy was expounded much more in Germany than in England or in the United States. It was in Germany that the Jews found it necessary to develop a philosophic statement for Judaism in terms of the philosophy of Kant, or the philosophy of Hegel, or the philosophy of Schliermacher. This is the type of thing that I mean by a rational interpretation.

w.b.: In applying this rational interpretation to Judaism, are there, or were there, any dangers?

■ BLAU: There are always dangers in rationalism. One ever-present danger becomes apparent in a phrase that we often use when we talk about rationalism. We call it "sterile rationalism," and there is always the danger in rationalism of sterility, of getting oneself involved in the ins and outs of the logical argumentation for its own sake. The sheer beauty of the logical argument leads one away from what the logical argument is directed toward, what its conclusion means in terms of human life. This is always a danger.

A second danger is specific to rationalism when it is applied to religion. Religion is, it is true, a matter of the head, but it is not a matter of the head alone. Religion is a matter of the heart as well as the head. Religion is a matter of knowledge, but it is also a matter of emotion. And knowledge without emotion is dead. Emotion without knowledge tends to be ill-directed. The ideal, I suppose, would be some kind of perfect balance between the emotional and the intellectual aspects of religion, but of course no group ever does develop this perfect balance. Every religious group tends to accentuate the intellectual more than the emotional or the emotional more than the intellectual. As you move toward the accentuation of the intellectual, the religion becomes dry and heartless. It becomes more a system of doctrines, where the interconnection of the doctrines is more important than a way of life. And it is this that seems to me to be the greatest danger in rationalism as applied to religion.

w.b.: I read, some time ago, a very interesting interpretation by a Chasidic rabbi that illustrates this very point in relation to the putting on of the phylacteries. The *Shel Yad* which is put on the arm is close to the heart. The *Shel Rosh* is put on the forehead. And his interpretation was that religion, in order to really achieve its great goal, must be a happy combination of both the head and the heart.

In Jewish history and Jewish religious development there has been another kind of adjustment to tradition and innovation. You call this *allegorism*. What is allegorism?

■ BLAU: Allegory is a method of interpretation that makes a text say something entirely different from what it seems to say on the surface. I wish I could be more specific than this; it is a very difficult thing to interpret. Let us say that allegory is a level of interpretation in which a secondary and concealed meaning is hidden, or is claimed to be hidden, behind the literal surface of the text.

w.b.: You have written: "There are two manifestations of allegorism. The Philonic is close to rationalism; the Cabalistic is almost completely irrational. What unifies the diverse interpretation is that there is an assertion that the language of the tradition invariably asserts something different from what it appears to assert." Please explain this.

■ BLAU: Consider the atmosphere of Alexandria. It might be worth mentioning that there were, in Philo's time, over a million Jews in Alexandria—an entire section of the city was given over to the Jews. This was not, therefore, a little fragmentary community; it was a great center of Jewish life. And it was a center that had developed its own Halachah different from the Palestinian Halachah. In this atmosphere, the Platonic school, which had originally developed in Athens and had moved in later years to Alexandria, was the general currency of intellectual life in Alexandria. This version of Platonism was based, not on works like Plato's *Republic* or his *Socratic Apology*, but on one of his most difficult and most confused works, the one in which he went into his cosmology, the *Timaeus*. Now, in the *Timaeus*, Plato sets up a structure in which there is one God, but that God is remote from the world. And He creates by means of an intermediary. Plato calls this the "demiourgos." The demiourgos was the actual workman in creation, and Plato has been interpreted as feeling, whether he himself believed it or not, that any anthropomorphic, any human characterization of God, was just plain bad theology.

This gave Philo two problems. First, the text of a good part of the Bible, and particularly of the Book of Genesis, is full of human expressions describing God. God walks in the garden at the cool of the day; God supervises Adam and Eve with a kind of patronizing landlord's air; God sits down with Abraham. Plato was understood to have said that God had no manlike qualities. Philo had to interpret these references to human qualities so that they no longer asserted that God had human qualities. And he did this by finding a second meaning behind the text. An entire treatment of the Book of Genesis, which is one of the longest treatises that we have from Philo, is a process of taking up text after text after text and showing that these anthropomorphic expressions convey a secret meaning.

The second problem that Philo had was to account for the Creation in terms of some intermediary between a very remote God and this very material earth that we have around us. He did this in the tradition of Plato's demiourgos on the one hand, but also in the tradition of the Bible on the other, by saying, not *demiourgos*, but the *word*, the *logos*. In the first chapter, God speaks the words "Let there be light." So it is the word that does the actual creation, and *word* in Greek is *logos*. Here is a situation in which the Word becomes the intermediary between God and man, between God and the material universe.

In both these cases, he was allegorizing, but in one case he was doing it to delete the human expressions used about God and, in the other case, he was doing it in order to establish an intermediary between God and His Creation here about us.

The second case is the Cabalistic works, and here, of course, I am talking most particularly about the major document of the early Cabalistic tradition, the Zohar. The Zohar takes the form of a midrash on the Book of Genesis. It gives allegorical interpretations of the Creation, translating the Creation that is written about into a doctrine of immanence. God is everywhere. But if God is everywhere, there is no room for the world. So God voluntarily contracts Himself in order that there shall be room for the world. The whole process, in the Cabalistic treatment of the Creation, is a process of allegory.

w.b.: Is allegorism used today?

■ BLAU: There are some traces of it in the thought of Martin Buber and in the thought of Abraham J. Heschel, and of course there is still some survival of it in some of the Chasidic groups whose heritage goes back to the Cabala.

w.b.: The final adjustment in terms of tradition and innovation has been *hermeneutics*. What does this mean?

■ BLAU: The word *hermeneutics* is originally a Greek word meaning *interpretation*. Since I was using the word *interpretation* generally for all these different types of interpretation, I had to use the specific Greek word here. What I mean by *hermeneutics* is an interpretation of the text in terms of the text itself, as well as certain techniques for dealing with the text. In other words, you do not import a philosophic structure to interpret the text; you do not import an allegorical view to help you interpret the text; you study the text in its own terms according to a set of rules of textual interpretation.

Not the logical principles of interpretation but the rhetorical ones, rhetorical principles that were used in the Greek law courts. These principles of interpretation—the *Midot*, the hermeneutic rule—were structured by Hillel in seven rules and later were developed into thirteen rules, or, for midrashic purposes, into thirty-two rules. They have been the acceptable techniques within the hermeneutic tradition in Judaism for making adjustments. These involve, for example, such things as being able to make a decision between a major and a minor law. For example, that which is forbidden on the Sabbath but is not specifically forbidden on Yom Kippur must be forbidden on Yom Kippur as well, because it is the Sabbath of Sabbaths. On the other hand, something that is specifically permitted on Yom Kippur must be permitted on the Sabbath because, again, Yom Kippur is the Sabbath of Sabbaths.

W.B.: You have said that the use of hermeneutics has been the most characteristic method of adapting Judaism to changed cultural surroundings. I would like you to explain something you have written. "Another way of using hermeneutic techniques," you say, "is to determine what a satisfactory innovation would require and then use hermeneutics to justify these predetermined conclusions." Then you add: "In Jewish thought the Reconstructionist movement exemplifies this type of self-conscious adaptation."

■ BLAU: The type of hermeneutics that has been carried on within the Jewish tradition is, of course, very similar to the type of legal hermeneutics carried on within our American Constitutional tradition. It has always been the case that the judges, in producing interpretations of the Constitution, produced new law. However, it is only in the last fifty or sixty years, since the influence of Justice Brandeis came to be felt, that the justices have sometimes decided what would be a socially desirable conclusion for them to reach and have then used their extreme skill and knowledge, or the extreme skill and knowledge of their legal clerks, to discover the hermeneutic justification for this. Now basically, in the history of Judaism, it seems to me that what happened is the first type of legal interpretation—the type in which hermeneutic principles were used by the rabbis in cases where they did not consciously say "This is the way it ought to come out; let us find a reason for it."

But when Mordecai Kaplan began the Reconstructionist movement some forty-five years ago this is precisely what he did. He considered what the end result should be. He laid out the principles of a modern Judaism and then he worked to discover a traditional basis on which he could hermeneutically get to the principles that he had decided on first. I do not know whether this could have been done by anyone less brilliant than Dr. Kaplan, but he certainly did it in a masterful fashion. So far, at least, no one who has come into the movement has had a comparable mastery of the tradition and a comparable ability to create new Halachah by the deliberate interpretation of the old Halachah.

w.b.: What you say reminds me of an old classic Yiddish story in which the *yeshivah bucher* burst into the room and said in Yiddish, "*Fregt mir a frage, ich hob a teiyeren teretz,*" which means, "I have a good answer, ask me the question!"

My final questions concern the state of religion among our young people on the campus today. Are they for it, are they against it, or are they indifferent? Is there a revitalized interest? What do you find in your very wide experience on campus?

■ BLAU: There is a tremendous interest, tremendous. There is, of course, a certain amount of indifference, but I think that even among the indifferent there is interest in religion but comparatively little interest in religious institutions, if I may make that distinction. For one thing, I suppose younger people do not feel the need for the institutional affiliation that they probably will as they get older. For another thing, our young people today are very critical and, may I say, in most instances, rightly critical, of all our institutions. They do not trust our institution of government, they do not trust our educational institutions. They do not trust our institutions of urban life. They are sure that we have made a mess of things. And as I look around me I see that there is considerable mess, whether we made it or whether we inherited it. There is considerable mess and I seem to recollect that, some forty years ago, I was blaming my parents' generation for the mess they made of the world.

One way in which this interest is reflected is in the number of students who take courses in religion wherever these courses are offered. We have a comparatively new department of religion at Columbia. [*Editor's note*: Today this department is well established and flourishing.] There was something on the books for many years of course, and the Bible was taught by the chaplain or someone like that, but it is only within the last twenty years that we have developed a full-scale department of religion. Thus we find that in our undergraduate body, which is one of the smallest undergraduate bodies of any major university in the country, every year from five to six hundred students take our courses in religion with no compulsion, no requirement to do so. They take these courses on a purely voluntary basis. We have a graduate department that is newer than this; as a department it is just five years old. And we now have on our books about a hundred graduate students in various stages of completing their work. Some seventy of these will receive their doctorates within the next few years and will be ready to teach in the field of religion. The other thirty, at present at least, plan to finish with the master's degree and then perhaps work as educational directors with religious organizations, Sunday school directors, and positions of that sort. Some who have specific training in sociology will work with denominational organizations in research capacities.

In the past few years we have been particularly delighted that applications have been made by others besides Protestant students. We gave our first Ph.D. in Religion to a Jesuit last June. We have given several Ph.D.'s to some fine Jewish scholars, one of whom I am particularly proud of because I expect that he will soon be recognized as one of the outstanding Jewish scholars in the world. He is Dr. Jacob Neusner.

Dr. Neusner received his Ph.D. from us several years ago. Dr. Malcolm Diamond, on the faculty of Princeton University, received his doctorate from us. We have had and we today have working with us six or seven Jewish doctoral candidates who, when they have completed their studies, will be, like Dr. Diamond and Dr. Neusner, able to go out into the secular universities of the country and teach religion.

Now this is a great triumph. It has happened in every other academic field, but of course the last field in which it would happen would be the field of religion. Today we can say that there is not just a supply of Jews to teach religion in the colleges and universities of this country but there is beginning to be a real demand. A study made by Arnold Bann showed that some ninety-two institutions offered some kind of work in Jewish studies.

My particular concern, and the thing for which I have been fighting, not only at Columbia but in the various organizations in which I have a finger to stir around, is that this work that is being done in Jewish studies be done as completely as the work that is being done on Buddhism, on Christianity, on Hinduism, on primitive religions. This is why it is important for us to think in terms of developing a core of able Jewish students who will go into the field of the teaching of religion in the secular colleges and universities, scholars who have knowledge and insight into Judaism itself as well as the other religions. And they should have whatever comes in the way of special moral emphasis that is gained by their immersion in Jewish tradition and Jewish culture. This is one of the ways in which we can begin now to do our part in the academic work that is going on in this field. It is going to be increased tremendously in the next few years, because publicly supported colleges and universities are beginning to recognize that teaching *about* religion is not the same as teaching people *to be* religious, and while teaching people to be religious may be forbidden by the First Amendment, teaching people about religion is not.

W.B.: Judaism has always said that one should sit at the feet of a scholar. I think that this discussion has been a rare and unusual treat. To sit at the feet of a great scholar who is a source of great pride not only to the Jewish people and to Jewish civilization, but also to America and to the academic world, has been a rich and rewarding experience.

PART II

Different Jews, Different Views

❧ Introduction

There are three kinds of answers (at least!) to the question, What is a Jew?

"Being Jewish" is not always simple, depending, as it does, on the sociological definitions of what makes a person a member of a group. There is a sad story about a man, totally assimilated into the non-Jewish world and rejected by his Jewish circle, who was found by a former friend having lunch at a kosher delicatessen on New York's East Side. "What are you doing down here?" asked the friend. "You know that you are not exactly welcome in this neighborhood."

"Well," came the response, "It was my father's *yahrzeit*, and I felt that I had to do something. . . ."

Intended as a joke, but actually a commentary on today's America, the story illustrates one person's struggle for some kind of self-identification—the response to "What is a Jew" given by the person who "feels Jewish."

Such a person may or may not give religious expression to his or her Jewishness, may or may not be educated in Jewish history, culture, or belief, may or may not choose to associate with other Jews or to identify with Jewish communal activity. No matter—this person is to himself or herself "Jewish."

Then there is the identification imposed by others. It is not important that a person does not consider himself or herself "Jewish." If the outside world says that one is Jewish, the label sticks. German Jews, many of them assimilated for generations, found this to their dismay when the Nazi thugs were at their doorsteps. On a lighter note, some non-Jews today discover that their local United Jewish Appeal has (for one reason or another) identified them as Jewish and hence as appropriate recipients of solicitations for funds.

More "reasoned" or "scientific" definitions of "What is a Jew" are formulated by scholars and leaders in various fields of Jewry. Every so-called expert has personal criteria about the qualities that make someone else a Jew. These may be based on one's own interpretation of traditional Jewish norms. Some institutions have employed social scientists to devise yardsticks against which to measure Jewishness. These may be questionnaires about the nature of individual *Shabbat* and holiday observance, the scope of Jewish communal participation, the types of Jewish association the individual prefers, and the like. Basically, such yardsticks are an attempt to quantify the unquantifiable.

Who is to determine which of these types of response to the question "What is a Jew" are the more valid? Only the individual can do this for him- or herself. Some notable figures have come to their own conclusions on the matter. Perhaps the discussions that follow will provide material for individual thought.

6. ❦ Religion and Psychiatry

Dr. Mortimer Ostow

W.B.: Both religion and psychiatry deal with the mind. Religion speaks to the individual through his experience, his faith, and his emotion. Psychiatry uses the methods of science to probe into the psyche. Both seek to enable the individual to achieve greater fulfillment as a human being. However, there are practitioners of each discipline who mistrust the other, who see in the practice of the "opposing" system a threat to the accomplishment of their own objectives. Religion has come under searching, if sympathetic, analysis by doctors who seek to understand and use all of the complex facets of the human mind in their work; while psychology, as you know, has become firmly established in many pulpits, with clergy eager to take advantage of every aid of modern science in serving their congregations. Nevertheless, there are still certain questions that must be answered. For example, is there a conflict between psychiatry and religion, and is this conflict an extension of the classic opposition between science and religion? If there is no conflict, what strengths can each one lend to the other? What answers do each—psychiatry and religion—give to the person who wants to know who and what and where he is?

To answer some of these fundamental questions, I have invited one of the leading men in his field to discuss these matters. A practicing psychoanalyst of national prominence, Dr. Mortimer Ostow is an author of note, and in addition to his many writings and his practice, he is Edward T. Sandrow Visiting Professor of Pastoral Psychiatry at the Jewish Theological Seminary of America, and the Department Chairman.

I would like to begin, Dr. Ostow, by asking you to define a few terms. What is the place of psychoanalysis in the general field of psychiatry? How well established is it as a science?

■ OSTOW: You have asked what psychoanalysis is and how it relates to psychiatry in general. This is an elementary question, yet the confusion is so great that it pays to be specific about it. Psychiatry is a medical discipline, a branch of medicine. It can be considered in the same category as orthopedics, or pediatrics, or allergy. Psychiatry is that branch of medicine that treats mental illness—that is all it is. Any physician who treats mental illness is a psychiatrist. Psychiatrists have existed for perhaps a century and a half, ever since the beginning of the nineteenth century. During most of the nineteenth century they concerned themselves primarily with the treatment of mental illness in hospitals.

However, in the last decade of the last century a brilliant Jew named Sigmund Freud said that not everybody who is troubled by mental illness is, or should be, in a hospital. There is much suffering from mental illness among people who are not so seriously disturbed that they have to be hospitalized, and this suffering can be alleviated. With this, he introduced us to the concepts of neuroses and character disorders. And he went further: he said that people who have strange ideas, who have strange compulsions, who have unlikely fantasies, can be helped. If you take what they think and what they say seriously, no matter how foolish it may sound, very often you can find out what is troubling them, and this knowledge is enough to set them free. Knowing what is troubling them helps, in many instances, to relieve them of their suffering. Freud devised a technique that he called psychoanalysis and that was primarily intended for the treatment of neurosis, for the treatment of the kind of mental illness that can make a person miserable but does not necessarily require him to be hospitalized.

So psychoanalysis is a specialty, a subspecialty, in the practice of psychiatry. Most people think that *psychiatrist* and *psychoanalyst* are two names for the same thing, but this is not true. There are in this country about 18,000 members of the American Psychiatric Association, but only about 1,000 members of the American Psychoanalytic Association. Of these, about 300 are in New York City. [*Editor's note*: These figures may have changed since the time of this Dialogue.] Most psychiatrists are not psychoanalysts.

The situation is further complicated by the fact that Freud learned that some of his best pupils in Europe were people who were not physicians. Psychologists, philosophers, and teachers studied Freud's method of psychoanalysis and learned to use it. They were particularly good in the treatment of children. So there are many laypeople, nonphysicians, who also practice psychoanalysis and who are quite competent to do so. A psychoanalyst may, therefore, be a physician, or he may not be a physician. A psychiatrist may be a psychoanalyst, or he may not be a psychoanalyst.

w.b.: We hear many different terms that I think need clarification. What do you mean by *mental health, normal behavior, neurotic behavior, psychotic behavior?*

■ OSTOW: I am not an expert on health. I do not deal with healthy people. I deal with sick people, so I can tell you about sickness. I can tell you what mental illness is, but I cannot tell you what mental health is, any more than an internist can tell you what physical health is. He can tell you what physical illness is, and he can tell you that the absence of certain signs and symptoms gives him the right to consider you healthy, but he does not really know whether you are healthy or not. All he knows is that he cannot find any illness.

Let me say that mental illness is illness, in the sense that we understand physical illness. Physical illness is illness in the sense that it is a disease. Disease means that the person who is sick is uncomfortable; he does not function properly; he feels miserable; something hurts; something bothers him. The same is true of mental illness. In mental illness something hurts; something bothers the individual. He cannot sleep; he cannot enjoy life; he has symptoms that disturb him. If the symptoms are so severe that the individual abstracts himself, detaches himself from the world of reality as we conventionally call it, if he believes that black is white and white is black, then we say that this person is psychotic or insane. If, on the other hand, he merely suffers inwardly, but on the outside can function fairly well, then we say that he is neurotic. Then there are some individuals who have a talent, not for suffering, but for making other people suffer. Everyone has encountered them. This we call "character disorder."

w.b.: Perhaps this next question may be too large to ask at the outset, but nevertheless, to really set this frame of reference before we turn to specifics, can you briefly indicate the differences between the religious and the psychiatric view of what is normal and desirable for mental health?

■ OSTOW: The question is a difficult one, because I do not really know whether I can see it as a proper question—at least, not proper for me. I could list for you a set of criteria that constitute mental illness, from a psychiatrist's point of view. I do know that in Jewish literature there are a number of discussions about mental illness, primarily in terms of responsibility—under what circumstances is a Jew no longer responsible for his behavior? For example, if he tears his clothing, or if he forgets things, if he doesn't know his name. These criteria have varied from time to time and from place to place, and I am afraid I cannot give you well-organized answers. When religion looks at mental illness, it is primarily concerned with the circumstances that mitigate a person's behavior, so that he or she should not be considered responsible for or guilty of misbehavior. When should someone be freed of religious obligations, for example? I know that it is a Jewish principle that a suicide may not be buried in a Jewish cemetery except when the suicide was committed as an act of mental illness; therefore, religion wants to know how one can identify mental illness for the purpose of qualifying or disqualifying a suicide.

Now actually, while psychosis or insanity renders a person incompetent to carry on his normal obligations and responsibilities, nevertheless most mental illnesses, most neuroses, and most character disorders do not, and should not, by any reasoning that I am familiar with, exempt a person from responsibility. In other words, the fact that someone has a neurosis or a character disorder, is not an extenuating circumstance in the question of whether that person is criminally responsible, or civilly responsible, for anything that he or she does. We have an entirely different set of criteria in terms of who is ill and who needs treatment.

W.B.: Both psychiatry and religion have a great deal to say about certain basic problems of personal living. One area of concern is the matter of guilt. Will you define for us the difference between normal and neurotic guilt?

■ OSTOW: Guilt is perhaps one of the most interesting and pivotal links relating psychiatry with religion, because both the psychiatrist and the rabbi deal extensively with this. There are two sets of circumstances under which a person may experience guilt. In one instance he or she deserves it, and in the other instance does not. That is a very simple but very important distinction. There are times when a person has done something wrong and feels guilty, and it is not strange that he should feel this way. This kind of problem is of no interest to the psychiatrist or the psychoanalyst. It is *not* his or her business, and if the person is troubled by guilt and wants to consult someone for assistance, the one to consult is the rabbi. If the situation ended there, there would be no problem. Unfortunately, it does not end there.

Everyone has known occasions when they themselves or people close to them have expressed feelings of guilt for certain things for which they were not at all responsible. For example, when someone close to us dies, we often feel that in some way or another we were responsible—we did not call the right doctor, we did not call the doctor soon enough, we did not call the most expensive doctor—that if we had done something else for the person who died, things would have been different. The extreme of this situation is seen in severe depression. Certain people who become seriously depressed accuse themselves of having committed every crime in the book, or, if not of having committed them, of having wanted to, and thus being responsible for all kinds of damage. This is pathologic or abnormal guilt, and it comes about as a result of illness. It is one of the most common components of mental illness.

You may remember from the Book of Job that Job was one

of the *tamim* of his generation, one of the perfect men of his time, and God rewarded him with prosperity, with children, and with *parnasa*. He was successful in everything that he did; he was a great man. Then the devil talked with God and teased him about Job's behavior. God agreed to test Job by depriving him of all his possessions, by arranging for his children to die, and for Job himself to suffer a most miserable, painful illness. Job sat there in a profound depression, and the clinical description of depression in the Book of Job is beautiful. One cannot find a better description in a psychiatry textbook today.

Job personified the picture of melancholic depression, but there was one interesting exception. Job himself did not feel guilty. His friends asked how he could explain what had happened to him, the most righteous man that they knew. They said that he must have done something wrong. Job said that he had done nothing wrong, he did not know why this had happened, he could not figure it out, but, "It's not because I'm guilty." Professor Sholom Spiegel says that this book was written to demonstrate that visitation of misfortune and illness does not prove that a person has sinned. In other words, if a person becomes depressed and accuses himself of misbehavior, we are not necessarily obligated to believe him or to accept that self-accusation. A man may suffer through no fault of his own. Suffering and depression in human beings automatically brings on guilt. Nevertheless, the guilt may be undeserved.

You know, in the *siddur* we say, *U'mipnei chata'einu galinu me'artzeinu:* "If we were exiled from our land, it is because of our own sins." But this kind of guilt feeling is not necessarily a deserved one.

w.b.: In your book *The Need to Believe*, you say that guilt is one of the most powerful tools of religion. Would you care to elaborate on this?

■ OSTOW: Guilt is probably present in every one of us. We all have reason to be guilty. As time goes on, we all get a little bit mellower, we begin to become a little more tranquil, a little less excited, a little less ambitious, a little more content. We begin to feel responsible for a great deal, a little depressed sometimes, and guilt accompanies the depression. So there is a certain amount of normal guilt that is undeserved. When people reach the middle forties and fifties, they start feeling discontented and restless. Religion particularly makes it its business to try to help the restless and the discontented among us. One way is by trying to help us get rid of some of these feelings of guilt. Since these feelings are undeserved, imaginary, brought on by fantasies and by unfulfilled wishes, religion, even without making any objective change in our lives, nevertheless has the power to make us feel more innocent. To illustrate this point most dramatically, I can ask everyone only to think back to how we feel on Yom Kippur at the end of a full day of fasting and sitting in synagogue. It seems to me that the experience of Yom Kippur—a day of *cheshbon hanefesh*, torment of one's soul and confession of one's crimes, real and imaginary, in the presence of one's friends and one's family, in the presence of the congregation, the whole *kehillah hakedoshah*— gives one a sense of renewal, a sense of invigoration, a feeling of being reborn. This is the power of religious ritual: to create a feeling of guiltlessness and of innocence.

W.B.:   Would you say that the concept, as you speak of it in your book, of the communal confession of Jews, the fact that we always speak as *Klal Yisrael* as the entire house of Israel, has greater therapeutic value in terms of communal identification than individual confession?

■ OSTOW: Your question raises a more important issue. Let me answer a different question than the one you asked. You asked whether it has a greater therapeutic value, and here there is a danger of confusing two issues. Religion is not, insofar as I have been able to ascertain, any kind of treatment for mental illness. It is *not* therapeutic. If a person is mentally ill, he requires professional treatment. No rabbi, or priest, or minister can or should treat mental illness. There is no technique that religion possesses that can or should be used as an exclusive or principal procedure for the treatment of mental illness. I think that the word *therapeutic* might be a bit confusing here, although I know exactly what you mean. The relative value of group confession over individual confession is a difficult thing to answer. I am Jewish, and I believe that group confession is superior. It has the virtue of making the individual feel, as he confesses, a member of a strong group, a group bound together with vigorous ties. Thus the individual feels, not more humiliated as a result of his confession, but more relieved and closer to the other people who have sinned with him. That is my suspicion.

You remind me of the story of the old woman who was taken to Bellevue Hospital in New York because she was confused, mentally ill. The doctor gave her a Rorschach test. She looked at it and looked at it and, still confused, she stumbled a bit and then turned to the doctor. She asked, "Doctor, you're Jewish? So give me a hint!"

W.B.: I would like to read something from your book that is relevant here: "When a person is caught in so deep an unconscious guilt, a thorough analysis can disclose its source. But there is another method for the handling of guilt of unconscious origin. The method is not as efficient in individual cases, but it can be applied to the large mass of humanity while analysis cannot. The other method is provided by religion."

■ OSTOW: This is really an extension of what we have been talking about. When guilt is pathological, a part of mental illness, it can be treated only psychiatrically. When, on the other hand, we are dealing with the kind of guilt that begins to pervade all of us from time to time, we are not necessarily mentally ill and we do not belong in a psychiatrist's office. But we do feel this heavy burden on us, and religion does provide a number of methods for easing our minds, making us feel lighter and more vigorous, so that we are not buried by the weight of an accumulating guilt.

You have referred to some of these methods—confession, self-denial. Sometimes, if we feel guilty that we have done something wrong, we try to make restitution, and so we give a gift to the synagogue. Without guilt, how would synagogues ever be built?

W.B.: How does psychiatry handle guilt or treat it?

■ OSTOW: This is asking me to discuss in three seconds how we treat patients, because guilt is not a disease. Guilt is a symptom, and it occurs in many illnesses, and one treats the illnesses. Since I co-authored *The Need to Believe*, we have acquired new and almost miraculous methods for the treatment of mental illness. These have been called the wonder drugs in psychiatry. They can accomplish for severe cases of mental illness what no other treatment could. They can accomplish quickly what previously required protracted treatment. It is interesting that with these drugs one can produce and dissipate at will not only guilt feelings but even religious sentiments. I have seen patients who have previously been uninterested in religion suddenly begin to vow that they would become religious. The family was amazed: they did not know where the patient got it from. So I said, "Wait, I'll change that." I took away the drug, and the religious fervor disappeared very quickly. But the interesting thing is that this can be done practically at will with these drugs, demonstrating that both a pathologic need to believe and a pathologic guilt are the consequences of mental illness and can dissipate when the illness disappears. But we must remember that this is pathological.

W.B.:   Many Jewish parents would like to discover such a pill for their pre-bar mitzvah boys to give them both the instruction and the inspiration overnight.

In *The Need to Believe*, you wrote: "A given bit of behavior may be seen as wicked or sinful by a clergyman . . . the psychiatrist may see it as a symptom." Is there a difference in the attitude toward morality between the clergyman and the psychiatrist? Is this difference of viewpoint important in affecting the moral behavior of the individual?

∎ OSTOW: These are very important questions. The subject has been the source of a great deal of misunderstanding in the past, and there is absolutely no need for this. It arises in the following way: clergymen very often insist—and I must say that this is happening less frequently with the young rabbinical students we are educating nowadays—that if an individual behaves badly, the psychiatrist must tell him that this is wicked behavior and must urge him to desist. The clergyman thinks that when a psychiatrist—and particularly a psychoanalyst—refuses to concern himself with the moral aspect of the problem and insists upon treating it as a clinical problem, the psychiatrist is falling down on his job.

Now this is based on a misunderstanding. It is not at all true. Guilt, morality, observance of standards are the clergyman's business; this is what he is supposed to supervise. It is his bread and butter. He is the expert. The psychiatrist, by disassociating himself from this area, is not denying its importance or its validity. Very often the psychiatrist in his own mind has exactly the same opinion about the patient's misbehavior as the clergyman. But when the patient comes to him for treatment, he is not coming for sermons. Very often the patient himself knows that what he is doing is immoral or incorrect, and to tell him so is foolish.

Just this afternoon I saw a woman who is very depressed and who is drinking large quantities of alcohol. She had been in treatment with a psychiatrist, and she had left him a few weeks earlier. I asked why she left, and she said, "I really didn't have a good reason, and I shouldn't have left, but I just couldn't stay. It took me several weeks to bring myself to the point where I could confess to him that I had been drinking too much, and when I told him I was drinking so much, he said that I shouldn't do that. I knew I shouldn't do it—that's why it was hard for me to tell him. So what was the point of his saying that to me?"

Well, this is the problem of morality as it is encountered by the psychiatrist and the psychoanalyst. It is not our job to tell someone that he has behaved badly, that he is immoral. He knows it. Can we help an individual to improve his behavior, to undo his impulse to commit acts which he feels to be wrong? The answer is that we can, but not by saying "You're a naughty boy; you should be punished for this." We can assist by trying to help him understand, by first confronting him with his own standards. I have never met a patient whose standards of behavior were so different from the standards of society that he did not know when he was doing the wrong thing. It is merely sufficient to say, "I believe that you yourself, if you saw someone else do it, would disapprove of it. How do you yourself feel about it?" The patient generally will say, "I shouldn't do it." Then the question comes, "Why do you do it?" And here is where the analyst can help him to discover why he does it and often help him to stop.

W.B.: I was fascinated by a chapter in *The Need to Believe* that dealt with the subject of ritual. It was my understanding that the effectiveness, meaning, and message of the ritual is really something that is of concern only to the clergyman. I don't have to point out how we as Jews emphasize the need for symbolism. Symbolism gives form and concretizes the ideal. To espouse belief in the synagogue, to espouse belief in certain ideas that Judaism propagates, and not to practice them, is a meaningless kind of Judaism. We have always preached that the deed and the mitzvah are important and that Judaism is a religion of action, not merely a religion of belief.

At one point you say: "Every last one of us is a reconstructed rebel. Of the instruments that society uses to maintain the community, ritual is one of the most important. . . . Ritual attaches itself to the basic activities and events of life, which are those that affect the emotions most deeply." Finally: "Ritual is to humans what the bit and the reins are to the horse. Ritual, in other words, is a practical instrument of ethics."

■ OSTOW: One of the basic reasons for finding a close tie, a close relationship between religion and psychiatry, is that both are concerned with irrational behavior. Religion sanctions behavior, requires behavior, that does not meet the test of reason. There is absolutely no reason in the world from a scientific point of view to believe that anything practical is accomplished by bowing the head and bending the knee. Yet doing so means a great deal to the individual who does it. This act has no real influence in a scientific, naturalistic sense, but it does have a real influence on the individual who does it. Not the psychiatrist, but the psychologist has discovered that we influence our feelings and our thoughts by the things we do that may not have any real practical value.

Freud's first paper about religion was written in 1907, and was entitled "Obsessive Actions and Religious Practices." In that paper he reported an observation that he had made about a patient who was using a ritual in a neurotic way; Freud noticed that this resembled a religous ritual in many ways. In the case of this patient, he found that the ritual had as its purpose the prevention of sexual misbehavior. Then Freud asked what function ritual could have in religion. He concluded that ritual in religion also plays the role of curbing undesired behavior and that neurotic ritual is primarily hostile to destructive behavior, which is curbed by religious ritual.

W.B.: Freud said, in *The Future of an Illusion*, that religion is an illusion born of the believer's need to see reality as colored by his wishes, and that religion is the obsessional neurosis of humanity. Do people in your field today accept this premise, or has it been reinterpreted? For example, you say, "Believing is almost as necessary to humans as eating."

■ OSTOW: To try to make everything that Freud says comply with everything else that he says is a problem in itself. To try to make it comply with what people think today is even more difficult. We have a problem with Freud's attitude toward religion for a very simple reason, which Freud himself explained. Freud was a grave *apikores* from the time that he was a child. When he got married he made it his business to force his wife to stop lighting candles; he couldn't tolerate it. His family had originally been fairly observant, but early in his childhood they apparently gave up many of their observances. He learned a great deal about the Torah, a great deal about the Tanach, but he learned very little about Jewish practice, Jewish literature, or talmudic Judaism. He was in a profession that *made* him an *apikores*. As a neurologist there was not much he could do with *apikorsus*. He was a great neurologist. When he came to psychoanalysis, he had an entrée for explaining and justifying his *apikorsus*. His book entitled *Future of an Illusion* is not a monograph about psychoanalysis, any more than the book *Moses and Monotheism*, which he wrote in 1937, is about psychoanalysis. *Future of an Illusion* is a book about religion, and it tells us that Freud had no use for religion because he believed that, in the future, when the Messiah comes, humankind will have no need for illusions or irrationalities, for wishes or beliefs, but will be able to lead a life determined entirely by science. Now this is Freud's belief, and it had nothing to do with psychoanalysis, but he used psychoanalytic methods and psychoanalytic results and findings to support his argument. This makes a certain amount of sense because one can use psychoanalysis to help understand things about art, to help understand archeology, and in 1937 he used psychoanalysis to try to help to reconstruct the history of the Jewish religion. He made many errors and, on the other hand, said a number of things that people have agreed with, but these should not be understood as the

"Torah" of psychoanalysis. This is not the integral body of psychoanalysis.

At a dinner party I was seated next to an attractive young woman whose conversation was making the dinner very pleasant for me until at one point somebody whispered to her that I was a psychoanalyst. She suddenly cooled off and moved to the other side of her chair. I was puzzled: I had not done anything to deserve this. Finally, she got up enough courage to say, "I understand that you're a psychoanalyst. Tell me, is it true, as I've heard, that all psychoanalysts seduce their female patients?" I said, "It may be true that some do, but it's not an integral part of the treatment." In the same way, *apikorsus* occurs among a large number of psychoanalysts, but it is not an integral part of the profession.

W.B.: You have written: "Psychiatry, or more narrowly, psychoanalysis, has a particular job of healing to do, whereas religion invigorates and directs in a general way. Psychoanalysis is aimed at individual neurotic problems, and religion at the unhappiness inherent in human life as we know it." Also: "For society to remain alive, it must feed on emotion. For an individual to remain happy and even alive he must hold some irrational or irrationally intense belief." While we have, in a way, touched on this, is there anything that you want to add on this particular aspect of the need to believe?

■ OSTOW: This is a very important problem because very often my patients will ask me, "How can I not be depressed when I read every day in the newspapers about the horrible death that is being prepared for all of civilization and that may very well come about with the next few days, weeks, months, or years?" "How can you tell me, doctor, that I should be optimistic if you know that all of my brothers and sisters have died of cancer in the past ten years and there is no reason to believe that I won't also?" "How can you tell me that I shouldn't worry about my children when there is reason to believe that mental illness may be inherited and therefore I have given illness to all of my children?" Behind every one of these pathologic ideas there is a kernel of truth. The fact is that everyone—nobody excepted—will die one day. The day may be tomorrow, or next month, or next year, it may be ten years from now. And yet, if a person wakes up in the morning and the first thing he thinks about is that he is going to die, this is illness. Most of us walk around with the illusion that we are immortal, that we are invulnerable, and that we will never die. We act as if we believe we will not die, and we almost seem to believe that we won't. Indeed, nowadays this takes a great deal of courage, in view of the present world situation. But take, for example—I think that we used this illustration in the book—the Jews in the concentration camps. What made the difference between survival and death? In the first place, accident, just pure chance. But almost as important as accident was the morale of the individual, the belief that he would survive, and that belief was an irrational belief against all odds. What was it that made the State of Israel possible? The conviction that *ayn breirah*— that there is no alternative, that you must believe, that you must be optimistic, or else you cannot possibly carry on. These are the illusions of normal life. Therefore, it is necessary to believe a lot of things that we cannot possibly prove in order to be able to carry on. And if we stop carrying on, we really become depressed.

W.B.: You say in *The Need to Believe*: "We have the need to believe and it is futile to think that many of us can be happy though thoroughly skeptical. One of the personally useful and mistaken beliefs that philosophers or scientists may hold is that they arrive at their philosophical conclusions on strictly rational grounds. The belief is personally useful but socially dangerous." You have written a very interesting monograph on the limitations of reason. Will you elaborate on this theme?

■ OSTOW: One of the first things that Freud learned when he started to listen to people talking was that the people he listened to—and the people whom psychoanalysts listen to nowadays—are not strange. They are not unique, or unusual. They are not the kind of people we do not know. For the most part they are indistinguishable in a crowd. For the most part they are not hospitalized patients or disabled. They are the people who do the work of the world, the doctors, lawyers, dentists, shopkeepers, and housewives whom we know. Therefore, what they say, think, and believe is probably very close to what *we* say, think, and believe. It is because these neurotic people are so very close to normal that we as psychoanalysts believe we have the right to make statements about what goes on in people who are not sick. Freud learned, when he began to listen to people and take what they said seriously, that their idea that they knew why they held certain beliefs, that they knew why they made certain decisions, that they knew why they did certain things, was an illusion. When it came to the most important decisions in life, people did not know what their true motivations were. People knew their true motivations only with regard to un-important decisions.

The small decisions—whether to have steak or roast beef for dinner, whether to go to this movie or to that one, or which stock is best to buy—can be made on fairly rational grounds. You use fairly objective criteria, and you come to a conclusion. But when it comes to questions of whom to marry, what to do with my life, what kind of occupation to follow, in what kind of neighborhood to live, whom to take as my model for behavior, what synagogue to join, should I observe *kashrut*—these decisions are made on the basis of entirely unconscious and unknown criteria and conditions. This was one of the first things that Freud discovered, and it is something that there is no reason to doubt at this point. Therefore we talk about the limitations of reason. Reason can solve only problems the outcome of which are not really very important to our lives. But reason is utterly impotent when it comes to the really important problems.

w.b: We have spoken about the role of the psychiatrist and the role of the clergy. You were the head of the Pastoral Psychiatry Department at the Jewish Theological Seminary of America. I think much more should be known about this department, what it does, when it was established, and some of its aims and purposes.

■ OSTOW: During the past decade and a half there has been a great interest in psychiatry, and especially in psychoanalysis, by the clergy of all faiths. Many Protestant seminaries offer intensive courses in pastoral psychiatry for ministers. This is being taken up at a more rapid rate now by the Catholic seminaries. Our Jewish seminaries are also paying some attention to the matter. We at the Jewish Theological Seminary began to be interested in this problem in 1954. Over the years we have built a program of education for the rabbinical student. Now, why do we bother him with this *narishkeit*—doesn't the student have enough in his head? Actually, it is very important for him. In the first place, the rabbi's job is behavior, helping people to behave in a way that he considers right. If you want to influence people's behavior, you have to understand what motivates behavior, what makes people do this rather than that. So in the first place, the rabbi is interested in the psychology of human behavior. In the second place, people come to rabbis with problems, with serious problems. As long as the problem is a *shaileh* about a chicken, he can answer it. But a rabbi is graduated at the age of 23 from the seminary, and is unmarried, and is sent to a congregation in *vay ich vus*, and the first thing that happens when he gets there is that a couple who are 40 years old come to him and complain of marital discord and quarrels. What is this 23-year-old boy supposed to do? In the Talmud he did not learn how to handle this problem.

The young rabbi is often called upon to answer questions that he is not equipped to handle. Therefore, we try to help these young men to understand what kind of problems they will encounter when they accept a congregation—the kinds of difficulties people run into with their marriages, their children, their relatives, their business partners, and their vocational choice. Many people who are mentally ill come to the rabbi first, and it is important that he be able to recognize what constitutes mental illness so that he himself can call for assistance and refer the individual for proper psychiatric help when he sees the need for it. Sometimes it is not very easy to distinguish a religious problem from a psychiatric one because religion becomes so involved in so many forms of mental illness.

W.B.: In a letter to the editor of the *New York Times* you comment on an article that the paper had printed regarding a unique, yet very frightening and real possibility, and you make some suggestions. You call attention to the grave danger to our country and to the world that would arise if mental illness should strike a president or his counterpart in another country possessing similar destructive power. The issue is so important that we should not be deterred by the difficulties. What has become a convention in presidential campaigns, the full disclosure of financial status and physical health, should be extended to emotional health. You suggest that, when a campaign is concluded, a responsible study should be authorized to determine what facts should be included in such a proper disclosure, what assistance can be offered by psychiatric consultants to political parties for the selection of candidates and to the citizenry for election, whether psychiatric opinion can be used in a responsible way to recognize identified dangers and destructive leaders—or whether managing this problem should be left to the normal processes of democracy—and under what circumstances a president's mental competence may be challenged and by whom. If we can work out some practical and sensible principles and procedures, perhaps other governments will follow our example. That is certainly uppermost in all our minds.

■ OSTOW: As you say, this has been so much on everyone's mind. The fact that such awesome power is now in the hands of so few people makes us realize how much danger this constitutes for human civilization. The fact that an individual may be moved by his own destructive impulses to involve a whole community and a whole nation in war is not new. Some of the warriors of past generations have been moved to fight primarily by their own needs and concerns. In an interesting article that appeared some time ago in the *New Yorker*, Daniel Lang investigated our nuclear war potential. He talked to the people in the Pentagon who are building nuclear armaments. He discovered to his great dismay—and the dismay comes through in his writing—that our government is committed, as firmly as the Russian government is, to the accumulation of larger and larger stockpiles of nuclear weapons without knowing when or where they are going to stop. There is no way of saying that at any point we can stop.

Fortunately our government is aware of the fact that there are people in strategic positions who can trigger a war if they so desire, and there are extraordinary precautions taken to prevent this from happening. There is, for example, an extensive program of psychiatric supervision of all the military and civilian personnel who have anything whatever to do with nuclear armaments. An individual who remains in this corps is not only tested when he gets in but is under constant surveillance. Certain areas are so sensitive that the people who are involved in them are never left alone; they must always go in pairs so that if one of them shows any kind of irrational or unusual behavior, the other can report it or correct it immediately. There is reason to believe that the Russians take similar precautions in the control of their own nuclear weapons. But the fact remains that there is one man who is utterly unchecked in his decision-making powers, and he is the President of the United States, whoever he may be. The fact that a man has been elected or appointed to public life does not in itself guarantee that he is thereby immune to mental illness.

Within the past twenty-five years we have seen a member of the Cabinet and a governor of a state become insane, psychotic, while in office, and do destructive things. This can happen to a president.

There is something even more important about which we can do even less. Most of the people who start wars are not psychotic; they are not insane in the sense that if they came to a psychiatrist's office he would term them sick and send them to a hospital. Anyone who is so sick would never be elected to the presidency, or would never be appointed to a high rank in government. Our major problem is not with psychosis. Our major problem is with destructiveness, with the kind of character disorder that makes destruction the primary goal, conscious or unconscious, so that an individual seeks to destroy everyone and very often himself too—Hitler or Stalin, for example. So far as I know, and I do not have the clinical data, these people were not clinically psychotic, but certainly they destroyed not only themselves but every bit of civilization they could reach. There is always the danger that such an individual will gain access to an important position. How in the world we can possibly prevent this, I do not know. I have no recommendations as a psychoanalyst in this area. We can only trust that our democracy, which is the best-safeguarded method of government that anyone has yet devised, will protect us from it.

W.B.: We look to a world redeemed, a world freed of pain and disease, a world that will become one as God is One. The laboratory and the sanctuary can become allies and creative partners in helping to bring that age of the divine a little nearer by learning to work together with mutual respect, mastering together the new secrets of nature and laboring together, in the words of an ancient Hebrew hope and prayer, "for the blessing of all, for the hurt of none, for the joy of all—and for the woe of none." We are thankful to Dr. Mortimer Ostow for all that he has done, both in the laboratory and in the sanctuary, to make this hope and this prayer a living reality.

7. ❧ Humorist with a Serious Side

Sam Levenson

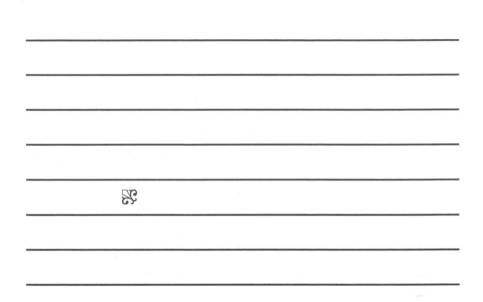

W.B: I think you will agree with me that few people can go through life without making at least one enemy. The process of achievement is by its very nature abrasive. To excel is to rise above others who are reaching for the same pinnacle, and we are reared in the tradition of competition—in business, in art, in sports. We try to assuage the loser by honoring good sportsmanship, which usually means to lose gracefully. But the psyche doesn't yield to slogans. Too often we envy the victor and we dislike him.

Our guest in this Dialogue is unique, not only because of his talents as a humorist and writer, but because of his scintillating, gentle, and beautiful personality. He has never said an unkind word about anyone, and as far as I know, nobody has ever said an unkind word about him. He combines sophistication and goodness, and he is genuinely loved. You all know Mr. Sam Levenson; let me begin without further ado.

Mr. Levenson—or, as you tell me to call you, Sam—I would like to ask you about two favorite persons in your life: your mother and father. You once said, "Mama lived with time, but not *on* time or *for* time." What did you mean by that?

> ■ LEVENSON: Mama paid no attention to the clock. In fact, she hated clocks. Anyone who was raised in the kind of home I was would understand that Mama was annoyed by the whole concept of "on time"—the idea that everything had to happen this second. To questions like, "Ma, what time is it?" she would say, "You have to know? If you know, what are you going to do with it?" She immediately turned everything into philosophy.

What she dealt with was eternal time, and it's amazing that here was a woman who, if you asked her about the word *eternity*, would not know exactly what it was that you were talking about. That's because she was a *Yiddishe mama* and was not literate in the intellectual or verbal sense of the word. But still she dealt with time, usually in relation to human feelings. If you asked her, "When was Dovidel born?" she would answer, "Dovidel was born on the night that the *Titanic* sank." For her, time was always marked in relation to some event. This one was born on *Erev* Rosh Hashanah, that one was born on another holiday, and so it went.

Now when it came to Papa, he dealt in two times: sacred time and profane time. Making a living, being a sweatshop slave sixteen hours a day—this was profane time. But came *Erev Shabbos*, with the candles lit on the table, and I could see my father change from a sweatshop slave into an angelic figure who had something to do with eternity and with sacred time. Suddenly the wrinkles left his face, and he became again a holy man who related to the whole universe and to God's destiny for humankind—which was greater than sitting over a sewing machine in a sweatshop.

W.B: Sam, what does the *Shabbos* and its sacredness mean to you?

■ LEVENSON: Well, to me, of course, it's full of beautiful memories. But even more than that, it's when I try to make time in my life to think and to meditate. I really feel that the concept of taking time out, taking time out of your life to think, is very fundamental. When I go to *shul*, I'm not always exactly following the Scriptures. I sit and think. I need some place that is dedicated to eternity. That is why I go to the synagogue. How many places will I find like this? I won't find eternity in a nightclub. I won't find it on the streets. Other than *shul*, there's no other place where people still talk about the beginning of things and the end of things.

W.B: Since you do go to *shul*, you know that one of the prayers we offer is for the country. What are your feelings about America at this time?

■ LEVENSON: Well, you know, Rabbi, we always say that we celebrated the two-hundredth anniversary of America, or this anniversary, or that anniversary. Now, when a Jew celebrates he always celebrates with spirit. You dance with the Torah, or you beat your chest, or you cry, or you talk of human failings, or you talk of dreams. That was, and is, a way of celebration. And this goes back to what we were just saying about the need to take time out to think. I have managed to make time even beyond *Shabbos*. For example, I refuse to work all year. I could make a lot of money if I did, but I need time to myself. I need time to think. I need time to meditate.

And I think this is what America needs, too—a little less American-style celebration and a little more Jewish-style celebration, a little bit more meditation. I once said this to a group of the Knights of Columbus, and you would have thought that they would have jumped up and said, "You're not a patriot, you're not a patriot!" But instead they immediately said, "Yes, you're right."

Now among Jews, we have one day set aside when we stop and think about where we are going. But the world, as a whole, should at least every hundred years sit down and say, *Where are we?* What were my dreams a thousand years ago? Are we closer to greater *menschlichkeit* today than we were then? Personally, when I ask these questions I am convinced that America today is in worse condition than it was in 1776. Absolutely. Everybody is afraid to say it, because they're afraid they won't be patriotic if they say it. Well, they have to say it.

Our holy teachings are not afraid to say when man turned evil. God is constantly saying to man, whether in Deuteronomy or Exodus or Kings or in the Prophets: "I told you a thousand times that's no way to behave. I have written out a good code and ordinance for you. Why can't you live up to these things?" And God is sure angry. Now, I'm not God, but I'm angry that after more than 200 years of golden opportunity in this country, we're afraid to walk the streets. Can you imagine coming to that in our lifetime? Would you call that something to celebrate? If you ask me, we should cry. We

should sit down and cry—lament like Jeremiah—over what
has happened to one of humankind's greatest dreams, to a
dream of democracy, equality, and a peaceful life for everybody.

W.B: I think you said that as a schoolteacher you would give America a
grade of 80 percent in patriotism. How did you arrive at the number 80?

■ LEVENSON: The reason I gave America an 80 is very simple.
According to the statistics of the government itself, we have,
in round numbers, 200 million people in America. After more
than 200 years of freedom and democracy, the government
admits that there are about 40 million people who live under
substandard conditions, who don't have enough to eat, who
don't have decent education, and who don't live like *menschen*—
to put it in the simplest terms. We always miss 20 percent.
From 200 million if you subtract 40 million, you get 160
million. You get 80 percent.

So the question is, *Vos tut men?* How do you handle this?
There are two ways. You can either take the way of the Left
and destroy the whole thing—you can say, "This will never
work" and start from scratch—or, following the more difficult tradition, you can say that it's the responsibility of
80 percent to see that the 20 percent are taken care of. By
"taking care of" I mean not just giving, but giving the opportunity not to *need* charity. This is what Maimonides suggested: that the highest level of charity is to give a man a job,
teach him a trade, put him in business, so that he will not
have to hold his out hand for charity. That is the greatest
charity there is. So that's why I gave America an 80.

Now it's my responsibility to take on the problem. How do
you teach others to take it on? The problem is that in the
schools we don't teach morality, *rachmonis*, compassion, or
concern for our fellow man. We teach reading, science, chem-
istry, physics, mathematics. We teach everything but my
responsibility for you and your responsibility for me. This
we learn in the great Jewish tradition as the goal of all
education. An educated man is an ethical man. A man of
understanding and wisdom is a moral man and a man of
compassion.

W.B: I couldn't agree with you more. However, while we can all agree on the need to achieve this goal, how do we do it? The synagogue and the schools are crucial. But what of the home and the family?

■ LEVENSON: Rabbi Berkowitz, let me answer you by talking about my own family. It's strange to say but true: I came from a home without money, but I never once felt poor. I came from a rich home, because it was a home that had books—lots of books, lots of culture, and lots of the devotion of our parents to us and to each other. My family didn't pursue happiness. That's a big mistake in America—the whole pursuit of happiness. The only people who get happy from the pursuit of happiness are the people who sell tranquilizers! They're the ones that have done very well. As for us, we believe in the pursuit of truth, of justice, of *yosher*, of God, of *rachmonis*, of peace, freedom. That's what you pursue. There is nothing written in our Jewish teaching about the pursuit of happiness. We pursue great ideals, but happiness is not an ideal. It's only a by-product of an ideal achieved. It's not an ideal unto itself.

To return to your question, What happened to the Jewish family? In my earliest years we lived in East Harlem, right across from Central Park in a cold-water flat. Home to all my ten brothers and sisters was a kind of temple, or sanctuary— a wonderful place to be, where you talked to your parents and they talked to you, and where you broke bread together. Today the hostility between parents and children is frightening. Absolutely frightening. What is that about? The new mood is to get away from home as fast as you can. When kids go to school they try to pick a college at least 3,000 miles away. And they go to college forever. But is it for education? Kids are staying in college today almost forever!

Take the average college student. Even when he gets his B.A., he doesn't want to go home. So he says, I haven't found myself yet. And he goes on looking for himself. The wandering Jew. He tries the B's first. He goes for the B.A., B.B., B.C., B.D.—and he *still* hasn't found himself. By this time the father finds himself broke. So then the youngster tries the M's—M.M.A., M.M.B., M.M.E., M.B.E. By now he's 37 years old, he has a B.A., an M.A., and a Ph.D.—but a J.O.B. he *doesn't* have! And with all his education, what he has tried to prove—and I resent it and fight back—is that his parents are his enemies. The parents frustrated him, the parents imposed upon him, we didn't understand him, we put our dreams upon him.

I just don't think that's true. I think that the words of the Fifth Commandment—Thou shalt honor thy father and thy mother—were absolutely profound and absolutely right. I have never known a more beautiful, absolute, uncompromising love like the love of parents for children.

There are very few in the world as willing to lay down their lives for another human being as a Jewish mother is. I know that. I have seen it. Of course, she has been misused and abused in contemporary literature. But if there were any gift I could give to an underprivileged child, it would be a Jewish mother—even if he isn't Jewish! Let him have one. I must tell you that this theme haunts me, because I go to so many homes where there *are* no children, where they don't come to sit and they don't come to visit, and don't come to break bread, and they don't come even for the *Yom Tovim.* They're always busy, busy, busy with a lot of *narishkeiten.*

Believe me, there are mothers and fathers with broken hearts who really gave their children the best of everything, who sponsored their children's education, only to hear from their children that their world is "extinct." I think that's a great offense. In humor you can find all the sadness and all the joy there is. Humor is a branch of philosophy. (Someday we'll discuss that as a subject unto itself.) A father once told me that his young son came to him and said, "Pa, I have a date Saturday night." "Good," says the father—"who's going to stand in the way? A young man has a date, he has a date."

"But I have problems," says the son, "I ran out of my allowance. Maybe you could kind of, you know, advance me a little bit of next week's allowance?"

"How much?"

"Well, Pa, today you take out a girl, you need $20." (And, by the way, I know it's true. I used to take out a girl for eight years and we spent 12 cents between us. We bought one ice cream cone and we used to lick from both sides!) Anyway, the father advances the son on his allowance. But it's not enough. "Pa," says the son, "today you can't take a girl on the bus or the subway, and you can't walk on the street . . . so can I borrow the car?"

"Sure, take the car," says the father.

"Pa, just one more thing. That new sports jacket you bought," he says, "I spotted it and it's a real beaut, Dad. I'll look like a smash. Can I wear it?"

"Sure, sure, take the sports jacket, take the car, here's $20." And as the son is leaving the father says to him, "Have a good time, son."

And the kid turns around and says, "Pa, don't tell me what to do!"

w.b: In Rabbi Morris Kertzer's book entitled *The American Jew*, he refers to you as "a comedian with a mission." Sam, just what do you find your mission to be? Is it influenced by Judaism?

■ LEVENSON: Rabbi Berkowitz, let me tell you this. The older I grow, the more I realize how profound my roots in Judaism are. What profound meaning there is in its history, ways, and spirit! I'm beginning now to understand why I'm alive. I confess to you that I didn't expect to end up doing what I'm doing, and yet there is meaning to it.

Let me tell you a story. Recently, I got a letter from a young man who said that I had saved his life. That's a good enough reason to live, isn't it? Well, how did I save his life? He reminded me that I had once visited Detroit. At that time he was a young man who was in a schizophrenic condition with profound depression. And his parents brought him to hear me, just to distract him. "At first," he said in his letter, "you meant nothing to me. Then suddenly I began to listen and suddenly I began to laugh, and then I broke into tears." He says it was a hysterical outpouring, but, he adds, from that moment his cure began: "I learned to laugh again. Your humor," he wrote, "made me feel that there are things worth living for—that if I laugh, I can hope." Today he's a practicing psychologist who takes care of others, and he felt obliged to send me this letter, years later, to tell me what *I* had done for *him*.

Now, of course, the question is, Where do we get the "why"? Where do we find the meaning beyond the meaning?

For me, the final answer is—God. God doesn't send anybody or anything to live on earth without a reason. There's a message that we all have to deliver to the human race. Let me give you an example from when I was a teacher. I remember I looked at classes full of kids—forty kids, thirty-seven kids, fifty-two kids—and some of them were geniuses and some of them were not such geniuses. But my Jewish tradition taught me that they wouldn't be alive without a purpose. There's something that every single *schlimazel* had to say or do, and it was my duty as a teacher to lead him to discover his own message.

Let me express it to you physically. When a baby is born and you look through the glass into the nursery, and you see the baby there, so red and funny-looking, the baby always has a clenched little fist. Watch them. Their hands are not open—they're always clenched. I've always said to myself, You know why? That baby's got in his hands a message to deliver, something to say to the human race. He doesn't have to be a doctor; he doesn't have to be a genius. Maybe he'll fix a radiator. Maybe he'll turn a bolt right. Maybe he'll be a carpenter. But it is only with love and affection that you will finally get him to release his little message.

W.B.: So you feel that in each one of us there is some spark of spirituality—a sense of potential to better the human condition.

■ LEVENSON: It was my father who first gave me that concept. My father used to say that when the Messiah comes, he won't be on a white horse, and he won't be dressed as royalty. I was raised to believe that the Messiah would be among the humble. That's why you had to be very, very careful how you treated a beggar who came to your door— because you didn't know which one of them could be the Messiah. And so you had to treat them all like the *Moshiach*. Well, that's how I began to look at the kids in my class. I had forty-seven kids in a class, each one a *Moshiach*. And that's the way I treated them, with sanctity, as though one had some holy message to deliver to the human race. And by doing that, that became my "why."

However, I was about 50 years old before I discovered why I exist. First I wanted to be a violinist. Failure. Then I became a schoolteacher. Good. Then I went on to show business. All right. And now writing! And suddenly I find that the more profound I am in talking and writing about myself, the more contact and communication I have with others. And then I'm delivering my message, and I really feel very fulfilled. Now I know why I am—and I can suffer anyhow, now that I know why.

W.B.: You referred to your being involved in writing. What impact has that had on you, and how has it involved your Jewishness?

■ **LEVENSON:** I don't have to tell you, Rabbi Berkowitz, that sitting down and writing is a part of our tradition. For me, in the past, I always wrote my own things, and I wrote them lightly. But as I grew older, I felt the obligation and the moral imperative to become more profound in my own writing. Because of this, I understand mysticism today much better than I did when I was a young college boy reading about it. When you go looking for the right words to express what you feel, you will not settle for mediocre words. You really find yourself turning inward. And that turning is almost a Cabalistic experience.

I found that out on many a lonely night, and it is a lonely business, because you're there all alone. But suddenly you begin to realize what the Jews meant by the wonder of the word . . . about how many meanings a word can have. And I found myself sitting alone and becoming, in my own way, like a Gemora specialist looking for what the French call *explication de texte*—looking for the explanation of an idea.

Let me give you an example. I was recently thinking about how, when you are a schoolteacher, you go from what they call the known to the unknown. That's how you teach. You start with the known and you go to the unknown. All of a sudden I got a thought. Here I am, sitting and looking at the word *unknown*, and I began to think that the unknown may know more about me than I know about myself, and that the unknown is greater than the known. Before long, I sat there realizing how little I know, and how the unknown is much greater than what I know or will ever possibly know. This gave me that feeling of the cosmos, and of eternity. This is just a bit of what you go through when you write. I now know more about myself than I ever knew before. It's very enlightening.

W.B.: Sam, we have spoken about meaning in life and about insights. I'd like you to share with us a theory that I think is unique to your own philosophy. You once asked, "Why do young people have to sniff glue when they can smell chicken soup and gefilte fish?" What did you mean?

■ **LEVENSON:** I meant that seriously. Just think what it was like to awaken in the morning in a home where something was always cooking or burning or frying or smelling. It made your senses come alive. Beyond that, take another example. Girls who were raised in the old tradition to be the future *balabustas* of the home had to know health, medicine, merchandising, child care; everything was taught to them. There wasn't a girl among them who had reached the age of 10 or 11 who hadn't already been taught by her mother to recognize just by touch what was cotton, what was linen, what was muslin. Remember how they used to bite the cotton? Everything was touch, the sensation of touch. Or take the smell of camphor balls in your pocket.

Then one day we dropped all of the real things like wool, and silk, and cotton, and wood, and we exchanged them for synthetics. Today everything you touch is plastic or vinyl or some other synthetic material. But what is the end result? Your sensations go dull. Today a kid can go through a whole day without smelling air because of the pollution. You can go to the park and see a stream, but you'll never see the bottom of it. You'll never see the little rocks. I remember in my time sitting at the lake on 110th Street when I could see the little fish ten feet down. I could see the brook, and I could see the brook running through the park when it still smelled like a park. Seriously.

Now a kid comes into this new era, and he doesn't smell anything. What about taste? He can't taste anything because it's been frozen to death. They warm it up a second after it comes out of the freezer.

And then they go to parties and have hors d'oeuvres and these taste like synthetics. Personally, I was a lucky kid. If anybody would have handed me LSD, I would have said, "Not like my mother used to make." You see, my senses were alive. And that's the way it's supposed to be.

One of the greatest gifts a mother can give a child is to *aromatize*—if there is such a word—to make their world aromatic. Have you seen the commercial where the woman comes in and says, "Oh, my kitchen smells. I'm going to kill myself!" Well, what's a kitchen supposed to smell like—a boudoir? It's a kitchen, and it's supposed to smell like a kitchen! If it was up to me, I'd do it another way. Instead of inventing deodorizers, I would put chicken fat in a can with aerosol and go around and *shpritz* the whole house with the chicken fat, and then when the kid wakes up in the morning—he'll know he's living! Why would he need to turn to drugs? Kids don't really die of overdoses of drugs. They die of *underdoses* of the joy of living. That is what they are really missing.

W.B.: You once said that "Papa wasn't a pal to his children, nor did I expect him to be one. He was my father. Now, today parents are pals. They go to the ballgame, they do this, they do that." *Shouldn't* parents be friends to children? Shouldn't they be pals rather than "he was my father"?

■ LEVENSON: A pal and a friend are not the same thing. A pal and a friend are really two different things. A pal is an equal, someone the same age, with the same interests; they play ball together and swim together and all that. I think that the best pal a kid can have is other little pals like himself. The father should be a friend but also a father figure.

Today the whole thing has changed, with the power shifted from parents to children. It used to be a patriarchy, right? And a matriarchy. But now we have a new thing: a *kindergarchy*. That means rule *of* the children, *by* the children, *for* the children, with the parents retained as unpaid servants. They can answer the telephone; they can pay the bills; they can send the kid to college. And maybe they'll get invited to the wedding—if there is a wedding.

But to get back to Papa—he was in charge. Papa said, "When I need your opinion, I'll give it to you." Was it democratic? Not at all. Papa was not democratic. He was Papa. He was an authority, an elder statesman. He was the senior citizen. He believed that he knew more than we did about life.

Maybe he didn't know about everything, but it didn't matter. Why? Because if you wanted advice about some profound matter in life—marriage, or work, or God—you could sit down and talk with Papa—when you had matured. Otherwise he said, "*Du vest amul farshtayen*"—"You just don't understand."

So we were used to waiting. For everything, we waited. We waited for getting new shoes. We waited for a haircut. We waited for *Yom Tov*. We waited for food. We waited for this and we waited for that. Now? They're not used to waiting, and that's part of the explanation. Today if you want something, you press a button that says *on, on, off, off*. Everything is quick. With Papa it was *wait, wait* . . . and we had to wait.

This, then, was my world—Mama and Papa and the children. I saw the cosmos this way. Papa was the sun, Mama was the moon. And the children were minor little satellites. For us, that's the way it was ordained. Always Papa was the top figure, and Mama got her light and direction from Papa, and we got the light and direction from both of them at different times. And that's the way the world seemed to me at that time.

However, I must tell you in all truthfulness: when we grew up, we didn't all follow in Papa's traditional steps. My father gave us the freedom, when we went out into the world and could sustain ourselves, to make our own choices. To make up our minds about what we wanted in life, and then, *Gay gezunterheit*. I remember he would say, "I will come as a guest to your house." And if you weren't kosher enough for Papa, he would refuse to eat in your house. And I remember the time when my father was still working in the shops. Joe, the number one son, became a doctor. But there was a bunch of us younger ones still having to make our way in life. I remember very clearly my mother said to each son as he became successful, "Now you have to contribute to the house to maintain your father. He maintained you all these years." Simple as all that. And there was no loss of dignity whatsoever.

W.B.: I would like to conclude this dialogue with Sam Levenson by quoting a story from Talmud. One day Rabbi Baruka was in the market of Lapet. On this day Elijah the Prophet, herald of the Messiah, appeared to him, and Rabbi Baruka asked Elijah whether, among the people of the market, anyone was destined to share in the world to come. Elijah looked about and replied, "There is none." Suddenly, two men appeared on the scene, and Elijah said to Rabbi Baruka, "These two will share in the world to come." Rabbi Baruka approached the men and asked their occupations. "We are comedians, humorists," they replied. "When we see a man who is downcast, we cheer him up, and when we see two people quarreling, we try to make peace between them."

My dear Sam, that you have ensured for yourself a place in this world is evident to anyone who has observed your fame, your best-selling books and numerous television appearances. But that you have ensured yourself a place in *the world to come* is equally evident to anyone who has been the beneficiary of your humor, which enlightens even as it entertains, which exposes our foibles even as it expresses your hope for progress through return—return to the ancient values that nurtured you and the entire Jewish people for centuries and centuries.

8. ❧ Champion of Pluralism

Professor Horace M. Kallen

W.B: The following is from a tribute given to Professor Horace M. Kallen on his eightieth year, citing him as one of America's greatest social philosophers and certainly the most outstanding one of American Jewry:

"Few Americans have contributed so much to American education and to the ideology of Zionism as Horace M. Kallen, philosopher, educator and author. Dr. Kallen has taught in some of the greatest universities in the United States and has been identified with such great Americans as William James, John Dewey, and Charles Beard. He has been a dynamic force in the founding of the New School and in its growing reputation as an outstanding institution of education in the United States. An eloquent, an inspiring exponent of cultural pluralism in America, Dr. Kallen has long been identified with the Zionist movement in the United States and was affiliated with Supreme Court Justice Louis D. Brandeis, when Justice Brandeis was a leader of the Zionist Organization of America. The author of an imposing array of significant volumes, Dr. Kallen has written frequently and movingly of Zionism, of the Jewish people, and of Israel. He has visited Israel, and he has written about it with the voice of a prophet and the understanding of a good Jew. Affiliated with scores of scholarly, educational, Jewish, and civil liberty organizations, Dr. Kallen has always been cognizant of the vitality of the Jewish people and the age-old dream of Jewish statehood and independence."

Professor Kallen, you are one of the great teachers of our time. Can you tell us something of your teaching experiences, something about the schools where you have taught, and something about your students?

147

■ KALLEN: Basically, I have found that the reward of a teacher is not the knowledge of the pupil. The reward of a teacher is the fact that after a while teacher and pupil become a cooperative team engaged in an intellectual adventure. If you were teaching, let us say, simple arithmetic, the notion that two plus two are four can be taught by a variety of methods, but the vital method, the most important, is that pupils get a feeling of pursuit, discovery, and illumination. Now, teachers who can arouse that feeling in their pupils do not have to be educated in pedagogy or anything else. It is partly a matter of what we technically call empathy, essentially a sense of the personality of the pupil and respect for this personality, so that he, the pupil, does not feel that he is under authority but is working together with the teacher in a common enterprise.

W.B.: What about some of the schools where you sought to effect this kind of relationship with your students?

■ KALLEN: I learned it first when I was an undergraduate at Harvard, from my own nearest and dearest teacher, William James. He had that quality, and it was contagious, not only to me. Later I went to many other places—Princeton, for example, and Wisconsin. I have been in a variety of other institutions, and I have been a member of many Jewish organizations. Sometimes it seemed to me that my chief function was to replace dogmatism and a certain kind of intolerance with this feeling of intellectual adventure through open inquiry, so that decisions would not be made before knowledge is gained but as knowledge is attained. I would say therefore that this aspect of my experience has not been primarily institutional, but rather that it became intrinsic to whatever I happened to have been doing. Of course, it has been so since the founding of the New School, focal in the enterprise of adult education—a pioneer enterprise when we started in 1919.

W.B.: You have known and worked with some of the great thinkers of our time, among them John Dewey, William James, and Justice Brandeis. Can you tell us how these giants among men have affected your thinking and philosophy?

■ KALLEN: Let me begin with Justice Brandeis. I came into contact with him through certain civic and educational problems in my home city of Boston. These made it necessary to obtain legal counsel; and his firm provided it for my group without charge. He figured then, in his career and in the distinction of his legal outlook, as a great American in the Jeffersonian sense. He was committed, as we all should be, to the principles of the Declaration of Independence. In consequence, his role in the political and legal economy of the country led to his being called "the people's lawyer."

As you know, his early personal history does not disclose any concern with Jewish identity or Jewish relations, certainly not Jewish beliefs. His uncle, Louis Dembitz, for whom he was named, was a mystic actually, of the Frankist denomination, and Justice Brandeis developed a curiosity about him. From this initiative followed an exploration of Jewish ideas, among them the Zionist idea and program, with the latter predominating. When the First World War broke out, we formed the Provisional Executive Committee for General Zionist Affairs. The offices in England and in Germany had to be closed down, and we asked Mr. Brandeis to take charge of replacing their functions. He did, with the consequence that the Zionist movement was converted from an interest of Yiddish intellectuals in the *Yiddishe Gass* into a great nationwide movement among Americanized Jews as well. The Americanization of the Zionist Organization was a direct consequence of the fact that Mr. Brandeis took over the leadership at that time.

W.B.: I understand that when Professor James passed away, you edited some of his writings. Please share something about your relationship with William James.

■ KALLEN: It is difficult to talk about these rather intimate and feelingful personal relationships. I first met William James when I was a sophomore at Harvard. I was at that time much more interested in the study and teaching of English than of philosophy and psychology as a possible career. However, the fascination of the man and the contrast between the theme and the method of his field with those I was encountering in literature and philology committed me almost at once, and in the course of the years we became very close. He left his unfinished work, entitled *Some Problems and Philosophy*, for me to edit. I did edit it. Indeed, our relations were such that I am disposed to call myself the only living, authentic pragmatist in the tradition of William James.

W.B.: Some years ago I did some practice teaching. At that time, the progressive method was quite in vogue, and I went to one of the schools that specialized in progressive education. When I walked into the classroom in which there were about ten or fifteen youngsters, one child was painting, another was throwing airplanes, a third was singing, and a fourth was playing the piano. When I spoke to the teacher, she said, "If ever I could get my hands on John Dewey!" You had a very wonderful relationship with Professor Dewey, and we would welcome a comment or two on that.

■ **KALLEN:** It seems to me that I have to comment on this anecdote. First I will remind you, Rabbi Berkowitz, about an Orthodox *minyan* in which every individual member of the *minyan* is addressing his God in his own rhythm and tempo. We can call such a *minyan* "Progressive Judaism," and condemn it for irreverent disorder. Similarly, the condemnation by teachers and others of the theory and practice of progressive education as disorder is a malicious fabrication.

You see, there are several ways in which teachers and pupils can be related. The first is the authoritarian way, in which the teacher has either a sharp tongue or a strap, as in many *chederim*, and where discipline is maintained by a sort of military coercion. This makes a problem for the pupil. He must learn how to deal with the teacher rather than the subject matter. The other way is the way that you have described, a sort of free-for-all. We could call it *laissez-faire*, as it is known in that very happy kind of economics that is mistakenly identified with capitalism, where everybody is left to do as he thinks right and good, and where order is incidental. There are many schools, not only "progressive" ones, where the teachers are ignorant and the principals are lazy, where *laissez-faire* is the easiest way to get on and to draw a salary.

There is also a third way. This is the democratic way. This is a way of achieving order without coercion. It is to have team play between teacher and pupil. John Dewey is the man most responsible for laying the foundations of such a technique of democratic teamplay in American education. There have been other experiments and other devices, such as those of Kurt Lewin, which confirm Dewey's.

I might also mention the Montessori Method in Italy and a whole collection of endeavors in Switzerland. However, not one of them has had the global impact—none of them has reached to Japan, to pre-Communist China, to Turkey, and especially to Israel—as has the educational philosophy of John Dewey. The School of Education at the Hebrew University is called the John Dewey School of Education. If nothing else can relieve you of your prejudices about John Dewey, this should.

W.B.: I should like to recall a most interesting note in your biography [in a publication put out by the New School for Social Research] before we turn to your philosophy: "Professor Kallen's faith is organically bound up with his practical experience as a newsboy, a farm laborer, a journalist, an editor, a social worker, lecturer, writer and teacher. His tasks brought him face to face with problems of political bossism in Boston's Wards Eight and Six, and the connection between such bossism and the public school system. As a youth, he met labor problems at first hand in the needle trades as well as on the farm. These made him very sensitive to the relation between labor, leisure, and citizenship, and the nature of man as a consumer rather than a producer. His residence in one of Boston's social settlements awakened him to the problems of the Americanization of immigrants in terms of group relations, especially the meaning of minorities in the cultural pluralism with which Horace Kallen in his earliest writing identified."

I think, Professor Kallen, that in order for us to understand more fully some of the areas we will discuss—the Jewish way of life, Jewish education, survival in Israel—we must turn to a definition of some basic terms. Professor, would you be good enough to define "cultural pluralism" for us? I realize that I am calling upon you to be like Hillel, to give us the Torah on one foot, but I know that you are more than equal to the task.

■ **KALLEN:** For this Torah, I would need to be a centipede. Cultural pluralism is as obvious a fact as the air you breathe, but we never think about the obvious. The fact is that all people are individuals who are different from each other. Each one is different from every other one, no matter how much they may claim to be the same. If you had an identical twin and everybody mistook you for your twin and your twin for you, you would still never mistake yourself for your twin. You would be sure of your own identity, and so would the police if they fingerprinted you, because fingerprints are part of the evidence of the uniqueness of body and psyche of every person.

So persons who live together are different from each other. There certainly has to be a woman and a child, whether or not there is a man, to make a family. You always can be sure who your mother is. Whether you can be that sure about the identity of your father is another question. You need to have greater faith in the identity of your father than you need to have in the identity of your mother, and the combination makes the family. All of you who live in families know that families are different from each other, whether they are all Jews together or Mohammedans or Roman Catholics or atheists or members of this congregation. You have these differences, but what good are they to anyone else? The good they are to you is that insofar as you are you, yourself, you are this by way of your difference. And insofar as your neighbor has any use for you, it is not because you already are what he is or have what he has. It is because you are not what he *is* and have not what he *has* that you are important to your neighbor. Your life together, all social life, is free trade, free communication in all the goods and services that make up our society. Where the communication becomes coerced, where it is unfree in any manner, the result is all sorts of vexatious political, economic, and psychological problems.

Thus, any society is made up of groupings of individuals. They form teams on different scales, from the family to the corporation, the school, the synagogue, and so on. These groups are the common instruments of our personal lives. You know what the Declaration of Independence says: "All men are created equal." *Equal* does not mean *the same*. Each one is different, but they are equal in sharing certain rights:

the rights to life, liberty, and the pursuit of happiness. Then the Declaration says: "To secure these rights, governments are instituted among men, deriving their just powers from the consent of the governed."

Now, what we call the "grassroots" of the life of any people consists of the endless and changing variety of groupings into which individuals enter and which they maintain. These groups have a biography analogous to the biography of the individual. Some have perished. Others live for generations a long historic life, like our own people. Groups, as they live on, change, just as you and I changed as we grew up and grew older. You are not the same as you were when you were a baby. If you were the same as you were when you were a baby, you would not be here tonight. You have become different from yourself, and yet you feel you are the same. What does this sameness of yours consist of? It consists of this ongoing nourishment of growth by the exchanges of a free trade, a free communication with people who are different from you. When you say *culture*, what do you mean? We each have an occupation—say, musician or pediatrician or garbage collector or archaeologist or what you will. But each depends on what the others produce and exchange for his product. The man of culture, the woman of culture, is a person who, having his or her own cultural center, his or her own characteristic individual group, nevertheless is able to respect, to understand, and to enjoy the productions of other people, and to exchange his or her own for theirs. I do not know how many of you are committed to eating kosher. But if you eat only kosher, what can you really know about the dietary values of kosher food? You are entitled to make the experiment, to discover the actual, not verbal, differences between kosher, *trefe*, and kosher-style, and then to decide. So, if you are a Conservative Jew, for example, and you think you are right and that the Reformers and the Chasidim and the Orthodox are all wrong, still, if you are really completely Jewish, your Conservative culture must be felt and realized together with the rest. Otherwise, you are only a Judaist.

I say Judaist because there is a difference between a Jew and a Judaist. I myself am not a Judaist. I am a Jew. Louis

Brandeis was not a Judaist, he was a Jew. Albert Einstein was not a Judaist, he was a Jew. Not only are Judaists often intolerant of each other, but they cultivate ignorance of each other and fight each other. Now if we are all Jews together, it becomes important that the Conservative should know, should understand, and should respect and appreciate the Reform, the Orthodox, the Chasid, the follower of Jewish Science, and so on, and vice versa, all around. There has to be free communication between the Judaistic denominations. If one is a Jew and not a Judaist, it is fundamental that he understand, appreciate, respect, and share the attitudes and the values of the different denominations of Judaism.

A large factor, therefore, in Jewish cultural pluralism would be the intellectual free trade, the spiritual free trade, between all the different varieties of Judaists in the country. Then, when you add "Jew" to Judaist, you add all that Judaism leaves out; you add what is called the secular culture. You add Yiddish, you add Ladino, you add Greek and Arabic. You add English, for English is today one of the major languages of the Jewish people. These modes of speech and thought are a heritage from the past.

Now this past is not present. What you have of it consists at present of books and other symbols. And what you as a man of Jewish culture need to do with these symbols is to absorb them into the quality of your own existence. To do this is to commit oneself to the totality of the Jewish heritage. Then, when you pass from your own community, from the different Jewish groupings to the other groupings that together make up the people of our United States, organized according to the principles of the Declaration of Independence and ordered in the terms of the Constitution, you enter a free, pluralistic society. This is a society in which culture, American culture, develops *E pluribus unum*, a one out of the many, a union of the different. The many become one, the way we Americans are one.

W.B: Dr. Kallen, please define Hebraism in terms of your own philosophy so that we will be able to apply it to some of the issues of contemporary Jewish life.

■ KALLEN: Rather than give you a definition, I would prefer to tell you how I came to use that word instead of Judaism and Jewishness. When I was a student, I was very largely an assimilationist, living under the handicap of being called a Jew. To be a Jew in certain American institutions of that time was not easy, and most of the young Jews in the colleges of my day were not visible as Jews; they tried to conceal the fact that they were Jews. I felt as they did, and I was quite certain, more certain than I am today, that Judaism was only a supernaturalist illusion that could not hold up before the progress of the sciences. I believed that the sciences of man and nature were bound to either nullify or radically transform the articles of faith of Judaists of every denomination.

Well, I took a course in the literary history of America with a teacher who afterward became one of my very close and very good friends. His name was Barrett Wendell. He has written a book that I want to recommend to you called *The Literary History of America*. In that course and in that book he indicated the role of what he called the Hebraic tradition—of Hebraism. He depicted the contributions of Old Testament values and ideas to the making of the Colonial and the pre-Revolutionary American mind. I learned that what I had been rejecting was one of the influences in the formation of what I had come to believe was the most important principle for the definition of human relations that mankind had ever conceived.

I couldn't accept that. I wrote a paper and took it to Mr. Wendell, and he went over it with me sentence by sentence. When he was through with me, I felt ashamed; I decided that I would do what I have ever since been recommending that everybody else do: learn the Jewish heritage, see the whole of it, and seek out the parts of it that are presently dynamic and important in the making of the ideal of a free, just, safe, and peaceful society of which "the American idea" is one expression. For all Jews it is important to study this heritage and to become aware of its dynamic relationship to their own position as members of a group called Jews, among many other groups called Negro, called Anglo-Saxon, called Texan, called Chinese, called even Russian. It is important for all Jews, indeed for all men, to understand how it is possible for people who differ from each other to the point of wanting to kill each other, somehow to find a way of living together in such wise that each would be more freely and more abundantly themselves than they could be if they tried to go at it alone. This way of life is the American principle. We do not embody it with the success that life requires, but the history of our country is certainly the history of a struggle to embody it, and often a bloody struggle, such as the Civil War was.

Think! We are celebrating the one-hundredth anniversary of an Emancipation Proclamation that was promulgated during a war unparalleled in the history of mankind, a war that a free people fought for the liberation of a slave people. History tells of slaves who fought for their own liberation. It tells of free men fighting to preserve their own freedom. But until the American Civil War there was no war recorded of a free people fighting for the liberation of slaves. And somehow this unique war has a root, a traditional root, in the Old Testament ideas of freedom and bondage. It does not have a root in the Greek heritage, since that took slavery for granted. For me, Hebraism became significant to these libertarian values. It could be contrasted with Hellenism and other "isms." This is why I prefer to use the term *Hebraism*. When we organized at Harvard the first chapter of what came to be known as the Intercollegiate Menorah Society, we made its objective "the study and promotion of Hebraic culture and ideals," for reasons that you can now well understand. After I left Harvard, and the contact of the Menorah movement with the wider Jewish community became greater, *Hebraic* was replaced by *Jewish*, and *Hebraism* by *Jewishness*. I do not quarrel with the substitution as long as it is clear that Judaism, which is only subsequent to Hebraism and has a large Greek component in it, is a part of the totality better called Hebraism. I make this point because there are certain philosophical notions implicit in the Old Testament and in the prophets that are suppressed by the Hellenized Judaism of Philo or of Maimonides and later writers. Moreover, Hebraism seems to me in intent much closer to the contemporary perspectives of the physical and other natural sciences. This is why I continue to prefer the word Hebraism, but *Klal Yisrael* is against me.

W.B.: Dr. Kallen, you have often said that survival is education and education is survival, that the first and last condition of Jewish living is Jewish education. You have also said that if the education of American Jews is to succeed in preserving Jewish living, it would need to be transformed from indoctrination in Judaism only. It would need to be shaped as an inquiry into the values of the entire Jewish cultural heritage, and as such extended to the secular educational establishments.

Based on that statement, I should like to ask this question, about which I have some strong feelings. First, would you say that it is true that Jewish education today is only indoctrination in Judaism?

> ■ KALLEN: You notice that I did not say *only* nor would I say *only*. I would say that Jewish education, generally and prevailingly, is indoctrination. Certainly the instruction in the elementary Jewish schools, and in such secondary Jewish schools that we have, is a process of indoctrination.

W.B.: What do you mean by *indoctrination*? What is indoctrination in Judaism?

> ■ KALLEN: Indoctrination is repetition of the formulae of a catechism—such formulae as we have, for example, in the Eighteen Blessings of the *siddur*, which we repeat, whether we mean them or not, every morning at Shachrit. Indoctrination imposes an affirmation such as the *Shema*, which we repeat regardless of what it means or whether we know what it means and implies. Indoctrination transmits a series of articles of faith neither argued nor demonstrated, but constantly reaffirmed and confirmed by repetition.

W.B.: This is one issue about which I feel very strongly. My own experience with Jewish education is that one of the weaknesses of Jewish education, in our elementary Hebrew schools and in our Hebrew high schools, is a lack of indoctrination, is the fact that although the youngster may recite the *Shema* or the *Shmoneh Esrai* and may have some kind of "catechism" in the course of his training, he does not really understand that these are essential doctrines of Judaism. I think part of the bankruptcy of Jewish education about which I have spoken on a number of occasions is that the youngster today emerging from

Jewish schools is not indoctrinated in Judaism, and thus he emerges ignorant of doctrine. He acquires some kind of feeling, some kind of emotional response, some kind of attitude, some kind of identification, but, aside from the day-school movement, if you were to discuss doctrine with the average afternoon Hebrew school youngster, he would be quite at a loss for words.

> ■ KALLEN: Before you continue, let me say that if you would put the word *successfully* in front of your word *indoctrinated*, I would agree with you. The point about indoctrination is not whether its victim knows a doctrine but whether he is either forbidden or prevented from considering the origins, background, reasons, and alternatives of the doctrine that is repeated. I would prefer the condition that you prefer. But we are not achieving it. All we have is a process of indoctrination that is unsuccessful.

W.B.: I agree with you, yet I think that as long as the youngster or the individual is given that information and given that doctrine, he can make the choice for himself. Unfortunately, however, because of his lack of knowledge, he does not make that choice.

In one of your essays, called "Ben Rosen and the Jewish School," you list, Professor Kallen, certain common objectives mentioned by Mr. Rosen as the aims of Jewish education: a feeling of belongingness, of dignity and security through understanding of the relevance of the past to the present; a desire to participate as a Jew in the home, in the synagogue, and in the community; preparation for the Jewish child to live in his environment and to withstand the effects of anti-Semitism on his personality; perpetuation of Jewish life and culture through education; strengthening of loyalties to American democracy.

This is built on the classic, ethical tradition of Judaism. Professor Kallen, you call Ben Rosen a path-finder and forerunner, and you say that it remains for the survivors to turn the path he blazed into a system of open roads. What do you mean by that specific statement?

> ■ KALLEN: I mean basically the formation of the American Association for Jewish Education and the support of its program.

W.B.: You also state that Ben Rosen did not think through and point up the responsibilities of the Jewish school for the education of Jews who are not or who do not wish to be Judaists. What is the definition of a Judaist as opposed to a non-Judaist, and what are the responsibilities of the Judaist?

■ KALLEN: A Judaist would be parallel to a Moslem or a Roman Catholic or a Congregationalist or any other person who is a member of a religious denomination and is committed to a certain creed and code that characterize that denomination. We Jews have, let us say, a denomination called Reconstructionists; we have a variety of Conservative denominations—although this is, I am afraid, denied by your hierarchy—and we have certain divergencies among Reform congregations. These types of organizations are not defined primarily by anything except the creed and the code establishing their relation to the supernatural. They are defined by certain rites they practice, and by certain rotes they repeat in the *siddur* and the *Machzorim* and the other books of prayer. All over the world you will have congregations of all sorts of creeds and codes defined by the way in which they worship together and by the way in which they follow certain taboos and proscriptions regarding what they eat, drink, and do about their bodies and their surroundings. They attribute these "commandments" to supernatural power. This is what Judaists do.

There is, however, so far as I know, only one organization in our country that is exclusively and solely Judaist. It is called The American Council for Judaism: it is utterly Judaist in that it defines itself by a minimal creed and perhaps by no code whatsoever. At least I am not aware of any ritual code. In addition, there are variations. But most Judaists are also Jews, although no Judaist has to be. For example, in Jerusalem there is the group known as *Neturei Karta*. They too are exclusively Judaists. They count themselves as aliens in Israel, and they receive support from the Williamsburg ghetto and from other parts of New York City. They are opposed to Israel's government and its works. They contain their lives within certain rites and rotes, and are perhaps the most uncontaminated instance of Judaists within reach.

Jews, on the other hand, are persons who may or may not be Judaists also. If they are also Judaists, they give their own Judaism a certain centrality but include with it the entire secular heritage of the Jewish people. That consists of all those aspects of the life of the Jewish people, all the content of the history of the Jewish people, which is not, and as a rule cannot, be identified with any Judaist creed and code, but can be and mostly is subordinated to the creed and the code. Most Jews in our country are recessive Judaists. There are very few dominant Judaists, very few, whether reformed or unreformed, who could parallel *Neturei Karta* in Israel or the Williamsburg group. The impact of the free world, with its free ways of life, necessarily tends to dilute and to dissipate the traditional aspects of the Judaistic heritage. In order to preserve any component of it, to keep it alive, it becomes necessary to assimilate the whole achievement of the modern mind into the Jewish heritage.

I say "assimilate." The word may shock you, but you know that it has two meanings, two forms for every Jew. In one form, the assimilators try to get themselves absorbed and digested in their non-Jewish environment. This is how they react to anti-Semitism—to the social handicap of being a Jew. In another form they endeavor to absorb and to transpose, to transvaluate into Jewish terms all that can be received from the rest of the world in exchange for their production as a Jew. That would include the arts and the sciences, and the various forms of secular culture of the non-Jewish world. It means the liberalization of the Jewish, including the Judaist, spirit. It means the sort of thing that I would like to believe Mordecai Kaplan refers to when he talks about Judaism as a civilization, but it must be either a civilization on the highest modern level or on the level of *Neturei Karta*. If it is on the highest modern level, it may not exclude anything. It must try everything. Just as you, personally—in eating and drinking, making your contact with the rest of the world, learning other languages, going to concerts, reading literary and scientific works—develop your own spirit, become a person of culture without suppression, and become one by absorbing into what you already are all that you are not yet and all you do not have yet, so in you and through you the Jewishness that you signalize will absorb and digest into its own identity the cultures of mankind. This is how the achievements, the expression, and the faiths of other people become a nourishment for the force and the growth and the survival of the Jewish people. That always was the case. It is the case now more than ever. The problem of Jewish education is the

problem of so altering the curricula that they will not alienate the young, that they will not reduce those who continue
to belong to a progressively smaller minority. It is the problem of winning and holding the commitment of the intellectuals and the artists who manifest the kind of "alienation"
that is part and parcel of the modern process. The function of
education is to solve this problem.

W.B.: In one of your books, called *Of Them Which Say They Are Jews,* you
ask the following question: Is there a Jewish view of life? You say that
the answer does not depend on the intrinsic character of the definition
nor on its historical correctness nor its religious sanctions. The answer
depends entirely on its consequences to the strength and the enrich-
ment of Jewish life. You also make the point that these consequences
belong to the unpredictable future, and you further say that the selection of a particular view by an individual may seem right and pertinent
in light of that individual's struggle and ideals. Now, Professor, what
ethical, moral, and religious guidelines does one then have so that we
are able to select at any particular time the view that is correct—or how
do we define the word *correct* in terms of a Jewish view of life?

■ **KALLEN:** I do not think I can define the term *correct* in advance. Primarily, everything you say and everything you
propose to do is a bet that you make on the future, and that
which you bet is your past. The more past you have, the
more varied your bet can be. Whether you win or lose does
not depend on your ability to predict the future, because if
you could do that, you would be infallible, and every bet
would be a bet on a sure thing.

Fundamentally, you look at the relevant part of the record
and appraise it. You hope that if you can make such and such
a design for living, for surviving, you will survive. There is no
guarantee that you will survive. For example, you undoubtedly had your dinners tonight; and in eating dinner, you had
faith that what you ate would be digestible, that it would
nourish you, that it might not add unwanted pounds, that it
certainly would increase your strength and well-being. Well,
you get away with it, but every so often you take something
that you enjoy very much but that gives you a terrible bellyache. You could not have predicted that bellyache any more
than you can predict the weather infallibly. In point of fact,
we always live dangerously. You are living dangerously at

this moment because you are having faith that your chairs will hold you up—it can happen, and I dare say there have been occasions when it has happened, that a chair has collapsed under one of its sitters. So we live and labor *by* faith and *in* faith. Faith belongs to secularity as to religion, for we do not know the future; we hardly know the past. Yet we do not presently possess any other tools than those that are drawn from the past, so that the formation of the future is a use of the past that transforms the past, because there is nothing else to change. You are your past. At this moment, if you are responding to what I am saying, you are responding with what you have learned yesterday and the day before and all the rest of your life. Your past is you. Lose, forget your past and you have lost your identity. But your response to what I am saying may consist of fighting it off and shutting it out. You-as-past may resist the future coming to change it. Or you may absorb the newly come. If you absorb it, the future will transform your past. This holds for all ideas, all systems of philosophy and theology that have a history. Their history is a record of transformations, not of repetitions of the same thing over and over again.

People talk about traditional Judaism. They talk as though they were talking about an unchanging Judaism. They deceive themselves. That which is traditional is something that is ongoingly changing. If it stops changing, it stops living. To live is to change and to change is to absorb novelties of the unpredictable future and of the residual present into the past, thereby to feed, strengthen, and enrich it, and, by strengthening it and enriching it, to transform it. This is what progressive education is supposed to do for its pupils.

W.B.: Dr. Kallen, what do you think are the prospects for religious freedom in Israel?

■ KALLEN: I am hopeful. I think that at present there are political exigencies that make for an allegiance between secularized and, I say, prophetic minds drawn from the kibbutzim and the moshavim of the old time, between those who are the present leaders and rulers of Israel, and the Orthodox contingent. The situation gives the Orthodox intolerants a position and privilege that they refuse to give others. I do not think that their predominance can survive. The Israel Declaration of Independence, which has certain analogies with our own, militates against it; and the modern world, regardless of political attitudes, has to be an intellectually and religiously free world. There is a *kultur kampf* in Israel. It has been going on since the foundation of the state. It was only potential before the foundation of the state. It is now explicit. It brings more and more public confrontation on the issues. It is already a fact that despite Orthodox resistance to setting up Reform congregations in various communities, the latter have been set up. I am very sure the fight is going to be a long one, but I think the future holds religious and intellectual freedom, especially in view of the fact that the security of Israel depends in the most definitive and absolute way on the achievements and the successes of the scientific mind in its modern terms.

W.B.: Can you tell us something about Israel the fact and Israel the ideal?

■ KALLEN: Well, you know the difference between an ideal and a fact: An ideal stands for what you may passionately or reluctantly wish and hope for; it stands for what you do not have but do want. A fact is a condition; it is a condition that you might want to alter, and a program for altering a condition is an ideal. An ideal is a design for living and changing toward the future. It looks forward. It does not try to preserve the status quo. Now there are three sources of the ideal for which the word *Israel* may be a name. The first is, of course, the Law and the Prophets, the Old Testament and the great Prophets, Jeremiah, Micah, Isaiah, and so on. You know how Ben-Gurion is always appealing to the Prophets and not at all or hardly ever to the *Shulchan Aruch*.

The second is Israel as a vision and a faith. A vision of a free and equitable society that is identified with the teachings of A. D. Gordon, who was one of the early, naturalistic pioneers, a Tolstoian who was a devoted inspirer of the formation of the cooperative communities called *kibbutzim* and *moshavim*. This faith is secular and is by its intrinsic nature easily orchestrated with the prophetic tradition. The two belong together; each suffuses the other; they grow into each other. It is difficult for a man in a kibbutz, even when he has had Communist derivations, to talk about the vision of the kibbutz without referring to the greater Prophets.

The third is the endeavor to implement this joint faith through the organization of the kibbutzim and moshavim themselves, and to use them as models, pilot enterprises. These are cooperative settlements endeavoring to achieve just that condition of the free association of individuals in such a way that each individual is freer and safer and lives more abundantly than he could by trying to go it alone. This endeavor has been arduous. It has a remarkable history of suffering and heroic effort. However, it is now in a very precarious condition. It needs to reconsider many of its assumptions in the light of the new and changing community of Israel, and in the light of the existence of the state as differentiated from the initial and developmental statelessness of those cooperative settlements.

They embody the ideal that the schools of Israel may communicate to the coming generations of the children of Israel. They are efforts to establish faith as fact. Theirs is the ideal that has its roots in the past and consists of a design for permanent reconstruction of the Israeli's ongoing life. But they embody an ideal working to reconstruct a very precarious and dubious fact, for the practical, the political, and the military security of Israel are always in doubt. To live in Israel is to live dangerously under any circumstances. Israel's very small population is surrounded by 40 million enemies who hate them. To stand alone without any helpers, to look abroad, to stand like Job before God, is something almost without parallel in history, certainly without parallel in modern history. Regardless of the harshness and severity of life in Jewish Israel, there is a quality of heroism about it that assuredly should have the admiration and the support of the world. Now, if Israel the fact should be defeated—and we cannot rule out that contingency—Israel the ideal endures. Jews envisioned it before Israel the fact came into being. It was there and theirs. Now it goes along with Israel the fact. But it is also capable of outliving Israel the fact. Of course, we need to do everything we can to see that the two live on together.

W.B.: "To believe in life in the face of death, to believe in goodness in the face of evil, to hope for better times to come, to work at bringing them about"—this quotation from Professor Kallen has been the essence of his life's work. He has celebrated his eightieth birthday, and according to the sages, *Ben shmonim ligvurah*—"When a man reaches his eightieth year, he reaches renewed strength." May God grant Professor Kallen the strength to continue to bring to all of us the many notable gifts of his mind and his glowing, truly great personality for many years to come.

Dr. Nahum Goldmann

9. ❧ Beyond the Jewish Façade

Dr. Nahum Goldmann

⚜

W.B: Dr. Nahum Goldmann, who has nobly blended into his life the character of a man of letters and a man of action, is one of the greatest leaders in Jewish life today, one who will certainly have a notable place in all of Jewish history. One of the clichés of our times is "Jewish survival" and we hear on all sides questions and opinions about how we as Jews can survive the contemporary pressures that envelop us. Dr. Goldmann deals with this subject, not as an abstract matter but in terms of the realities of today. As president of the World Jewish Congress [1936–1982] and of the World Zionist Organization [1951–1968] he has long been concerned with Jewish survival, not as a philosophy but as a factor in our lives.

For a long, long time we lived in one Jewish world. In fact, this living in one world gave rise to a Yiddish expression, *die velt zugt*, and when Jews said "the world says," they meant their world, the Jewish world. But along came a period in world history when the winds of new doctrines blew across Europe and when, with the French Revolution, Jews were granted emancipation, equal rights, citizenship. Suddenly they were hoisted from the one world into a second world, and ever since then we have been living in two civilizations.

Dr. Goldmann, you have said that there are no free gifts in history, and that emancipation has had certain very negative consequences for us. Please enumerate some of these negative consequences. What would you say that ghetto life gave to Jewish survival that our living in two worlds lacks?

■ GOLDMANN: I want to say at the outset that by nature I sin on the side of optimism, rather than on the side of pessimism. I have often proved this in my career because I have

169

believed in things that at the time appeared ludicrous: in 1941 I was certain that we would have a Jewish State after the war, and I believed, at a time when perhaps 2 percent of Jews thought it possible, that we would get tremendous amounts of reparations money from the Germans. I point this out in order to qualify myself as an optimist, yet when it comes to the question of Jewish survival, I repeat over and over again very grave warnings to my Jewish generation. I think that we are all living in a fool's paradise.

We are living in a world where the façade of Jewish life is more wonderful than it ever was. Jews are emancipated practically everywhere; they have equality of rights. Economically, Jews are probably living better now than ever before in any period of Jewish *Galut* history, including their glorious, prosperous period in Spain before the Inquisition and the expulsion. We have a Jewish State. So Jews generally feel that we are now living in a wonderful period. But the greatest danger for people occurs if the façade of life is not in accord with the real situation. In a certain way all of humanity lives today with a wonderful façade: people get richer and enjoy more material possessions and in general think that they are happier. Yet at any moment a silly decision, an error, by a leading statesman could bring the world face to face with a war that could be a catastrophe for all of us. So, we are living a better life day by day, yet all of us are dancing beneath a volcano.

W.B: I agree with your generalization that we cannot call our world happier or more successful because we possess more material things. I know that ministers of many faiths deliver sermon after sermon about the pursuit of the material. I am aware that we Jews desire the enjoyment of riches as much as anyone else. Because of this we are in danger, as must be all peoples who are mainly concerned with the acquisition of pleasures and possessions. There is a dangerous vacuum created by the loss of spiritual quality.

■ GOLDMANN: Yes, this is a general problem that applies to everyone. Jewish survival is our own particular concern, and it is a real concern. In my opinion, if nothing is done about it, we are more threatened now than perhaps in any other period of our history, and the existence of the Jewish State does not eliminate this danger.

Let me try to enumerate briefly. First, for the Jewish people to survive as a community it is necessary that Jews be able to survive physically. There must be no pogroms or massacres. Second, we must be allowed to survive not only as human beings but, more importantly, as Jews. If our whole problem had been one of survival as human beings, we Jews could have solved our problem many centuries ago. We could have been baptized or have become Moslems, and no danger would have threatened our physical survival. Survival as a religion, as a nation, or as a people or a community is another matter.

In many parts of the world there is a tendency today that endangers our survival as a Jewish community. We cannot discuss Jewish problems without always referring to the general situation of the world because we are dispersed all over the world. Whatever happens anywhere in the world affects us directly because we are everywhere. We are living today in what I regard as the last chapter of modern state nationalism. The modern form of nationalism that finds its supreme expression in the so-called sovereign state I regard as a disaster for history. It is an invention of the Prussian philosophy. The greatest philosopher of this tendency was Hegel, who proclaimed the state to be the climax of historical development, and I have always said that there is one very clear direct line from Hegel to Hitler. Hitler proclaimed that only one ideal required the loyalty of people—the state. No religion, no church, no family, no class—every loyalty belongs to the state because the state is the supreme being. I do not think there will ever be peace in the world as long as sovereign states exist.

W.B: Yet we fought and gave so much for the establishment of the State of Israel—*you*, particularly, did so much.

■ GOLDMANN: Do not be surprised to hear me say this, even though I was the political Zionist who fought for partition when most Zionists were against it. I said that Jews should make great sacrifices to have a state. Some of you may recall that Sholom Aleichem had a wonderful saying: A Jew should sell his last shirt to become a millionaire. So I said to my fellow Jews that it was worth fighting and sacrificing half of the territory of Palestine to have a state, because in a world where every people has a state, we needed a state too. We needed it to make sure of our survival and to have a home-land for Jewish immigrants.

But, generally speaking, this last chapter in world history is a very violent chapter. Nationalism today is more violent among the young nations than it ever was before. A general historical fact is that a class is always most arrogant the moment before it breaks down and is ruined by revolution. An idea is most violent the moment before it disappears from history or loses its impact on history. We are living, as I see it, in the last chapter of political state nationalism. This chapter can survive one or two or three generations because a chap-ter in history can be very long.

This rabid nationalism makes Jewish existence in many parts of the world very difficult. It denies the right of Jews to live their separate lives. I will come later to the Soviet Jewish problem; that is the quintessence of this problem. Jews are not massacred in Russia, and are not persecuted in the nor-mal sense of anti-Semitism.

As an example, take a country that is quite different, Tuni-sia. The leader of Tunisia was a Western-oriented democrat, Bourguiba, a very decent man. Some years ago he issued a decree that dissolved all Jewish communities. When we came to him he said, "I don't understand the whole business. As long as you lived in the ghetto, in Tunisia, you had Jewish schools and Jewish societies and Jewish youth organizations and so on. Now you are Tunisians, equal citizens. So I under-stand that you need a synagogue; you are not Moslems, granted. But that's the end of it. Why do you need your own schools and your own youth organization, your own sport organization, and your own women's organization? Mix, mix with the Tunisians, with the Moslems, with the others." Since the communities were real *kehillot* in the old sense and took care of every aspect of Jewish life, he dissolved them. He did not implement the decree, but this gives you an example.

Here was a modern democrat who believed that the price the Jews have to pay for their emancipation is the loss of their separateness.

W.B: It seems to me that in our country, many Jews take the same attitude. They feel that we should not separate ourselves from the general community, and that our Jewish schools and institutions are separatist organisms. Of course, Jews who simply allow these Jewish schools and institutions to suffer from neglect and lack of support are, in effect, taking the same line, even though they do not express it.

■ GOLDMANN: There are many American Jews who think the same way. It is a little bit better today than it was twenty years ago, but when you mention a Jewish day school, they say, "Oh, that's a ghetto, that's renouncing emancipation, that's against Americanism—we have to mix with the others." The problem of Jews today, as I once formulated it, is the contrary of our problem of the nineteenth century. In the nineteenth century we had to fight for the right to be equal. Today we have to fight for the right to be different. We have achieved equality; but many non-Jews who gave us equality and many Jews who took it think that the price of equality is to be like everybody else.

Real democracy and equality mean that people have the right to be what they are as long as it does not hurt their neighbors. If a Jew wants to have his own school or if he wants to join with Jews in a certain activity in his own Men's Club, or if he wants to develop Yiddish in the Argentine, or Hebrew teaching in other places, he has a right to do it. This has nothing to do with equality. As long as there is no conflict with the Jew's obligation and loyalty to the state, these pursuits should not concern the state. We feel this way in America, because here we are living in a very tolerant democracy. Americans cannot be radically or violently nationalistic, because here we have Irishmen, Italians, Hungarians, Germans, Englishmen, Catholics, Protestants, Jews, and everything else. If America took the nationalistic point of view, who would be the Americans? But in Latin America, in Russia, in North Africa, Jews are not, for instance, allowed to join international Jewish organizations. If Jews attend an international Jewish conference, the national press attacks them. They are said to be traitors to their country. That is all the result of this violent nationalism.

The last reason for my worry is that we have left our separate life in the ghetto. I do not preach going back to the ghetto. This would be nonsense; a line in history that has broken cannot be mended. I said once that there are no mended pants in history. We have to live as emancipated Jews with full participation in the political, economic, cultural, and social life of the countries where we have been emancipated, but as you said in quoting me, we pay the price for it.

As long as we lived our separate life, we had to worry about our physical survival, but there was no reason to worry about our spiritual survival. A hundred years ago a Jewish leader could have complained about pogroms and anti-Semitism, but he was sure that his children would remain Jews. They lived a Jewish life from morning to night because Jewish religion was not just prayer—it was a regulated Jewish life from the morning when the Jew got up until he said *El Melech Neemun Shema Yisrael* before he went to bed. A Jew in Casablanca and a Jew in Poznan and a Jew in Bialystok and a Jew somewhere else in the world lived more or less the same life, although they spoke different languages and did not know one another and had no contact.

This has disappeared. We mingled among the peoples of the world, which in many respects is a tremendous progress. We fought for this for centuries, but we paid the price of losing this tremendous framework of Jewish religion as a form of life, not only as a form of praying, that guaranteed our survival as Jews in the days of the ghetto or the Yiddish *shtetl* or the *mellah* in Morocco. So today we have to learn to secure our Jewishness within this framework of Jewish religion as the regulator of our life.

Even the loss of the threat to our physical survival represents the loss of a motive that secured our survival as a Jewish community. I am sure that many of you know the famous theory formulated by Arnold Toynbee—that a people exists as long as it has challenges to resist. When a people takes it too easy and lives too peacefully and contentedly and has no dangers that threaten its existence, then this people begins to disintegrate and disappear. The tremendous challenge of brutal anti-Semitism made for Jewish solidarity, gave Jews a feeling of a moral obligation to be loyal. I would not say this in the period of the Nazis, but today one can say it: Hitler killed six million Jews, but millions of Jews became better Jews in that period. They suffered when they saw the destiny of those who were massacred. They had a bad conscience: "Why them and not us?" This challenge is very weak today because Jews at the moment are not threatened and so they take it easy. They feel that there is no challenge to Jewish existence, and therefore we must teach the younger generation what this means. I said once that for two thousand years we learned how to remain Jews in bad times. We developed a tremendous genius for resisting physical dangers. Now we must learn how to remain Jews in good times. This is much more difficult, believe me.

w.b.: I would like to quote another of your theses. You have said, "No people ever was murdered; a people can disappear only by suicide." On another occasion you said, "If we lose the courage to stand out against majorities, we are lost as a people. If we keep this courage, we perform a great service not only to minorities and other nonconformist groups, but to humanity, in avoiding overpowering equalization through the modern state"—that same modern nationalistic state of which you spoke. Finally, you have said, "Our unique greatness is not alone in the great ideas, monotheism, prophetism. Every great people develops leading ideas. Our uniqueness has been the stubbornness with which we fought for our specific ideas, our nonconformism." Will you expand on this latter thought, and the importance of being stubborn in the right direction?

■ GOLDMANN: You have succeeded in distilling the quintessence of my ideas in a few very brief phrases. I used the term *uniqueness*, and this explains our survival. I am not the world's greatest historian, but I know a little about history, and I know of no other people that has survived in similar situations. There is no parallel. Our faith and our history are unique in the history of the world. There are people as old as we—the Chinese, for example—but they were not dispersed; they have lived these thousands of years in their own country. I do not know of a parallel in which people persecuted for some forty centuries, driven out of here and there, going back and forth, managed to survive. You know, there were periods in which the numbers of Jews were reduced to a million and a half, perhaps two million. Large numbers of our people were lost, but always there remained what we call in Hebrew *shearit hapletah*—"the remnant of the people"—and out of this remnant a new Jewish generation and a new period of Jewish history always developed.

This can be explained only by a great will to survive, which for Jews is a great moral obligation, because the uniqueness of the Jewish religion and its philosophy is that all the ideals in which Jews believe have to be implemented in this world; that is what the prophets taught. Christianity has made things very easy for Christians. There will be another world where everything will be done. In this world you may torture people, and persecute people, and lie to people, and exploit people, but it does not matter. The great ideals will be implemented somewhere else. Jews did not make it so easy for themselves. They said that God put us here, in this world, to implement His commandments. So when Jews had to survive, it was a great moral obligation. If it had involved only the instinct to live we could have found it much easier to survive.

But the bulk of the people refused to compromise, because for them it was a great moral obligation to remain alive and be an instrument—the Chosen People, or however you express it—to implement their ideals in this world. That is their unique stubbornness. That is why they were never afraid of the dictates of majorities. Conformism is one of the curses of our civilization. There has never been a period in history when it has been as difficult to be an outsider, a nonconformist, as it is today. That is the paradox of our world: we are divided more than in any period in history, yet technically it is one world. The same music that is being played here will be whistled a few months or a half year later in Soviet Russia, in Japan. This is a world that mechanizes everything and tries to create one conformist type of human being. This is the greatest danger to civilization. Civilization was always created by nonconformists, by individualists. The great ideas in history came from small peoples. Justice Brandeis wrote a notable book, *The Curse of Bigness*. He referred to economic bigness, to the big companies and monopolies, but there is a much deeper meaning in the curse of bigness. It is not proven at all that the numerically great peoples have created more civilization and greater values than the smallest peoples, such as the Greeks or the Jews.

W.B.: I worry that more and more Jews are conformists. You see it in the minor things: the sameness of dress, the patterns of living, the acceptance of status values that emphasize vulgarity rather than culture. You see it in more important things too—in the unwillingness to go against the mainstream of thought, even when this course is dictated by tradition.

■ GOLDMANN: It is too bad that there is this great tendency among Jews today to conform. For centuries we were the great revolutionaries in history. Many reactionaries accused us of it. We produced Marx; we produced great revolutionary theories; we were fighting with nearly every revolutionary movement; we were mostly to the left; we were progressives; we fought for minority rights. Whenever there was a great human problem—the emancipation of enslaved peoples, of enslaved minorities—we fought for that. We fought for ourselves at the same time, but we were never satisfied just to fight for ourselves. We were the pioneers in moral and intellectual progress.

Today, and I speak quite frankly, today in many parts of the world we belong to those who cling to the status quo, who have much to defend, who are not so keen about being on the side of human progress. This may be good, it may be bad. I am not analyzing the situation. It has to do also with this stubbornness. The greatest danger for our people as a classical minority is to be too impressed by the will of the majority. We must have the courage to be a minority if we know that what we feel is right. We do not say that we are against things just to be against them. I am reminded about the man who came to this country and as soon as he landed in New York's harbor asked his friend if there was a government here. "Sure," replied the friend. "Well then, I'm against it," the newcomer said.

It is not good enough just to be against, but when we feel that we have an ideal to defend, our own special entity to defend, our special character, we must not be impressed because the majority frowns on it, or does not like it or even opposes it. We must be ready to fight for it, to remain stubborn, and to remain nonconformist in our attitudes and in our relationships with the majority. Otherwise, we will lose the basic emotional, intellectual, and moral strength to survive in this specific condition in which we live.

W.B.: This leads to another aspect of survival. Do we know what "surviving" is? Do we know what we are keeping? To what extent do we understand this heritage of which we are the heirs? It seems to me that one of the key factors in Jewish survival is Jewish education. A long time ago a great rabbi, scholar, and teacher, Saadia Gaon, said: "*Ain anu u'ma anu, elo bizechut ha-Torah*"—"We are a people only by virtue of the Torah." The priority that Torah is given today in American Jewish life has changed somewhat. I want to quote something that expresses this, and that may give a hint about the state of Jewish education: "Our fathers were accustomed to kiss the Torah with their mouths and give with their hands, but nowadays, we kiss the Torah with our hands and give with our mouths."

In speaking of Jewish education, you have said: "There is only one method to save the loss of Jewish consciousness—build up a real system of Jewish education." On another occasion: "Jewish education is more important for our future than the primary issues of Jewish life in the past, anti-Semitism and Jewish relief." On a third occasion you said: "Jewish leaders must begin to change the system of priority in our public life and give the top priority, next to securing the existence and future of Israel, to the problem of Jewish education."

■ **GOLDMANN:** To add to that, I might say that I feel at times that our list of priorities in Jewish life has been all wrong. In the nineteenth century our top priorities were given to the fight for civil rights, because we did not have them, and to the fight against Jewish misery because the majority of Jewish people lived in naked misery. Jewish education in those days was more or less assured: a boy went to *cheder* and then to the yeshivah, and his Jewishness was fairly secure. Today all this has changed. Anti-Semitism is not a number-one problem in our lives, and I know something about this. Three weeks ago I spent three days in Sao Paulo, Brazil, because I was asked by the Latin American Jewish communities to participate in an urgent conference of all Jewish communities from Mexico to Chile. This may be the part of the world where anti-Semitism is at the moment most serious—and I know about the neo-Nazi movements in Europe. But right now I do not see anti-Semitism as a serious menace.

The top priority today is to secure Jewish survival, religiously, culturally, spiritually, and for this the beginning is education—Jewish education in all forms. I am not discussing problems of Jewish education. First of all, I am not an expert. I do not say which form, what slogans, what methods are best for Jewish education.

Let me give you an example in American Jewry. I think it is all wrong when you emphasize what American Jewry spends on "philanthropy," as it is called. Incidentally, this is a word that I hate in the bones of my body, because "philanthropy" is a very splendid thing, but throughout history no problem of a people has been solved by philanthropy.

If American Jews could give enough money for everything, and I believe that they could, it would be fine. They could give money to Jewish schools, to the United Jewish Appeal, to the Anti-Defamation League, to the American Jewish Committee, to hospitals, to many causes. But American Jewry's contribution is limited, and it is necessary to establish priorities. So I say that the fact that we spend millions and millions on philanthropic causes as compared to education is, in my opinion, all wrong—all wrong. American Jewry will survive, as Jewry in any other part of the world will survive. It will have a generation that will remain Jewish—at least a large part of it will. But it will not survive because there are more Jewish hospitals, or more wonderful Jewish institutions, clubs, or beautiful buildings. I am not speaking just for America. In Latin America they are sinning much more, because they became richer even quicker and their desire to be ostentatious is much greater than that of many American Jewish groups.

The main problem in American Jewish life is to ensure Jewish survival; this demands Jewish education. I think that the situation is much worse than most of us realize. First of all, there are Jewish communities around the world that are far superior to the American Jewish community in this respect. There are Jewish communities in Latin America where 60 to 70 percent of the children go to Jewish schools. You could not even begin to dream about such a state of affairs in

American Jewry. From the financial point of view alone, millions of dollars will be required. I know that great progress is being made—I follow it—but it is a drop in the ocean. Unless the Jewish community, which means the Jewish welfare funds that are the sources of money, change their policies to a large extent, progress will be minimal. There are some indications that change is taking place: we hear about "cultural foundations" and "Jewish schools," which just ten years ago or so were *trefe* to some of our Jewish leaders. But unless such a change is really brought about, I am fearful about what will become of the next Jewish generation.

Let me tell you about a survey that was made a few years ago among Jewish students. I do not know how many thousands of students were polled, but this is the significant thing: the majority said that they have no interest in being Jews. When asked why they remain Jews, the majority of those who indicated a certain interest said they did so in order to please their parents. This is what I will never forget; this made a tremendous impact on me. Because the consequence is that the children of *these* students will not have this motive. These students will not be displeased if their children are not good Jews. And so another motive for the survival of the Jewish community, as tenuous as that motive is, disappears.

W.B.: You have many contacts abroad. Have you heard anything that would indicate similar or opposing trends in other countries?

■ GOLDMANN: I can give you a much more tragic example that was a surprise to me, and I flatter myself in that I know something about Jewish life. The Jewish Agency has a department that has been doing a great deal of work in the field of education. Not in the United States—because what could this one organization with its limited means add to the great resources of American Jewry?—but in Argentina, in Brazil, in England and France, and all over the world. At any rate, some years ago the Jewish Agency Education Department called a conference of Jewish students from the best Jewish communities in Argentina, first- or second-generation immigrants, although there are a few third-generation Sephardic

Jews there. Argentina has a wonderful Jewish community with three Yiddish papers, with tremendous Jewish life and a wonderful Jewish school system. On this occasion, we did some research about the situation of Jewish students in Argentina—and they are a tremendous number because the Jews of Argentina have become wealthy and now everybody, every Jew, wants his boy to be a doctor or to study for some kind of degree. Some 15 to 18 percent of these Jewish students were Zionists. Thirty percent were Castroites—followers of Castro of Cuba. They call themselves "Castroites"—this means not yet Communist, but you know Castro. A small percentage were open Communists, and the rest were not interested in anything. They wanted to get a degree, to make a career, and to make a good living. That is all.

I must say that when I read this I could not sleep that night.

That was Argentina, and I am sure that if we were to make the same survey in Brazil, we would get similar results. If you begin to imagine what will happen twenty years from today, when the leadership of today's generation disappears and these students will be the ones who will bear the responsibility for Jewish life, then you begin to shudder.

W.B.: This reference to South America has taken us out of the United States, so to speak, and I would like to continue our discussion with reference to another aspect of Jewish life: the Jews of the Iron Curtain countries. One of Felix Frankfurter's good stories tells about the Jew in one of these Eastern lands who went to the proper authorities to see if he could get a visa to leave the country. They told him that no such visas were being granted; he should return in eight years. He said nothing but began to leave; then, before he walked out, he turned to the attaché and said, "When I come back in eight years, should I come in the morning or the afternoon?"

On this note of faith and hope and belief, can you make some comment about Soviet Russia and its Jews? You have said, for example, that here and there they make a gesture: suddenly they publish a volume of Sholom Aleichem in Yiddish. You said in another statement that it is nonsense to accuse the Soviets of pure anti-Semitism; the Jews there are emancipated, but they have no facility to live as Jews. You said on another occasion, "We will, I am sure, not give up hope that the great Jewish community of the Soviet Union will get at least facilities for Jewish education that other Jewish communities in Communist countries and Eastern Europe possess."

Finally: "This separation of Soviet Jewry . . . of losing three million after the Nazi period is the number one problem of our life." What is being done in this area, and what is the possibility, in your judgment, of subsequent emigration to Israel from Russia? [*Editor's note*: This Dialogue took place well before the liberalization of Russian policy regarding Jewish emigration.]

■ GOLDMANN: The problem is being kept alive by a statesmanlike public relations job, without exaggerating the problems, because this boomerangs. When we deal with Soviet Jews we should not forget that there are three million Jewish hostages in the Soviet Union. It is a very delicate problem. Also, Khrushchev's Russia is no more Stalin's Russia. Khrushchev would not so easily massacre a few million Jews or expel them to Siberia, as Stalin wanted to do before he died; still the same so-called more liberal Khrushchev has shown in Hungary what he can do when he is driven to the wall. So we have to be careful. We are playing here with the fate and the position of three million Jews who cannot do anything by themselves.

On the other hand, we have to keep this situation alive, and I think here we have made certain progress. The first gain is that the Soviet representatives are ready to talk about it. I am in touch with Soviet diplomats now since 1935, when I first met Litvinov and became friendly with him. Since then I have met, more or less, nearly every Soviet ambassador to the more important countries of the world.

For many years they refused to discuss the subject. They asked, "What business is it of yours, why do you mix in? Have you a mandate from the Russian Jews? Why are you coming to us?" Today they do not ask this of us any more. They do it, however, when Israel speaks: Israel cannot open its mouth. If Israel's ambassador were to mention the problem of Russian Jews, they would immediately expel him. Israel is a foreign state and cannot intrude in Soviet affairs. But with people like us who are not foreign diplomats, who speak on behalf of Jewish voluntary organizations, they are ready to discuss Jewish life in Russia. That is some progress.

They have begun to realize that there is a problem. For many years they had denied it, saying that it was nonsense, the Jews did not want to be Jews; they have all the facilities to be Jews if they want to. Today they do not say this, especially when you speak *tête-à-tête*. They try to apologize. They are generally in a defensive position. You have seen their statements: they give statistics and figures that never hit the point.

We do not say that Jews cannot become lawyers in Russia. Certainly there are many more Jewish lawyers or physicians than we might proportionally expect, but we do say that Jews are not allowed to live as Jews, that they cannot have synagogues, schools, teachers, literature, publications. The Russians answer that there are many Jewish lawyers and great Jewish scientists and great Jewish academicians. That is true, but they never react to the real problem; they defend themselves, and this, of course, shows certain progress. What the chances are of forcing Russia to change its attitude is another matter entirely. I would say that there is no hope for Jews in trying to force Russia to change. If America cannot easily force Russia to change its ways, certainly we cannot. But there is a chance in trying to persuade Russia that it is an idiotic policy from their point of view. A few months ago I talked to an important Soviet ambassador and he said to me, "When I listen to you, Doctor, I begin to feel that we act like idiots." I quote him. He is a very outspoken man—quite a new type of Soviet diplomat.

How would it harm the Soviet Union if Jews had three hundred synagogues and not thirty, and had five Yiddish papers as well as one monthly, or could publish Hebrew books? Would the cohesion of the tremendously powerful Soviet Union be in danger? It's nonsense. On the other hand, by pursuing their policies they are antagonizing millions of Jews and millions of non-Jews. There are large Communist groups that are furious. The French Communists have intervened several times and asked, "Why do you do it? It is silly." The Italian Communists are completely against it. Men like Bertrand Russell make statements condemning this policy.

So the only hope is to convince them that from their point of view it is foolish to antagonize the liberal and progressive public opinion that is with us in this problem.

W.B: There remains one additional factor of solution—emigration to Israel. If there are Jews in the Soviet Union who cannot abide living in that kind of society, and who would be happier out of it, why not let them go? Of course, I am well aware of the many reasons why the Russians will not let Jews go to Israel, but would this not in the long run be a better way out for the Russians as well as the Jews?

■ GOLDMANN: As far as emigration is concerned, I am sure it will come one day, because the logical solution for the Soviet Union would be to do what Poland and other Communist countries have done. They have permitted those Jews who cannot be digested, who do not want to integrate and who want to remain Jews, to get out. Thus they have solved the problem. Those who remain, of course, will integrate. I am not hopeful that emigration from the Soviet Union will be permitted soon. One of the main reasons for this policy is Soviet Russia's hostility to Israel. They know that those Jews who are good Jews in Russia are very much attached to Israel, so Israel is for the Soviets an enemy country. They call it the fifty-first state of the United States of America. A Soviet ambassador once told me that there is no difference between Texas, Oklahoma, and Israel.

The Russians know that emigration of Jews to Israel would immeasurably strengthen Israel: this is the best human material that Israel could get. On the other hand, emigration would naturally antagonize the Arabs. So the Soviets play the Arab card against Israel. As long as there is no rapprochement between the Arabs and Israel, and no rapprochement between Russia and Israel, I am not hopeful about emigration from Russia to Israel.

The day will come, I am sure, when the Soviets will open their doors and permit hundreds of thousands of Jews to go to Israel or elsewhere, just to get rid of an element that they cannot assimilate, cannot annihilate, and cannot digest because these Jews want to remain as Jews. It will happen, but it won't be next year, or the year after, or the year after that.

W.B: On the subject of Jewish rights, I have a document in front of me that I would like you to comment on in a general sort of way. The document—written in 1963—was addressed to His Eminence, Augustine Cardinal Bea, the Vatican, Vatican City, and it reads as follows: "As chairman and co-chairman of the World Conference of Jewish Organizations, we have the honor to transmit the accompanying memorandum and respectfully do request that you be good enough to submit it to His Holiness the Pope, and bring it to the notice of such officials and organs of the Church as may seem appropriate to you. Appended to the memorandum is a list of the organizations on whose behalf we have been requested to transmit it to you. We beg Your Eminence to accept the assurances of our high consideration and remain: Dr. Nahum Goldmann, President, World Jewish Congress; Label A. Katz, International President, B'nai B'rith."

This memorandum was presented to the Ecumenical Conference. Can you, in a few words, give us the gist of this document, as well as your own feeling on whether there will be a new cycle in Christian-Jewish relationships?

■ GOLDMANN: The document was intended to urge the Ecumenical Council to make a very clear statement against racism, condemning anti-Semitism and promising to purge the textbooks and the literature of the Catholic Church of all anti-Jewish passages. This would be of tremendous importance, especially in countries of Latin America, where the Catholic Church dominates the field of education and where millions of Catholic children grow up being taught that the Jews are the murderers of Jesus, that they are an accursed people. There is a chance that this will be changed because the new pope is, as you know, liberal-minded. He himself has eliminated two passages in traditional prayers that contain derogatory references to Jews. But this is only a drop in the ocean, because Catholic literature, and especially their textbooks, are full of these references. So we submitted the memorandum, and the pope appointed a special commision to study it. The commission is headed by Cardinal Bea, one of the leaders of the progressive wing. We have hope that a resolution, which has been worked out by a subcommittee of his commission and has been kept secret for the time being, will finally be submitted.

We cannot be sure that this will happen, because the reactionary wing is opposed to it. For them it is dogma that the Jews crucified Christ and are therefore an accursed people. This wing fights all changes in dogmatic teachings, and they are fighting this one, too.

Which group will be the stronger remains to be seen. We will know this only at the end of next year, because the

Council adjourns in the middle of September. In the meantime, we discuss it with the cardinals, in order to gain the support of the cardinals and bishops from all over the world who will finally have to vote on the matter. Despite all of the difficulties, which I do not underestimate, I am hopeful, because the pope is in favor of it. You know that the pope does not have to bring this to the council but can make decrees himself; however, the action will carry weight if the Ecumenical Council adopts the resolution.

I am hopeful that, despite great resistance by the reactionary group, we may finally get a statement that could be of tremendous importance from the point of view of fighting anti-Semitism and also have a great impact on an improvement of Catholic–Jewish relations all over the world.

W.B: Yes, that would certainly open the gates to a new age of understanding, peace, and enlightenment.

We have had our men of letters and our men of action. Dr. Nahum Goldmann is that rare phenomenon, a combination of the two. Both student and doer, Dr. Goldmann is one of the major world figures in Jewish life today, with a remarkable insight into issues vital to contemporary Jewish life. It is good to know that the affairs of the Jewish people throughout the world are in good hands, just because they are in the hands of people like Dr. Nahum Goldmann.

10. ❧ A Great Novelist

Isaac Bashevis Singer

W.B: Our guest is the first Yiddish writer to receive the Nobel Prize in Literature. He has written many novels and short stories, including *The Slave, Short Friday and Other Stories*, and *Enemies: A Love Story*. His latest works include *Shosha, The Manor, The Penitent*, and *The Death of Methuselah*. His books have been translated into English and many other languages, and all have received wide acclaim. He has received the award of the National Academy of Arts and Letters, marking the first time that this honor was accorded an author who does not use English as his original language.

Isaac Bashevis Singer has spoken about his own works and about Yiddish literature to many and varied audiences, and he is rightfully credited with awakening a wide and sympathetic interest in Yiddish literature.

To set the background for our discussion on the Jewish book, I would like to pose these questions: Speaking in broad terms, what do Jewish readers want from books? Do they want images of themselves? Do they desire to take stock, to see where we are now and where we came from? Or are Jewish readers concerned with a quality of reassurance— that is, Jewish books that assert Jewish worth and attest to Jewish survival?

   ■ **SINGER:** I cannot speak in the name of all readers, but since I am a reader myself, I can say what I like in a Jewish book. What I really like to see in a Jewish book is quality. This means that it has to be a good book. If it is a good book and it deals with Jewish people, Jewish heroes, it is enough for me. I do not think that a Jewish book has to take stock, as you said,

189

to offer a summary of the Jewish question and of the Jewish situation, because no book, of fiction especially, can do that. To me a good Jewish book is a wonderful thing, for it is a great achievement for Jewish literature, no matter what the topic. I think that many do not understand this simple thing, that a book has to be good. If it is not good, no matter what its other qualities are, it has no value and it does not deserve to be reckoned with.

w.b: The whole idea of reading, the whole lengendary fascination of the Jew with books, has a certain aura, shall we say, of a kind of holiness. Does this kind of aura still crown the average American Jew?

■ SINGER: I would say that it does to a degree. But this is also true, I think, not only of the Jewish reader but of all readers. We all have an illusion that we will one day find a book that will show the way. This illusion grips every reader, and when we stand in a bookstore and we look over its books, we always have this silent hope that maybe here we will find not just a book but *the* book—the book that will point a way that will show us how to live. And since the Jewish people have more problems than any other people, since they are really *Am ha Sefer*—the People of the Book—I would say that a Jewish man, a Jewish woman, who goes into a bookstore has more of this illusion, has more of this hope than others. But also with this illusion comes disillusion. No matter how many books we read, we always come to the conclusion that this is not "the book," unless we read the *Sefer ha Seforim*, the Tanach. In other words I would say that the desire in us to find the book that shows the way is a little greater than in other readers, but I still believe it exists among all good readers.

w.b: I have an interesting quotation here, and I wonder, based on your own experience, whether you agree with it: "In traditional Jewish culture, it was the man who hovered over books, the sancta of his existence. Today there is a curious transposition. It is women who constitute the study and literary circles. They buy the books. They act as tastemakers, and with missionary zeal they get their husbands to read worthwhile books." In your travels have you found that it is the woman who sets the pace for the man in terms of Jewish reading?

> ■ SINGER: I almost have the feeling that these words were written by me. It is true that most of the people I see in bookstores are women. There is no question about it. As far as fiction is concerned, the woman goes first. She is still more interested in a novel and even in a short story than the man. It is true about Jewish women, and I think about women all over the world, that they are the real customers of the fiction writer. They are the ones who push or pull their husbands to partake of literature.

W.B: If we were to make a study of publishing houses and bookstores, we would probably find that Jewish books are very saleable these days. In addition to your own books, there are the works of Harry Golden, Leon Uris, Saul Bellow, and others. Why are Jewish books so "big" these days when other forms of minority literature—books about Italian Americans or Irish Americans—have disappeared in America?

> ■ SINGER: My impression is that the first generation of Jews who came to this country had the idea that America was a melting pot. The immigrants came here to forget their origins, to forget the Torah, the Talmud, their customs, and to begin a new life about which they knew nothing. I do not know how much this idea of the melting pot disappointed other minorities, but it has certainly disappointed us. We have convinced ourselves that assimilation does not work with the Jewish people. We do become assimilated, but there is always a limit.
>
> Another factor was the tragedy in Europe and the establishment of the State of Israel. All these things awakened in us the desire to continue our Jewishness, so I would say that we are in this respect more an exception than the rule. We have stopped believing in the melting pot. This is the reason that the Jewish book has such power among the Jewish people as well as among others. We may in this respect show a way to other minorities. In other words, what we are beginning now may soon take place among other people.

W.B: To have Jewish books, naturally, we need Jewish writers. Do we have writers dedicated exclusively to Jewish writing?

> ■ SINGER: There are certainly many people who write Jewish history and all kinds of religious books, but I will speak only about fiction because this is the field in which I have experience. There are a number of American writers who call themselves Jewish writers or are called Jewish writers. But I would not call them this. To me a person is not a Jewish writer merely because he is a Jew or because he writes about Jews. He must have a very deep background in Jewish tradition to be a Jewish writer. From my own point of view, this excludes a person who does not know Yiddish, who does not know Hebrew, who does not know our history, who does not know our customs and our laws. I would not call such a person a Jewish writer even if he happens to write about a Jewish storekeeper or a Jewish worker or a Jewish doctor. From this point of view, I would say that there are very few fiction writers in English whom I would call Jewish writers.

W.B: Would I embarrass you if I were to ask you to name names?

> ■ SINGER: I will give you an example. I would not call Henry Roth, the man who wrote *Call It Sleep*, even though this is supposed to be a Jewish novel, a Jewish writer. He just lacks the experience that a Jewish writer should have, the way I see it. To me a Jewish writer is a person like Yosef Agnon, like David Pinsky, a person who has really lived in Jewishness all his life and this is the very air he breathes.

W.B: Now let me read a quotation and an interesting comment that you have made. The quotation first: "It has been said that simple economics makes it almost impossible for one to be devoted exclusively to the field of Jewish writing. It offers pitifully meager rewards. It cannot even begin to compete with non-Jewish fields." Then, in an interview after you had received a very good fee from a magazine, you said: "One should not pay writers so much. I do not believe in it. They get conceited and they think every word holy."

Do you feel that the fact that Jewish writers are not able to make a living is a deterrent, or do you still feel that the Jewish writer should not be paid so much?

■ SINGER: I did not say that Jewish writers should not be paid so much. I said in *Harper's* that we have too many rich writers, and some of them are poor writers. This I said about writers generally. They are rich and poor at the same time. As far as Jewish writers are concerned, either the Yiddish or the Hebrew writers, there is no danger whatsoever that they are going to be overpaid in the next ten or twenty years. So this problem does not exist.

If they are underpaid, this is no deterrent. If a writer has talent he will go on writing. Let us not forget that such great writers as Dostoyevski and many others suffered need. It did not deter them from writing masterpieces. This idea in this country that with the power of money we can create literature, that foundations by raining money on writers can create a great literature, does not hold water.

W.B: I have heard it said by many people that writers are set apart from other people. What is your opinion about this?

■ SINGER: Certainly not. Writers are the same people as all others. And what is true about writers is also true about scientists. The great scientists, the great inventors, the great creators of scientific theory, were not motivated by money. Every creative person has the desire to create. It is within him. He needs to create as he needs food or he needs air to breathe. It is true about every man of spirit. If he has something to say or something to do he will say or do it. Naturally, in science, money is sometimes needed for laboratories and so on. But when it comes to writing, all the writer needs is a piece of bread, a bed on which to sleep, and paper on which to write. I think that a poor writer can do as well as a rich writer, and experience shows us that the poor ones did even better. It may be because they were in the majority. I do not know what the reason is.

W.B: In an interview, you were asked, "Don't you think that writers, of necessity, have to be lonely?" You answered, "I suppose that is true. All artists are basically rebels, not against society, but against God. They have a quarrel with the Almighty, and this is because a real artist is a builder. Destruction and death are something he cannot understand or accept." Would you want to elaborate on this?

■ SINGER: There are people, especially in Jewish life, who would very much like the writer to take part in all activities. I have heard complaints, in Poland and here, that I did not become a member of this party or the other party, that I did not work for the schools, and so on. My feeling is that all these activities, even though they are useful, are not good for the writer. If a writer continually deals with people, with "real life," with the real troubles of life, he may lose the energy that he needs for his work.

But this is not enough. Somewhere, I would say that every writer has a quarrel with the Almighty. The quarrel is the Great Builder's quarrel with the power that builds and destroys at the same time. Because of this, there is something strange about the creative man. He belongs to the world, but also does not belong. I once said that a writer is both a son of humanity and its stepson and, because he is a stepson, I think he has certain privileges, certain rights that the others do not have. I would say that the more we leave the writer in peace, the less we demand that he be active in prosaic kinds of work, the better it will be for the writer and also for society. The writer who has become too active, as a rule, becomes too lazy or too passive when he sits at the table and he has to do his main work. The writer's battlefield is still his desk.

W.B.: It has been said that Jewish writing includes negative and positive writing. Please comment on what you consider negative and positive writing.

■ SINGER: All my life I have heard people speak about positive and negative writing—not only our people but other people as well. For example, when Dostoyevski wrote *The Brothers Karamazov* and *Crime and Punishment*, the critics complained bitterly that he was a negative writer. They asked why he wrote so much about Russian murderers and not about decent people among the Russians. Why did he write two huge novels about murderers? The same thing was true about Guy de Maupassant, who used to write about unfaithful women all the time. He was obsessed with this topic, and the critics complained bitterly. They asked whether there weren't any faithful women in France. I must tell you that in his time there were many faithful women, even in France. The Jewish critics, especially, deal with this theme of positive and negative. Positive writing would be the kind of writing that would make propaganda for Zionism or for socialism or for religion. The question is what one considers positive and what negative.

To me this whole question does not exist. We know now that Dostoyevski did not bring shame on the Russian people—just the opposite. When we want to say something good about the Russians we say that they produced a Dostoyevski. When we want to say something good about the French, we say that they have produced a de Maupassant or a Flaubert. The same thing is true in every literature and should be true also in Jewish literature. In other words, if a writer wants to write about Jewish murderers or Jewish thieves, he can be just as important a writer as if he wrote about Jewish saints. To me the main thing is the quality. Another thing—where shall a Jewish writer find his topics if not in his own people? Let us say he wants to describe a thief. Should he describe a Portuguese thief? If he wants to portray a prostitute, he will describe a Jewish prostitute, and if he wants a saint, he will describe a Jewish saint. To demand of the Jewish writer that all his positive heroes be Jews and all the negative heroes Gentiles would not be just to literature, and not just from an ethical point of view.

w.b.: Here are two statements you have made that seem to contradict each other. First: "I write about Jews. It is not that I think that they are special, but that I know them best." And yet you also say in a very beautiful passage: "I do think that as a philosophy Judaism has unrevealed treasures which no other religion has, and it has never before happened in history that a nation has been exiled for two thousand years, then came back and formed a country. This proves that the Almighty has a purpose for the Jewish people."

■ SINGER: There is no contradiction. It is true that I write about my people because I know them best. If they were an inferior people, I would still write about them, because no writer can write about "other" people. Once in a while, I will travel and I will write a story about other people, but you know that the great writers have always written about their own. At the same time, I may have the idea or perhaps the illusion, call it what you will, that we are an exceptional people. No people have been exiled and stayed in exile for two thousand years and returned to its land, to its language, and to its culture. So the fact that I happen to belong to an exceptional people, and all peoples are exceptional in their own way, is no contradiction to the fact that I write about my own people. These two statements go very well together, I think.

w.b.: Yet you say, "I write about Jews. It is not that I think that they are special . . . " It was this that I felt might have been a contradiction. On the one hand you speak so glowingly, and yet you term the Jewish people "not special."

■ SINGER: I meant the idea of Jews as topics for writing, the idea that writing about Jews will create better literature than writing about other people. In this respect, I think we are not special. A great writer will always write great books, and a bad writer will write bad books, even if his people were ten times as special. So this is the reason there is no contradiction. When I said special, I meant special as far as literature is concerned, and there are no people who are special for literature.

As far as the great destiny of the Jews is concerned, certainly I believe in it. But I do not believe that literature has to lead there. Literature has to reflect this greatness or smallness. It has to reflect what we have accomplished and what we have not. But I do not believe that literature has a mission in the sense that it should show the way as people sometimes hope it will. Maybe nonfiction may do it, but never fiction, because fiction is written after the fact, not before the fact.

w.b.: Now as a religionist and as a rabbi, I want to take up another aspect of Jewishness. In speaking of yourself as a Jewish writer, you point out that you are not a particularly observant Jew. What you feel constitutes a Jew is someone whose Jewishness is his life. This person is to you a *maximum* Jew. You say there are *maximum* and *minimum* Jews. Now I cannot accept this definition because I cannot agree that what constitutes a Jew is merely someone whose Jewishness is his life. This ignores the whole tradition of religion, custom, and ceremony. So, would you more exactly define for us what you consider to be a maximum and a minimum Jew?

■ SINGER: I consider a maximum Jew a person who really lives with Jewishness. It is his whole life. When I think about a maximum Jew, I think about my father because I knew him best. For this man, being a Jew and being a human being were the same thing. When my father wanted to say that a person has to eat, he would say "a Jew has to eat"—not because he thought that the Gentiles should not eat, but because a Jew and a person were for him synonymous. To our parents and grandparents, this was their life. Jewishness was actually the very air they breathed. Because of this, many of the men did not go to business. They let their wives sit in the stores or work for them. They sat all day long studying. Such a man I would call a maximum Jew. But on the other hand, to say that only such a man is a Jew and others are not, would be not just. Because of this, I think there is a minimum and a maximum. A minimum Jew to me is a man who calls himself a Jew, even if he does not observe. There are many grades of Jewishness, and I think that this is the way also that our sages have understood it, because they said, "*Yisrael aff al piy she'chata Yisrael hu*"—a Jew, even if he has sinned, is still a Jew. And even a man who has converted to Christianity is considered a Jew from the point of view of religion. This is the meaning of maximum and minimum Jews.

W.B.: You have said that your brother was your teacher and master. What has been his influence on you and your writing?

■ SINGER: My brother was a number of years older than I, and he began to write in Yiddish and also to paint. I always looked up to him as my teacher when I was a child. When he became a writer, I began to dream about writing myself. Later, when I began to write, he pointed out to me certain rules and certain views that are of value to me today. So when I call him my master and my teacher, I do not do this because of modesty but because I really feel that he has taught me a lot. One of the things that he taught me, and he taught me many, is that a writer must above all state the facts before he indulges in commentary. He was very much against commentary in writing. He always believed that too much commentary can kill literature. In this respect and many others, he was my master and teacher. His books, *The Brothers Ashkenazi* and *Yoshe Kalb* and the others, were always an example for me as far as construction was concerned. I think that in this area he is really without a peer. I could never learn his way of telling a story. I still try hard.

W.B.: In the introduction to a reissue of I. J. Singer's *Yoshe Kalb*, you tell of your brother's desire in the late 1920s not to write in Yiddish—that he no longer thought of himself as a Yiddish writer. And in a review of the book in the *Saturday Review*, the reviewer says: "What I. J. Singer was trying to escape was not the grammar and syntax of Yiddish, but the milieu in which the language was spoken, a culture that he had come to regard as narrow, decadent, stultifying. In his own words, 'humiliating.'" Could you elaborate on what is meant by this?

■ SINGER: I do not agree with this reviewer. He did not understand my brother. It is true that my brother was disappointed for a time in Yiddish literature, but not because he considered it decadent or too petty. His disappointment was with the Yiddishist milieu of his time. It is no secret that, in the 1920s, especially, Yiddish literature (and the Yiddish reader with it) was in danger of almost disappearing into the Communist sphere. There was so much Communism, there was so much belief that the "Red Messiah" was going to come and that Yiddish was going to lead to him, that I would say there was almost nothing else left in literature. This was the time that so many people who went over to Soviet Russia came out and said that Yiddish was for them only a way to achieve the revolution. The revolution had become everything, and Yiddish had become only a means to it. Such writers naturally persecuted men like my brother, and even me, though I was only a beginner. For them we did not lead in the right direction. So my brother became very much disgusted, not actually with Yiddish but with those who misused and misunderstood Yiddish literature. For a moment he had the illusion that if he could run away from the language, he could also run away from the atmosphere that these people had created.

But as I point out in my introduction, no writer can run away from his language, because the language of a writer is his fate. My brother soon convinced himself that this was not possible, and he returned to literature and wrote *Yoshe Kalb*, *The Brothers Ashkenazi*, and *Comrade Nachum*, as well as a number of other books. So the fact is that my brother was disappointed. I understand him very well. I myself was, and still am, disappointed in those writers who think that Yiddish is nothing but a means for Red propaganda.

W.B.: Here is what I think is a very beautiful statement by Maurice Samuel: "I call Yiddish a knowing language because of the special intramural hints, allusions, interjections in which it abounds. It is also that because of intonation and gesticulation." Let me add a classic story to show the power of this kind of intonation. Two Jews meet, and one turns to the other and asks, "How are you?" The other says "Feh!" Number One asks, "And how is business?" The answer: "Be-meh!" Then he asks, "And how are the children?" "Eh!" Finally he asks, "And how are things in general?" "Mmm!" So the one who was asking the questions says, "Well, friend, thanks for filling me in on the details." The Yiddish version of this line is *A mechaye az m'redt zich durch.*

Maurice Samuel wrote that Yiddish was a language with a policy. He said: "Classic Yiddish writing derives its stylistic strength and charm from the deliberate emphasis on Hebrew phraseology. Yiddish had a policy which gave it full character and that was to keep Hebrew alive. Classic Jewish writers—Peretz, Sholom Aleichem, Mendele Mocher S'forim—have loaded their Yiddish so heavily with Hebrew over and above the common usage that it is impossible to read them intelligently without a good knowledge of Hebrew, and the beauty of their style springs strangely enough from the naturalness of this bias." He concludes by saying: "We speak Yiddish not only to convey our transient thoughts, but to keep in touch with the eternal language."

■ **SINGER:** I agree with Maurice Samuel that Hebrew words give Yiddish much of its zest and charm. The Yiddish language could not exist without the 10 or 20 percent of Hebrew words, or even Aramaic words, that it uses. But I would also say that this is true in a great measure about Hebrew. It is true that the Hebrew language, modern Hebrew, does not use Yiddish words, but it uses so many Yiddish idioms, so many Yiddish ways of expression, that I would say they have taken from us as much as we have taken from them—perhaps even more. To me, since these two languages express the same Jewish person, they are not only sisters, they are twin sisters. Both express the Jewish spirit. I personally believe that someone who does not know Hebrew, who does not know the Talmud, does not really know Yiddish. The same is true about Hebrew. A person who does not know Yiddish does not know Hebrew well. To know what a Jew is, to know Jewish literature, one has to know at least these two languages. This is also the reason that I consider those people who write in English and do not know either of these languages not really Jewish writers but English or American writers.

W.B.: Yiddish has been spoken of as a "jargon" without grammar or extensive vocabulary. A lot of people do not agree, and I am sure that you do not.

■ **SINGER:** Many people who call Yiddish a jargon do not know that English and French were also at one time called jargons. All these languages that are today the beauty of Europe were called vulgar languages. English was called a vulgar language. The English scholars some five hundred years ago, seven hundred years ago, wrote in Latin. English was the language of the peasants. This was true of Italian, it was true of French, and it was certainly true of Russian and Polish. As far as Russian was concerned, the Russian aristocrats boasted that their children did not know a word of Russian. They were afraid to teach their children Russian because it was a vulgar language, and they were afraid that it would spoil their French accents.

What happened to those languages also happened to Yiddish. It is only a question of time. Other nations saw their mistake sooner and corrected them. We still have some fanatics and snobs who call our Yiddish language a vulgar language. Yiddish is as far from being vulgar as English and French and German are. There is no such thing as a vulgar language. The language that people call vulgar contains, very often, the very vitality of the human spirit.

W.B: I have found in my own experience that if one speaks before a group and throws in a Yiddish word or two that is not humorous in itself, it evokes laughter on the part of an audience. Is there any reason for this? Have you found this to be the case?

■ SINGER: It is true that if a language is half forgotten and one suddenly throws in a word that reminds the hearer of this language, it somehow evokes humor. I once received a letter from Conrad Richter, an American writer. It seems that he knew Pennsylvania Dutch and he told me that when they translated *Hamlet* into Pennsylvania Dutch, and performed it, the moment the hero said "To be or not to be" in Pennsylvania Dutch, everybody in the audience began to laugh. They were not accustomed to use these words in this connection, although Pennsylvania Dutch is used in the villages for everyday talk. Because we have forgotten Yiddish, many of us laugh when we hear a word, in the theater, for example, that is somehow familiar and at the same time strange. But I do not think this is only a quality of Yiddish. This would happen also to English if English became to some people a half-forgotten language.

W.B: You have been traveling around the country, and I know that you have made a tremendous impact on students at a number of colleges. What is it that you do? Is there a renaissance or a revitalized interest in Yiddish culture, in the Yiddish language?

■ SINGER: I would not say that there is a renaissance in the respect that young people really intend to begin to speak Yiddish. It is too late for that, but at least they have learned that Yiddish is a rich language and that great works were created in this language. They are as eager to know it as our parents and grandparents were eager to know what was created in Hebrew. Hebrew was in my time a dead language, a language of the book, and Yiddish was a living language. I am afraid that now the roles are being reversed. Hebrew is now more and more a living language and Yiddish may become for a time the language of the book. People will have to study Yiddish because nobody will be able to understand the last 500 or 600 years of Jewish history and Jewish creativity without Yiddish. In a way it is happening right now. Some people learn Yiddish not for the sake of speaking the language, but to understand what is going on in Jewish life and what went on for hundreds of years. In this respect, there is a great revival and a great renaissance. I was told at the Hebrew Union College that they are going to get a professor to teach Yiddish there. I gave a lecture at that college which I called, "The Autobiography of Yiddish," and the hall was filled not only with students but also with members of the faculty.

There is a different attitude toward Yiddish because we finally understand that the melting pot idea does not work and that we are too rich to lose ourselves. As far as culture is concerned, we are millionaires.

W.B: For a long time in the establishment of the State of Israel there was a struggle about which language was to be the language of the state. It was so intense that the Hebrew zealots said: "There will never be a Yiddish word spoken in *Medinat Yisrael* until such time as Hebrew is assured as the prime language." Here is what you have said: "I am a Yiddish writer. That is one reason that I could not live in Israel. They have a wonderful thing, a miracle, and I think it is wonderful that we have our own country again, but I could not live there because it is too small and because they are against Yiddish." Would you like to comment on the change of policy toward Yiddish in Israel? I know there are many Yiddish theatrical groups and several Yiddish dailies have already appeared.

■ SINGER: It is true that in the beginning those who built Israel felt that Yiddish might be a very dangerous competitor to Hebrew. They were really afraid that Yiddish would remain the language of Israel. Since they had returned to the land of their fathers, they also wanted to return to the language of old, of Abraham and Jacob and David. But I think the fear of this competition has now ceased in Israel. They already have a generation that speaks Hebrew, and there is no danger that Yiddish will become the first language in Israel. But many Israelis are now also convinced that Yiddish must become the second language in Israel, because if it does not, Hebrew itself will not be so vital a tongue. In other words, they are coming to the same conclusion that many writers have come to, that Yiddish and Hebrew are two sides of the same coin, and that the knowledge of one must go with the knowledge of the other. Because of this, I think that the whole situation has changed.

However, for me to go to Israel and to live under the shadow of Hebrew would not be a very pleasant thing. Still, I never know. Things may change for the better.

W.B: I would like to turn to the problem of translation. In Maurice Samuel's book *The Prince of the Ghetto*, there is a chapter called "Translators Are Traitors." A few sentences from this chapter may set the background for our discussion: "It is impossible to penetrate the Yiddish word by mere translation. There must be on the part of the reader a willingness to devote some attention to the peculiar revealing character of Yiddish, to whatever extent this character can be conveyed in English. Every language has its genius which is nontransferable and on one level. Yiddish differs from English and French and Italian, just as these differ from one another." Then he cites illustrations: If you were to say in German *"die Schnur des Rabbiners,"* it does not mean the same as the Yiddish *"dem rebbens schnur."* Another example is the use of the word *staitch*, which can best be described, if described at all, as "an expletive of expostulation." Or he speaks of personal names that have a fascinating spiritual mold. A name such as *Shprintze* or *Yente* or possibly the extreme example of a name found in Yiddish, *Feivish*, when one couples it with *Yukel*, to make *Feivish Yukel*, it is perhaps the most comical-trivial man's name in the Yiddish-speaking world. Samuel points out: "When Jews speak of the impossibility of translating Yiddish into English, they have in mind just those differences of spirit and idiom which are the ordinary barriers between all languages. They will ask, for instance, how on earth can you say in English *hayre uff tzu hacken a tchainik?*—literally, "to chop, or wallop, a teakettle." To make it harder they will say, *Er hot gehackt a tchainik off vos die velt shteit*—"He walloped the teakettle on which the world stands." Other phrases are difficult in translation, and I think these are very interesting. For example, a certain type of Jew is described as a *shadchan*, a *badchan*, a *ganei*, a *lamden*, a *Yid*. Go translate these, or, *Gott die neshomoh shuldig.*

You have said that you always write so that you do not lose too much in translation. You write in Yiddish but you go over the translations and sometimes, as in *The Slave*, you help to translate. Would you share with us your thinking on the subject of translation?

■ SINGER: I do not agree with Maurice Samuel that Yiddish is an exceptional language in the respect that it almost cannot be translated. I would say that each language has idioms that cannot be translated, phrases for which one cannot find an equivalent. If you do not find the best one, you find the next best, because sometimes there is no best. It is true that *Hack mir nit kein tchainik* cannot be actually translated into English, but there are a million English expressions which cannot be translated into Yiddish.

As far as losing is concerned, all writers lose when they are translated. The greatest losers are humorists and poets. Poetry almost cannot be translated. As far as humor is concerned, we know that a joke in one language sometimes sounds very serious or very silly in another language. I think this is the reason why it is so difficult to translate Sholom Aleichem. He is a man of humor, and humor cannot be translated. Writers who are full of folk expressions are also very difficult to translate. For example, consider Nikolai Gogol. It is almost impossible to translate him. I would say that he loses about 50 percent of his value in translation. However, he is so rich that no matter how much he loses, he still stays rich.

I take part in the translations myself, and because of this I see the difficulties of the translators and how much they suffer until they translate something right. I must say that I have a lot of compassion for translators, but I also have to watch them very carefully.

Even good translators sometimes make bad mistakes. Some time ago I wrote in one of my stories that my father in the time of the war was poor and went to the rabbi to ask him for a loan. The rabbi did not have any money, but the rabbi's wife gave him her ring. I said that my father put this ring into a *schketele*, which actually means a jewelry box. The translator read it not as *schketele* but *schteckele*, which means "stick," and he translated it: "And my father came home with the ring and put it on a stick."

W.B: Notwithstanding the difficulties of translation, your message to Jews today, about their Yiddish heritage, comes across clear and strong. We have long been known as the "People of the Book," for we are a people whose life and destiny is molded not only by the Bible, the Book of the Ages, but by the numerous volumes that have flowed from the Bible. Throughout history, the Jewish writer has contributed to the literature of the world, in many languages as well as in Hebrew and in Yiddish. However, just as the Hebrew language is saturated with Jewish values and has bound together many generations and many countries, so too is Yiddish and Yiddish writing a repository of the Jewish ethos, the Jewish wisdom, the Jewish pattern of life. We owe a debt of gratitude to Isaac Bashevis Singer for revealing to us our cultural roots and enriching our lives and those of many to come.

11. &? The Glorious Jewish Past

Max I. Dimont

W.B.: In any field, distinction comes to very few. It is a rare gift, one that requires total service and dedication. This is especially true of the historian, for the study of the human journey upon earth is an unremitting struggle to extract the fullness of human experience from the voluminous records that have been left behind. To gain distinction as a historian one must have a deep and sympathetic understanding of humankind. Thus the writer must be a full human being, for his greatness as a historian and his greatness as a human cannot be separated. This happy and noble combination is found in our very distinguished guest, Mr. Max I. Dimont.

I am sure that many of you are familiar with his book, *Jews, God and History*, a modern interpretation of a 4,000-year-old story. But what about the man behind the pen—the human being. Let us begin our Dialogue with something about you and your background.

■ DIMONT: There is not much to tell. My parents were born in Russia and they settled in Helsinki, Finland, where I was born. We were one of 1,200 Jewish families in Helsinki. In 1929 we arrived in the United States along with the stock market crash, though we had nothing to do with it. During World War II, I served in the Army Intelligence Service with the 18th Airborne Corps and the 82nd Airborne Division and saw service in England, France, and Germany, all the way to the Russian border.

W.B.: You have selected as your contribution to the world of scholarship the field of Jewish history. Would you comment on your interest in history in general and, more particularly, the development of your interest in Jewish history?

■ DIMONT: Ever since I was a little boy I have been reading history—mostly Finnish and Swedish history. When I got to the United States, I found out that Sweden and Finland were not the centers of world history, and I was quite disappointed. Until then I thought that the Finns had the most important history in the world. But since then I have continued reading the history of every civilization, every people. I have found it most fascinating, and, of course, Jewish history was always a main interest. I always try to correlate Jewish history into the history of other peoples and other civilizations.

W.B.: I am sure that in your study of Jewish history, you read certain classic authorities in the field. When you read Jewish history, did you find something that presented a special problem to you? More specifically, did you in your own teaching or lecturing experience find an event that directed your attention and your thinking toward the kind of book that you wrote?

■ DIMONT: As a matter of fact, yes. The idea for this book grew ten years ago out of a very curious incident. Hadassah in St. Louis had asked me to give a series of six lectures on a new Jewish history book that had appeared then, *The Great Ages and Ideas of Jewish History.* Twenty hardy Hadassah ladies showed up at my first lecture, and I lunged into what I call the "Oy, Oy, Oy" history of the Jews, modeled after the "Oy, Oy, Oy" school of Jewish historians. By this I mean those historians who present Jewish history as nothing but a 4,000-year tragedy, a travail, a sorrowful burden. I was so accustomed to reading this kind of history that I unconsciously presented the same thing. In five minutes my audience of twenty ladies was asleep, and my ego could not take it. So I threw away my prepared script and launched into a different kind of Jewish history, an off-the-cuff kind of psychoanalytic, psychological, sociological, economic interpretation of Jewish events. That woke them and, after the lecture, they kept asking questions for an hour.

They asked *why*? Why did it happen that way? Why did the Jews survive? Why is Jewish history different? Why did Jewish culture last longer than anyone else's? I did not know the answers, but I promised to have the answers for the next lecture. For the subsequent lectures we had a full house. Over a hundred ladies showed up, and the questions they asked kept me on my toes.

I kept a list of these questions, and I thought that it would be a good idea to write a book that would present these questions and their answers. That was the genesis, the idea for this book. I did not know, of course, that it would take me seven years to do it.

W.B.: Almost everyone is familiar with Graetz's classic treatment of Jewish history. What would you say about his approach?

■ DIMONT: Not to single out Heinrich Graetz, Jewish historians as a rule treat Jewish history as a linear history—as one line from Abraham to Golda Meir, a 4,000-year straight line. They do not take into consideration the fact that Jewish history is not linear. Jewish history is really a series of six histories, because it developed within six alien civilizations. Then, too, they do not explain Jewish history in terms of the interaction between Jewish civilization on the one hand and the alien civilizations within which it enfolded itself.

For instance, the reader who reads the ordinary Jewish history learns about Jews in Babylon. Before he knows it, the Jews are having business dealings with the Persians. Now, where did the Persians come from? What happened to the Babylonians? The next thing the reader knows, the Jews have the Greeks to contend with. What happened to the Persians? How did the Greeks get into the act? What was the interaction between the Greeks and the Jews? Then suddenly, the Greeks have vanished, and now we are in the Roman Empire. Then the Roman Empire disappears without our knowing why, and suddenly we have the Golden Age in Spain. Where did the Golden Age in Spain come from? How were the Jews catapulted from the Near East into Spain? What historic and social forces catapulted them from one civilization into another? What economic circumstances gave them the wherewithal to make such a shift? What was the psychology that permitted the Jews to make this kind of adjustment— from a Babylonian society to a Persian society to win a contest with the Greeks, to survive the Roman Empire and to become businessmen and statesmen in the Islamic era?

This is what I mean by writing Jewish history in a vacuum instead of explaining Jewish history as a living, dynamic force.

w.b.: How was the book actually put together?

■ DIMONT: The first thing I did was to tell my wife, "Look, from now on you won't see me very often. I'm going to start writing a Jewish history book." Then I decided to write the framework for the book—what I wanted to say, what questions I was seeking. I began to write a chapter outline first, and then a skeleton outline for each chapter, and then whenever I did not know the answers I just left big question marks. I kept on writing, even if it was wrong. I said, "I'll come back and clean it up afterwards." It took a year and a half to get the framework for the book so that it would stand. Then I began a five-year hunt for facts.

w.b.: Many students and people who have had experience in writing may wonder why you did the outline first. Why didn't you sit down and read up on the various facets of our history and then develop your outline?

■ DIMONT: If there is one people who has written more than anybody else about itself it is the Jews. I was afraid that if I did a lot of research, the material would overwhelm me, and I would come out with another Graetz opus, which I did not want. So, in order to prevent my material from directing me instead of me directing my material, I decided that the best thing to do was to have an outline first. It is a very painful thing when you have a beautiful theory and you search for facts to support it and do not find them. You have to abandon a beautiful theory that doesn't work, and that is a very, very painful thing. I hope that I succeeded in eliminating theories that were not supported by facts.

After the outline came five years of research into all kinds of books, not just Jewish history books, but books on economics, sociology, geography, and many other subjects. I tried to explain the Jewish experience from different facets of history—not just a succession of kings, wars, monuments, but Jewish history as a clash of ideas. Then came the marriage between the structure and the material, and that was a two-year struggle. Finally, after this seven-year labor, this book came out. Even that was not the end. After that came another year of fighting with scholars. The publishers sent it to four different scholars of different sects and denominations to punch holes in the manuscript. Every three months I got the manuscript back with all kinds of comments, all kinds of protests from scholars that "this isn't so—where did you get that!" And then I had to justify my work. After a year of these bloody battles, the book stood on its own and went to press.

W.B.: When you are dealing with as vast a field as Jewish history, you have to do research in many languages, not only Hebrew, but Aramaic, Yiddish, German, Polish, and Russian. Now, how does one as a historian handle all this? Must one be versed in every language? Must one be fully versed in primary sources, or can one use secondary sources in doing research?

■ **DIMONT:** This may be rationalization, since I do not speak Polish or Russian, or Aramaic, or Spanish, or Portuguese. I, of course, maintain that it is not necessary always to draw on primary sources. Fortunately, others have done the digging for you.

Consider this: In Jewish history you are dealing with 4,000 years of history that developed in a dozen different nations, with a dozen different languages. The Jews have left the record of their history in these languages. To acquire all the languages and to read all these primary sources would take a thousand years. We have scholars who have devoted their lives to one segment of Jewish history, to the study of the primary sources. In thirty years of reading, I have read most of these scholars' books, these people who have devoted their lives to giving the reader one facet, one aspect of Jewish history. I synthesized them. Whenever I feel, however, that something is wrong, I want to see what the original sources say.

For instance, were the laws of the Roman Emperor Constantinus anti-Semitic, or did they merely have restrictive clauses about the Jews? I did not believe that anti-Semitism existed in Roman days, and I wanted to know exactly what the laws of Constantinus said. The Harvard Library has the original, and there are translations. It is like being a good lawyer; one has to know where to look for material and then read it in translation. Then you read the original documents to see if your theories are substantiated. In the case of the laws of Constantinus, I discovered that most scholars had taken one paragraph out of a fifteen-paragraph edict that dealt with Jews. The laws of Constantinus, for instance, were not directed against Jews only—they were directed against any people who did not belong to the Christian religion. The same restrictive clauses were directed against pagans, fire-eaters, Zoroastrians, and a few other groups.

W.B.: From my own experience, when I conclude my sermon on *Shabbos* I begin thinking about what I am going to preach on the following *Shabbos,* and one of the great problems is the question of the title. It reminds me of a young rabbi who came to a congregation for a trial weekend. Not having had any experience and not really knowing what he was going to preach about, the only thing he could think of was the title "What Now?" He delivered a very eloquent sermon, and they were so impressed that they invited him back for another weekend. On Thursday they called him and asked for his sermon title. He thought for a few moments and said, "Well, the only thing I can come up with is, 'After Now, What?'"

Jews, God and History is a particularly good and appropriate title for your book. Can you tell us something about the title's genesis and development?

■ **DIMONT:** This is a very painful subject because originally the title was *Jews, Jehovah and History.* I used *Jews* and *Jehovah* for alliteration. A very prominent scholar read the book in its manuscript form and liked it very much, but he said that he would never buy the book with that title because I was forcing him to use the name of God against his will. He said, "Why don't you change it so that the title won't be objectionable to many Jews?" I thought that he had a very proper complaint, so I came up with *Jews, God and History*. Here I had two monosyllables and then *History*, and it sounded equally good. But a more important reason for choosing this title was this: in essence, Jewish history is a dialogue between Jews and God, with the entire world as a very interested eavesdropper. This dialogue, which began four thousand years ago between Abraham and God, has been a continuing one and, as you know, the world has practically taken it as its own today. I titled the book *Jews, God and History* as an indication that these are the elements that have created Jewish history, this continuing dialogue.

W.B: This view of Jewish history, as a continuing dialogue between Jew and God, between humans and God, leads to a very fundamental question. What are the unique distinctions that single out Jewish history from the histories of other peoples?

■ DIMONT: There are four unique differences. There have been twenty to thirty civilizations, depending on how you classify a civilization, in the history of man. None of them has lasted for longer than 500 to 1,000 years, yet we find that Jewish history is a continual cultural development for four thousand years.

No people, no nation that has been exiled, that has lost its country, has ever been able to continue for long as a recognizable ethnic entity. The only exception to this is the Jewish people, who have been for 2,000 years without a country of their own, yet have lived as a recognizable ethnic entity.

No people in exile, no people that has been disfranchised from its country, has been able to produce a culture. They have truly become what Toynbee calls "fossils of history," and have stagnated into a meaningless existence. Again, we find that the only exception are the Jews. As I indicated earlier, we have had a history that has developed in six alien civilizations—that is, in six civilizations of other peoples, and yet within these six civilizations we have been able to establish a culture of our own.

Whereas every people, every civilization, every culture has left a record of its experience, of its history in one language only, the Jews have left a record of their history in practically all the civilized languages of the world. They gained very great fluency in these tongues so that they have been able to express themselves in many foreign languages.

W.B: We have thus established the premise that Jewish history is unique, and this leads us to the history itself. Can you first give a brief summation of the main events contributing to Jewish history in the ebb and flow of world events?

■ DIMONT: Let me begin by asking that you step out of the usual chronological framework of history and look at human history from a vantage point out in the universe. You will see history unfolding itself as a series of tidal waves of civilizations. You will see first the Sumerian–Akkadian civilizations and the Egyptian culture, sweeping to the shores of the planet Earth. Then you will see these civilizations inundated by the Assyrian and the Babylonian civilizations. Then the Persian civilization floods in where the Babylonians and the Assyrians once were. You will see the Greek civilization take over the Persian, and the Romans step in. Then you have the Islamic civilization, the Byzantine, the early feudal, and then, finally, the modern age wading in on the stilts of industrialism and capitalism.

Then you ask yourself, "Well, where are the Jews? Here are all these civilizations, and there is no mention of the Jews. Where are they?" If you look more closely, you will see the Jews in a very, very peculiar position. They are riding surfboards, so to speak, on the crests of these civilizations. You will see the Jews riding in on history, on the crests of the Assyrian and Babylonian civilizations. Yet you will also note that each time, as these civilizations mature and die, as they fall into a sea of oblivion, the Jews who are within these civilizations also fall into a sea of oblivion. But whereas the other civilizations remain submerged, Jewish history reappears again on the crest of a subsequent new civilization. So we see this fantastic aspect of Jewish history—the ability to survive where all these other mighty empires and civilizations died.

W.B: Your thesis is that Jewish history is a succession of ideas rather than of events, names, and dates. Please elaborate on this view.

■ DIMONT: Let me first outline the events themselves. It is a most incredible succession of events even when we comprehend the ideas behind them. Let us stay for another moment out in the universe and let us focus the lens of history on the Jews themselves. We see an incredible succession of events take place. We see Jewish history begin with one man, Abraham, who introduces a new commodity into the world: faith. From this we begin to see the wandering in Canaan, enslavement in Egypt, and then Moses leading the Jews out of Egypt, giving them the Torah. We see Joshua taking them into Canaan, and the establishment of the Jewish state. We see destruction by Assyria, captivity by the Babylonians, a return under Cyrus back to Palestine. We see the establishment of the Maccabean kingdom. We see a clash with the Greeks, oppression by the Romans. We see the Jews emerge as scholars, poets, and philosophers in the Mohammedan age in the Islamic empire. We see them as a business class in the early feudal age, as children of the ghetto in the late feudal age. We see them as avant-garde intellectuals, as generals, as prime ministers, as cosmopolitan capitalists, and as concentration camp victims in the modern age. Then they return after a 2,000-year absence to where they started from, to Israel.

This is an incredible succession of events, and the question we must ask ourselves is whether it has any meaning. Is it just a mishmash of things, did it just happen haphazardly, accidentally, or is there a meaning to it? And if there is a meaning, what is it? Is it what philosophers call theological meaning? That is, is it purposive? If it is purposive, who drew the blueprint—God or man? Or is it nonpurposive, just one event following another?

Therefore, what we want to see is whether there were ideas motivating these events, or whether these events just accidentally, haphazardly followed each other.

For instance, take Abraham's concept of monotheism. We are not concerned now whether it was Abraham who thought of it himself and retroactively attributed it to God, or whether it was God who gave the idea to Abraham. This is for theologians to debate, not for historians. The point is that once the concept of monotheism was introduced, it did away completely with the pagan concept of the world and it did away with paganism. The idea of a sexless Jewish God did away with the sexual rivalry among the Gods so prevalent in Greek and Roman mythology. Because there was only one God, it did away with warfare among Gods. Because God was invisible, it meant that God had to be worshiped in an entirely different way; instead of worshiping God with one's hands and trying to fashion idols, one tried to comprehend God with the intellect, thus developing human intellectual instincts.

The Torah was a very pragmatic document. In the history of other people, the state usually appears first, and then out of the state develops the law. Not so with the Jews. First the Jews got the law, and then they had to fit the state within the framework of the law. In the Mosaic code, there is the beginning of democracy, the separation of church and state. The Torah sets down the basic relations between humans and God and between citizens and state. The concept of the Jewish king, when the Jewish kingdom arose, did away with the divine right of kings. The king had no special exemptions; he had no special rights.

With the prophets we find the beginning of the universalization of God—that God was not a fragmentary thing, the possession of only one people or only one nation. God was universal in scope, and He was God of all people on earth. Here we begin to find the concept of human brotherhood.

As you look about you now, these are the concepts that rule the civilized world. This is what I mean when I say that ideas motivated Jewish history. When the Jews survived, it was not merely to survive as Jews, but to bring about a vision, an idea.

W.B: I think that this is a very fresh and enlightening approach to Jewish history, because it enables the student and the reader to comprehend ideas and concepts rather than merely amassing facts. If history is taught from this particular standpoint, it will become very much more meaningful to the student.

Let us imagine that this room comprises all of Jewish history; in this room are packed 4,000 years of Jewish achievement and Jewish homelessness. We can look into this room through various windows, each one giving a different view. In your book one sees Jewish history through these different windows. They may not completely explain Jewish history, but they help.

■ DIMONT: It is not just Jewish history that must be viewed through these different windows; it is all history. Some historians, like the Marxists, try to explain history by giving it an economic interpretation. They view history as economically determined. Then there is the psychological window to history. The personality cult views history as a result of the impact of certain personalities. There are the sociologists, like Max Weber, who think that the way we organize our society, the interaction between peoples, determines our history. Of course, we have the political historian, who says that wars, battles, monuments, and kings make our history.

Now, it is true that all these factors did determine history, but not exclusively. It is the interaction of all these things that shapes history, and each one of these will explain a certain aspect of Jewish history or of any history. We can view what happened to the Jews in the Hellenic times through economic eyes, because when the cultured Greeks took over Palestine, they brought a new economic system, they brought a new social class, they brought a new philosophy, and this had a tremendous impact on the Jews that changed their ways, which in turn changed the Talmud, which in turn changed its contents, and changed the Jews.

The Jew who lived in the Islamic empire was as different from the Jew who lived in Hellenic times, as we are from the Jews who lived in the ghetto two hundred years ago. We are the product of the American economy, of American society, of American democracy. We have developed because of it. Yet we ourselves have brought certain things to this American democracy and to this American economy that made us both American and Jewish in a unique sort of way. We have contributed to America and America has contributed to us. This is what I mean by the interaction.

Nevertheless, this interaction itself does not explain the totality of Jewish history, because Jewish history is not the sum of its individual parts. It is that plus something else, plus some vision, plus some will, plus some accomplishment. The

Jews coalesce into an entity that defies analysis by taking it apart and simply saying this is economic, this is political, this is social.

w.b: Earlier you posited the thesis that there are four distinct, unique aspects of Jewish history. You have just said that there is something else unique that made Jews survive. You discuss this in your book along with Spengler's view, Toynbee's view, and the Jew's defiance of all views of the past.

■ DIMONT: I am glad that you have introduced Spengler, because I am a Spenglerian, and let me explain what I mean by that. I left a facet out, and that is the philosophical or the metahistorical concept of history. The metahistorian tries to look at history as a living thing, not a succession of events, but as a cycle of events, a cycle of ideas. He tries to find out if it has some meaning. The greatest metahistorian, in my opinion, is the German philosopher-historian Oswald Spengler. In 1918 he wrote a fascinating book called *The Decline of the West*, giving an entirely new approach, a new concept of history. He views history as a succession of civilizations. To him, a civilization is not an accident; a civilization is a totality. He considers a civilization in the way he considers the life of an individual. It has a birth, it has a period of adolescence, it has a period of maturity, and then an old age, and finally, death. Spengler's view is that all history is predetermined to die, and civilizations die just as human beings die.

He calls these four phases *spring*—that is, the birth of a civilization; *summer*—the adolescence of a civilization; *autumn*— the maturity, the full growth of a civilization; and the last phase, old age, he calls *winter*. He shows how each of the civilizations went through these stages. However, he does not know what to do with the Jews. They will not fit into his neat categories. Every other history fits except that of the Jews.

Toynbee has a different concept of history. He views history as not exactly linear, as not exactly cyclic, but as an evolution from a lower to a higher form. So, in a sense, a civilization can, by implication, endure forever if it responds successfully to certain challenges. Yet Toynbee also excludes

Jewish history from his system. Therefore, the primary question we must ask is, Why have the Jews not continued on to their decline? Why have they not gone on from their birth, through their spring phase, to their summer phase, to their autumn phase, and, finally, to the winter phase? Why do they not die like all other civilizations?

Here we have to introduce a new concept, to make a distinction between a culture and a civilization, and here I draw upon another historian, a Frenchman, Amaury de Riencourt. He defines culture this way: Culture is really the first of these stages of Spengler's system—spring, summer, and autumn. Culture is the stage that generates new ideas, that gives birth to a new religion, that gives birth to new vitality, new thinking, new sciences, new psychology, new art forms. When culture has been developed to its maturity, what happens—to use Toynbee's terminology—is that the people tend to "rest on their oars." They become satisfied with their institutions. Then civilization sets in. The culture that has been productive is sponged off by the civilization that is uncreative and that can last only so long before it dies out.

But what happened to the Jews? The Jews progressed from their spring to their summer and autumn phase. Then, just at the point when they reached the height of their culture, the autumn phase, came the wars with the Romans, and the Jews were driven out into the Diaspora. Spengler very perceptively sees this, and he asserts that this war with the Romans freed the Jews from history. But he did not understand the function of the Diaspora.

In the first 2,000 years of Jewish history, fittingly or unfittingly, by accident or by design, the will to survive as Jews had been hammered into them. It had been hammered into them by Moses; it had been hammered into them by a succession of prophets. They had a mission to perform, and this mission was constantly hammered into them. Then they were catapulted into the Diaspora, and this freed them from decay. Having this will to survive as Jews, and having the accidental factor of a Diaspora, which prevented them from declining, which prevented their maturing into the winter phase and the final death phase, they now had a succession of what I call "Diaspora designers"—people who said, "Here we are; if we want to survive, let us ask ourselves what are the challenges, and then let us respond to those challenges."

You have, then, in this metahistorical way of looking at history, an explanation of why the Jews are here, although archeologists, by this time, should be rediscovering us and holding us up as exhibits in the Smithsonian Institution.

W.B: Can this material that we are talking about—this 4,000 years of Jewish history—be arranged in some kind of order? Is there something in Jewish history that reveals a purpose or meaning? You have said that you view Jewish history as a Cabalistic drama in three acts. What do you mean by this?

■ DIMONT: The Cabalists were early Jewish mysticists, a very fascinating breed of Jew who began to speculate about mind and matter and who began to look at history as a succession of ideas. As far back as the third century C.E., the Jews began to speculate on history, while others, to use the phrase of the Irish historian William Edward Lecky, "were groveling in the darkness of besotted ignorance." I believe, as a Hebrew scholar has pointed out, that all Christian history rests on ideas that the Jews devised back in the early Middle Ages. Jews began to speculate on the nature of history in the third century and came up with some fantastic conclusions. They viewed history as the result of social and economic factors. They speculated about the causes of the downfall of civilizations and wondered why the Jews reappeared over and over again. They began to think that the Jews were exempt from the natural laws of historical decay that applied to everybody else. In about the sixteenth century a Jewish mystic philosopher, Isaac Luria, had a fantastic concept of the evolution of mind and matter. He thought of the evolution of mind and matter as having three stages. The first stage he called the *tzimtzum*, the *contraction*, or in modern terminology, the *thesis*. This thesis he saw as the bringing together of all the distant elements, taking people here, people there, uniting them into a nation, uniting them into a civilization. The second stage he called the *shevirat ha-keilim*, "the breaking of the vessels," or in modern terminology, the *antithesis*. In this stage he conceived of all mind, all matter, being torn asunder—everything that he had brought together in the first stage was torn asunder and thrown into the world, into an exile, so to say. The third stage he called the *tikkun*, or the *restoration*, in which everything would be brought together again into a new totality, a new meaning.

W.B.: Let us consider these three ideas—the *tzimtzum*, the *shevirat hakeilim*, and the *tikkun*—and interpret Jewish history in these terms.

■ DIMONT: Let us view, then, Jewish history in three Cabalistic acts, each act 2,000 years long. In the first act, the *tzimtzum* or the *contraction*, we see Jewish history begin with Abraham and end with the destruction of the Temple. Here you see Jewish history as a succession of six scenes, much like a Greek predestination drama, with God as the "author" of the script. We see Him hand the script to Abraham to proclaim the monotheistic God. Then we see the script handed to Moses to proclaim the Torah, proclaim the Law within which the Jews are to operate. Then we see the script being handed to Joshua, to lead the Jews to the Promised Land. Then comes a succession of prophets who predict exile for the Jews. And even as they predict it, they predict a return from that exile. The prophets now universalize the Jewish God, and the script is handed to Ezra and Nehemiah, who caution the Jews against being swallowed up in this universality, for they still have a mission to perform. Finally, we see a new sect appear, the Christians. Jesus is proclaimed the Messiah and in essence the Jews are told that they have fulfilled their mission and Christianity has come to take over.

It seems almost as if the prediction of the prophets is right. The Romans destroyed the Temple, the Jews were dispersed into the Diaspora, and the curtain comes down on the first act. Here, then, we see the *thesis*—the unifying of one idea into a nationhood with a universal message to proclaim. Catastrophe follows: the Jewish state is destroyed, the Jews are dispersed, the Temple is destroyed, and this act ends. We have now come to "the breaking of the vessels."

W.B.:   What is the second act?

■ DIMONT: The second act would include, of course, our history from the destruction of the Temple to the restoration of the State of Israel. If the first act proceeded like a Greek predestination drama, the second act proceeds like a French existentialist drama. Jean-Paul Sartre, the French existentialist, says that the history of each human being is the sum total of his choices. Each time you or I make a choice, we limit the field of possible future choices we can make, because by choosing the things we are choosing, we are telling ourselves what we are, what we want to do, and what we want to become, until, finally, we checkmate ourselves into a position where we no longer have these choices. We must then act out the destiny we have already chosen for ourselves by the choices we have made.

The Jews at the beginning of the second act had an existentialist choice to make. They could have denied the past; they could have claimed that all that happened in the past was just coincidence, an accidental series of events that meant nothing. They could have said that the Jews were not different from the Assyrians, the Babylonians, the Persians, or the Greeks; it was their time to disappear. On the other hand, the Jews could have said, "No. It cannot be that way. We were given the Torah; if we have a mission to fulfill, then we must continue." At this point God cannot add to the script any more because the Jews themselves have canonized the Old Testament; nothing else can be added, so the Jews must write the script themselves. This is a complete reversal in Jewish history. Before it had been God who had directed Jewish destiny; it is now the Jews who are deciding their own destiny. In the yeshivahs, throughout the Talmud, they hammer out a succession of laws. The Talmud in the early days was a very liberal document that changed and conformed and tried to adapt itself to changing socioeconomic conditions of new civilizations. We find again this incredible succession of Jewish history as it continues through the Islamic period, through the feudal age, into the modern age. Through this hammering out of new concepts, new laws, new ideas in each age, we have codification. We have the ideas of Maimonides, of Josef

Karo, of Rashi—all reinterpreting Judaism in the image of the times within which the Jews then lived, all making it fresh. So we come to the twentieth century and the reestablishment of Israel.

This brings us to the end of the second act, in which all these exiles come together again in the freely constituted State of Israel. And now we have two Judaisms as we had at the end of the first act, Judaism in the Diaspora and Judaism in Palestine. Now we are repeating ourselves; we have brought the theses together now toward the beginning of the third act, toward the *tikkun*, toward the restoration. Again we face the same dilemma. We have a Judaism anchored in Israel and a Judaism anchored in the Diaspora, and the curtain comes down on the second act. We are awaiting the third act. We have this question to answer: What is the function of the Judaism in Israel and what is the function of the Judaism in the Diaspora? *Does* each have a function to perform, and if so, what?

W.B.: You have just returned from Israel. What would you say are the two or three fundamental needs facing Israel at the present time?

■ **DIMONT:** The only reason I dare give such a report is that I became an "expert" in two weeks; as such I dare tread where experts would shy away. What Israel seems to need are two things: industry and religion.

Industry is needed because people are constantly pouring into Israel even now. They are coming in from many, many parts of the world, and they need industry to sustain their economy. Religion is needed because I find an Orthodoxy that is a fossil of the past, a strict Orthodoxy that is out of date because the ghetto is out of date. The modern Israeli Jew cannot accept that Orthodoxy any more than we here can accept the Orthodoxy of our grandparents of the *shtetl*, because we do not live in the *shtetl*. Israel is seeking for a meaning outside of nationalism.

They are very intensely nationalistic, intensely proud of what they have accomplished, and very rightly so; but behind the braggadocio, behind this pride, is a search for identity. They feel that they must have a *raison d'être*—a meaning for existence—a meaning for continuing as Jews, just as we here must have a meaning, a *raison d'être* for continuing to survive as Jews. If we do not have a mission to fulfill, if we do not have a purpose in life, then why survive as Jews?

W.B.: What is the function of the Jew in the Diaspora?

> ■ DIMONT: This I do not know. We have changed from an age of faith to an age of reason, and the modern Jew, like the modern Christian, can no longer be held with the ideas of the faith of the past. He must have a twentieth-century faith. What that will be, what it is that will tie us together in the twenty-first century, I do not know. But I do know this: There have always been "Diaspora designers" in the past; there are going to be new ones in the future. If we can just keep the chain going, if we can just keep the links forged until we have new Diaspora designers who will tell us what our philosophy is, how we can survive with a meaning in the twenty-first century, then we will survive. I have no doubt that these men will come, just as Moses Mendelssohn, Rashi, Maimonides, and others came at the right time.

W.B.: What about the relationship of the Diaspora to the State of Israel?

> ■ DIMONT: I think that both must exist, for this reason. Twice in history, the Jews in Israel have lost their country. Twice it has been the Diaspora Jews who have reconquered and re-constituted that country. Without the Diaspora Jews there would have been no Israel, there would not be an Israel today.
>
> On the other hand, we have an Israel to which Jews in the Diaspora can go should we face another crisis like the Hitler era. We have a place to go, a sanctuary, a national citadel. But there is something else too. Now that a segment of the Jews are back in Israel, we must ask this metahistorical question: Will the Jews in Israel now become victims of Spengler's law of decay, just as all other civilizations have? They went there in their autumn phase; they have only one more phase to live, the winter phase. How long can they last as a civiliza-

tion, unless for some reason they become exempt from the laws of historical decay? So, if we believe what Spengler says, we must have the Diaspora, where Jews can remain eternally young instead of dying out in a country of their own. Yet they must have a country of their own in order to have a national homeland.

There is another consideration. Jews today live on five different continents. Should Western civilization be doomed, as Spengler says it is—Spengler's contention is that Western civilization today is in its winter phase—the Jews can be, if I may coin a phrase, the "civilization hoppers" of history. Because they live in many civilizations, they can continue to exist in an emerging civilization even as another one dies.

So I feel that both should nurture each other, Israel and the Diaspora. We must have both, until we reach whatever the *tikkun*—the third act—has in store for us, until the mission has been accomplished, after which we would have no reason for existing separately.

W.B.: Your book *Jews, God and History* has sold 30,000 copies, and the paperback edition is now beyond 250,000. Why do you think it has been so successful?

■ DIMONT: I think the reason it has been successful is that it has discarded the view of the Jew as an underdog, as a martyred being, as a person plagued by trials and tribulations, as a persecuted man. Instead of this concept I have maintained that the Jew has had a grand history, that the Jew has been one of the proudest men in the history of man, and that he has one of the most glorious histories of any people. The mail I receive indicates this. For instance, much of my mail comes from young Jews who tell me that they have read the book and for the first time in their lives they are really proud to be Jews. I get mail from Christians. One letter from a lady in New Orleans said, "Mr. Dimont, after reading your book I realized that I should be a Jew, but I have been a Christian for so long, I can't change. Will you please forgive me?" I forgave her.

The question now is, Which is the correct view? Am I inventing an image for the Jew which is nonexistent, or have the other historians erred about their image by depicting the Jew as a downtrodden, persecuted individual throughout history? The answer is—neither. Each age portrays its history in its own image. Let me illustrate it this way: When the British historian Carlyle wrote the history of the French Revolution, he did not portray the French aristocrats as sheep marching to the guillotine. He did not ask why they did not fight back. Instead, he depicted the French noblemen as walking proudly up the steps to the guillotine, looking with contempt into the eyes of the revolutionary mob.

Now, how have we treated a similar episode in Jewish history? I am talking about the concentration camps. So many of us ask why the Jews did not fight back. As I see it, this was one of the most heroic chapters in Jewish history. As I read diaries of concentration camp guards, Nazi officers who saw these executions, there was one thing that astounded them continually: the Jews did not beg for mercy; they did not quail; they were not convulsed with fear. What struck the Nazis was that the Jews marched proudly, as the French aristocrats did. The Jews marched into their tomb looking with contempt at their persecutors.

Now this, I think, is grandeur. This, I think, is greatness. This, I think, is courage. And I think that this is the true image of the Jew—that, rather than go down on his knees, he goes to his death proudly. So again, it is how you look at history that determines what facets of history you select. An event has no meaning in itself; it is what you bring to that event and how you view it that counts. I view the Jew as one of the proudest beings of history, as a man who has suffered longer because he has survived longer.

W.B.: I believe this is an appropriate thought with which to conclude: It is not wealth, it is not station, it is not social standing and ambition that can make us worthy of the Jewish name and of the Jewish heritage. To be worthy of them we must regard ourselves as their custodians, and every Jew must feel that he is the trustee of what is best in Jewish history, a history that has lasted for 4,000 years and, Spengler and Toynbee notwithstanding, will continue to live forever.

PART III

Six Million Were Murdered. . . .

❦ Introduction

Ours is the generation that was seared by the Holocaust, the singular tragedy that ushered in an era of bestiality and defamed the word *human*. Now, a half-century later, we still feel the shock to our souls, the assault on our senses, the blow to our intellects. Our world—*the* world—can never be the same. In response, we ask with Job: "Why?"

We may never find a satisfactory answer to that question, but we have given the world the only answer we have: *zachor*, "remember." We remember, for the sake of the generation we lost and for the sake of generations to come. We remember, not in order to wallow in morbid self-pity but to celebrate the faith and courage of those who fell. Although the storm somehow, fortunately, passed us by, we are its victims nonetheless and we have the mission of safeguarding our people, and the world, against future such cataclysms.

Make no mistake, we cannot relax. It is horrifying that, fifty years after the event, we are still faced with difficult challenges that demand thought, vigilance, and activism against the winds that seek to engulf us.

We have recently been witness to the growing trend of trivialization of the Holocaust and the demeaning of its tragic message. We see a growing revisionism in history. To our horror, we hear serious assertions that the Holocaust never happened. Concentration camps never existed, we are told; the ovens were built only to bake bread, the "showers" were only for hygiene. A neo-Nazi propaganda machine publishes thousands of booklets with these and other outrageous distortions of the past.

But the menace goes beyond propaganda. A *Kristalnacht* anniversary in Germany is the occasion for a Nazi rally. Austria elects Kurt Waldheim as its president despite his acknowledged Nazi activities during World War II. In Germany, neo-Nazi computer games—with names like "Concentration Camp Manager" and "Cleaning Up Germany" (players win points by eliminating Jews, Turks, homosexuals, and gypsies)—have been developed. Gangs of Nazi-oriented youths surface in American cities and in the American countryside. Not too long ago, a proposal for federal funding of an eighth- and ninth-grade Holocaust studies curriculum was rejected by consultants, who wondered why it did not also represent the Nazi point of view. A Ku Klux Klan leader and avowed American Nazi is elected to the Louisiana State Senate. And so it continues.

We must remember, and we must be alert. We must be firm in keeping faith with those whom we have lost, those who said, with Job, "Though He slay me, yet will I trust in Him."

We can take our stance, gain our strength, from the last words of the Warsaw Ghetto heroes, who—after an incredible fight against overwhelming odds—sang as they went to their deaths:

Oh, never say that you have reached the very end
Though latent skies and bitter future may portend—
Because the hour for which we yearned will yet
    arrive,
And our marching steps will thunder: *We survive!*

12. ❧ Nazis Face Justice

Judge Michael A. Musmanno

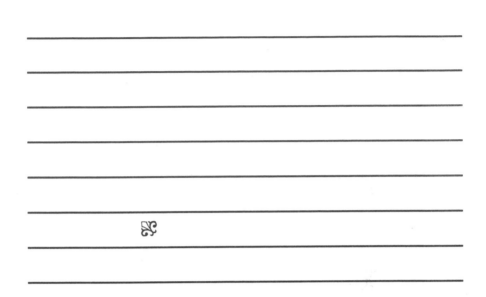

W.B.:   In a courtroom in Jerusalem Adolf Eichmann sat on trial, accused of being responsible for carrying out the Nazi program of annihilating the Jews. Confronting him was the accuser, the State of Israel, born in a generation of pain and misery. At the very opening of the trial, the Attorney General for the State, Gideon Hausner, said: "When I stand before you, Judges of Israel, I do not stand alone. Here with me at this moment stand six million prosecutors, but alas, they cannot rise to level the finger of accusation in the direction of the glass dock and cry out *J'accuse* against the man who sits there, because their ashes have been piled up in the mounds of Auschwitz, in the fields of Treblinka, or spilled into the rivers of Poland."

Mr. Hausner went on: "And their graves are scattered throughout the length and breadth of Europe, and their blood cries to heaven, but their voices cannot be heard. Thus, it falls on me, representing the State of Israel, to be their mouthpiece and to deliver the accusation in their name."

Justice Michael A. Musmanno is eminently qualified to analyze the meaning of the trial that followed that dramatic beginning. He was a Justice of the Pennsylvania Supreme Court; he was a judge at the Nuremberg war crimes trials and a witness for the prosecution in the Eichmann trial; he is the author, among many books, of *The Eichmann Kommandos*. He is a human being who, day to day and week to week, month to month and year to year, in a glowing career has been one of the noblest exponents of the biblical injunction, "Justice, justice, shall ye pursue."

Justice Musmanno, can you tell us something of yourself and your career as an introduction to our discussion of the Eichmann trial?

■ MUSMANNO: I might begin by relating a little episode that occurred early in my public career. In 1926, I was a candidate for the Pennsylvania legislature in an area that was interspersed with districts that reeked of intolerance. You can gather from my name that I am of Italian lineage. In this legislative district, anyone with an Italian name was regarded as being rather lowly. In one particular township it was said that "It would be absolutely ruinous for us to send this man to the legislature because he is not even an American. His name is obviously not American." I decided to go into this township. They did not know me, had never seen me, and knew only that I was a candidate.

I attended an open meeting in a school building. I asked the chairman not to announce my name, but, when my turn came, to say only "And this is the next speaker." He did not know who I was. I was about number fifteen on the list and finally was called upon. I stood up before the crowd of about two or three hundred people, and said, "I have come here tonight to speak for a candidate who is truly an American. He was born on the banks of the Ohio River only about ten miles from this very schoolhouse. He attended the local schools and then went to Washington, D.C., the capital of the nation, and graduated from four universities, attaining five degrees. He volunteered in World War I as a private and emerged as a captain. He wrote a book on the Constitution of the United States that was adopted by Congress as a national document. There were four brothers in his family, all of whom served in the army. One made the supreme sacrifice on the battlefields of France." I was about to go on when one man stood up and asked, "Who is this man you are talking about?" I said, "Michael A. Musmanno."

A sort of mute horror pervaded the room. No one said anything, and then the questioner continued, "Well, why doesn't he come himself to speak?" I said, "He did come." He said, "Who are you?" I said, "I am Michael A. Musmanno." I could feel the shock in the air and then I heard a little scattered applause. The election followed about two weeks later. There were 1,200 votes cast in that district. I got 78. Many of the voters had seen me, they knew that I did not have "horns." I had told them of my American background, but still the spirit of intolerance was so ingrained in them that they yet felt I was not an American.

I was defeated, but I was elected in my next campaign. I served in the Pennsylvania legislature for two terms, then I was elected to County Court and then the Court of Common Pleas. I served as a trial judge for twenty years in all. I enlisted in the Navy when World War II broke out; I had served in the Army in the First World War, but I learned that they fed you better in the Navy, so I joined the Navy in the Second World War. I went in as a lieutenant commander and came out as a rear admiral. Then I was elected to the Supreme Court of Pennsylvania in 1951, and I have been on the bench ever since. President Truman appointed me as a judge at the War Crimes Trials in Nuremberg. I think that brings us up-to-date.

W.B.: We can operate, Justice Musmanno, on the premise that most of this audience have read about the Eichmann trial and have been keenly interested in its development. So let us turn to the first question area: the great amount that has been written and said in objection to the trial itself. The first objection is that this was a case of *ex post facto*. Would you care to comment on this and explain what *ex post facto* is, in relationship to the Eichmann trial? Is this a valid objection against holding any such trial in Israel?

■ MUSMANNO: When Prime Minister David Ben Gurion announced to the world that Adolf Eichmann had been captured in Argentina and had been transported to Israel for trial, a clamor of protest arose throughout the world. It came mostly from theorists, chronic obstructionists, and people who believed that the world should stand still. They complained, to begin with, that it was illegal to try Adolf Eichmann because he was to be tried under what Rabbi Berkowitz referred to as an *ex post facto* law.

In 1950, Israel enacted a law known as the Nazi and Nazi Collaborators Law. Eichmann was to be tried under this statute. It is obvious that this statute was passed after the crimes were committed. So therefore, the objectors said that he could not and should not be tried under that law. Now, an *ex post facto* law is a law that declares to be criminal an act that was not criminal when actually committed. For instance, if

Congress were to enact a law today that anyone who goes to Cuba will be punished, certainly they could not arrest a man and charge him with having violated the law because of a trip he made to Cuba five years ago; that would obviously be *ex post facto* prosecution. But what many of the critics overlooked or were ignorant of was the true meaning of *ex post facto*. Some of the critics were college professors and some were even lawyers, but most of them, I think, got their law from Perry Mason's TV show. The simple fact of the matter is that there was never a period of history when murder was not a crime. Therefore, it is ridiculous to speak of Eichmann as having been tried under an *ex post facto* law.

W.B.: Now we go to objection number two. Many people asked how a man could be tried by a state that did not exist when the crime was committed.

■ MUSMANNO: These people reveal their ignorance in that they overlook the fact that Israel is a successor to Palestine, which has had over 3,000 years of existence. Let me give you an illustration to show just how absurd that criticism is. Let us suppose someone in the colony of Pennsylvania, before the Declaration of Independence, on July 3, 1776, committed a murder. On July 4, 1776, Pennsylvania ceased being a colony of England; it became a state. Let us suppose that on July 5th this man, who had committed the murder on July 3rd, was arrested. It would be preposterous to say that he could not be tried because the crime he committed occurred when Pennsylvania was a colony of Great Britain. A crime is a crime, regardless of the political complexion of the nation in which the offense occurs.

The crimes that Eichmann committed were not directed against this little tract of land that is bordered on the west by the Mediterranean Sea, that is hammer-locked on the north and on the east by Syria and Jordan and Lebanon, and is separated from Egypt by sand dunes. No, his offenses were directed against Jews, against six million of them. These Jews did not live in Israel, but they formed part of a Jewish community scattered over some twenty nations. The crime that he committed was not a geographical one; it was directed against humanity and particularly against six million Jews.

W.B.: Let us put objection number three in this fashion: suppose that Eichmann were an American citizen and suppose that because of him and his gang six million Americans were murdered. Would the United States be justified in seizing him for trial even if he were in some foreign country? Was Israel correct in the manner of its capture of Eichmann by kidnapping him from Argentina?

> ■ MUSMANNO: Those who wailed so loudly about the kidnapping of Eichmann overlooked the fact that no mass murderer has the right, morally or legally, to escape over a sea of blood that he himself has filled. If Eichmann, in the hypothetical situation described by Rabbi Berkowitz, had murdered six million Americans in twenty different countries outside the continent of North America, there can be no doubt that the United States would have seized that man wherever he might be and brought him here for trial, assuming that the United Nations did not do anything, as the United Nations had not acted in the Eichmann case. The United Nations at the very outset should have assembled an international tribunal to try Eichmann. But it failed to do this. Germany was not interested, Argentina was not interested; Great Britain, of course, was not concerned; the United States itself did nothing. Was this man, accused of the most heinous and gigantic crime in the history of mankind, to go free because there could be no tribunal to try him?
>
> To get back to this hypothetical question, Article I, Section 8 of the Constitution of the United States says that Congress is mandated to enact laws to punish offenders against the law of nations. Eichmann's offenses were offenses against the laws of nations—in other words, international crimes. A pirate may be tried in any nation that has custody of the pirate, no matter what the sea or ocean may be on which he committed his offense. There can be no doubt that the United States would be justified, duty bound, and there is no question that it would act to prosecute Adolf Eichmann, had he killed six million Americans outside the

borders of the United States. And what the United States would have the right to do, Israel as a sister nation in the family of nations certainly had the right to do.

w.b.: We have read a great deal about the reactions of people from all walks of life—emotional reactions—to this trial. You were in Pittsburgh when you were invited to go to Jerusalem to testify for the prosecution, and you left your chambers to take part in the trial. Would you care to share your reactions with us?

■ MUSMANNO: If you would like me to share a very personal reaction, I will tell you how I felt about the Eichmann trial emotionally, intellectually, spiritually, and professionally. I testified at the trial for one full day, but I was at the trial for a month, at the end of which I returned to the United States. When I finally got back to my home city of Pittsburgh, I felt an emotion that is almost impossible to describe. At that time, as is true even today, there was a great deal of discussion in the papers about a contemplated trip to the moon. And I felt then that had I made that trip to the moon and successfully returned, the emotions that I would have experienced on such an epochal voyage could not surpass the emotions that seized me in recollecting what I experienced at the Eichmann trial. If I had made that fantastic trip to the moon, I would have found myself hurtling through space at thousands of miles per minute observing the stars, comets, and meteors whirling in the heavenly orbit, witnessing the sunbeams bathing the whole planetary system in golden light. The experience would be overwhelming, and it would be breathtaking in its infinitude and intensity. But it would, after all, be merely a phenomenon in the divinely organized system of God's world. But entering into the world that was the Eichmann trial baffles the intellect, staggers the senses, shocks the soul, and makes the human spirit stand against the horizon, a sky-high interrogation point. Dante Alighieri, in all his melancholy verses on his imaginary journey through the inferno, never described anything that could approach the horror of the real hell that was stoked, fueled, and kept blazing by the satanic Nazis through the twelve dolorous years of 1933 to 1945.

There at the Eichmann trial I listened to evidence that was so horrifying that there were days when I had to avert my consciousness as one would attempt to avoid a blast of scalding steam. I heard witnesses describe projects and enterprises that had but one objective, and that was to produce unspeakable horror, unbridled terror, and inconsolable pain, anguish, and misery.

In the latter part of the Nazi regime, six million innocent men, women, and children were murdered. Can you visualize six million murders? It is impossible. It is beyond human comprehension. It is like trying to hold in one's hand a sphere that is too large for the hand to enfold. The fingers slip, the hand loses traction, and you become aware of something that is physically unattainable. Can you hold in your hand a globe made up of the incalculable phenomenon of death? What is death? How often I thought of this as I presided over the trials of Nuremberg and as I sat there at the Eichmann trial in Jerusalem. No one can really understand death without a realization of the sweetness of the divine essence of life. And what is life? We can only get a glimmering of the treasure of life when someone near and dear to us passes away, and in the depth of our misery and as we try to grope through the veils of mystery that surround us, we become aware that something we thought could never be severed from us has been taken away for all time, and we can never, never be wholly happy again.

That is one tragedy. Multiply that by six million, if you can, and you begin to understand a little of the significance of this unspeakable crime that was committed by Adolf Eichmann and his confederates.

W.B.: Most of us during the trial sat before our television sets each evening to watch the proceedings. We looked at this man, Adolf Eichmann, sitting in his cage with the earphones on, taking notes; each of us had his own feelings, his own point of view. Here is a reaction that might at first seem strange. I was talking with a friend and he observed that when he watched the Eichmann trial on TV and saw this man sitting in the cage, he began to feel sorry for him. Having caught himself in this feeling, he had a sense of guilt about it and tried to rationalize it. He said that Jews, by virtue of their own history and background, have always been the underdog; automatically he fell into a position of sympathy for this man who was now in that position even though he was well aware of the magnitude of Eichmann's crimes. For a moment he felt sorry and then he realized just who it was that was staring at him from the TV screen. Mr. Musmanno, what kind of man would you say Eichmann was?

■ MUSMANNO: I was considerably amazed and still am by people such as the man you have described, and others who have said that Eichmann is a very ordinary-looking person. I remember one press correspondent saying that Eichmann looked like a bank clerk. I know that if I went into my bank and I saw a man looking like Eichmann behind the grated window, I would not wait to take my money out of the bank, but would run for the police at once. Eichmann is not ordinary-looking. No one could descend into the foulest depths of depravity as that man did and still look ordinary, and still retain the image of the man that he was originally created to be.

When I sat on the witness stand I was only about fifteen feet away from him, so I had an opportunity to observe him rather closely. And on an occasion or two when some questions or answers were rather lengthy and a little time was consumed in listening to the translations, I jotted down my impressions of what Eichmann looked like. Later on, I wrote a series of articles for some newspapers, and I would like to quote a paragraph that I wrote, describing how he appeared to me as he sat there just seven or eight paces away: "I see an individual with beady, snake-like eyes sunk in the deep sockets of a startling skull over which the yellowish parchment of his skin is drawn tightly and therefore crinkles and almost crackles as the unseen tongue rolls about within the cadaverous cheeks. His thin lips curl, twitch, and bunch into either side of a mouth which any fox could call its own. All the cunning, craft, and rapacity which one ascribes to the fox can be seen there in that cage."

W.B.: Let us go a little deeper into the character of Eichmann, if we may. As he listened to the testimony and was forced to recall all that had been perpetrated in his time and under his administration, do you think that there was any feeling, any sense, any idea that he felt sorry for what he had done?

■ MUSMANNO: There is no doubt that he was sorry that he was caught. But as I watched that predatory countenance for a month, I could not see any regret in his face for the millions who had been reduced to ashes in the furnace of his hatred. There is no doubt whatsoever in my mind that if he were free and heard once again the screeching voice of Adolf Hitler, and listened once again to the beating of the drums of racial prejudice, and if the atmosphere of Germany were once again befouled with the cries of *"Nieder mit den Juden!"* that he would once again leap into his black SS uniform and his gleaming black boots and put himself at the head of the jeering column and march once more to unloose the holocaust that froze the blood of the world.

W.B.:   When the Eichmann trial began and the fifteen-count indictment was read accusing Eichmann of crimes against the Jewish people with the intent of destroying them, of crimes against humanity, of war crimes, of Nazi crimes, Adolf Eichmann, in answer to the question "How do you plead?" answered "Not guilty."

What was his defense? It was that he had taken the oath of an SS officer and had followed orders, that he was a mere cog in the machine and a victim of history. In his own words, "I was small fry bound to carry out Hitler's orders regarding the final solution to the Jewish problem. I was too insignificant to have a voice in policy matters. As a soldier of the fatherland, I simply had to obey. If someone had told me, 'Your father is a traitor,' and I had to kill him, I would have done it. I obeyed orders blindly and this gave me a sense of fulfillment and gratification. But never did I ever give an order sending Jews to their death; I only provided the transportation."

The court interrogator pursued this, stating, "You keep on saying 'I got orders from above, I was not responsible.' If you were not, why does the fact emerge in all these documents that you were in fact mixed up in it, that you were in fact responsible in a way?" Eichmann replied "Yes, but these were all matters connected with evacuation." The interrogator continued: "Without evacuation, there could have been no gassing; the transports were ordered, the people were delivered to their deaths."

Eichmann admitted, "Naturally, from a legal point of view I am guilty of being an accessory; I see that myself." The interrogator: "We are not talking about a legal point of view. We are talking about bare facts. In all your statements you keep on trying to pull yourself into the background, to hide behind 'That was not my department, that was not my sphere; these are orders that I received that came under the Reich

Railway Administration, and so on.'" Eichmann: "I have to do that, because as head of my department I really was not responsible."

Mr. Justice, what is your view on the question? Is Eichmann alone responsible for these crimes?

> ■ MUSMANNO: Eichmann is what he is, but he alone could not have accomplished the gigantic program of massacre and horror that was described from the witness stand. Adolf Eichmann had, for his avid confederates and bloodthirsty conspirators, hordes of wolves that bore the same claws and the same fangs as he. And they sucked from the same swollen teats of the dragon of racial prejudice. Some of those confederates were intellectual, some of them were primitive; some of them were cultured and some of them quite aboriginal. But they were all imbued with the same thought, they all enacted the same role that has disgraced the human race down through the centuries: anti-Semitism. The Eichmann trial has established above everything else what horrible crimes, what brain-staggering offenses, what heart-rending deeds can be perpetrated by the twin beasts of racial and religious prejudice.

W.B.: Judge Musmanno, your last comment brought into sharp and agonizing focus a period when people descended to the depths of human—or inhuman—experience. And this is the point of my next question. One of the great concerns about this trial was that it could evoke new winds of anti-Semitism. Might it not have been better, people ask, to let sleeping dogs lie, to let the criminals reap their richly deserved punishment in some other world, at the hand of One who judges us all? As painful as it has been to open old wounds, might it not also have created the danger of awakening a new wave of terror around the world? What effect will the trial have in this area?

> ■ MUSMANNO: The trial was most salubrious; it cleared the atmosphere. It has done a great deal for mankind, not only for the Jews. It exposed the hypocrisy, the meanness of the spirit that still attempts to distinguish between the Jew and the non-Jew. I know people who regard themselves as quite honorable, who stand pretty high in society, who will tell you that they have no prejudice against the Jews. They will even tell you, almost confidentially, that "some of their best

friends are Jews," not being aware that this is but one of the most obnoxious forms of anti-Semitism.

I got to know Eichmann's attorney, Dr. Robert Servatius, in Nuremberg and, of course, in Jerusalem. And he has my professional respect. Above all, it required more than a little bit of fortitude to defend a person so universally reviled. But I was considerably disappointed in him when he cross-examined Professor Baron of Columbia University, who had given a brilliant exposition on anti-Semitism down through the centuries. In his cross-examination Dr. Servatius put a question that could be paraphrased in this way: "Dr. Baron, is it not a fact that there is something supernatural about this phenomenon of anti-Semitism, and that the Jews are just fated to have a hard time of it?"

Now, my answer to that question is, of course, a resounding negative. There is nothing supernatural about anti-Semitism. Anti-Semitism is the product of the grossest passions of man. It is a lust for power, a mania for self-exaltation through an assumed superiority and greed—yes, greed. As one reads the history of the Jew and follows the sad story of his maltreatment through the ages, one sees that as the aggressor struck with one hand, he always had his other hand in the victim's pocket.

In the early stages of the persecution of the Jews in Nazi Germany, the first aim was despoliation. Jews were made to pay exorbitant charges for services that were rendered gratis to others. Staggering fines were imposed upon them for no reason at all. And then came the all-inclusive, all-embracing confiscation of every type of property—without compensation, of course. Throughout the whole program of Jewish persecution in Nazi Germany that has disgraced mankind, you find that robbery and pillage accompanied every step. There was first the humiliation of the wearing of the badge, the yellow badge, accompanied, of course, by robbery. Then there was the deportation, accompanied by robbery. Then there was commitment to the concentration camps, accompanied by robbery. And then finally there was murder, accompanied by robbery.

I sat on three trials in Nuremberg, the *Einsatzgruppen* trial,

244 Nazis Face Justice

and the trials of the administrators of the concentration camps and of those who were charged with slave labor. And throughout these three trials, which lasted about a year and a half, evidence was constantly being presented on the confiscation of Jewish property. Documents were introduced in evidence that, in their totality, made piles higher than this ceiling. The story of the robbery of the Jews under the Nazi rulers is something that staggers the imagination and makes the fabled story of the pirates of the Spanish Main fade into insignificance. If I had not seen those documents, if I had not heard the witnesses who described how every item of possession was taken—factories and railroads, automobiles, household furniture, and every piece of wearing apparel down to little, tiny baby shoes, all listed, businesslike—if I had not seen that documentation, I could never believe that so gigantic a program of thievery could be worked out and carried into fulfillment. The Nazis wanted to become rich by killing off the Jews. There was no great principle of ideology involved. There was no great philosophy involved. No Nazi leader ever made a speech, or ever wrote a book, or ever delivered a dissertation in which he showed that in some way the Jews had harmed Germany. The Jews fought in all the wars on the side of Germany, until this holocaust. The Minister of Justice of Israel, a wonderful man, told me that he had been an officer in the Kaiser's army. The Jews all were good citizens. Why, then, was there this persecution?

I remember the first trial in which Goering and Ribbentrop and Raeder and Keitel and others were defendants. I attended that trial as an observer for the United States Navy. I interviewed practically all of the defendants. I went to their cells and talked with them, and invariably I put this question: "Why did you commit this horrible crime against the Jews? I can understand your jealousy of France and desire to invade France as you have done three times in history now. I can understand many of these things; but what about the Jews?" And they would say to me, "Well, the Jews were getting too powerful in Germany. They had taken over the newspapers; they had taken over the theaters; they had taken over the banks."

The persecution of the Jews by the Nazis was strictly a matter of jealousy and greed. The Jews were willing to work, they were frugal, they were economical, they lived according to God's laws, and whatever they acquired they got honestly. But the Nazis were not disposed to exert themselves in that fashion and to acquire the good things of life honestly, so they decided to take the property away from the Jews.

I spoke to Funk, the Nazi Minister of Finance, in his cell at Nuremberg. He apparently knew what I was going to question him about, and although the interpreter had not yet arrived, Funk at once began to speak in German, counting off on his fingers as the others had done, enumerating the fields in which the Jews had succeeded and had outdistanced the Germans. He regarded this as the crime of the Jews. So you always have to come back to the proposition that the Nazis persecuted the Jews out of greed for their possessions: The Nazis would not work as the Jews did, but they did want what the Jews had honestly obtained.

Rabbi Berkowitz has read to you from the testimony at Jerusalem in which Eichmann said that he just had to obey orders. During the *Einsatzgruppen* trial, one of the defendants, Willi Siebert, was accused of having murdered a few thousand Jews. His defense was that he was under orders. His attorney, in order to establish the point that the defendant was under orders and therefore had to obey, said to him, "Now, Mr. Siebert, is it not a fact that the Kaiser once issued an order that if a soldier is ordered to kill his own parents, he must execute the order?" And Siebert, seeing a way out, said: "That is right, that is right. Yes, you have to obey." And the attorney felt that he had proved his point and walked away from the witness stand.

Then I put a question to the defendant. I said, "Let us assume now that you do get an order, a military order, that you are to kill in cold blood your father and your mother. You are to shoot down your father and then stab or otherwise kill your mother. You have an order, it comes right down from the Kaiser. Will you fulfill that order?" He saw at once that he could not say he would kill his father and his mother when I personalized the matter, because that would reveal him as being rather bestial. So he hesitated and demurred. He said, "Well, I do not think there would be such an order." I said, "Well, now, let us assume that there *was* such an order. Would you kill your father and your mother?" He was throwing dagger glances at his lawyer for having put the question to him in the first place, because he was now really in a very precarious situation. Finally, he said, "I will need time to reflect upon this question." I said, "How much time do you want?" "Well, I do not know; I really do not feel very well." I said, "All right, we will adjourn court. You think it over and then tomorrow morning you can answer the question."

The next morning he took the witness stand—you could see by looking at him that he had not slept that night—and I put the question to him again. "Your attorney said that if the Kaiser or anyone under him ordered you to kill your own parents, you would have to do so. Now, I am asking you, would you kill your father and your mother?" He said, "Your honor, I would not do it."

"All right, let us go one step further now," I said. "You now admit that you would not kill your father and your mother even though ordered to do so. Let us assume that a man and a woman, husband and wife, father and mother of children, are brought before you. They have committed no offense, they are not charged with any crime, but you have an order to kill them. Their children are there begging you not to kill their parents. Would you do it?" He said, "I would not do it," thereby exploding the whole theory of superior orders.

As a matter of fact, this may sound a little strange to you, but it is true: no one was *compelled* to kill an unarmed civilian. Not out of compassion for the individual or out of sympathy for the sensibilities of those ordered to do the killing, but just because there were many more who were willing to do the job. If an individual felt that he could not kill in cold blood, he was simply considered an inefficient soldier. He was sent back, and others took his place, because these new ones knew that the more Jews they killed the better chance they had for a promotion, a bigger car, a gaudier uniform, increased authority, more underlings to tremble before their greatness. And so it was with Adolf Eichmann. He could easily have withdrawn from the chiefship of the Department of Jewish Affairs. Anyone could have been excused from committing murder by stating, "I cannot do this and I ask to be sent to the front," and they would have sent him to the front. But no, Adolf Eichmann enjoyed the luxury of his position. He had homes, he had villas, he had expensive apartments in Paris, in Berlin, in Vienna, and in Budapest. He was only a lieutenant colonel; he lived like a king. He had no sense of justice, no conscience. To kill a million people meant nothing, so long as he could continue to enjoy his fine wines, his champagnes, his big automobiles, and his mistresses in all these various places. Greed, lust, and a desire to be important at the expense of others; there you have the principal causes of anti-Semitism.

W.B.: I think at this point there is one question that must be answered, and it bears on the larger issue of the relationship of world civilization to the whole matter of genocide in general, and this special tragedy of the Jews in particular. Judge Musmanno, what was the responsibility of civilization in this holocaust? Who was at fault, if anyone?

■ **MUSMANNO:** The Western powers were greatly at fault. As one reads of the persecution of the Jews in contemporary and past history, one can only feel shame that the human race has been so disgraceful as to permit the torturing, the pillaging, and the massacre of an unoffending, God-fearing people down through the centuries. The Western nations, to their credit, have in their history occasionally gone to the defense of oppressed nations. They should have acted in 1936 when Hitler gave conclusive proof of his determination to annihilate a race. The United States, England, and France particularly should have served notice on Hitler that if he did not desist and did not abandon the program that he had announced, he would be forcibly required to desist. And it would have been an easy matter in those days. It would have been simply the matter of curbing and restraining a mad dog, which he was.

But the Western nations, the populations of the world, were too interested in prosperity, too intent on good living, too indifferent to the sufferings of humanity to undertake the defense of humanity. They did not want to undertake a conflict that was later forced upon them anyway.

The Eichmann trial revealed more than anything else the blunders of the Western nations in this respect. Had they restrained Hitler in 1936, there would have been no Hermann Goering, there would have been no Heinrich Himmler, there would have been no Joseph Goebbels, and there would have been no Adolf Eichmann with his murder machine that in cold blood killed six million innocent men, women, and children. And had the Western nations—and I answer your question directly, Rabbi—had the Western nations lived up morally, ethically, and legally to the standards of civilization, World War II would not have happened.

W.B.: Jews have been persecuted throughout the ages and never were able in any country or in any age to stand up and try their persecutors. There were the Egyptians and there were the Babylonians; there were the Greeks and there were the Romans; there was Torquemada and the Spanish Inquisition; there were the massacres of the Middle Ages and there were the pogroms of Czarist Russia. Finally, there was the Germany of 1933 and its determination to exterminate, once and for all, the Jewish people. Yet in our age, in Jerusalem, the man, Adolf Eichmann, who was in charge of this extermination has been tried and judged by those he once condemned to death. And there in Jerusalem, in the Holy City, in the capital of a Jewish State, the eyes of the world were fixed on a trial by law as Israel presented its case, not only on behalf of the Jews of the world or the citizens of Israel, but on behalf of six million dead.

Revenge does not enter into this triumph of humanism over Hamanism at its worst. In the land of a people that Adolf Eichmann tried to destroy, he stood on trial before the world and one can truly say this is an accounting of history.

13. ❧ Intrepid and Selfless People

Marie Syrkin

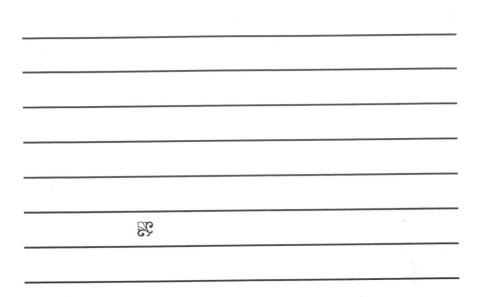

W.B: Within our lifetime, a great and unforgettable personality appeared on the Jewish scene. His name was Dr. Nachman Syrkin, a socialist and Zionist theoretician whose contributions are still acclaimed today. His daughter, Dr. Marie Syrkin, has earned in her own name an international reputation as an author, as an editor—in particular, of the *Jewish Frontier*—and as a lecturer and teacher. For many years she was Professor of Humanities at Brandeis University. She has served with great distinction and devotion as a member of the Executive Board of the Jewish Agency for Israel.

The pages of Jewish history are filled with incidents of resistance, of people or groups of people determined not only to live their lives but to carry on a way of life and a mission that centuries before was given to them as a mandate at Mount Sinai. Too often we associate Jewish resistance movements and Jewish bravery with something in the far distant past, something in a history book. Yet in our time we have seen Jewish resistance in Palestine. There, a handful of people were determined to survive. They said, "We shall live; we shall create a new Jewish state." And create it they did, with great glory and valor.

Also, we were witnesses, some of us even participants, in a resistance against the most diabolical force of evil that the world has ever beheld: Nazi Germany. This was a struggle that often ended in death, but that was fought with bravery, honor, and courage.

While Dr. Syrkin has written several books, I want to concentrate on only one because of its historical value and its insights as to what went on in the lives of our people during one of the most tragic periods of Jewish history.

In 1947 Dr. Syrkin wrote *Blessed Is the Match*, unquestionably one of the most stirring and meaningful documents of the Jewish resistance movement against Nazi Germany. Dr. Syrkin, why and under what circumstances did you write this book?

■ SYRKIN: It is always very interesting for someone who has written a book to be asked to tell what prompted the writing of it. Like most Jews in America during those terrible years in the 1940s, I was concerned by a question that began to trouble us subsequently even more. The more we heard, in the early part of that decade, of the destruction, the more anxious I became to find out whether there had been any attempts to act against that destruction.

In 1945, the war with Germany had already been concluded and the war with Japan was practically over. About that time I heard from many Palestinians about a remarkable young female parachutist, Hannah Senesh, who had perished in Hungary after she had parachuted in from Palestine. She had written a poem that became the theme song of Palestine in 1945, "Blessed Is the Match That Is Consumed in Kindling Flame."

W.B.: I would like to read some of the poem's lines:
Blessed is the match that is consumed in kindling flame,
Blessed is the flame that burns in the secret fastness of the heart.
Blessed is the heart with strength to stop its beating for honor's sake,
Blessed is the match that is consumed in kindling flame.

■ SYRKIN: That poem seemed to me so wonderful. The sense of something slight, a match, that cannot be very much but that can be consumed in kindling flame, seemed the absolute essence of sacrificial heroism. I remember asking a man who had been a prominent member of the underground to visit me and tell me about Hannah Senesh. As he talked more and more about Hannah Senesh I was very thrilled. Then he suddenly said to me, "I have to make an important telephone call." He went to make the call and came back into the living room saying, "I have to go now. Besides, why should I tell you about it? Go to Palestine and find the people who were engaged in the Resistance." At the moment it seemed completely logical and reasonable. The thing to do was to go there to speak to the members of the Resistance and to those who had emerged from the ghettos and escaped and made their way to Palestine. It was a little hard to get there. One could not get a plane, and it took three weeks by boat, but that was not important. I got there. And that book was the result of interviewing those people who had been in the Resistance and who had lived through it. I wrote the story immediately, as I remembered it.

W.B.: Did you limit your research and documentation to Palestine alone, or did you go elsewhere before writing the book? Did you visit the DP [displaced persons'] camps at any time?

■ **SYRKIN:** Remember, this was the summer of 1945. Movement was limited. The only place to get material—directly from the people who had experienced it, the people who had been active in the Resistance—was in Palestine. There was no exception to this. Subsequently, a year and a half later, I went to the DP camps and got much more material, but by then the book had already been written.

W.B.: Let's turn to the book and the chapter called "The Underground Network." In speaking about the wartime rescue of Jews from Europe, you stated: "At the outset the entire rescue operation was a Jewish one. The great powers displayed no active concern in the drama being enacted behind the Nazi curtain, the deliberate scientific massacre of six million men, women, and children." You also wrote: "It is important to stress this point, not for the purpose of leveling an accusation against the world's incomprehensible indifference with regard to history's great crime, for no accusation can be bitter or grave enough, but so that one can appreciate with what limited strength and by what few hands the work was done."

You have a fascinating chapter called "The Office in Istanbul"—could you tell us about this office, and, in particular, how the code using Hebrew names fooled the Germans?

■ **SYRKIN:** The office in Istanbul consisted of Palestinian Jews who had made their way to outposts. We must remember what the situation was. Europe was a Nazi fortress, with much of it in Hitler's hands. At certain points there were attempts to bore from the outside in. This was not the situation that existed after the war, when some frontiers were down and there were attempts to go illegally over other frontiers. During the war the continent was hermetically sealed under the control of Hitler's armies. The Jews in Istanbul were individuals—few in number but great human beings with so little at their command—attempting to establish contact within. I have sometimes thought of the parallel of miners who have been entombed, where the people above are knocking and listening and trying to contact them, and when they are lucky, hearing some kind of an answering sound. It was the same process. This was an awesome attempt to get to the heart of Europe, particularly Poland where the great misfortune was raging at its utmost, in order to establish contact or even to get them out. To get someone out did not necessarily mean to get them out of Europe, but to get them perhaps from one depot to another depot, or from Poland to Czechoslovakia. From Czechoslovakia one could get to another country, farther away from the Hitler terror.

Now, they had their *shlichim*, their couriers, who at times managed to penetrate. A Palestinian could not suddenly just appear in the heart of Europe. How was it done? At times they engaged German businessmen who cooperated with them. These businessmen had the right to travel, and they usually got as far as Poland, for instance, with messages. They did it for pay—rarely for idealistic reasons. Sometimes this was successful. In the office in Palestine, where I was looking for material on this, they had somehow received code communications from the heart of the Warsaw Ghetto. An example of the code they used was to write the Hebrew words for "Uncle Gus is with us," or "Auntie Sarah is in our midst this moment." Or by using the Hebrew words for Simon: "Simon so-and-so is with Auntie so-and-so." It was a simple code, and it is hard to understand how the Germans were fooled by it.

But Resistance members were able to communicate by using just a few words allotted to them, so that somehow a pretty clear understanding of conditions within the ghettos reached Istanbul and Palestine. Even when it came to the Warsaw Ghetto uprising, somehow they got the message to Palestine.

W.B.: This reminds me of a friend who tells of a member of his family who received a letter from relatives in the Soviet Union. It was a very enthusiastic and glowing report of life in Russia. It said that Jewish life was flourishing—that not only were they able to study Yiddish, but Hebrew, and all the things that go with it. And at the very end, the letter was signed *Moishe Kapoire*, which, read as Yiddish, means "the other way around." Perhaps by this time the Politburo has learned what this means.

Dr. Syrkin, you wrote of the period of the Jewish resistance movement, "They too were zealots and visionaries, consumed with the passion to reach the Jews of Europe." You were speaking of the Palestinian Jews. Then you said, very movingly, "As I sat there with them [referring to the Palestinians], I could not help asking myself for the hundredth time, 'Why was there no such inner compulsion among the Jews in America?'"

Dr. Syrkin, what evidence do you have for this? Why was this so? What comment would you like to make today with respect to this statement of some years ago?

■ SYRKIN: The evidence is that the Jews of America did not act, they just did not. I do not think that this is a matter I must in any way prove. Of course, there is the question "*Why?*" I think it would be presumptuous of me to answer. It is more significant to give the answer that the Palestinians gave us. We have had many discussions on it. There were 600,000 Jews in Palestine who were consumed by the feeling that it was their business to do something about the Jews in Europe. They saw to it that the British government sent the parachutists. It was not much, but it was as much as they could do. Subsequently they organized the illegal immigration; they did all these things. Here, with five million Jews in America, we had protest meetings.

The Jews of Palestine explained this to us. The U.S. had five million Jews, many of them rich and powerful, while there were 600,000 Jews under the British mandate—not even in a free democracy, yet they infiltrated the Axis. Why the difference? The difference, as they themselves said, was that they were 600,000 who had to fight *as a people*. They were accustomed to think as a people, and when a group thinks of itself as a people, they act as a people. They did not say, "We are only 600,000 individuals, what can we do?" They said, "I am a member of a people, and my people is being tortured and destroyed. I cannot be indifferent to what is happening to my people because I *am* that people." They did not ask, "Is it possible, is it reasonable, will it be successful?" They did what they had to do out of their passionate concern.

I do not think we can exempt any of us, we American Jews. What was our situation? In the first place, it took a long time for us to believe that what was happening was actually true. The Jews in Palestine, because of an entirely different psychology, because of the historic reasons that had led them to Palestine, were much more psychologically prepared to believe what was happening. In addition, the first witnesses were among them. By the time it began to percolate into our minds, we also felt that we were good American citizens and we had to do what the American government wanted us to do, and the last thing the American government wanted was disturbance, uproar, change in immigration quotas, anything they thought would impede the war effort. We did nothing to rock the boat. With America in the war, with inconvenient demands and questions, we wanted to cause no problems. The Jews in Palestine did rock their boat, and they never worried about it. They had been rocking the British boat for a long time. They were doing it for themselves and out of their enormous sense of national responsibility.

Very simply, if you were a Zionist in Palestine, you obviously had a more consuming sense of national responsibility. If you were an American, you had to face the fact that this is what had happened historically, and you were not at all certain that it would not happen again. In a similar crisis, in a great crisis, what would be the reaction today of American Jewry and what would be the reaction of Israel? We can take it right down the line. Who catches Eichmann and tries him? Not the respectable American Jew; he would not do anything unlawful. It is Israel. And I think that this feeling of national responsibility is the basis of the nation.

W.B.: In your book you have a chapter called "Eichmann Makes an Offer." What is this about?

■ SYRKIN: When you try to piece a story together, as I did in this book, you go to all sources. I went to the mother of Hannah Senesh, and she told me about how she had seen her daughter in a Hungarian prison. I went to a Palestinian, a friend of Hannah Senesh, and heard another part of her story. One day, someone came to me in Tel Aviv, a very interesting chap. He did not seem to be doing much then, but he had a very interesting history. His name was Joel Brand, and he claimed to have negotiated with Eichmann. This was in 1945. I have a special reason for mentioning this now. He died several years ago, but all of this happened many years ago. I met him, he told me his story, and I put it down as he told it to me. You are familiar with the story. It was late in the war, and he was told by various intermediaries that Eichmann had made an offer that for 10,000 trucks for the Russian front, plus a certain amount of medicine and other things, the Germans would release a million Jews. Negotiations began with Eichmann, who said—and I remember the words this man told me—*"Blut fur Waren, Waren fur Blut,"* "Blood for goods, goods for blood."

The people in Palestine notified the Jewish Agency and brought it to the attention of the British authorities, who in turn told Roosevelt. It was dismissed as an attempt to divide the Allies. Russia was our ally, and the trucks would have been used on the Russian front by the Germans. The British and the Americans argued that this was an obvious attempt to create division among the Allies and not a serious offer. Even if it had been possible to raise the money, no Jewish organization could have followed through. It was a question of delivering trucks to Germany to be used on the Russian front. Obviously, no one could have gone to the Joint Distribution Committee and said, "Here, we have 10,000 trucks." They were in no position to hand over trucks to Germany. It could only have been done if Great Britain and America were willing.

When I met Joel Brand I asked him, "What do you think? Could anything have been done?" The question thus came down to, Would the strengthening of the German war machine by this amount have been so dangerous that it was not worth the sacrifice of hundreds of thousands of Jewish lives? Joel Brand said, "The cost to the Allies would have been infinitesimal if measured by the extent to which the German war machine might have been strengthened. If, however, political division had ensued between Russia and America, that might have been a more serious matter. In any event, the tragedy was that nothing happened."

The reason I mentioned this—remember, this is what he told me in 1945—is that within the past few years, those of us who have followed the literature have seen book after book appear that made the following accusation: "The Jewish Agency—in other words, Ben Gurion and the leaders of Palestine—had a chance to save the Jews, a million or at least hundreds of thousands, and they did not take it." You see, the tragedy was made into a constant political argument against Moshe Sharett, and against Ben Gurion, by groups who claim today that more could have been done to save the Jews of Europe. Joel Brand himself, as time passed, came under the influence of political groups who used him to make capital against the parties in power, and he lent his name to some of those accusations. For that reason my interview with him, given in 1945, before any political issues came up some ten or fifteen years later, is, to me, tremendously valuable. At that time it was so clear in his mind, as he said, that whatever the Jewish community could have done, they did. It was wholly in the hands of Great Britain and America, and neither was prepared to act. That a tragic incident is turned into the vicious political capital of a decade or fifteen years later is one of the minor tragedies, but is, nevertheless, a tragedy of Jewish contemporary history.

w.b.: In Slovakia in 1942, another person tried to negotiate with the Nazis: Gisi Fleischman. Who was she, what did she do, and what were her negotiations with the Nazi leaders?

■ SYRKIN: Gisi Fleischman's story is a smaller version of the Joel Brand attempt. She was very valuable, very devoted, and she perished, of course. Her negotiations were with a German named Willy von Wislitzeni, who said that for a certain price he would let Jewish children escape from Czechoslovakia. The tragedy of these attempts is that on a large scale they failed. But there was a constant attempt, as you read the documents, to save, perhaps, ten children, to get them from one spot to another until that one became dangerous, then to another until that was threatened. What is significant was the constant pitting of the human spirit and intelligence, under the most incredible circumstances, in attempting to do something.

So when one reads that the Jews in Europe were passive, that they let themselves be slaughtered, it is written not in malice, I am sure, as much as in total ignorance of these undying efforts. What could they achieve? A person here and an individual there, this one or that one would perhaps be captured in the next place to which he could go, but the attempts—by ransom, by hiding, by every possible means— were utilized, not only by a few but by a whole network of individuals attempting to do what they could.

W.B.: This is what you meant, then, when you wrote, "The breathtaking schemes of mass salvation prodded by such optimists as Gisi Fleischman and Joel Brand never materialized, but the loss was not total." You say that between 1939 and 1940 the chief obstacle to rescue was lack of ports of entry. The Germans then permitted their victims to escape if they could, but there was nowhere for them to go. Then you write, "By the end of 1941, however, the Nazi temper changed." Do you think that if Jews had been able to be rescued and ports of entry could have been found, that the Jews could have left Germany, and if so, how many?

■ SYRKIN: It appears true that in the initial stages the Germans were not so committed to an extermination program. They wanted to get rid of the Jews. The Jews could have left, and they were prepared to let them go. An issue of the now defunct *Look* magazine tells how a ship had gotten out with hundreds of people on it, but in North and South America, no country would let them in. It was a question of quotas. That was the horror and the shame. It is undoubtedly true that there was a stage when Germany *would* have let Jews out. It might have cost money, but it was possible to get them out. But no country would give shelter to them; there was no place to go.

Later, undoubtedly, as situations hardened, the pathology of Hitler increased. When the Jews had been on the shores of salvation, there were no saviors to take them in. So apparently the world was not outraged. Consequently, the world almost appeared to consent to Germany's acts. It is a terrible thing to say, but certainly the Germans felt that if the outrage of the world was not great enough to save the Jews when they could be saved, then the next step was not so enormous. They had a kind of tacit permission from the world, almost, psychologically.

And then, of course, as things got worse, undoubtedly Hitler and his entourage felt, first, that if they could achieve nothing else, they could at least achieve this, the extermination of the Jews, and second, they were already so drenched in blood, so deep, it would be better to go on than retreat.

This changed for a few at the very end of the war when there was an attempt to show, by some, that they were "good" Germans, but not for Hitler and his entourage, who were concerned with completing the business and, if possible, with wiping out all signs of what they had done.

W.B.: In writing about the Warsaw Ghetto, in the chapter "The Struggle of the Spirit," you have two poems by children. One little boy, Motele, wrote:

From tomorrow on I shall be sad—From tomorrow on! Today I will be gay.
What is the use of sadness
Tell me that?
Because these evil winds begin to blow?
Why should I grieve for tomorrow—today?
Tomorrow may be so good, so sunny, tomorrow the sun may shine for us again;
We shall no longer need to be sad.
From tomorrow on I shall be sad—from tomorrow on!
Not today, no! Today I will be glad.
And every day, no matter how bitter it be, I will say:
From tomorrow on, I shall be sad, not today!

Here is a poem by Martha, a little girl, that reads:

I must be saving these days (I have no money to save),
I must save health and strength,
Enough to last me for a long while,
I must save my nerves,
And my thoughts, and my mind and the fire of my spirit;
I must be saving of tears that flow—
I shall need them for a long, long while.
I must save endurance these stormy days.

There is so much I need in life: warmth of feeling and a kind
  heart—
These things I lack; of these I must be saving!
All these, the gifts of God, I wish to keep.
How sad I should be if I lost them quickly.

These were written by children in the Warsaw Ghetto.

> ■ SYRKIN: I found these poems in the *Gazeta Zydowska*, a
> Ghetto paper. They were written in Yiddish and I translated
> them. The first poem was by an 8-year-old child. The second,
> which is much more mature, is by a little girl, Martha, aged
> 11, I believe. Of course, they both perished. Look at what
> that child asks for. She asks for thoughts. She asks for saving
> of thoughts and to have a kind heart. You see in that poem
> the whole desire of the Ghetto not to be brutalized, not to be-
> come what the Germans tried to make them. This is a tremen-
> dous, conscious struggle to remain human, which is expressed
> so marvelously in the lines of this child, which does not ask for
> bread, does not ask for warmth, but for human qualities. That
> a child of 11, under conditions of such terror, which I do not
> have to describe to you, could create this dream to remain
> human—this is the greatest triumph of the spirit. This is
> heroism and nobility. This is one answer to the question,
> "How did they resist?" This is resistance, deep and profound in
> nature. The child perished, but she is alive due to this desire.

W.B.: I am equally moved by the other poem. Dr. Syrkin, I would like
you to describe briefly the community that inspired these poems. What
was the Warsaw Ghetto Council?

> ■ SYRKIN: The Council played a very equivocal role in the life
> of the Ghetto. The German authorities set up the Ghetto,
> and then they designated a certain number of people to be
> the Jewish representatives vis-à-vis the German authorities.
> These Jews were the Council. I believe that in the beginning
> the Council acted in completely good faith. They acted as a
> buffer between the Ghetto and the German authorities.
> Whatever miserable rations were available, whatever work
> could be doled out, whatever sanitation took place, there had
> to be some kind of authority—an authority that dealt with

the Germans. Of course, the great horror began when the Council was asked to furnish Jews, to deliver them to the Germans, and the Council members at some point became aware that the Jews they were delivering were not for labor but destined for death. And the selection started.

If you read the diaries of the Ghetto that exist—there are famous diaries, like the Lieberman diary, the Kaplan diary—you will notice that in the beginning they saw the Council as very ordinary people. The bitterness against the Council increased with time, of course, as their functions became clearer and clearer. In the case of the Warsaw Ghetto, when the head of the Council discovered what was really going on, he committed suicide. There were different kinds of councils in the Ghetto, and some, when certain demands were made of them, refused to collaborate. There were probably others, under the threat of guns, that did perform the bidding of the Germans, probably with the rationalization that in any case there would be a selection in the Ghetto.

I think it is impossible for us to judge them. We here cannot judge what the Council was doing then. But I think there is something that we must understand: selection for death was implicit in the Ghetto from the first day. For instance, there was something in the diaries of Dr. Emanuel Ringelblum that I cannot forget. Ringelblum was the archivist of the Warsaw Ghetto, a historian, and a marvelous human being. Certainly he was the last person to be a collaborator. He had a page in his diaries that goes something like this: "All night I heard the crying of children outside, freezing to death in the snow. In the morning, people came and took away the corpses."

You say to yourself when you read this, "All night he heard the crying of children, dying—why didn't he get up and bring them into his house?" You say this, now and here, in America. The whole point is that there was limited warmth, limited food, and one person existed at the expense of the other. Ringelblum had nothing to give the child who was dying in the snow, probably not even a bit of space to spare. There were too many dying in the snow, and this was going on throughout the Ghetto.

He describes situations and discussions that show that those still alive in the Ghetto were thinking and saying, "We have just so much left of food; should we say that we will save perhaps ten while the others perish, or shall we *all* perish in doling it out? And whom shall we save? Shall we try to find ten children? But the children may be too weak to live. Shall we try to find ten young people who perhaps will be able to survive, to achieve something?"

This selection, which you see in its ultimate form when the Council selects, is already an essential part of the existence of the Ghetto. The most delicate soul, the most marvelous spirit, the most dedicated beings are engaging in selecting. Even when you think of illegal immigration, it is a selection of those who will get on the boat and those who will not get on the boat. Part of the tragedy of the existence of European Jewry is that selection is, from the start, implicit in the conditions.

w.b.: Dr. Ringelblum in his diary writes the following: "Know then that the last surviving educational workers remain true to the ideas of our culture. Until their death they hold aloft the banner of culture in the struggle against barbarism." He concludes: "We doubt whether we shall ever see you again. Give our warm greetings to all our leaders of Jewish culture, writers, journalists, musicians, artists, all builders of modern Jewish culture and fighters for the salvation of Jews and all humanity." This was written when people knew they were going to die, the next day, the next week, the next month.
What are some of the activities that went on in spite of and against the barbarism?

■ SYRKIN: Dr. Ringelblum organized a group called *Oneg Shabbat*—Celebrants of the Sabbath. They were determined to keep a record of what was happening. It is interesting how they maintained their historic sense, a people that was doomed. We learned so much about the Ghetto because of the people who kept the records. They buried their papers, they smuggled them out, and the record remained as written by Ringelblum, Kaplan, and others.

They also kept trying to organize activities. They had lecture series on Sholom Aleichem, on Moses Mendelssohn. This is interesting. These were Jews from all over Europe who were in the ghetto in Warsaw. Many of them had been assimilated Jews. Now they were beginning to learn and speak Yiddish for the first time.

And there is a moment when Ringelblum must pause in his diary because they are giving lectures in Yiddish on Sholom Aleichem, or when they are discussing Socialist Zionism, Marxism. "Who knows?" he says, "this may mean the revival of Yiddish." Can you imagine, at such a moment, to have this notion that the language is going to be revived?

They gave courses that they thought would be practical. For example, in the early stages, a lot of them were studying English for the day when they would be able to get out and use it. There was a course in cosmetology; these were practical things, you know, the desire to train for something.

A diary has appeared recently that was written by a young boy; it was found and translated. The boy was named Moshe Flinker. He was killed in Belgium at the age of 17. This is very different from the Anne Frank diary. This boy's family had decided that they would save themselves, not by hiding, but by living openly. They were well-to-do and lived openly in Belgium, thinking that perhaps they would get away with it there. They were captured. Young Moshe left a diary in Hebrew. I think it is one of the most remarkable ever written. The boy—remember, he was keeping his diary in the 1940s—was a great Hebrew student, but he decided that he must learn Arabic because he sensed—in 1944, mind you—that there would be a Jewish state, and he wanted to be a diplomat for the Jewish state. So he had to know Arabic as well as Hebrew. You can picture this young boy, with the doom of death on him, sneaking into libraries in a Belgian city to get Arabic grammar books.

One more thing, which has nothing to do with the book, illustrates again the Jewish spirit in its intensity. I went to the DP camps for a very interesting reason in the beginning of 1947—you have to keep the date in mind to understand. There was no State of Israel yet, and things looked very black. The Hillel Foundation here had persuaded American universities to allot a certain number of scholarships to young Jews in the DP camps. The American government had agreed to let about 300 above the quota go to American colleges. I was involved in choosing the applicants for this project.

I would like to tell you about the most remarkable examination I ever proctored, when I was picking the lucky 300. I went to the DP camps and the question, naturally, arose—here were young Jews gathered from every part of Europe; how could we choose from all the thousands? They had no documents; those had been destroyed long ago. In the past few years they had not been going to college, they had been in ghettos and concentration camps. So we had to go back a few years to where their education had been interrupted, and we decided that the only way to choose was to give an examination. We could not tell all of them that they could go to America. We announced that an examination would be held in Munich and those who passed would go to America—to Columbia, Vassar, or wherever they chose. The next question was, In what language should we test? These were people from Hungary, Poland, and other countries. The examiner, of course, had to be able to read the answers. A general question on literature or history had to be answered, in depth, in French, German, Yiddish, or Russian, because those were the languages that I knew. I could not read any others. A question in physics or mathematics, of a general kind, could be answered in those languages as well as in Hungarian and Rumanian, because the examiner who marked those knew these two languages also.

Then there was another question. If these boys and girls were to go to an American university, they had to know some English. They had to be able to write a paragraph in English on why they wanted to go to America. I will never forget that day as long as I live. Young people came from all the DP camps in Germany, and they sat there—hundreds of them—and the questions were given to them. Many of them looked at the test and stood up and left. They had forgotten—years and years had passed. Others began to weep. Most of them remained. Then I saw something that I had never seen in my life before: they broke out in the most horrible sweat. A beautiful blond girl, I recall, burst into tears and left. She was supposed to be very good in mathematics, but she said that she could not remember anything. Finally, they got through with the examinations. It took much longer than we expected. We had expected that it would take about two hours, but it took all day. Then came the question of grading. We could not give grades of 98, 97, or 96. We had classifications: Class 1, 2, and 3.

Eight years ago at Brandeis University I met a young professor of physics who had been in Class 1. Another—who had been the blond girl who jumped up and ran away—I saw as a graduate student at Harvard. These were among the successes. But there were many more failures. I tell you this story for the courage and the zeal it shows. This examination, written in three or four languages, was taken by people who had not even looked at a book for four years. This tells much about a people and their spirit.

W.B.: One question on the Warsaw Ghetto that has been asked should again be answered: Why did the Jews of Europe begin to resist so late? Why did the Warsaw Ghetto fight back only when a mere 30,000 were left and over half a million had been massacred?

■ SYRKIN: Because many of them still hoped. They hoped for the victory of the Allies, they hoped that there would be some kind of deliverance. They knew that resistance meant the finale. As long as there was an element of hope in their minds that something would intervene, they waited. They were mistaken, but who are we to say that they should have acted otherwise? Early resistance would have doomed them. It is the greatest delusion to assume that if they had started six months earlier, they would have succeeded. They would have been liquidated that much more rapidly. With the Nazi war machine against them, they had no chance. And they waited, hoping that perhaps the Allies would do something, that the Germans would be defeated, that some change would take place.

W.B.: In addition to the Warsaw Ghetto, there were Jewish partisans throughout Eastern Europe. What about them?

■ SYRKIN: In Vilna, particularly, there was an active group of partisans, people who had fled to the woods and attempted to fight. That was one type. There was also an attempt there to establish a community in the woods, not to fight but simply to live. You might ask, Why did they not all go to the woods? I spoke to one of the heads of the Vilna partisans.

If the young men, for instance, had left the ghetto and gone into the woods, they would have had to completely abandon the old, the women, and the children. Only the young men and the strong could go into the woods in winter and operate from there, and those who went did so knowing that they were free to leave the ghetto and their people. But many felt that they could not leave the ghetto and all it meant: women, children, family.

The Vilna group was very active as partisans. But there was another tragedy: they were alone. They could not tie up with the Polish partisans, for instance, or the White Russian partisans, because these hunted the Jewish partisans. The Jews were as alone in the woods as they were alone in the ghettos. Anti-Semitism was so entrenched that Polish partisans attacked the Jewish partisans. There were many instances of that.

w.b.: You have a phrase in one of your chapters: "Rescue Is Resistance." I think it is an unusually telling phase. Who were the rescuers in some of the countries of Europe who were also part of the resistance movement?

■ SYRKIN: In Holland and in Denmark the situation was much brighter than in Eastern Europe. There were Gentiles who assisted the Jews. There were really heroic figures who attempted to smuggle Jews out, hide them, and it is really a question why the people in these small countries showed so much more valor than those of Eastern Europe. Even in France there were not as many rescues as there were in Holland and Denmark. The smaller the country, the more valor there apparently was in the attempts to actively assist in the rescue of Jews.

w.b.: Dr. Syrkin used the phrase "a woman of valor" as part of the title of her book on the life of Golda Meir. I should like to use the same words to describe and characterize Dr. Syrkin herself, in her noble life and work. But I believe we would have to have one more element, one more word, one more phrase, and that is the word *ahavah*—the concept of love, for this is a concept that is fundamental to all that Dr. Syrkin has done. She has, through a lifetime of service, indicated her love for her people and for the land of Israel and for its culture.

14. ❧ The World Watched, Uncaring

Arthur Morse

W.B.: The murder of six million Jews by the Nazis was the most cruel, sadistic, and bestial crime in the history of civilization. Many have written about this, but few have investigated and documented the guilt of the democracies in the mass murder of Jews. In a book titled *While Six Million Died*, this aspect of one of the world's greatest tragedies is seriously and deeply investigated. Arthur Morse wrote this volume after years of research, which included a period during which he worked in a locked room in the National Archives in Washington. In addition to interviewing more than a hundred participants, he studied records in London, Paris, Rome, Stockholm, and the Roosevelt Library in Hyde Park. The culmination is a volume that has been read and discussed by many thinking and sensitive people in which the nations of the world are accused of indifference and apathy while six million died.

Why did you write *While Six Million Died*, Mr. Morse?

■ **MORSE:** I am not really sure that anyone can honestly explain his own motives. He can guess at them, but he may not be quite accurate. I am a journalist. I spent some years at CBS in documentary television, and in writing magazine articles about social questions. It seemed to me that the Nazi destruction of European Jewry, or the attempted destruction of it, was the most significant event of our times if one is interested in human capabilities—in the possibilities for human error, on the one hand, and human nobility on the other. It also seemed to me that if we are going to prevent genocide in the future, no matter who the killers may be, no

271

matter who their intended victims, we have to know how it happened in the past. There has been very little literature about this question.

W.B.: How does one go about writing a book like this?

■ MORSE: The techniques I had used in television and in writing for magazines were not very much different from those used in the book. The problem was to get the material. Much of it was classified as secret, although it is difficult to understand why, so many years after the event. There seemed to be no threat to national security. But to get to these secret archives I had to have clearance—and this took eight months.

You may be interested in a personal anecdote in this connection. My family lived in Stamford, Connecticut, for a while, and we had some very pleasant neighbors, people we liked but with whom we had very little social relationship. Some months later, after we had moved to Westchester, I met my former neighbor, who asked (rather hopefully, I thought), "Are you in some kind of trouble?" I asked "Why?" and he said, "Well, a man came to our door and flashed a badge and asked me questions about you and asked if I thought you were loyal to our form of government. I told him that I thought you were loyal but not very sociable." So if you are going to try to get clearance from the State Department, be sure your relationship with your neighbors is sociable.

Once you have clearance, the State Department, though wrong in many ways—I think it is fair to say that it is the villain of my book—is very generous. It is more generous than the State Departments of other governments in opening materials. In most countries one cannot get any material for fifty years after the event. In the United States, generally, it is twenty years after the event.

W.B.: How long did it take you to write the book?

■ MORSE: About two and a half years to research and slightly over a year to write.

W.B.: Has it appeared in other languages and in other countries?

■ MORSE: Yes. It was published in Germany with the title *Die Wasser Teilen Sich Nicht*, which means, I gather, "The Waters Did Not Part," which seems to be a rather eloquent title. It has been published in eight countries up to now.

W.B.:   The book documents an involved, long, and complex chapter of human indifference and lack of involvement in the rescue of millions of innocent men, women, and children. You write: "In the years between 1933 and 1944 the American tradition of sanctuary for the oppressed was uprooted and despoiled. It was replaced by a combination of political expediency, diplomatic evasion, isolationism, indifference, and raw bigotry, which played directly into the hands of Adolf Hitler even as he set in motion the final plan for the greatest mass murder in history."

How do you explain the fact that our American tradition of sanctuary was reversed during this era?

■ MORSE: In general, this period from 1933 to 1944 was marked by a departure from the American past in the field of immigration. We absolutely reversed the whole tradition of this country as an asylum for the oppressed. It was also marked by the fact that for perhaps the first time in American diplomatic history, we made no overt diplomatic intercession in order to aid people who were suffering through no fault of their own. Between the time that Hitler came to power—in January 1933—until December 1942, there was not a single American protest to the German government about their treatment of the Jews. This is utterly at variance with the way in which we responded to similar problems that occurred in the past. Many times in American history we interceded: in the Czarist pogroms against the Jews; the Kishinev massacre, which led to Theodore Roosevelt's intercession; the Turkish persecution of Armenians in 1915, which led to strong American protests. We broke the treaty of 1832 with Czarist Russia because of Russian pogroms, even though that meant a loss of income to the United States government. The House of Representatives voted 300 to 1 to abrogate the treaty of 1832. There always had been a past pattern of American humanitarian intercession.

I am not speaking of the ordinary people but of the government. Almost every aspect of government, it seems to me, violated our tradition during the period from 1933 to 1944.

Of course there were reasons, which we cannot go into. Unemployment, as you will recall, had its impact on immigration. Congress was dominated by fairly extreme reactionaries, and there was an increase of anti-Semitism as well. But, nevertheless, during that period we turned our back on our tradition.

w.b.: Some time ago the entire world was stirred by a play that appeared in America and Europe, called *The Deputy*, an accusation against Pope Pius XII. In your book you comment on the role—or lack of role—of the Pope: "The apathy of Pope Pius XII became the subject of numerous dispatches to Washington from Myron Taylor." Further on, you say, with regard to the Pope, "The self-imposition of the most delicate reserve begins to look very much like abdication from his leadership." Do you want to add to these comments?

■ MORSE: During this period, approaches were made by Myron Taylor, American representative to the Vatican, in collaboration with a number of other governments, to induce the Pope to take a position threatening the Nazis with excommunication if they continued their deeds. All of these efforts were of no avail. The Pope refused to take action. The evidence, which I have seen in American archives, seems to me to bear out in large measure the accusation in *The Deputy*. But having said that, one must also add that we cannot extend the apathy of the Pope to the whole Catholic Church or the whole Catholic population, because the history of Europe during this period is filled with examples of heroism on the part of churchmen, of nuns, of many lay Catholics who sheltered Jews.

We may wish that there had been more of them, but nevertheless we cannot forget that there were many. One of the things my book does is to reveal for the first time the role of Monsignor Angelo Roncalli, who became Pope John XXIII. He rescued at least 50,000 Jews. He was then the Apostolic Delegate in Istanbul, and he was approached by Ira Hirschmann, who represented the American War Refugee Board. Mr. Hirschmann described the plight of the Jews, and Monsignor Roncalli, who was aware of it, said that since the Germans were not killing anyone carrying a baptismal certificate, he would issue a great number of them for the

Jews in Budapest. He said that he hoped they would accept this in the spirit in which it was offered, as a method of saving lives, and not as a way of recruiting converts. Hirschmann said that he thought they would accept it. Some 25,000 of these certificates were distributed in Budapest. In addition, the future Pope John, who had been the apostolic representative in Bulgaria before the war, learned that Hitler had ordered the King of Bulgaria to send the 25,000 Jews of Sofia to Auschwitz. Monsignor Roncalli sent a letter to King Boris saying that if he sent the Jews to their doom, the King would face eternal damnation. King Boris, who, by the way, was not a Catholic, dispersed the Jews of Sofia into the Bulgarian countryside, where they lived in safety for the rest of the war.

There were others who helped during these episodes, but the man who was to become Pope John XXIII was indeed a most significant friend to the Jews.

W.B.: In this period there was one great personality, a towering human being, physically and spiritually, who is not remembered too often. I wonder how many of us recall the devotion and dedication, the dynamism and commitment to the Jewish people of Dr. Stephen S. Wise?

■ **MORSE:** During this period, Rabbi Wise was president of the American Jewish Congress and spiritual leader of his own congregation. He was in the forefront of every effort to try to awaken the United States government to its moral obligations and was constantly badgering the President, albeit in a respectful way, to accomplish this. He led delegations repeatedly to the White House. He helped author a document called "Blueprint for Extermination," which was a very detailed report of what was happening to the Jews based on materials coming in from occupied Europe. It seems to me that in every respect he worked tirelessly. Unfortunately, it was a very lonely effort. Nevertheless, if he had been listened to, I do not think that all that happened would have occurred.

W.B.: In your book you write that in November of 1942 Secretary of State Sumner Welles summoned Rabbi Wise to Washington and that the Secretary showed the Rabbi affidavits from Switzerland that supported the revelations of the leader of the World Jewish Congress. Just a few weeks before, the President had made an important announcement that the United States would join Great Britain and the other allies in establishing a War Crimes Commission. What was the War Crimes Commission?

■ MORSE: That War Crimes Commission, which I think origi- nated in 1942, was one of a whole series of façades—façades with nothing to back them up. The War Crimes Commission was first suggested, oddly enough, by Roosevelt to Winston Churchill in Washington. The idea was to set up a group of legal specialists who would begin the work of sifting through the war crimes and who would establish the judicial require- ments for treatment of war criminals. The hope was that publishing this would inhibit the criminals from carrying out their actions. In fact, the United States, which had first proposed the idea, was so dilatory that it had not sent a representative to London six months after the first meetings were held. Finally, the President chose a man named Herbert C. Pell. Roosevelt chose him because he had been a loyal political follower.

To me, as a writer, the evolution of Herbert Pell is a fascinating illustration of the possibilities of human develop- ment. Judging from the manner in which he was chosen and considering his background, one would have expected him to be ineffective. As a matter of fact, once he got to London and to the sessions of the War Crimes Commission and began to read about the Nazi atrocities, he became more and more inflamed. He realized that the War Crimes Commission really offered the possibility of punishing the Germans for their mistreatment of the Jews, because there was no prece- dent in international law for punishing a country for the way it treated its own citizens. He also realized that the worst perpetrators of these crimes might thus go free. So he began a personal crusade, growing angrier by the day, and as he did he aroused the antagonism of the State Department, which was opposed to this sort of action.

It was fascinating, because eventually Herbert Pell was told that there was no longer any money in the budget for him to continue as a member of the War Crimes Commission. He said then that he would serve for nothing, but he was told there was no precedent for that. His firing led to a wide public awareness because all the newspapers picked up the story. This led eventually to the later American position and a determination in the War Crimes Commission that Germans could be punished for the mistreatment of other Germans.

W.B.: In discussing Roosevelt's Secretary of State, you write:

> Hull had neither the time nor the conviction to go deeply into the refugee problem. He became short-tempered and rigid when faced with opportunities for rescue. For example, in 1940, a refugee ship carrying Jews who had escaped from France before the German occupation was turned away from Mexico. Mexican authorities ruled that the passengers' visas had been sold illegally, and the Jews were ordered to return to Europe for certain doom. When the ship made a brief stop for coal at Norfolk, Virginia, a delegation of American Jews, encouraged by Eleanor Roosevelt, visited Hull. Among them was one of Rabbi Wise's colleagues, Dr. Nahum Goldmann, a persuasive and tough-minded Zionist. Goldmann urged the Secretary to grant the refugees asylum, although they lacked U.S. immigration papers. Hull swung around in his chair and pointed to the American flag behind him. "Dr. Goldmann," he said, "I took an oath to protect the flag and obey the laws of my country and you are asking me to break those laws."
>
> Goldmann reminded Hull that several weeks earlier, a number of anti-Nazi German sailors had leaped overboard as their ship departed from New York. Since the United States was not as yet at war with Germany, the Coast Guard had picked up the sailors and had given them sanctuary at Ellis Island. Goldmann suggested that Hull might send a telegram to the refugees in Norfolk and ask them to jump overboard. "Surely," he said, "they will not be allowed to drown. The Coast Guard will pick them up and they will be safe for the rest of the war."
>
> "Dr. Goldmann," said Hull sharply, "you are the most cynical man I have ever met." Unabashed, Goldmann replied, "I ask you, Mr. Secretary, who is the cynical one? I, who wish to save these innocent people, or you, who are prepared to send them back to their death?" Hull dismissed the delegation, refusing to shake Goldmann's hand, but in the end he yielded to Mrs. Roosevelt's intervention and the refugees were admitted.

Can you comment on Secretary Hull?

■ MORSE: Cordell Hull, from my studies at least, was not generally an ill-intentioned man. He was a Tennessee lawyer, a very significant force when he was in the Senate because he was used by Roosevelt to bring together the recalcitrant Southern senators with the more liberal Eastern senators. However, he was totally focused on questions of reciprocal trade and ending tariffs. He had very little time for the question of humans in distress. There was some conjecture that the fact that his wife was Jewish played a psychological role in his attitude. I cannot say whether it did or not, but it is an interesting thought.

In this connection, when the German ambassador returned to Germany in the 1930s, he sent a note to his colleagues in the Foreign Office saying, "You know, we are made to look ridiculous in the United States because we accuse all important Americans of being Jews. There are enough important Americans who are Jewish so that we can be accurate about them." He made up a list—Herbert Lehman, Henry Morgenthau, and so on, who were Jewish. The name of Cordell Hull had an asterisk next to it. The footnote at the bottom of the page noted that Mrs. Hull was Jewish. But I do not know how important this was in Hull's life. In any case, the most charitable thing one can say about Cordell Hull is that he was a man of very narrow vision and grasp, and that he was uninterested in the problem. I am certain he never regarded himself as anything but a friend of the Jews. He could not relate this problem in any way to the American tradition.

W.B.: You mention in your book the names of people responsible for the evolution of the American policy. One was Robert Borden Reams, another was Breckinridge Long. Who were they?

■ MORSE: Breckinridge Long was a product of very socially prominent Virginia–North Carolina families—the Breckinridges and Longs. He married an extremely wealthy woman and used his money to cement his own relationship with the Democratic Party. One hears he contributed $130,000 to the Democratic campaign. He was not the most perceptive of men. I might mention that his thesis at Princeton was entitled "The Impossibility of India's Ever Becoming Independent." His career from that point on was an unbroken series of misjudgments. He was the American ambassador to Italy and wrote that line that people think is apocryphal—the one that says that Mussolini made the trains run on time. Of the Italian–Ethiopian war, he wrote: "This is a war in which there is no moral question that I can find." With that background, he was appointed by Franklin Roosevelt to be the Assistant Secretary of State in charge of every division of the State Department dealing with refugee problems.

Among his subordinates was Robert Borden Reams, a graduate of Allegheny College. He had been a hotel clerk in Washington, had taken the foreign service exam, passed it, and became a Foreign Service officer. He was put in charge of the "Jewish question." All matters dealing with refugee problems passed under his benevolent supervision. I interviewed him for several days, and in response to my questions he said, "Well, you know I was only a master sergeant." That may have echoes for you of a certain trial in Jerusalem. In fact, there was something in that: he was a very zealous master sergeant. He was important because he read all the incoming cables from American diplomats. When an American ambassador, such as Anthony Drexel Biddle who was the ambassador to Poland and a fearless, eloquent opponent of Nazism, sent in his telegrams, they were initialed by all of the men who saw them. Reams was one man who had read and initialed all the documents coming in from occupied Europe; and yet, whenever he was asked whether there was, in fact, a Nazi plan for the extermination of the Jews, he invariably replied, "That information comes from Jewish sources," tending to cast discredit on it.

In one instance, the President of Costa Rica, shortly after the beginning of the "final solution" in 1942, sent a telegram to Cordell Hull asking whether it was true that a Nazi plan existed for the extermination of the Jews and was being carried out. If this were true, he said, his government wanted to make formal protest, but he was not in possession of the information. Hull forwarded the telegram to Reams for reply, and he, in turn, sent a telegram to the President of Costa Rica, saying, "The source of that information is a Jew in Geneva." In fact, the source of that information was a wide variety of people of all faiths all over Europe.

These were two of the people who were on a lower level. Before we castigate them too severely, we must remember that they were carrying out American policy, carrying it out more cruelly, I am sure, than the President realized, and with more duplicity than he realized—but they were carrying out official American policy.

W.B.: Let us look at a higher level, the very top level. From 1933 until he died, Franklin Roosevelt was a favorite of the Jews. What role did President Roosevelt have in all of this?

■ MORSE: Let me say that this was one of the more painful parts of my research, because I had always related people who had nasty things to say about Roosevelt to the extreme hate-wing of the country. I do not have nasty things to say about Roosevelt. I use the documents. I use his own words and try not to give my own interpretation. Having said that, I think it only fair to say that however great he was in many other aspects in life—and he was certainly great—one does, in measuring Roosevelt's performance in this particular crisis, find him wanting. On his behalf, however, one must also put this in the context of his times.

One must recall the years when this country was engulfed in a terrible depression and there were more than 20 million unemployed, when Congress was dominated by men like Martin Dies and Senator Robert Reynolds of North Carolina, people who wished to eliminate all immigration. One must remember that our quota permitted at least 150,000 immigrants a year, although we never really fulfilled it. And one must realize Roosevelt's problems in marshaling this country's resources to overcome the Depression, to make Americans aware of what was happening in the rest of the world, to rearm a country that was isolationist in spirit—and at a time when anti-Semitism was, I think, more prevalent than today. His role was an extremely difficult one.

It is certainly not my intention in my book to imply that Roosevelt was an anti-Semite or that all our appraisals of Roosevelt are incorrect. I think it was probably Mrs. Roosevelt—and you will be happy to learn that none of your feelings about her will in any way be disturbed by this book—who put it perhaps most accurately when she wrote: "Franklin often fails to fight for those things in which he believes because he considers the political realities. That was the reason he never opposed the poll tax, or fought for anti-lynching laws, although certainly as a human being he was opposed to those."

Roosevelt was a political animal and operated as such, and I do not use the word *animal* disrespectfully. To me, a very touching example of the ideological split between the President and Mrs. Roosevelt was in 1939, when there was a proposal before the Congress to admit 20,000 German children and not to charge the numbers against the quota. There were thousands of American families who were willing to adopt these children, and a Quaker was going to be in charge of this nationwide program. It was beautifully organized, the labor unions were assured that the children would not compete for jobs, and so on. There was not a word from the White House in support of this bill. The President was off on the cruiser *Houston* on his birthday, and Mrs. Roosevelt sent a telegram, which I will have to paraphrase, but it was something like this: "Happy birthday, Darling. I hope you are having a lovely cruise. Can I tell Sumner [Welles] that you favor the child refugee bill?" There was no answer, and there was never any presidential support for the bill.

w.b.: In the Roosevelt era there was another great personality, a man who was Secretary of the Treasury, and in later years became exceedingly active in the Israel Bond organization. What was the role of Henry Morgenthau in helping to rescue refugees?

■ morse: Perhaps I can begin this with an anecdote that I thought was charming. It was told to me by Morgenthau's former secretary, a Jewish woman who was very disturbed because the Secretary of the Treasury was not really interested in Jewish affairs. Because of this, she tried to proselytize him.

One day a distinguished-looking rabbi, who shall be nameless—a tall, imposing, bearded man—came into the anteroom of the Secretary of the Treasury's office without any appointment and demanded to see the Secretary on important business. Mr. Morgenthau's secretary said that he was going off on vacation, and since the rabbi did not have an appointment, he could not be seen. At this point the rabbi began shouting that while these terrible things were happening to the Jews of Europe, the Secretary of the Treasury, himself a Jew, was going off on vacation and did not have time to see a rabbi bringing the story to him!

The shouting of the rabbi brought Morgenthau out. He was a very delicate man who did not like disturbances. He immediately summoned the rabbi into his office and tried to explain to him privately that he really could not see him that day and would see him within the next week or two. At this point the rabbi put his hand to his head and fell on the floor in a faint. Morgenthau was desperate. He summoned the Treasury Department doctor and his chauffeur, and he had the rabbi escorted down the corridor by the rabbi's young assistant.

Now, Morgenthau's secretary did not look Jewish. She was following them down the corridor when the rabbi turned to his assistant and said in Yiddish, "How did I do?" The secretary decided not to tell Mr. Morgenthau the story because it would only make things worse, and she said that this was the one secret she ever kept from him.

From this quiet beginning, Morgenthau, in late 1943, became a tiger, and the incident that touched off his wrath and played a very profound and positive effect on American policy had to do with what I think is probably the most disturbing episode in this disturbing book. In March 1942, the dictator of Rumania, Ion Antonescu, deported 185,000 Rumanian Jews to a terrible group of concentration camps in the Ukraine. These Jews, riddled with typhus and hunger, clothes ripped off their backs, brutalized by the Rumanian police, dwindled down to 70,000. In 1943 the German armies were in retreat before the Soviet counteroffensive, and in the path of the retreating Germans were the 70,000 Jewish survivors. Suddenly, Antonescu became a humanitarian. He realized that if the Jews were killed, with the tide of war now turning and an Allied victory in prospect, he would be regarded as a war criminal after the war. He therefore let it be known to the United States and the World Jewish Congress that he would be willing to bring back the surviving 70,000

Jews from the Ukraine, provided the United States sent food, medicine, and clothing. There was no bribery involved; this would go to the people. The money could be placed in a blocked Swiss account, where it could not possibly fall into the hands of the Nazis. It was to be repaid after the war.

This offer was reported to the U.S. government. It took nine months for the United States to authorize the transmission of the first payment of $25,000, because a license was necessary in order to send money overseas. This license had to be authorized by both the State Department and the Treasury Department. The Treasury Department agreed immediately to the license; the State Department refused.

As a result of the State Department's refusal, three officials of the Treasury Department, all of whom happened to be Protestant—Randolph Paul, Josiah E. Dybois, Jr., and John Pehle—drafted a detailed documentary report on these nine months of indifference. They titled this report "The Acquiescence of This Government in the Murder of the Jews." This report is printed for the first time in *While Six Million Died.* They gave the report to Morgenthau, who read it and was shocked by it. He retitled it "Report to the President," and made an appointment to see Franklin Roosevelt. He and the three authors of the report went to the White House on January 16, 1944. They handed the report to the President and sat there while he read it. That day President Roosevelt set up a rescue mechanism, the War Refugee Board. It was January 1944, eleven years after Hitler came to power, seventeen months after the United States had definitive information about the Nazi order for the extermination of the Jews. The War Refugee Board, without diverting a single American serviceman, without firing a shot, without sending a bomber or a fighter, without spending taxpayers' money because they used the funds of Jewish philanthropies, were able to rescue about 400,000 people within the next nine months.

w.b.: In connection with the War Refugee Board, you mentioned a number of names, among them Dr. Nahum Goldmann and Ira Hirschmann. What was Ira Hirschmann's work in connection with the War Refugee Board?

■ MORSE: The War Refugee Board sent representatives to each of the neutral nations. Ira Hirschmann was sent to Turkey; Roswell McClelland was sent to Switzerland; a Unitarian minister, Dr. Robert Dexter, was sent to Portugal. Regrettably, the American ambassador to Spain, Carlton Hayes, refused to allow a War Refugee Board representative to serve in Spain. He was the one American ambassador who refused.

Ira Hirschmann was responsible for the release of the 48,000 Jews who remained in the Rumanian camps. He did it very simply. He called on the Rumanian Minister to Turkey and said, "If you do not release the remaining refugees from these camps, you will be executed after the war as a war criminal." The Rumanian Minister asked if he could get a visa to the United States, and Hirschmann said he would try. And the Jews were released. That's how simple it was to effect rescue in this case.

W.B.: One name often in the news at that time was Joel Brand. What does your book have to say about him?

■ MORSE: You may remember the proposal that Eichmann was supposed to have made to Brand to trade one million Jews for ten thousand trucks. That story is rather widely known. It is a tragic story because we will never know whether or not Eichmann had the power to keep the bargain. Joel Brand said repeatedly before his death that it had not been crucial to him whether Eichmann could do so, but what was important was to keep the dialogue going in the hope that lives would be saved in the course of it.

Joel Brand was captured—that is a strange word to use, but that is exactly what happened. He was captured by the British and was imprisoned in Cairo. All the while he felt that he was responsible for the lives of millions of Jews. He was not sent back to Budapest, so one is unable to tell whether or not any lives might have been saved. Actually, even during the period when he was engaged in discussions with Eichmann, there was a slowing down of the transports to Auschwitz.

What is new information in my book, I believe, concerns something we have never understood—why this dialogue between Brand and the Germans was terminated, because there seems to have been no objection on the part of the United States to the deal. We know that the British captured Brand, but there seems to be more to it than that. The mystery seems to be cleared up by the fact that Andrei Vishinsky told Averell Harriman, the American Ambassador to the Soviet Union, that the Soviet Union would not countenance any discussion regarding the rescue of the Jews between representatives of the German government and Joel Brand. It was this message that was sent to the U.S. Secretary of State that terminated the dialogue.

Ira Hirschmann, in a very heroic bid, went to Cairo and forced his way into the office of Lord Moyne, the British High Commissioner, and demanded to see Brand. He was able to see him, and he submitted a character report on Brand that matched the report that Moshe Sharett, whom the British had allowed to come from Palestine, had also sent about Brand—that Brand was a man of great courage and very pragmatic, who seemed to know what he was doing, a man who realized that Eichmann's offer was probably a trick but was willing to go along with it to delay the proceedings against the Jews. The Brand case, of course, is a tale of failure. Nevertheless, the idea of a dialogue with the Germans was continued by a man named Saly Mayer, representing the Joint Distribution Committee. With the help of the War Refugee Board, he conducted negotiations with the Germans on the Swiss border, never giving them anything, but always showing and negotiating with Swiss bankbooks. The Germans did not know that Mayer could not release funds without the signature of the State Department. Yet Mayer was so skillful that many lives were saved during the course of these negotiations with Germans who thought they could get rich by releasing Jews.

W.B.: What is very distressing and disappointing is that one gets the feeling that people—Americans, even Jews—just want to block out this period. That we are not interested in hearing about those atrocities, or concerned enough. Perhaps this stems from an awareness that we did not do enough. I do think that what we are doing here—reminding and reawakening ourselves—is very important and necessary. There were other attempts to negotiate with the Germans in trying to save lives. What were the discussions with Hjalmar Schacht?

■ MORSE: There were attempts during the 1930s to see if freedom might not be bought for the Jews from the Nazis, which is really what it amounted to. It posed a terrible problem, because the Jewish organizations that were prepared to raise a great amount of funds were not prepared at the same time to fuel the Nazi war machine. This put them in a very difficult ethical dilemma. It soon became clear that what the Germans were asking for would only strengthen Nazism and Hitlerism, and so the problem became an extremely sensitive and difficult one. In addition, one could never be sure whether the Nazis were really serious and would carry out their agreements.

In the 1930s, complex negotiations were carried on with Dr. Hjalmar Schacht, who was Hitler's financial chief. At one point we seemed to be getting close to an understanding that was feasible—that in return for substantial sums of money, but not sums of money that would have made much difference in terms of Nazi power, Jews might be released after actually undergoing training in Germany for Palestine and other areas of resettlement. But when it appeared that Schacht was close to coming to an agreement with a man named George Rublee, an American who was the law partner of Dean Acheson, Schacht was suddenly removed from his job and another man put in his place. All these efforts came to naught, and to this day there is no reason to think that any of these plans were really feasible.

A distinguished delegation of British Jews visited the United States in the 1930s. They agreed to put up a third of an enormous sum to rescue the German Jews, although British Jews represented one-twelfth of the number of American Jews. This came to nothing because always at the critical moment the Germans introduced some new element. One cannot be sure that any German offer was really serious.

W.B.: You wrote that in May of 1939 the Gestapo permitted representatives of the German Jews to visit London to plead for immediate action with the Intergovernmental Committee. Why was this done?

■ MORSE: The Intergovernmental Committee was one of those endless committees set up with a noble charter and no resources, with the people at the head of this group really having no interest in what they were doing. What had happened was that discussions between Schacht and representatives of the Jewish organization went stumbling along month after month. The Gestapo became disturbed by the fact that there did not seem to be enough interest on the part of the Jewish community, and allowed representatives of Berlin Jewry to come to London to this meeting. It is a terrible story. The representatives of the Jews of Germany, in the privacy of a room with the two Englishmen who headed the Intergovernmental Committee, said, "You know that you don't have the funds and we know that the Germans may not mean it. All we ask is that you give us a note to the Gestapo saying you are interested in continuing negotiations and are serious about them." Lord Winterton, who was the leader of the Intergovernmental Committee, said, "You will not tell us how to conduct our business." They refused to give these people even a note and simply sent them back empty-handed to the Gestapo.

W.B.: With all that was going on, you said, "One factor that enabled Roosevelt to maintain his discreet silence without losing political support was the disunity of American Jewry. This was reflected most sharply in the conflict between the American Jewish Congress and the American Jewish Committee."

■ MORSE: Perhaps it is my fault in writing it that way, but if you take these individual sentences out of the body of the work, it leaves one with a false emphasis. It was clear to me that all of the Jewish groups, however differently they responded to the problem, did respond in their own ways and they did respond sincerely. Influential, well-to-do, highly placed Jews in this country chose to work more behind the scenes to influence the President, whom they knew socially. This was their way of trying to help. Others, more militant people, were not afraid to demonstrate and hold rallies.

My own idea is that while it was true that for part of the period there was disunity, most of this ended in 1938 with the *Kristalnacht*, when the Jewish organizations did come together. The feeling I have is that, given the attitude of the government at the time, it probably would not have mattered much whether the Jewish community was totally united or not. Apart from that, my own conviction—with which you may disagree—is that Jews, the same as everyone else, are very different from each other. They perform differently and their notions of how to operate under given situations vary. They are not a homogeneous mass. At that time they had different political attitudes, on foreign affairs and everything else.

I do not think this is the critical part of the problem. I do not think that people should beat their breasts now and say, "If only we had done differently," because it appears that all the cards were stacked against a successful approach. I really believe that.

W.B.: Isn't it true that part of the cards stacked against the Jews was America's immigration policy of that time?

■ MORSE: Before I comment on that, I do want to make a point that is out of sequence in our discussion. I am acutely aware that when we talk about the book as we are doing now, what we have is an endless saga of despair. We say, "My God, how terrible, how awful! Nothing but blackness!" Because of the nature of this discussion, we do not have time to go at length into the work of the War Refugee Board, although we touched upon it. I would like people to remember this: the War Refugee Board demonstrated that when the government of the United States makes the decision to take a positive approach to a problem that seems difficult, it can overcome the most incredible obstacles, and we did at that late period. It seems to me that we must always keep this in mind. This is the only thing that will prevent despair from overwhelming everything else.

The question really is, How does one get the government to do what it did in 1944, and did not do in 1936 or 1937? That is the lesson for the future. It is important for us to know how apathy and indifference and government failure lead to the loss of innocent people's lives. Yet we must not forget, and I would not want this saga of despair to make one forget, that when this government decided what it wanted to do, it did so exceedingly well.

Now, your comment about immigration demonstrates the reverse of this. Here is an example of how we missed an opportunity. Between 1933 and 1943 we admitted 1,200,000 fewer people than even our restricted immigration quotas permitted. In 1933, when Hitler came to power, the quota for Germany was 26,000. We admitted 1,700 of all faiths, not just threatened Jews. A year later, as the lines lengthened around the American consulates in Germany, we admitted 3,000. In 1935 we admitted roughly 4,000. Not until 1938 or 1939 were we even filling the German quota. At one time we had five times as many applications from Germany alone as we could give to the whole world. So this country of immigrants and sons and daughters of immigrants completely turned its back on its own tradition during that period. Every time we turned away a refugee ship, one could always find within a day or two the German press asking, "Who are the beasts, we or you?"

Some of you may have had terrible first-hand experience with this. As examples of how people were rejected, I was able to get some of the immigration case histories. Let me read you just one, which is, I assure you, similar to so many others.

This is a report of the American consul in Rotterdam, who in 1933 received seventy-four requests for visas to the United States. Sixteen were granted, and of the fifty-eight refusals, fifty-seven were based on the "public charge" provision of the immigration law—that is, that no one was to be admitted who was likely to become a public charge. Let me read to you about one of these likely public charges, a 33-year-old German physician and his 30-year-old wife. They had $1,600 and three affidavits of support from a sister, a cousin, and a friend in the United States. It was claimed that a second sister in the United States owned $70,000 worth of property and had $12,000 in additional resources. This was the consul's analysis of that case: $1,600 was insufficient; the greater part of the resources listed on the affidavits was unproved; and the number of dependents of the cousin, sister, and friend signing the affidavits was unstated; the cousin, sister, and friend had no direct obligation to the physician and his wife. The couple was refused admission to the United States on the grounds that they were likely to become public charges, and this went on and on. The public charge provision was misused, and so were so many other provisions, some of them written in the late 1800s to prevent the immigration of indentured servants and so on. These were later used to justify the rejection of Jews who, in every respect, fulfilled American immigration requirements.

W.B.: There is an important point that you stress in your book: "Of course, not all the actors in this drama practicing silence and inaction were bad guys wearing black hats. There were both nations and groups who wore white hats. There were the Danes, the Swedes, the Bulgarians, the Dutch, most of the French clergy, the American Quakers."
You single out some individuals for their special role in helping or trying to help. One of them was Prince Johannes Schwarzenberg. Who was he and what did he do?

■ MORSE: Prince Schwarzenberg was an Austrian nobleman who escaped from Austria at the time of the *Anschluss*, went to Switzerland and became an official of the International Committee of the Red Cross, which, I might add, had a dismal record during the war. But Prince Schwarzenberg broke the International Red Cross pattern. He decided that there was some way to get through to the concentration camps, and through great resourcefulness and ingenuity, he built up a list that began with sixteen people in Oranienburg and later was extended to more than 55,000 people who received food packages.

W.B.: Who was Roswell McClelland, the Quaker?

■ MORSE: He was the representative of the War Refugee Board in Switzerland, a man of enormous courage and resourcefulness, responsible for getting materials to the German underground and for working with Saly Mayer on the Swiss border.

W.B.: Raoul Wallenberg?

▪ MORSE: Raoul Wallenberg, one of the most extraordinary characters of this period, was a member of one of Sweden's great families, the Wallenbergs, a great family in banking, military, and clergy. They are not Jewish. He was sent by the King of Sweden in 1944 to throw a Swedish protective umbrella around the 100,000 Jews in Budapest. He rented, borrowed, and begged for thirty-two apartment houses and placed the protection of the Swedish crown over thousands of people who had no remote connection with Sweden. He later was captured by the Russians, allegedly our allies at that time, disappeared in the Soviet Union and is presumed to have died in prison. His family still lives in Stockholm.

W.B.: I would like to read a tribute that was made to Raoul Wallenberg: "The time of horror is still fresh in our memories when the Jews of this country were like hunted animals and thousands of Jewish prisoners were in the temples preparing for death. We recall all the atrocities of the concentration camps, the departure of trains crammed with people who were to die, the suffering in the ghettos and the attacks against the houses that had been placed under international protection. But also we remember one of the greatest heroes of these terrible times, the Secretary of the Royal Swedish Legation, who defied the intruding government and its armed executioners. We witnessed the redemption of prisoners and the relief of suffering when Mr. Wallenberg came among the persecuted to help. In a superhuman effort, not yielding to fatigue, exposing himself to all sorts of dangers, he brought home children who had been dragged away, he liberated aged parents. We saw him give food to the starving and medicine to the ailing. We shall never forget him and shall be forever grateful to him and to the Swedish nation, because it was the Swedish flag that guaranteed the undisturbed slumber of thousands of Jews in the protected houses. He was a righteous man. God bless him."

You write about another, totally different type of person, an American, a Jew whom you admired, Eddie Cantor.

▪ MORSE: Eddie Cantor was one of the most active people in the plan to adopt Jewish children from Nazi-occupied Europe. He told the U.S. State Department, "Don't worry about finding homes for the children; I can find 10,000 myself." Unfortunately, not much attention was paid to him in the White House. There is a sad little note that the President sent to his secretary, saying, after one of Cantor's innumerable letters to the White House about the adoption of children, "Send him a nice letter because he is very important in the National Foundation for Infantile Paralysis."

Nevertheless, Eddie Cantor was one of thousands of Americans, of all faiths and from all over the country, who were prepared to do anything to help. They had no power to bring children out of occupied Europe. They could only express their willingness to shelter them.

w.b.: Are there modern evidences of a Nazi era today? If so, what can we do about it?

■ MORSE: Unfortunately there are such evidences, and there are things that we can do. The lesson of the Nazi period can serve us in good stead. In fact, perhaps—if we can determine what can be accomplished now—this is really the way to memorialize the people who died. Consider the fact that the United States had the power, imagination, and resources to feed the children of Biafra [during their famine] and did nothing. I think it is a disgrace that we in this country, suffering more from overweight than any others, were unable to figure out how to get food to them when we knew one million innocent children would die in that country. I know there are all kinds of political problems, but when one thinks about it, the political problems are much simpler than they were in other periods of history. It was unbelievable that the Nigerian government could stand before the world and literally try to shoot down American planes bringing only food. I am sure that if some other government had threatened to shoot our planes down if we brought food supplies to a hungry population, we would not have reacted as quietly as we did to the Nigerian threat.

A second thing can be done. The United States is one of only two major powers on earth that has not yet [at the time of this Dialogue] ratified the United Nations Genocide Convention. This is the first attempt to consider genocide an international crime, to define it, to provide provisions for the return of genocidists who try to escape from one country to another, the first step toward an international court to treat cases of this kind. We actually helped to draft that convention in 1948, and no American president since Harry Truman in

1948 has called upon the United States to ratify it. The Genocide Convention should be ratified. There is a move afoot in this country to stimulate public support of the Genocide Convention. It is another concrete way in which we can try to see to it that legal provisions are adopted that would at least make such an event in the future less likely.

W.B.: I mentioned before what I consider to be the great value of your work: that this was one of the tragic eras of Jewish history, but that the reminder of how things were in those times can be valuable to us if such recollection can help us to spot the danger signals and avoid another such human catastrophe.

It is inspiring, I feel, to see a person gifted in a craft such as yours devote his abilities to the benefit of his people. For two and a half years or more, television and the printed page suffered a loss while you used your skills as a researcher and writer for this important work. It has proved to be a small loss, for the information that you uncovered and the lesson you point up will be valuable for generations to come. You have indeed added to the literature of our people.

15. ❧ Seeker after Justice

Elie Wiesel

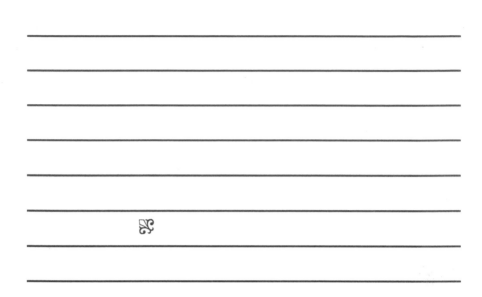

W.B.: Elie Wiesel's burning lucidity has had an indescribable impact on our generation—a generation that was seared by the Holocaust and yearns to discover some hope in the brutal darkness of our time. Mr. Wiesel's profound eloquence as spokesman for the silent millions unable to give utterance to the singular tragedy of our century has stirred the conscience of people around the world. As messenger of the mystery and majesty of the Jewish condition, his voice and vision extend far beyond the world of literature, encompassing the spectrum of the contemporary humanities. He is more than writer, speaker, and distinguished university professor and Nobel Laureate. He is one of the major figures of our time, instructing and leading humanity toward finding the lantern that will help us discover the way. It is an honor and privilege to speak with Elie Wiesel.

Mr. Wiesel, we have recently begun to notice a frightening phenomenon in the world and even here in America: the resurgence of neo-Nazism. In Frankfurt, Germany, for example, on the anniversary of *Kristalnacht*, a Nazi flag was flown at a rally of 800 neo-Nazis. We hear of increased Nazi stirrings. Moreover, we read of indifference to Nazi war criminals the world over. Worse, even in New York and Skokie we have had our share of indifference to the neo-Nazi resurgence. How do you respond to this resurgence in Europe and America? Why is it happening today? And does it frighten and disturb you?

■ **WIESEL:** I am frightened, because of the indifference to the resurgence of Nazism, fascism, and anti-Semitism. Admittedly, there are cranks in our midst. But people are indifferent to these cranks, and that is disturbing.

The fact that fifty years after the Holocaust there should be people in America and France and England and Germany who are not ashamed to be called Nazi is baffling. I am appalled that there are people in Nebraska who belong to a Nazi party, that there are two Nazi parties in Chicago, that there is a Nazi propaganda movement that publishes hundreds of brochures with the most vicious lies, with the most vicious distortions of our past; that they can publish pamphlets today claiming that the Holocaust did not take place, pamphlets called "The Lie," "The Big Lie of Auschwitz," "The Swindle of Six Million"; pamphlets that try to "prove" that the Jews invented Auschwitz simply to make business, to get money from Germany. And there is no outcry. That is what hurts me; that is what offends me. I find this all outrageous and ugly. Nothing is more vicious than when the victim is being deprived of his memory. Many of the survivors and some of the murderers are still alive. It is beyond me why we don't see a million Jews in the streets on *Yom Hashoah*, or any other day, to say simply *we believe* and *we suffer*, and *we remember*.

Am I afraid for the Jewish people? I said it a couple of years ago, and I say it now. Of course I'm afraid. I'm a *galut* Jew. I live in fear. But beyond the fear there is a certain hope, and beyond the hope there is a certain pride in being Jewish. These three feelings are not contradictory. But I am much more afraid for the world.

W.B.: I recently gave a talk to a Zionist group in Long Island, and after I concluded my remarks a man came up to me, very excited, and said, "You know, Rabbi, you mentioned Auschwitz and the Holocaust five times in your talk." And I said to him, "I really didn't count." And he said, "Yes. I sat there and I counted—five times." And then he began in a very strident tone to say, "Can't you forget about this whole business already? Isn't it enough?"

Have you found people saying to you, "It's enough already, we've heard too much about it"? Have you found that people want to forget about the event? And in particular, have you found Jews wanting to forget about it? If so, why?

■ WIESEL: Occasionally, yes. Once in Canada I was on television, and the interviewer, who was not Jewish, asked me: "Isn't it enough?" Well, such people are sick. What can I say?

Amnesia is a form of mental illness, and those who want to forget are suffering from moral amnesia. I remember a couple of years ago I read an article written by the Executive Vice President of the Jewish Telegraphic Agency, an agency that we support with United Jewish Appeal money. And this man who gave his official title in the article simply said, "Why not forget the whole thing? Isn't it enough?" And he went on to say that the tragedy was not only a Jewish tragedy, other people suffered as well. And then he added— and this proved that this man was sick—"after all, there was even music in Auschwitz." This man was a leading figure in American Jewish life, and the Jewish community supported him and tolerated him. I am ashamed of that.

W.B.: I have here two items. The first, from the bulletin of a California synagogue, announces: "Join us at our temple show of Jewish fashions through the ages modeled by our congregants. We will feature a multimedia cavalcade showing the mode of dress of Jewish men and women throughout the Dispersion from biblical times through the Holocaust and up to the present time."

Item two: At a special convocation of Johns Hopkins University, a very distinguished rabbi delivered the benediction on the occasion when an honorary degree was conferred on former chancellor Helmut Schmidt of Germany. Among other things he said, "It is gratifying to note that Germany has learned to stretch out the hand of brotherhood to all who are anxious to foster cooperation and friendship in a world torn by dissension and strife. What could be more welcome than to find Germans again in the vanguard of the forces of enlightenment and goodwill striving for the improvement of the human lot everywhere. These noble objectives coincide with the ideals of our United States of America." He then went on to praise the former chancellor lavishly. When you come face to face with items such as these, Mr. Wiesel, do you feel that the Holocaust is being forgotten, or being cheapened? Do you feel that one of the most tragic chapters in all of Jewish and human history has been diminished?

■ **WIESEL:** Yes, unfortunately, it has been cheapened, and I don't know how to cope with the situation. I don't know what to do. There was one phrase, one expression, on the lips of Jews who were there—do you remember it? "You will never understand." And these words are still valid: *You will never understand.* Those who were not there will never know what really happened. And those who were there somehow don't speak. Even those of us who try to speak, do not speak. We say certain words in order not to say other words. One day we shall speak, and that day the world may tremble. But that day hasn't arrived yet. For the moment, we are diminishing our own tragedy. We say less because we wish to be believed. If we were to tell the whole tragedy, we would all go mad—all of you and all of us.

How can I communicate so many tears and so many flames? Therefore, we speak less, but even those few words uttered by survivors have already been misused, have already been cheapened. I'll give you a shocking example. Some time ago I saw a movie. I don't go to the movies very often; I prefer books. But someone said, "You must go; it's about the Holocaust." So I went to see *The Seven Beauties*. What can I tell you about it? How do you handle vulgarity? How do you cope with obscenity? I don't know. You walk in the street and a drunkard spits at you. What can you do? What can *we* do? This is what we feel: we are being spat upon. Now, of course, we could keep quiet; we could just go on living. And I might go on teaching literature or philosophy or Jeremiah. But then what do you do when you feel that you survived only to communicate certain things? That too is part of madness.

So I confess, Rabbi Berkowitz, that I have no answer. I don't know what to do. I feel that to speak was not good, and not to speak was not good. No matter what we did, something went wrong. I used to believe that Judaism was a protest against vulgarity. I used to believe that Abraham was the first man to protest against obscenity. I used to believe that Judaism is a set of esthetic values, that there is beauty in it, that there is beauty in Jewish history. I used to believe that a Jew cannot but cling to that concept of beauty. Unfortunately, there are some people who don't share these views: they are vulgar. What can I do? What can we do? I don't know.

W.B.: Mr. Wiesel, in a brilliant and striking piece on the Op-Ed Page of the *New York Times* some years back, titled "Ominous and Unspeakable Thoughts," you said: "I feel threatened for the first time in many years, I feel that I am in danger. For the first time in my adult life I am afraid that the nightmare may start all over again, or that it has never ended.

Since 1945 we've lived in parentheses; now they are closed." Do you still feel the same way today? In the atmosphere that exists today, do you also feel that the Holocaust could happen again?

■ WIESEL: Yes, I do sense danger, more and more so. At the same time, I repeat what I said in that piece: I do not believe that there will be another Holocaust. Dangers will come, but massacres will not happen. The enemy will not slaughter Jews in the street. My fear goes beyond the Jewish condition. Whatever happens to the world happens to us first. That is true in all areas of human endeavor. The world discovered God, but we discovered it first. The world accepted, or pretended to accept, the Bible, but we accepted it first. Whatever happens in history happened to us already. Whatever they—the enemies—did to us, they—the enemies—will do to themselves. And this time they will do it to humankind. In other words, the world is in danger.

Look at what is happening today—the corruption of ideas, the poisoning of anything beautiful. The United Nations has become a farce, a sad comedy—sad because the United Nations, to my generation, represented a grandiose symbol of hope and faith. We really believed that somehow out of our great suffering, out of our anguish, a message of humanity and of hope was communicated. Now it has become a joke that is not even funny. The United Nations has no power, no prestige, no moral standing. It has nothing except a huge office building. It is sad, very sad. One more ideal has failed, one more illusion has faded away. The U.N. one generation ago was an altar, an altar shrouded in saintliness. There were people who believed in the U.N. There was something inspiring about it—peace, harmony, equality, liberty, freedom, justice. The charter of the U.N. is an exciting, prophetic message of hope for humankind.

Now what has become of the U.N.? Take the U.N. resolution that equated Zionism with racism. I took it seriously. I was concerned. Why? Because we have learned something in our history. Whenever the enemy—and the enemy may be an invisible enemy in the beginning but will become visible later on—plans to do something against our people, they begin with words. They plan first. In a way, they try to legalize their subsequent acts by formulating an idea, and the idea is that it is permitted, if not commanded, to persecute the Jewish people. I say the Jewish people because I do not allow them to make a distinction between Zionists and Jews. It is not for them to give me definitions of anything that has to do with Jews. We and we alone have the right to say who is a Jew and who is our enemy. That is *my* philosophy, not theirs. So they proclaim that to be a Jew, to be a Zionist, is to be a racist; that's bad enough. But it's also stupid. If there is one culture in the world that is hospitable to the stranger, if there is one civilization that is an answer to racism, it is the Jewish tradition and the Jewish civilization. Any person, black or yellow or green, regardless of color or race, any person who accepts the law of Moses and of Israel becomes a Jew at that moment. A Jew distinguishes himself not by the color of his skin but by his memory, by his moral commitment, by his sense of history and justice, by his solidarity with his people.

For the U.N. to accuse us of racism is indecent. Why did they do it? They wanted to call into question the Holocaust. They realized that the Holocaust is our strength: it's paradoxical, but true. We have been shielded by it for a generation. For some thirty years it wasn't fashionable to be an anti-Semite. Ten years ago, nobody would have said, "I don't like Jews," because of the memory of the Holocaust. So what did they [the U.N.] try to do? They tried to turn it around, to take it away from us, and to say, "You were victims of racism, but you yourselves are racist." That's where the danger lies. The next step? I don't even want to say it in words.

W.B.: Mr. Wiesel, some time ago you made the following very strong statement: "Today we live no differently from the absolute point of view than we did 500 years ago. We are no safer now than we were then. There is a danger, a very acute danger, that the Jews will again be blamed for the past, for everything that is wrong in the world, for all the suffering in the world. I can easily imagine Christians saying, in a crisis, *It is the fault of the Jews*. On the political plane, the accusations against us are liable to be related to Israel. What if tomorrow an American president were to declare, 'We could bridge the gap between ourselves and Russia or China if it weren't for Israel. Israel is the stumbling block.' Then the Jews would be a menace to the peace of the world. Here and there you can hear State Department officials complaining that were it not for Israel the U.S. would have good relations with the Arab world. The cry may yet go up, 'We've lost out because of you!' More and more they may hold us responsible for all the evil in the world. That is what frightens me."

You were frightened about this some years ago. Does it still concern you now?

■ WIESEL: I have exactly the same fears today. I have the feeling we are heading toward difficult times, a critical period in our history. Why? Never before have we been so united, which is good. And yet never before have we been so vulnerable. Something is happening to this society. It's a criminal society in which the leaders of the world openly say that they do not believe in values, and take the cynical approach to politics.

Colonel Muammar al-Qaddafi is a clinical case of madness, and yet nations on two or three continents say "amen" to him. Do you remember when Qaddafi came to France? The late President Georges Pompidou received him as though he were a king, with all the pomp and honors due a king! And Qaddafi didn't hesitate to say on French soil—it was reported in all the world papers—that the only solution for the war in Israel is to annihilate one of the belligerents, Israel. And, he added, the survivors will be welcome in Libya. You heard him say it, and nobody protested.

We know one thing: that a man determines his fate in small gestures from the beginning. It's the first step that counts, the first lie, the first crime. Then, it's too late. The very fact that today the entire world yields to Arab oil and other blackmailers is a bad omen not only for us but for the entire world. And of course, at some point, I am sure everybody, or some people, will turn against us and say "It's your fault."

Yes, I foresee dangerous times.

W.B.: Mr. Wiesel, you spoke about the relationship of the world to Jews and Judaism as well as the need for internal strengthening within the Jewish community. Let us turn to the state of Soviet Jewry. I was fascinated by something you once said about Arnold Toynbee, the noted philosopher and historian. Toynbee, you said, indicated that the only philosophy that could defeat communism is Judaism. What do you think Toynbee had in mind?

■ **WIESEL:** Toynbee hated Jews, and he didn't mean it as a compliment. *I* meant it as a compliment. Communism was conceived as a universal religion, as was Judaism. What was communism if not Messianism without God? We can understand why so many Jews were caught up by the communist idea. Parenthetically, when I was young in my hometown, I spent all my days and nights in the yeshivah. Only later did I find out about things in my town that I had not been aware of. I didn't know, for instance, that we had yeshivah students who secretly were communists. They would meet at night with the communist agitators and read Marx, Hegel, and so on. I understand why it caught their fancy. There is something in it—to redeem the world, to change humankind, to give freedom to those who have no freedom, to give bread to those who are hungry—it appealed to Jews, to those who were persecuted for 2,000 years.

Now one thing is clear. Communism failed. Judaism won. Judaism is alive despite our troubles, and we have many. But it is still alive and creative. The fact is that young students in Russia, fifty years after the Revolution, became Jewish—not only nationalistically Jewish but religiously Jewish. I remember when I came back from my first visit to Russia. I went to Paris and met with people like Manes Sperber who were former communists and had left the Party in the late 1930s. They are as antireligious now as they were then. I told them of the thousands of young people who come to sing and dance in Moscow on Simchat Torah. In *The Jews of Silence* I wrote about it and I stressed the joy, the Jewish joy above all. These former communists had arguments with me. "Why do you make it a religious issue?" they asked. "These youngsters are not religious. They come there because they want to liberate themselves politically."

These old-liners were wrong. Most of the young Russian Jews who come to Israel now come with *yarmulkes*. For them it is an important dimension to rediscover Judaism. This, to a Nikita Khrushchev or a Leonid Brezhnev, was the most painful insult one could imagine. Three generations of communism and of a communist regime. Read their manifesto, platform, and constitution. They knew what they wanted to do. They wanted to create a new man, a new *homo sovieticus*, the Soviet man who was supposed to be different, a man immune to anti-Semitism, without hate, without class struggle, without bitterness—a happy, good, peaceful man. Yet that dream failed. Each young Jew who dances in the streets of Moscow on Simchat Torah and studies Hebrew and wants to go to Israel is the living proof that communism was defeated. This is the reason, I believe, that the Russians were so involved in the Yom Kippur War. The Egyptians had thrown the Russians out some years before. So why did the Russians come to their rescue? Why were they so determined to punish Israel? In addition to the political considerations there is a psychological one. They wanted to punish Israel because of the Russian Jews. And here again we are facing the question of unity. What we do in Israel affects Russian Jews. What we do in Russia affects Israel. What we do *here* affects Jews everywhere. Today we live in a time when what a Jew does anywhere has repercussions much beyond his sphere.

w.b.: In one of your essays you point out that Jews in medieval times were wiser than we are today, indicating, for example, that when the Jews in France suffered, the Jews in Germany trembled. You make the observation that in the past there prevailed a sense of interrelationship and solidarity with regard to the well-being of Jews the world over. In light of this concept, what did you think of the effectiveness of the demonstrations that took place in America for Soviet Jewry?

■ WIESEL: Of course I quoted the example from medieval times, when communities were concerned for each other, in contrast to what happened during the Holocaust. There was a kind of eclipse in Jewish life during the Holocaust. The Jewish heart was not Jewish, or not Jewish enough. While Nazis were killing Jews, chasing Jews, humiliating Jews in Europe, other communities overseas were not concerned enough. Today it's not the same. Today when Jews are persecuted, we do something about it, or at least some of us try.

As for demonstrations, I am a bit of a skeptic. Of course I am for demonstrations, but I want them to be big—very, very big. In a city like New York, with three million Jews, we cannot get out half a million for a demonstration. Why can't we? Maybe it has something to do with the mentality of the American Jew. I always come back to myself as an example, because I speak of what I fully know. We were 15,000 Jews in Sighet, my hometown. When refugees arrived from Galicia, thousands of Jews would come to the train with bread, cake, and other food. No one remained at home. Imagine, if the third assistant to the vice consul of Israel had arrived, 15,000 Jews would have gone to welcome him. We would have even kissed his garb! How many Jews here would come to greet the prime minister of Israel? How many would take three hours of their lives to go to LaGuardia or Kennedy airport, or to fill the avenues? It may have to do with the atrophy of some fibers in some American Jews.

In the beginning we couldn't move the American Jewish community to help Soviet Jewry. *The Jews of Silence* came out in 1966. That year I returned to Russia, and when I came back I went to the American Jewish leaders to plead with them on behalf of Soviet Jews—unsuccessfully. You just couldn't move them. Do you know who moved them? Do you know what made the difference? Young people, our brave young people. They are our pride, our secret weapon. Young Jews were the first to organize demonstrations. They were the ones to shout, and they were the ones to urge their parents to come too. Their parents didn't come. They stayed home. Just like in Russia, in the beginning. Who rebelled in Russia? Not the old people. The old people were afraid. Not those of their sons who were former communists. But their younger sons, the 18-year-olds, the 20-year-olds, they were the ones to rebel, and they were the ones who defeated the Kremlin.

Imagine the poor Russian anti-Semites. They could die out of spite, they really could, as they saw humiliated, persecuted Jews who managed to do what no one else had done! Young Jews managed to change the policy of the Kremlin. Think about it: Jews were convicted and sentenced to death, and because of other Jews abroad, their sentences were revoked. Jews were sent to jail, and because of other Jews abroad, they were let out of jail. The Russian government never thought of allowing Jews to go to Israel. And then, because of some young students who dared to sing and dance, to shout and protest, the Kremlin opened the gate and let them go to Israel. During the Yom Kippur War, I was in Israel visiting the front and military hospitals. Then I went to Lydda to

welcome somebody, and I couldn't believe my own eyes.
There was a plane with 150 Jews who arrived from Russia
during the fighting! It was absolutely insane. On the one
hand, the Russians were sending missiles and weapons and
tanks to kill Jews, and on the other hand, they were sending
Jews to Israel!

w.b.: Some time ago, there was a debate raging over the issue of the
noshrim, Soviet Jews who were at that time dropping out in Vienna and
going to the West instead of Israel. A committee deliberated this very
complex issue of the dropouts. What was your reaction to this?

■ **WIESEL:** I am for education. I would like to educate these
Jews in Russia and show them what *aliyah* to Israel is and
what it used to be: a Messianic concept, a Messianic movement. And when I say a Messianic movement, I mean it. It
would be the second time in our history that there was such a
movement. The first came during the Spanish Inquisition.
And we must admit it: the Spanish Jewish community actually yielded to conversion. Very few left. Those who did were
an exception. The majority of Jews stayed in Spain. True,
they wanted to remain Jewish in hiding. But do you know
what happened to those who became Marranos? Substantially, they forgot their origins and kept only a few symptoms and symbols of their origins.

The same thing occurred in Russia, where in the beginning
the Jews were communists. Those Russian Jewish communists wanted to submerge, wanted to immerse themselves in
Russian history and disappear. What happens now? These
very Jews who then wanted to leave us are coming back! And
if they don't, their grandchildren come back. This is an extraordinary adventure, with Messianic undertones.

w.b.: Mr. Wiesel, having spoken movingly about Soviet Jewry, will you
now turn to the State of Israel? At the time of the last tragic war, the
Yom Kippur War, you flew there. Why?

■ **WIESEL:** I believe that to be Jewish is to have a Jewish consciousness. And that means that the Jew must always see
himself related to history. The Jew without history cannot be
fully Jewish. History, therefore, goes back to the beginning.

That's what I have tried to do in my writings and lectures. I've tried to show that Moses was not a mythical figure. Moses lives here. What he taught us is relevant to us. I've tried to show that Abraham, Isaac, and Jacob are Jews who are here today. Their problems are our problems. Their fears are our fears, and their defiance is our defiance. The same is true of the present; whatever happens to the Jewish people in the present touches every Jew, not just me. When I felt in the 1960s that history was going through Russia, naturally I had to go to Russia. In the early 1950s I went to India to see the last Jews of Cochin, and I went to Morocco to see the last Jewish communities in the Atlas Mountains. I went to Algiers where there was a sovereign Jewish tribe in the eighth century. I am obssessed with our people, and I am haunted by its powers.

Whatever I have to give, I have taken from our people. And that is why I am always so full of gratitude when I think of the people of Israel. On Yom Kippur [in 1973] there was a war. I felt I must go there—not to fight, for I have never fought. But during the Yom Kippur War I felt I must be in Israel. Let me tell you something that may sadden you. The day after the war started, I phoned a few Jewish leaders and I said, "We must go. If I go alone, it doesn't mean a thing." When Israel is at war I think we should show Israelis that at least *we* are with them. The results? I am ashamed to tell you. I suggested that we charter a plane for 100 passengers so as not to take away the El Al planes that were carrying ammunition. I said don't worry about money, I'll get the money from rich people. I was disappointed—they didn't want to go. They had all kinds of excuses. They were needed here. They had a business to run. They were needed to raise funds. I pleaded with them: Let us go and celebrate Sukkot with the soldiers in the desert! Imagine what it would do for them and us to celebrate Sukkot in Sinai? I used all kinds of romantic arguments and pictures to fire their imaginations.

Finally, I got twenty people who said, "All right, we cannot charter a plane, but we'll go with you." So I began to buy medicines and transistors for the soldiers in the hospitals. But then the twenty became seventeen, the seventeen became twelve, the twelve became seven, and the seven became two. The other one was a friend, a survivor, Sigmund Strochlitz. Of course, who am I to accuse them? There was a war going on, there was danger. Yet I felt sad. That was the overriding feeling even after we arrived in Israel. That war was different: it began on a note of sadness. Maybe the 1967 war was a different war because it erupted before Shavuot—a joyous holiday celebrating the meeting of God and His people—but in 1973 we were in a Yom Kippur mood, and it lasted well beyond Yom Kippur.

I remember Tel Aviv during the blackout, and being afraid to call friends because they all had children on the front. What will they say? What news will they give me about whom? There were many, so many, casualties . . . but then somebody said something beautiful and moving: "If a family is not afraid to pick up the phone, you shouldn't be afraid to dial." So we dialed. And then, of course, came the first visits to people who had lost their children. You know, usually whatever I feel I write. And usually what I write I try to publish. But not about this war. There was simply too much sadness. Something happened to me there. Something happened to Israel. Something happened to the Jewish people that year. Yet I wouldn't have wanted to miss it—if I had not gone, I would have felt deprived. When Israel goes through any experience, how can a Jew not be part of it? So in a way, I am thankful I was there.

W.B.: Today one of the pressing issues is that of the Palestinian Arabs. In your book *A Jew Today*, you write a letter to a Palestinian Arab. What do you say?

■ WIESEL: I try to explain to him why I feel sympathy for his suffering, but why I cannot accept the responsibility for what he is doing with his suffering. I cannot share responsibility with anyone who uses his suffering to commit violence, who kills at Maalot, who organizes the massacres at Lydda and Kiryat Shmoneh, and so forth. In spite of my sympathy for the suffering children among the Arabs—and I do feel sorry for them—I am afraid, as I say in my letter; I cannot go further and add that because of all that I am with you. I am not with them because they have misused their suffering against our people.

W.B.: In a recent interview you made a profound statement about Israel: "I believe Israel can and should personify a powerful message to the world, a message for the great powers." What is this message?

■ WIESEL: No doubt the message of independence, sovereignty, and humanity. This is the message we always try to communicate. Israel, strangely enough, has never been an empire. It has always been a victim of empires. Somehow Israel was never attacked by its neighbors—always by distant empires, by distant armies. Israel survived those empires maybe because it never wanted to become an empire, except in imagination, or in history. Our obsession was not geography, but time, history, memory. So I believe that even today when we are assaulted by so many powers, big and small, there is something that Israel can do. Israel can show how to resist forcefully and yet gracefully. And Israel can show that in spite of the pressures from the outside, we maintain our identity. We maintain our concept of ourselves, the image that we have of ourselves. This image may ultimately reflect the world at large.

W.B.: You have traveled across America. In your lecturing you have visited many synagogues and institutions. At one point in your travels you said, "I foresee a serious spiritual crisis in this country. The American Jewish community is going to go down." Do you feel that way today? And if so, why?

■ WIESEL: I oscillate. Often I oscillate between hope, extreme hope, and dark despair. That day must have been one of dark despair. There may come a crisis. Suppose next year, or the year after, there will be pressures on Israel to accept a settlement, to give up territories. Suppose the President of the United States were to go on television and say, "My fellow Americans, we are friends of Israel and always will be, and now we want to preserve the security of Israel, and Israel says no. And because of that, world peace is in danger." What do you suppose would happen to the American Jewish community? Will we have the strength to stand up and say, "No, it's impossible! It's wrong. The pressures are wrong, the timing is wrong." I'm giving you an extreme example.

Let me tell you that a crisis for our community may be dangerous because we have not been strengthened from within. I think the Jewish community is not strong from within basically because it lacks leadership. That is the problem. We have no moral leadership. We have had many presidents and vice presidents, and who knows what kind of presidents we had. But people who speak on behalf of a collective vision of history, of a moral concept of history? That we don't have. Because of that we don't really know what to do with ourselves. Education is not stressed enough. And the real education is to have our children study and discover the beauty in study and discover themselves in that study, and to assume all the world that they learn about, and to claim kinship with all the people that they read about. This can give us the strength we need. But we don't do that. So if a crisis comes, it may be a dangerous crisis.

w.b.: I fully agree with you. We are desperately lacking in dynamic Jewish leadership, and I believe that much more has to be done to develop it. In this context, in an interview with the French magazine *L'arche* some years back, you said, "The most representative international Jewish organizations preferred to adopt the philosophy of the ostrich." What did you mean by this?

■ WIESEL: I remember that interview. It was in France in the early 1960s before the 1967 war. I was referring specifically to European leadership, which usually yielded to the government. French Jews didn't want to anger the French government. Belgian Jews didn't want to anger the Belgian government. They felt so insecure that they adopted the policy of not seeing in order not to be seen. I think it has changed. I think that the Six-Day War in 1967 produced a major upheaval in history and a major psychological change in the Jew. And the Yom Kippur War only reinforced that change. Today even American Jewish leaders manifest less awe than their predecessors.

w.b.: In a magnificent address delivered before the Jewish Agency in Jerusalem, you said: "I am still worried. Because of others? No. Because of our enemies? No. Perhaps I sound naive, but the Russians don't frighten me, neither do the Arabs, and not the Chinese. But the Jews do." Why do the Jews worry you?

■ WIESEL: Because of the lessons of our history. Most Jewish catastrophes were preceded by a certain process of Jewish weakening from within the community. Jeremiah actually announced and denounced the weaknesses before the catastrophe. Take *Churban Bayit HaSheni*, the destruction of the Second Temple. You recall the terrifying example of Kamza bar Kamza. The blows came from the outside—but from the inside we were prepared to receive them. I am not afraid any more. We are beyond fear. What can the world do to us that it hasn't done already? What else can it do? In a way, we are immune. In a way, we are shielded by the event of one generation ago. The danger comes when Jews stop being Jewish. When they turn away. That is the danger. When they decide it's enough. When they decide to forget. When they decide, why worry only about ourselves when there are so *many* people to worry about—as if there were a conflict between the two! As if there were a conflict between being human and being Jewish! This is what disturbs me. As long as we shall remember the recent past, the danger is not real.

W.B.: In this context of Jewish destiny, what do you see as the uniqueness of Jewish history that distinguishes it from other histories and other people?

■ WIESEL: Vitality. I am constantly astonished by the vitality of our history. We cannot die. Strange, the Jewish people cannot die. Even if it wants to, it cannot. Our killers died, our enemies died, mightier nations than us have died, but we cannot die. This is part of our mystery. The immortality of our destiny. The *netzach Yisrael*, the eternity of Israel. I believe in it with all my heart. There is something, especially today, that corroborates this impression. For the first time, Jewish history and universal history coincide. For so many centuries they were parallel. Sometimes they were in conflict. Now it's the same history. And whoever does anything to the Jewish people is doing it to himself. If the world wants to destroy the Jewish people, I am convinced it will mean the end of the world. So that is Jewish destiny: to keep destiny alive. Somehow it is ironic. We have been hunted, we have been persecuted more than anyone by more people than any other, and here we are again in the position and the situation to force others to survive. And teach them the art and the necessity of survival. That sense of irony: it cannot but make me smile.

W.B.: You speak of Jewish education and of kinship with Jewish figures being the key to Jewish strength. As you look back and reflect on your own life, who had the greatest influence on it in terms of your thinking and commitment?

■ WIESEL: There were more than one. One was my grandfather, Dodye Feig, a Chasid who taught me Chasidism. Whatever I know about Chasidism, Chasidic songs, Chasidic stories, or Chasidic passion and compassion, I have from him. Then I had a teacher, Kalman, in my little town. And Moshe—the madman. And then in Paris I had another crazy character, Shushani; he left an indelible imprint on me. Actually every encounter is important in a person's life, to enrich it and give it a density that it hadn't had before. Some stand out. Today, for instance, my master is Professor Shaul Lieberman, the greatest teacher of this generation. I imagine that my *rebbe* in Israel would certainly also qualify, or rather his children would. The Lubavitcher Rebbe has had—in the meetings we've had—a very profound influence on me. Strangely enough, there are great people among us today, they are true guides and teachers. But who is here to listen? I try to listen. I try to listen to those voices that are still being heard and to those voices that have been muted. A Jew is he or she who listens.

W.B.: In a recent television interview you said that you were pessimistic about humankind, but optimistic about the Jewish people. What did you mean?

■ WIESEL: I don't make a distinction really, except for the purpose of explaining these attitudes. I believe that for a Jew the only way to be human is through his Jewishness. But if one is not Jewish, of course, he has his own way to fulfill himself. For a Jew, humanity goes through his Jewishness.

When there was a conflict, the Jewish people did not come out of the tests of history too badly or too poorly. We withstood the test. We withstood the trial. . . . We all know that the real tragedy occurred to the soul. It was a test over our souls: Were we going to yield to the executioner and accept his rules, or not? We did not. We were killed, and we shall be mourning for many generations and for many eternities because the losses were so great. But we refused to yield. Yet if today we don't have leadership, what is it if not the fact that a generation ago we lost so many teachers, so many rabbis, when they still were children? A million and a half children! How many among them would have become scholars and geniuses, violinists and scientists, writers and artists? That is it. It will take a generation or more to realize what we lost. But still we did not come out too poorly. The world that permitted those events to take place, that world failed the test then as it is failing the test right now. What kind of world is this? So much hypocrisy. So much cynicism. So much bloodshed. Today, for the first time in history, there isn't a single place under the sun where there is hope for humankind. There is no hope invoked as a movement or as an idea. There is no hope anywhere except in Jerusalem. And so, why shouldn't I have more hope for our people? We do invoke hope for our people, and we shall share it with humankind as a whole.

W.B.: Let me conclude with a Chasidic tale that best expresses what we all feel and think. Long before the great Levi Yitzchak of Berditchev became a rebbe, he traveled to the court of Rebbe Schmelka of Nikolsburg to inquire about the meaning and essence of a new phenomenon called Chasidism that was sweeping so many communities in Europe. When he arrived at the court of the rebbe, he was immediately ushered into the inner chambers. The old rebbe sat before Levi Yitzchak and listened as he asked, "Tell me, what is the meaning of this new movement, Chasidism?" Reb Schmelka, in turn, asked the young man if he knew how to study Torah. Suddenly, overwhelmed by the power of the Torah, Levi Yitzchak replied: "Ah, Torah, wonder of wonders!" And again Reb Schmelka asked the young man, this time, if he knew what the *Shabbos* meant. Suddenly, overwhelmed by the power of the word *Shabbos*, Levi Yitzchak could only reply: "Ah, *Shabbos*, wonder of wonders, Ah *Shabbos*, Wonder of Wonders! But what is Chasidism?" the young man persisted in asking. And all the old rebbe replied was: "Tell me, do you know what is the love of God and Israel?" "Ah, the love of God, Ah, the love of Israel," answered the young student. And with this he rose, knowingly, and left—to join the Chasidic movement.

You see, ends the tale, this is the secret of Chasidism, the secret of Jewish living and, may I add, of Jewish listening: the "Ah" that is evoked. The "Ah" that is offered. The "Ah" that is felt and transmitted. For equally as important as what we receive is how we receive it. How we respond to it.

To you, Elie Wiesel, great master, great teacher, great luminary, I would like to link this tale of Levi Yitzchak by exclaiming: Ah!—for what you have taught us over so many years in your writings and your lectures but also, most importantly, in your person and by your presence. For if I would have to choose today a Jewish Renaissance man, it would have to be you—scholar, teacher, writer, activist, committed Jew, concerned friend—*Ah*, for this we thank you. *Ah*, for this we praise you. But most of all, *Ah*, *Ah*, for this, Elie Wiesel, we bless you.

Professor Emil L. Fackenheim

16. ❧ Averting a Second Holocaust

Professor Emil L. Fackenheim

W.B.: In this Dialogue we turn to a world that is no more. I recall the unforgettable words of the late and lamented Rabbi Milton Steinberg in his immortal address, "When I Remember Seraiah": "There was piety in that world, and learning and reverence. Bread might have been scarce, but not books. It was a merciful world. But you and I know that that world is no more. Its old synagogues, where generations worshiped God, are in ruins. The books it composed and treasured, for which it dreamed and saved and scrimped, are all in ashes. And even its cemetery, where my forefathers sleep, has also in many places been erased. And so have its Jews, of whom there were six million—men, women, and children, some saints and some sinners, some learned, some untutored, some wise and some not so wise, but all eager to live, all undeserving of the fate that overtook them. They are gone."

In this Dialogue we will do something that we have been told by our tradition to do—to remember, to recall. Tradition says that we must understand, we must come to grips with the greatest catastrophe that has ever befallen the Jewish people. It was followed by the greatest event in 2,000 years, the rise of the State of Israel. We come together to understand one against the other, to understand why. Why did this happen? Dr. Fackenheim, in order for us to better understand your thinking and your observations on the Holocaust and the rise of the State of Israel, will you tell us about yourself?

■ FACKENHEIM: This is a very unimportant subject, so I will deal with it very briefly. I was born in Germany and left just in time in 1939, not because of my superior wisdom, but

319

because of what some people might call luck and others might call good fortune. I got out just in time.

Perhaps I should say a word on how I became a rabbi, and how I came to be here. My response to the events of 1933 was that I had to become a better Jew. I never really knew why I wanted to become a rabbi. I didn't last very long; I was a rabbi for five years. But I did know that I wanted to become a better Jew, and for this you had to know something. Around 1935 or 1936, when I was a rabbinic student in Berlin, we were perhaps not too dissimilar from the idealistic American Jews of today. You have to follow your conscience, be authentic. We arrived at the conclusion that for us there were only two authentic choices: either we could become *chalutzim*—pioneers—or we could become rabbis or scholars. If we chose to become *chalutzim* we had to abandon all aspirations to be rabbis or scholars. They don't need scholars in Israel, we thought then.

If we wanted to pursue our goal of becoming scholars and teachers of Judaism, we had to stay in Berlin and study. What was so foolish about it is that we imagined we had the choice. Fortunately, we didn't really know that Hitler was at the door. I think that if we had known, we would have been driven mad, and we would not have been able to study. That is why we made the choice we made. Some five years ago, a non-Jewish student in a mixed audience asked me, "How can you talk to us the way you do, and you are not in Israel?" I told him what I just told you. That's why I am here. But I said that I had never questioned whether perhaps I made the wrong choice until the Six-Day War. Now, I think that maybe I made the wrong choice.

A lot more could be said, of course. I think that if a German rabbi wants to know what he can ultimately believe, he becomes involved with philosophy. That is something that Americans can learn from the Germans—that there are too few Jewish philosophers in the world today. In Israel there are not many philosophers—they have too many other things to do—but in America there might be a few more Jewish philosophers.

I might dramatize it a bit, so perhaps I will add just two more points. My father was a lawyer trying to rescue—by legal means—Jewish property from Nazis who had stolen it. My father must have been succeeding too well with his legal cases, because one night he did not come back. Just to show you my youthful innocence at age 18, I went down to Gestapo headquarters and asked them, "Where is my father?" The S.O.B. there said, "He'll stay here overnight." I said, "I beg your pardon, you can't do that. I demand to see my father." And he said, "If you don't get the hell out of here, we'll keep you too."

That was the beginning. My father was let out after a few months, but not until the Gestapo had robbed his clients of their property. The end of my studies was the notorious *Kristalnacht*, when I was thrown into the concentration camp of Sachsenhausen. This, in this absurd world in which we live, was a blessing for me in two ways. As I said before, I didn't realize the real evil of Nazism. Did any of us realize the extent of the threat? When I came out three months later, I knew that I had to get out of Germany as fast as possible. I was in one of those prewar concentration camps that were meant only to torture and intimidate us, and, being a philosopher, I have never stopped trying to understand what that machinery really was.

w.b.: Your books deal with fundamental themes: philosophy, theology, the Holocaust, Israel. Let's start with a story. A theological student was told to read a book entitled *Seekers after God*. He went from bookstore to bookstore and was told everywhere that the book was out of print. He lived in Chicago, and he was advised to write to the publisher in New York to see whether they had a copy of the book. So he wrote, saying, "I am interested in securing a copy of a book you published, *Seekers after God*. Can you help me? The next morning, he received the following telegram, which read: "No seekers after God in New York—try Philadelphia."

We are all seeking God, each in our own way with our own understanding. You have written on this. Professor Fackenheim, what does it mean when we speak of God's presence in history?

■ FACKENHEIM: The idea that God can be present in history is an affirmation that I think came into the world with Judaism. The Greeks said that God can be present in history, but that is a very different thing. They had many gods, and in the Homeric epics some gods were fighting with the Greeks, others with the Trojans. Since the Greeks were men of great genius, they sooner or later decided that this made a certain fundamental theological term necessary. The gods one day said, "What are we doing, behaving like mortals, fighting against each other?" They decided to let mortals stew in their own juice, and the gods turned their backs on history.

Ever since, the Greek concept of God has been one that assumes God is not involved—that is, not present—in history.

At first sight this seems to be logical, because one thing can be said about history: it is full of cruelty and evil, of injustice, of starvation, of the suffering of the innocent. So how can one say that God is present in history? Not the puny gods of the Greeks, but God with a capital G? That's absurd. One must have either a very lowly conception of God, which the Jews did not have, or a very naive notion of history, which only some Jews had—for instance, the friends of Job, who said that if you get it in the neck, you must deserve to get it in the neck. With such friends, who needs enemies?

Now, the point I am making is that the Jews know as well as anyone that history is a tragic theme—so much so that we say it stands in need of redemption. The Jew is like a man who hangs on to history with one hand and hangs on to God with the other, and prays to pull the two together. I ask myself, why? Because we have had certain root experiences in our history that we cannot forget, that we must refuse to forget. The key root experiences are the Exodus and Sinai. These are the two events that give us evidence that God was present in history. The Midrash says that at the splitting of the Red Sea, the lonely handmaidens knew more than the most exalted prophets ever knew; even Ezekiel and Jeremiah saw only visions of God. But the handmaidens and the whole people, at the edge of the Red Sea, saw God Himself.

Martin Buber explains it thus: "How did they see it? On the verge of catastrophe, the Egyptian army behind, the sea in front, and then to their most radical astonishment, a sudden relief." Buber goes on to say that what made this a basic religious experience was that it wasn't just a fortunate coincidence. It was an astonishing experience, a presence we never forgot—a saving presence. I might go on from here to the commanding presence at Sinai. But these were the root experiences that formed Jewish consciousness. Ever since, the religious Jew asserts that, however sporadically, or however enigmatically, God is present in history.

W.B.:   In effect you are saying that these two root experiences that are fundamental to Judaism—the crossing of the Red Sea and the giving of the Torah—made the awareness of God's presence in history manifest to everyone, including the lowest handmaidens.

■ FACKENHEIM: The problem that then arises, of course, is this: What do you do when history has become a dead past? Then people say, "It is so long ago, it doesn't matter." As the young of today might say, "It's irrelevant." And they are right in demanding relevancy. What does relevance mean? It should be an experience for us.

What are we really doing, for instance, on Pesach? The seder seems to be one of the most marvelous, one of the greatest of Jewish celebrations. Indeed, Jewish theology is essentially celebration. We are reminded of old stories. We are supposed to re-live them. I am reminded of a most moving account that was reconstructed as a result of the impact of the fact that the Warsaw Ghetto uprising started in Pesach. The story goes something like this: It's Pesach, the uprising is starting, and as they wait for the Germans to come on the next night, one man suddenly asks—because they have other things on their minds—whether they realize what night it is. Someone answers that it is the first seder night. Another retorts, "Don't give me that. Who cares? The Nazis are outside." Then in the middle of the night, the same person says, "Maybe you have something. You lead us in the seder."

The first man responds, "Who? Me? I know very little. Besides, where are the matzohs?"

"Never mind matzoh; isn't the bread we have here miserable enough for you?" the other replies. And then he starts to remember: "This is the bread of affliction that we ate in the land of Egypt." Someone adds, "and You liberated us." Someone else says, "What do you mean 'liberated us'? Is it still true?" And the story ends—yes, it is true. We are miserable, but we are free, because in spite of the worst of all hangmen in our history, worse than Pharaoh, we die free.

I give you just one of the greatest examples that I can think of, of how the Jew can make the past live in the present because there is always the question, Can the past still be reenacted? Or has the present reality, for better or worse, made it irrelevant? I think that is a perpetual challenge to Jewish faith.

W.B.: You have explained about the root experience; you have explained about God's presence in history. Let's move to the period of the Holocaust, a period that all of us lived through. I have a question that *I* don't ask, but that so many other people ask, the same very fundamental question. How do you answer people who say that God wasn't present, that He had nothing to do with the Holocaust?

He gave man freedom, and man abused it; it is man's fault—that is one side of the coin. On the other side, how can we pray to a God and worship a God who allows six million Jews and seven million Christians to be destroyed? Can we believe in such a God? How can you continue to confirm His presence in history?

■ FACKENHEIM: You are giving me all the nasty questions. I feel honored, but I also feel on the spot. Let me begin by saying something autobiographical. It took me many years to get around to writing anything about the Holocaust. As a result of my personal experience, I can answer in two different ways, but without knowing whether I am right. One group of people says that the longer the Holocaust is past, the more it will be forgotten. I disagree with that. On the basis of my own experience, I say the opposite is true. The Holocaust was such a trauma that it will take perhaps another whole generation before Jews can really even face it. Perhaps more than a generation. The great scholar Gershom Scholem said that after the expulsion from Spain, the greatest Jewish catastrophe prior to the Holocaust, it took much longer before the Jews were able to give a religious response to it—Cabalistic mysticism.

This may sound like an evasion of the question. But I would say that the time is not yet ripe for an adequate religious response to the Holocaust, and I totally disagree with Richard Rubenstein, who said "God is dead." The op-

tions are only two or three, like playing around with mathe-
matical possibilities. They don't increase with the passage of
time, he said. I say that that is not the way a religion and a
faith works. Let me say what my earlier view was and what
happened. Martin Buber, whom I have already mentioned,
coined in the fifties the expression based on earlier Jewish
thought, that there is an "eclipse of God." It means neither
that we are blind nor that the sun has disappeared, but
rather that something has come between us and God. In this
case, of course, it was the Holocaust. There is also the
imagery, the implication of the hope that, just as an eclipse
will pass, the time will pass when this eclipse will be over.

I must say that this idea sustained me for many years. It
would answer all the questions you have asked me. Certainly
you can pray to a God who is in eclipse. The Psalmist asks,
"Wherefore doest Thou hide Thy face?" But he goes on
praying. Nothing is explained, and you certainly have not
committed the sin of attributing to God the killing of a
million children in the Holocaust for no good reason. I would
always have rejected that. So it seemed very satisfactory and
also in line with Jewish tradition.

But, this is the stumbling block it created for me over the
years: One might ask, and this is going to sound quite brutal—if God is not present when we need Him most, who
needs Him? That was my stumbling block.

W.B.: Was that the reason—excuse the interruption—why you did not
write for a period of twenty years?

■ FACKENHEIM: That was only one reason. I would say that
the uniqueness of the Holocaust is a shocking and scandalous
thing. We are now off on a tangent for a moment, but I think
it is very important. When I first came to Canada during the
war, I found that my fellow Jews took great comfort in the
fact that Jews were not the only ones whom the Nazis persecuted.

Even from the standpoint of the non-Jews, it was a very
good thing to emphasize that although the Nazis were racists—and, of course, they were—they weren't racists of an
ordinary kind. They singled out Jews for special treatment.

With the exception only of the Gypsies, all the other supposedly inferior races were maltreated, but they were not "exterminated"—that was reserved for Jews and Gypsies.

But let us get back to the subject. It seemed a more comforting notion, for one thing, not to be singled out. One thing finally made me realize that it is necessary to talk about the Holocaust. You know the saying "Where there is smoke there is fire." I think that this is the most terrible concept related to the Holocaust, because it means that one blames the victim: If the Nazis hated the Jews all that much, then there must have been something in the Jews that caused it. We were afraid that in stating the truth about Nazi anti-Semitism, we would increase anti-Semitism elsewhere—as well as Jewish self-hatred.

Let me say, totally and flatly, that I don't think any kind of anti-Semitism has anything to do with what Jews do. Anti-Semitism has absolutely nothing to do with what Jews do. It is really a Gentile problem. It is our problem only because we are the victims.

If you decide that you are not going to tell your children about the Holocaust because it is a great trauma, you should know that they are going to learn about it anyway. And when they do, they will think that you didn't talk about it because you had a guilty secret. What was the guilty secret? Where there is smoke, there is fire. I think this is the most dreadful distortion. It is profoundly untrue, and therefore it is necessary for us to speak of the Holocaust.

I couldn't face it myself. The religious reason, of course, was one factor. If one faces the fact that whatever the sins of the Jews might have been, the punishment of the Holocaust was totally and absolutely out of proportion, it becomes a terrible problem for one's faith. It is terrible to face the Holocaust and believe in God.

At least Jews have some small freedom of action that Christians generally do not have. It is very important to understand this great difference between Judaism and Christianity. The general, normative Christian teaching is that humans can never be right against God. God is always right. Therefore, to protest against God is a sacrilege. Theologians ignore the fact that Jesus, acting as a Jew, once in the New

Testament protests against God, saying, "Oh, God, why hast Thou forsaken me?" In Judaism, protest against God is there all the time. Abraham says, in connection with Sodom, "Should the Lord of justice not be just?" Job protests his innocence and says, "I may deserve punishment, but not this." And so it goes throughout all of Jewish history. Our very name, Israel, means "one who wrestles with God."

So I think we have to be very careful here to try this within a Jewish framework. The real problem it raises is how much protest, how much wrestling with God is humanly possible? To this I have as yet no adequate answer, but perhaps the time is too soon.

W.B.: You wrote, "The Nazi Holocaust has no precedent in Jewish history." What about those who lived in the Chmelnitzki period and who were destroyed? Wasn't that as traumatic as the six million? What about those who lived in 1492 with the Inquisition; was this not equally traumatic for the times? You further say: "There is also no precedent for the Holocaust in general history. Even actual cases of genocide still differ from the Nazi Holocaust in at least two respects." How can you, in looking at history, say that this particular period has no precedent in Jewish history? How did the Nazi Holocaust differ?

■ FACKENHEIM: Let me first make one thing as clear as I can. I have been misunderstood time and again, particularly when I compare this tragedy with non-Jewish tragedy. I am seen as some kind of Jewish chauvinist who thinks it is a worse tragedy when Jewish children are murdered than non-Jewish children. That is not in any way the truth.

Let us just contrast general tragedies with this particular Jewish tragedy. What I mainly intended by that statement was to stress the effect the Holocaust had on Jewish faith. Let us suppose, for example, that Martin Luther King alone had not been murdered, but that genocide had been committed against his people. Religiously, it would not have constituted a problem for those of his faith. His people would have been murdered because of their race, not because of their faith. In 1492, and during the Crusades, the Jews were murdered for their faith, and, of course, many Christians were also murdered for their faith. That is the category known as martyrs. What is meant by martyrdom? In Judaism and

Christianity both, and I think Islam also, there is a concept that a glorious moment, albeit a terrible one, comes when a person chooses to die for his convictions rather than become an apostate. Now what was the uniqueness of the Holocaust? The uniqueness of the Holocaust was that the Jew was not murdered because of his faith, but for reasons that had nothing to do with his faith. He was murdered because of the Jewish faith of his great-grandparents. If these great-grandparents in pre-Nazi Europe had not obeyed the minimum of Jewish faith, bringing up Jewish children, then their distant offspring might not have been among the murdered at Auschwitz. This is the terrible unprecedented trauma.

You might say that Chmelnitzki came a little close to it, but his wasn't a rationally conceived enterprise to try to murder even the last of the Jews. The Crusades are in an entirely different class because they gave Jews a choice. But in the Holocaust it was as though the devil himself had plotted for four thousand years how to make an end to Judaism. How do you make an end to Judaism? What if they killed you for being a Jew? They would make a martyr out of you. But if the victims of your Jewish faith are your great-grandchildren, that is a dirty trick, to put it mildly.

This creates a dilemma that is so horrifying that there is no precedent. Shall I follow the religious commandment that I bring up Jewish children? Or shall I follow the *moral* commandment?—and then I shall not expose my great-grandchildren to being murdered. Just as the atomic bomb created a new situation for humankind, so the Holocaust created a new situation for Jews. Five generations ago, people knew that there were anti-Semites. We knew that there would be the occasional pogrom. We knew that there were Jews who might be exposed to choosing whether they wanted to be apostates or pious Jews. But they didn't know that there would be a system that would systematically kill everyone who had Jewish great-grandparents.

We know now that it has happened, and therefore it is possible. We are therefore confronted with the post-Holocaust faith. How can you cope with this contradiction? It is morally impossible to expose one's grandchildren to being murdered. Yet it is necessary for us as Jews to bring up

Jewish children. We must follow either alternative or deny either alternative. How can you overcome this contradiction? I know of only one way: A hope and an iron determination that there shall be no second Holocaust. A commitment as holy as Israel itself.

W.B.: Do you really feel today that the world has finally learned? And that a second Holocaust is not possible?

■ FACKENHEIM: We should not ignore that there is perhaps a glimmer of hope. Let me first say that the world has not learned very much. There was a debate between Richard Rubenstein, whom I mentioned before, and someone else, whose name I have forgotten, in print some years ago. The question was this: "As a result of there having been a Holocaust, is it less likely or more likely that it would recur?" Rubenstein, being grim and dark, asserted that it is more likely, and I think he made the better case. To say that it is less likely is to indicate that the world has learned a moral lesson. To say it is more likely is to say that an evil once done becomes easier the second time.

If you look at the evidence since the Holocaust, you find as much to encourage one side as the other. Who is willing to call himself an anti-Semite today? Remember the days when people gloried in being called anti-Semitic? So, superficially, there has been a tremendous advance, but actually it is only skin deep because the anti-Semite has learned to use code words. Instead of calling themselves anti-Semites, they call themselves anti-Zionists.

If there is any guilt in the world about the Holocaust, there is a very neat way of neutralizing it. I think it was Toynbee who said it first: The Israelis are the new Nazis. And ever since he said it, the forum of so-called moral verity has gone lower and lower and lower. The United Nations has become the world center of anti-Semitism. That is how bad it has become. Nobody calls it anti-Semitism. Anti-Zionism is the tactic of a shocking band of scoundrels. We might say that Americans still pay for it, because it is anti-American too. The whole center has shifted. Anti-Semitism has been exported to countries where there are no Jews. It is a sinister instrument in China, where there are virtually no Jews, and in India.

If you analyze the phenomenon of anti-Semitism, you'll see that there is always a core of confirmed anti-Semites, and then all the opportunists who cluster around them. We see this unholy combination in newly found oil power plus fanatics. And let us not forget all the Nazis who went to Egypt and other Arab countries to influence policies there. This goes right back to the Grand Mufti, who was an honored guest in occupied Jerusalem. All these things fit together, and I think we are faced with a grim reality.

The world is buckling under, and the first people they are selling out are once again the Jews, this time in the State of Israel. I make one prediction; not that it is particularly hopeful—it is a grim prediction. I think that few predictions are safe. When Chamberlain said, in 1938, "Peace in our time," I was only a young student and politically naive; but I knew Nazis, and I was in Germany, and I knew it wasn't true. He was not going to succeed in buying peace for England by selling out the Jews. I think it is absolutely certain that the Western world will not succeed in buying peace for itself by selling out Israel for Arab oil. From this, of course, we can take small comfort. Once before it was too late for us. Hitler was defeated, but the Holocaust had been perpetrated.

It is hard for me to say that I should make optimistic predictions. When I say there must be no second Holocaust, that is not a prediction, that is not a prophecy; it is a commitment. An essential part of that commitment is the integrity and safety of the State of Israel, a living symbol that there must be no second Holocaust. And as far as we are concerned, it must mean this: there can be no Jew who backs away from the State of Israel in its hour of trial. No one. Let us use all of our strength, however little it is, to avert this eventuality. I say be faithful, stand by the State of Israel in its hour of trial, because there is the collected testimony against the evil that Hitler wrought. The world wants to forget it, the world wants to distort it. We cannot let them. We must have the faith that we can pass through this period of trial. These are the days when we are often on the verge of despair—the few against the many. How often has this happened before? Then we need endurance, and then a new miracle comes, but this doesn't mean that you can count on miracles.

The Israelis know it so well. It means that just as we have sudden surprises that are terrible, you might say the whole of Jewish existence is bound up with the opposite—namely, that there are also happy surprises. We have survived; it's a miracle. The name Israel is found on a victory column of the Egyptian King, Menenptah, who reigned several thousand years ago, and it says that if Israel is destroyed she will never rise again. Have you ever heard of Menenptah? Maybe 2,000 or 4,000 years from now Jews still will live, and people will ask, "Have you ever heard of Arafat?"

W.B.: One of your most quotable statements was that in addition to the 613 commandments that it is incumbent upon the Jew to fulfill, you advocate one more, and that commandment is: "Thou shalt survive." The fact of the matter is that there is a great difference between 1933 and 1940, and today. The times are different. We have learned a great deal: We have learned from Soviet Jewry; we have learned the political game; we have learned to express ourselves in an entirely different way. I sincerely believe that the key to solving the Middle East problem lies in Washington, and nowhere else; that is where the key is to be found.

Now, when we speak of Jewish survival, I would like to know what is wrong with our Jewish intellectuals. Do they suffer from self-hatred, or do they think that they are going to stand under a greener umbrella? Why is there this ambivalence? What's wrong with the Jewish intellectual?

■ FACKENHEIM: I would not say that your statement applies to all Jewish intellectuals. The chairman of my department, who is not Jewish, said this about John Foster Dulles, who is not remembered very fondly by many people: "Dulles went to Harvard. When you go to Harvard, they don't cure you of your stupidity; they make a system out of it." I have found in thirty years of university professorship that the intellectuals and professors are very intelligent people, but they can combine intelligence in their own fields with the most exasperating lack of common sense in all other fields. It is really most amazing. So then when they get involved, they make such a mess out of things that you end up wishing they *hadn't* gotten involved. They will say that if Jews are entitled to Jewish nationalism, then Palestinians are entitled to Palestinian nationalism. So there is a conflict between two nationalisms, and this conflict is tragic.

A tragic conflict is not between right and wrong, but between right and right. What do you do about a tragic conflict? There is no perfectly just solution; in fact, there is no perfectly just solution to anything in history; there has to be compromise, give-and-take on both sides. In this story, the Jews have done all the giving and the Arabs have done none. Palestine was supposed to be a national home for the Jews. The details weren't quite clear, so they divided it up in 1922, and what is now Jordan became the Arab part; then they divided it up some more when the Arabs were not satisfied.

Again the Jews accepted. Then the U.N., different from what it is now, underwrote the Jewish State when the Jewish State declared itself. The next day several Arab armies invaded it.

These facts everybody knows. Why didn't a Palestinian state come into being afterward? Because the grandfather of the present King Hussein of Jordan took over. And so it has been to today. Yassir Arafat [head of the P.L.O.] brings us right back to where it started, because not even the most stupid intellectual doubts that a state for all—a secular state—means the destruction of the State of Israel. I ask myself, How can the intellectuals be so stupid? The ordinary businessperson understands it. I really have no answer to this. Again, as the head of my department used to say, "The more logical you become about some things, the more illogical you become about others." But there is a deeper thing; we are talking about Jewish intellectuals. What I said before really applies to non-Jewish intellectuals. I met a colleague the other day who asked me, "How are you?" I said, "Terrible, because Arafat is going to speak at the U.N." "You think he shouldn't speak?" my friend asked. "No, because he is a murderer. He wants to destroy Israel, and I don't think such a person has a right to a forum," was my answer. My friend had never thought of this before. I don't know whether it made any difference.

Now we come to Jewish intellectuals. I think that Jewish intellectuals in large numbers are sick; they are sick in a Jewish way, and you might say that it is not their fault. They are Jews from hard-working families who have a 100-year history of "liberation," and they look to the university as the great institution of their fulfillment. Many of them come from good Jewish homes. Then they come to the university, and what do they find? English studies, French studies, Russian studies, but Judaism is represented only by the so-called Old Testament, which, of course, is a propaganda term. In a Christian theological seminary, that is proper—to them it *is* the Old Testament. To call it by a Christian name at a nonsectarian university is propaganda.

So, there have been 100 years of the traumatic experience of young Jewish people thinking they are somebody, and then entering universities only to see that the subject of Judaism doesn't exist. This is an academic anti-Semitism, and it has been permitted to go on for too long. The result is that today we find Jewish professors of history who tell students who want to study Jewish history that there is no such subject.

But I wave my hand and say, I am here, I am alive, so there must be Jewish history. Jews belong to German history, French history, and American history, but there is no Jewish history. It is a sickness that is part of a general sickness in the modern world. The Jews are supposed to be an anachronism. It is all very well to tolerate Jewish individuals, acknowledge their contribution to civilization, but it always has to be somebody else's civilization.

It is time to put an end to this. You have to look beyond the present crisis. Jewish studies have to come onto the map of every campus in America. Let me quote somebody I don't very often quote. Norman Podhoretz describes how he came to Columbia University and after a while an English professor took him aside and said, "Look, it is time you gave up all this parochial Judaism and begin Universalism." Podhoretz reports the incident and adds, "What they call *Universalism* is just parochialism." That was a great insight. It is about time for Jews on campus to become a little more militant on behalf of Judaism. It adds up to a very sad thing. The leadership that we should be getting from most Jewish intellectuals, we get from only a very few.

W.B.: You spoke some time ago at St. John the Divine. The address was to have appeared in the *Encyclopaedia Judaica*. I believe they asked you to write on the theological significance of the State of Israel. Instead you spoke—delivered a paper—on "What Connects the Holocaust with the State of Israel." Can you just give us a rough outline of what you said?

■ **FACKENHEIM:** I rejected the original great subject because of a sudden fear. We grapple with the question of survival. We are almost tempting God when we speak at this point in history of the theological significance of the State of Israel. I think what one can say is this: What connects the Holocaust with the State of Israel? I don't mean to give an historical explanation. I mean that there is a moral imperative. After the Holocaust, a moral imperative exists that there must be a State of Israel. When you go to Israel you ask yourself, Where do the people of Israel get the strength to hold out on all those many fronts? You see the day-to-day inflation, the astronomical fact of being daily in danger. Where do they get the strength? There are many answers, of course. The Orthodox have theirs; the *chalutzim* have theirs; but what binds the people together? I can think of no better answer than Kibbutz Yad Mordecai. Mordecai was one of the leaders of the Warsaw Ghetto uprising. When he felt that he was close to capture by the Nazis, he feared that they would torture him and extract secrets, and he committed suicide. That uprising, about which I have spoken in a different context, was an extraordinary, inspiring, and also mystifying thing for us to contemplate. It mystifies us that when these people had no chance, they held out longer against the Nazi army than had the entire British Army. Just imagine that—starving, without ammunition, and without hope. Why? Mordecai said in his letter, "We do it for future generations. And I die satisfied and happy."

The kibbutz was named after him. It was founded in the same year; and five years later to the day, it held off a huge army of Egyptians for five long days. The poet Abba Kovner, who was also a resistance fighter, has graphically described the scene for us and for future generations: You see the place where the resistance fought, a little hill. A sign tells that there were two American guns, one Canadian gun, two Czech guns. There are other images in the darkness, those many Egyptians. How did the Jews manage to hold out for five days? And why? You wander to another hill and you find your answer: There is the statue of Mordecai, larger than life. Behind him they have preserved the water tower that the Egyptians smashed—a mute symbol that the hatred of the Jews—the hatred from the days of the Holocaust—had not yet come to an end. But that is behind the statue, not in front. In front are fields, flowers, cows, peace—things Mordecai could only dream of. Then you understand that the battle for Israel began in the streets of Warsaw. This is the deepest inspiration, and it holds us all together.

W.B.: There is a saying on the stage that it is good theater to end on an upbeat note. This is hardly the stage . . . hardly theater. During the course of this Dialogue, we have lived with the reality of our recent dark history, guided by a most perceptive scholar. But Dr. Fackenheim, who knows better than so many others the impact of that history on our people, has given us the upbeat note on which we end. It is not, however, a cheery platitude to send us all away happy. It is, instead, a solemn charge, an admonition to remember who we are, what we are, and why we are here. It is, indeed, a promise that we will prevail over all events so long as we draw on our tradition for strength.

PART IV

Israel: Crossroads of the World

ॐ Introduction

The State of Israel is not only a sovereign political entity. It is, for the rest of the world, a state of mind. Hardly any other nation, especially one so tiny and remote, is the focus of so much global attention. In the farthest reaches of the South Pacific, in the central Amazon basin, and probably in the frozen North, people who have seldom, if ever, seen a Jew (much less an Israeli) hold strong opinions about the Middle East and Israel's role there.

Today, against the headlines from Jerusalem and other Middle Eastern capitals, this is especially true. Sadly, an old joke has been translated into twentieth-century politics: Members of an elementary school class were given a homework assignment to write essays about "The Elephant." The youngsters' compositions included some that focused on the circus, some on ivory, some on animal behavior—in short, they covered every possible aspect of the subject. And one little Jewish boy wrote on "The Elephant and the Jewish Question."

Today, almost every ripple in world affairs is examined for the "Israeli connection," whether it exists or not.

Much of the feeling engendered by anything that Israel does arises from the nature of the State and its people. Israel itself is a strange anomaly—a modern Western democracy, with its roots in one of the world's great religious traditions, struggling to survive in a Byzantine world.

The people who are building the land are no less complex by nature. Jews are full of faith, yet they are questioners; they are kindly, yet they are stubborn; they are strong, yet they are tender; they are creative, yet they are pragmatic. Without this admixture of traits there may very well have been no Israel, but the differing facets presented by its people to the world sometimes confuse Israel's friends and foes alike.

No Israelis exhibit the diverse and often conflicting qualities that mark these people quite so much as the

339

leaders whom they choose to represent them. Neither is anyone better qualified to appreciate these qualities than those same leaders. So, in order to gain any insight at all into the twentieth-century State of Israel against its biblical background, to get some sense of the direction that the nation might take in the years to come, one must speak with the leaders. This is one land in which the leaders do not merely represent the people; they come from the people. Israel is still young enough, still democratic enough, so that the upper echelons of government were not so long ago in the same streets and shops and schools, pursuing the same kinds of lives, as the citizenry around them.

Any dialogue with a high-level government figure in Israel is likely to be a dialogue with a man or woman who played a significant role in the Zionist effort to create the State. The Israeli "past" lives very much in the present thinking of these people; the problems and hazards they faced not too long ago must shape the thinking that they bring to their tasks today. Among this group—who not only called themselves "pioneers" but who truly *were* pioneers—the memories are long and vivid.

Yet the quality of balance is never lacking. As much as Israelis look back on the days of clearing swamps, fighting arid soil, helping illegal immigrants to land on midnight shores, and plotting physical defense, they live and act in the present. The problems have shifted focus: they now spring from the demands of neighbors, the pressures exerted by major world powers, the complexities of current economics. Still, the willingness to grapple with seemingly impossible tasks, and the ability to bring skill and imagination to bear on them, remain Israeli characteristics.

And over it all, in talking with these people, one is impressed by the way they look forward to the time when they, and especially their children, can devote their energies to peaceful and productive activities in a land that bears out its promise of milk and honey.

17. ❦ Self-Silenced Leader

Menachem Begin

W.B.: In the world of diplomacy and politics, this man enjoys the enviable reputation of being a statesman with deep integrity and honor, one who has never exchanged conviction for compromise and whose leadership has shown, not the conviction of power, but the power of conviction. In the world of Zionism and Jewry, he is respected and revered as a fearless fighter for the survival and well-being of the Jewish people and its historic homeland, *Eretz Yisrael*. His years of service on behalf of this sacred cause have earned for him, from friend and foe alike, a special place in the pantheon of Jewish leaders as one who acts like a man of thought and thinks like a man of action. But even beyond all these vital areas of concern, he is best known as a unique human being and a Jew. He is a humble man, yet a dogged, determined leader. He is a deeply devoted family man, yet universal in his concerns for the entire household of Israel. He is courtly and gentle in manner, however strong and decisive in achieving his goals. And finally, his powers of persuasion coupled with his warm, charismatic personality have made him a uniquely beloved personality among Jews in Israel and abroad. It is an honor and privilege to join in dialogue with Menachem Begin. [*Editor's note*: This Dialogue took place a few months before Menachem Begin was elected Prime Minister of Israel. He was then the leader of the opposition party, the Likud.]

Mr. Begin, you've said that people have called you dogmatic or an extremist. Do you feel you *are* dogmatic or an extremist? If not, how do you respond to these charges?

■ **BEGIN:** I am not impressed with name-calling. Yes, in the course of our struggle in the resistance during the 1940s for our just cause there were people who called me an extremist.

343

What do these words mean? We the Jewish people have been persecuted, tormented, tortured, and almost physically destroyed. What looking-behind should we have done during the 1940s when we heard from afar the trains running from all over Europe toward one destination: death to the Jew, whether at Auschwitz, Treblinka, Babi Yar, and all the other places where the process of killing a nation continued for five long years.

The world did nothing to try to rescue any of them. At the same time, *Eretz Yisrael*, the Land of Israel, the land of our forefathers and of our children, promised by the British as a national home for the Jewish people, was being subjugated by the British, and its gates were shut to the Jews. When does a human being need a home more than at the time when he is being not only persecuted but also physically destroyed?

Therefore, we rose in revolt against the British. We did it to make it possible for the Jews to come home under conditions in which never again a bloodthirsty two-legged beast would try to destroy a Jewish child. We had to fight for statehood, for national liberation, to ensure the salvation of the Jewish people. Is this dogmatism? Or is this devotion to a just cause and the simple love for a people?

Our fight was for personal liberty and political independence. Otherwise, we would have been handed over to the Arab majority, and the end would have come to the existence of our people. This was more than just a fight for individual liberty. It was the fight to save a nation from complete and utter physical destruction. This is why there hasn't been a fight for liberation as justified as ours in the annals of humankind.

There is nothing dogmatic about it, but some people assume that if a group fights for liberation, then it believes in force. This is a complete mistake. Such people never believe in the great moral values of a free human being. Had they believed in force, they could not have started the fight and they surely couldn't have continued in it, because force is always on the other side—the side of the enslaver.

In this struggle, we were *again* the few against the many, the weak against the strong. We didn't believe in force. We *do* not. We detested physical force. We believed, with Abraham

Lincoln, that right is might, not vice versa. Only because of this could we have continued fighting. At one point a certain equilibrium is created in history between the forces involved. On one side is brutal physical force; on the other side, faith in the justice of a human cause. With that equilibrium, one molecule of self-sacrifice decides the issue, tilting the scales, and the just cause wins. There is nothing dogmatic about this.

w.b.: How would you reply to those who have said that Menachem Begin is an extremist?

■ BEGIN: There is nothing extremist about this point of view. We have never been extremist. What did we want then? What do we want now? Let us take the attitude of the Arab countries vis-à-vis Israel. The Arab people, whom we respect, now have twenty-one sovereign states with an area of twelve million square kilometers. The land of Israel belonging to the Jewish people is a very small country, and yet the Arabs want even this country. Where is the justice in that? Should they have twenty-two states, and the Jewish people have no country whatsoever?

After nineteen centuries of dispersion, persecution, and humiliation, we cannot live without Israel. It was true in previous generations, but it is especially true now, because on Israel depends our national security; and so, if you ask, Is it extreme to believe in the right of one's people to their own country? I can only reply that there is nothing extremist in this. For a Jew to love Zion is moderation, because Zion is the faith of our people throughout the centuries that the land of Israel should be the land of the Jews. If this means extremism, then we should ask ourselves: Are we considering the Bible when we use that word? Is the Bible extreme? When we use that word, are we considering all the teachings, all the history, all the suffering of the Jewish people? Let us make it clear that whoever loves the Jewish people and the land of Israel and stands for the right to do so is no extremist. He's just a patriot.

w.b.: In addition to calling you dogmatic and extremist, people also have accused you and the Irgun of being a group of terrorists. How do you counteract the accusation of some people, even those who may have believed in the principles you espoused, that the Irgun was a terrorist group?

■ BEGIN: Times change, and many people who called us those names at that time now admit that perhaps they were mistaken. This is why I was invited by the very people who called us those names in 1947. We worked together for three years in good understanding in a government of national unity with these same people, with the disciples of Ben Gurion, the members of the Haganah, and the Palmach.

Now about that horrible word *terrorism*. That word stems from the Latin *terror*, meaning fear. Indeed, throughout history there have been people who used terror. The word in its political sense stems from the French Revolution, when there was in-fighting between the various groups that overthrew Louis XVI and tried to build a republic. All of them died under the guillotine, and that was called terror. In other words, people were arrested or their heads fell in order to terrorize and instill fear among the French.

A century later there was a group in Czarist Russia that used personal assassination of the czar or a governor to instill fear in the Czarist government. The Russian people considered them heroes. They risked their lives. They died on the gallows. Many went on fighting because they faced an oppressive regime. But admittedly they took upon themselves that word.

We never used terror. We never wanted to instill fear into anybody's heart. Ours was a classical fight for liberation. We never used personal assassination. In the Irgun we carried out *military* operations against an overwhelming force of 100,000 British soldiers equipped with heavy guns, tanks, and planes, and supplemented by 30,000 British policemen. When we started our fight for liberation at the end of 1943, we were 388—less than 400 men. We finished with 10,000 fighting soldiers. Thousands of our members and those who helped us were arrested. Some were executed, while others were deported to Africa to concentration camps. Therefore, that term *terrorist* does not fit us at all. Otherwise, all fights for liberation should be called *terror*—including the war of liberation by the American people. They, too, rose in revolt, arms in hand, to gain independence. No one would dare to call that terror.

I would like to add that if anyone should again use that word *terrorist*, applying it to our struggle for liberation, he takes upon himself the risk of dividing the fighters of the Jewish people, which include the Haganah, the Irgun, the Lechi, the volunteers of 1948, and the members of our victorious army. We never made a distinction between our fighting group and the others.

But if a person should repeat that word in connection with Jewish fighters, he takes upon himself the peril of artificially making a comparison with those who today are referred to as the so-called Palestine Liberation Organization [P.L.O.].

We fought to save a people. *They* shoot in order to destroy a people. Look at the methods we used. We did whatever was humanly possible to *avoid* civilian casualties, sometimes at the risk of the lives of our own fighting men. We warned away any and every civilian, whether Jew, Briton, or Arab, from the zone of danger in advance.

What do they—the so-called P.L.O.—do? They make the civilian population the target of their bloody attacks. They never express regret or sorrow when they have "succeeded" in killing an innocent Jewish man or woman or child. On the contrary, they rejoice in it. That is the difference between fighters and killers. That is the difference between the Jewish underground and those killers of the so-called P.L.O.

For the sake of the dignity of the Jewish people, and indeed of all who have fought for liberty, never use that cursed word *terrorist*. Always make a distinction between authentic, humanitarian fighters for liberation and the terrorists who want to kill every man, woman, and child in Israel. That difference should always be remembered by every person who respects the truth.

W.B.: Mr. Begin, I have in front of me several books. One is *The Revolt*, written by you. The second is entitled *Days of Fire*, by Shmuel Katz, who was a high-ranking Irgun member. The third is *Perfidy* by Ben Hecht. All these books speak of a ship named the *Altalena*. I was fascinated and disturbed by this incident. I must confess to you that although I grew up in an intense, informed Zionist home, I do not recall hearing much about it. Moreover, I have spoken to any number of people, contemporaries of mine in the Zionist world, who do not recall hearing too many details about this ship either. Even older, veteran Zionists seemed to shrug their shoulders concerning the incident. So I come to my questions: What happened with the *Altalena*? And why the lack of knowledge about it? Could it possibly be that this tragic story was somehow suppressed from the Jewish people?

■ BEGIN: Let me start with a principle in which I believed all my life. I have always said *veritas vinci,* "truth will prevail." Some time ago, one of the closest disciples of Ben Gurion came to me and out of his own initiative said, "We have reached the conclusion that Ben Gurion was misled concerning the incident of the ship *Altalena.*"

Think of it: twenty-five years had passed since that ship was bombarded by guns and set afire. I was there on board with many young volunteers who came to help Israel fight for survival. All of us could have been killed instantly. In fact, some young Jewish boys who came from as far away as Cuba were killed. The others somehow survived. After twenty-five years this man, whose name I cannot mention, came to me. I asked him to permit me to say who he was, and time and again he said, "No I cannot do so." So I will guard his name as my commitment to a promise not to disclose it.

I can assure you that he was one of the closest men to Ben Gurion, *zichrono livrachah* [may his memory be blessed]. He assured me that Ben Gurion's order to use heavy guns against a helpless ship standing at the shores of Tel Aviv was the result of his being misled.

Altalena was the *nom de guerre* of the Irgun leader Zev Jabotinsky. That is why we gave our ship that name. In 1948 we received arms from the French government for use in our struggle for survival. This ship was to bring these arms to *Eretz Yisrael* before the State was proclaimed, some time in April or the beginning of May. If they had sent the ship then, there would not have been any problems. But delays always happen, and the ship was delayed time and again. Our friends in France wanted to help us. They knew that none of us—neither the Haganah nor the Irgun nor the Lechi—had arms. And they knew that the day after the U.N. General

Assembly resolution was adopted, the Arab groups would shoot at us and kill our brethren.

Therefore, the call for arms was the call for the survival of our people. Our enemies had tanks and heavy guns and machine guns and ammunition. We had a few mortars—they were our so-called artillery. In fact, we had one gun that we had to send from front to front. Of course, later we received more arms, and *Baruch HaShem*, thank God, we won the battle.

But in the beginning we were not only the few against the many; we were the very few weapons against the many weapons of our enemies. Therefore we looked for weapons, and, thanks to the people of France and even some in the French government, we found them. On board the *Altalena* were 5,500 guns and 3 million pieces of .303-caliber ammunition. I mention this because the commander of the Haganah, with whom we were in agreement and with whom we were fighting shoulder to shoulder, one day asked me, "Can you help us get .303 ammunition for the rifles and the machine guns?" We did. That ship was a storehouse of arms, with ammunition, armored cars, even bombs for planes we didn't have. In those days it all meant salvation for us.

One day, while listening to the British Broadcasting System [BBC], I heard that the ship had sailed for Israel. This worried me because that day was either the first or second day of the cease-fire. Now, the cease-fire conditions entailed one specific condition about arms: neither side was supposed to bring in arms for themselves. So, obviously, this was a breach of the cease-fire. I was deeply worried in my heart. I knew that if the ship came and the Arabs learned about it, they would say it was a breach of the cease-fire agreement and they would start shooting again. I then said to myself, as long as we in the Irgun fought on our own, we could take full responsibility for whatever we did. But this time we were fighting together with others, and we could not cause a breach of the armistice agreement, which might have caused an Arab war involving the members of the Haganah as well. As a result of my concern I sent a cable to Shmuel Katz, who was our representative in Paris: "If *Altalena* did not yet sail, don't let her sail." I later learned that the cable came three days late. Why? To this day I don't know, but the *Altalena* had sailed from one of the islands of France toward *Eretz Yisrael* without our knowledge. Subsequently, Katz cabled me, replying that he got my cable only after the *Altalena* was in the waters of the Mediterranean.

We in *Eretz Yisrael* had a little radio, and as soon as we got the cable we radioed the ship night and day every hour with the following cable: "Keep away. Await instructions." We did not want them to come before there was an agreement that they should. After Aryeh Ben Eliezer, *zichrono livrachah,* came from France giving us the details about the ship and its arms, I called Mr. Levi Eshkol at 2:00 in the morning. He was then the director general of the provisional government's defense ministry. I also called Mr. Galili, who was then the *de facto,* if not *de jure* deputy prime minister for defense. I gave them all the details about the ship and even the numbers of armaments and said, "You decide whether *Altalena* should come or not during the ten days of the cease-fire. If you decide that it shouldn't come, we shall send it back. It's up to you to decide."

The following day at 10:00 in the morning I received a call from Mr. Galili with this reply: "The government has decided that the *Altalena* should come as soon as possible." There was great rejoicing in the room. We sent a cable to the boat: "Full speed ahead." There was then a consultation between the specialists of the Haganah and the specialists of the Irgun about where the ship should land, so that the observers of the U.N. should not see it. We originally thought it should land in Tel Aviv, but it was decided by agreement that it should land at Kfar Vitkin, which is a moshav where all of our former opponents were living. It landed, and the arms unloading began. There was only one conversation about what to do with the arms. We wanted part of the arms to go to Jerusalem, which was besieged and beleaguered, and that was agreed on. The other part we thought should go to all the battalions—the Irgun battalions, as they were still called during the transition period, as well as the other battalions, without any discrimination. *That* was not agreed upon, and I got this news: "If those are the conditions, we won't help you in unloading the weapons." That was all. There was no warning. We were told that the *Altalena* should be at the shore at

Kfar Vitkin, and so we began to unload the weapons for all our fighting men. And suddenly, the *Altalena* was fired upon and people were killed. That is the explanation.

Some people have heard that the *Altalena* was an attempt to take over the provisional government by force. To say that is a *Chillul HaShem*. It never occurred to us to do something like that. How can one make a so-called *coup d'état* when he informed the government in power about the ship? How can one make a so-called *coup d'état* when he informed the government in power about the details of the armaments, even agreeing where the ship should land?

Everyone should remember that after five years of fighting the British, we [the Irgun] formed battalions in accordance with the agreement with the provisional government for the transition period. We joined with the Haganah even though there were times when we were persecuted, and even though we, the men of the Irgun, were handed over by the Haganah to the British police. Nevertheless, we joined with the Haganah.

We don't remember wrongs. What's more, all the time we avoided fratricidal fighting. We learned from history about the fate of the Second Temple state. It was destroyed not so much by the Romans as by the internecine, fratricidal warfare of those tragic days. We in the underground said that whatever the price, whatever the sacrifice, we would always avoid fratricidal war. Even when we were handed over by the Haganah to the British police, our men received instructions not to raise their hands against their brethren although persecuted by them. There was never fratricidal war in *Eretz Yisrael*.

We won the battle because we all stood together despite all our differences and throughout all the tragic days. This was also the way we handled the problem of the *Altalena*. We prevented the fratricidal fighting from breaking out and said on that tragic night: "Don't raise your hands against your own brethren—although ours were killed." The main thing now is to stress that it was not an attempt to take over the government by force. Everything was disclosed in advance to the government.

Let me conclude on an optimistic note—a personal story that tells us never to despair about our people, for wounds can be healed. My wife and I went to Brussels for the Conference on Soviet Jewry. Mr. Ben Gurion was also there. You know that we were opponents, sometimes very sharp opponents, but as you remember, before the Six-Day War broke out, I suggested that a government of national unity be formed. As there was a deep crisis that had to be avoided between the government and the high command of the Army, out of my own initiative I suggested that this national unity government be headed by Ben Gurion. Although we had been opponents, I felt that at this juncture of crisis and danger we must restore the confidence between the commander of the army and the civilian government that must rule the army. This is the first principle of a democracy—the supervision of the armed forces by the elected civilian authorities. I went to see Prime Minister Eshkol, *zichrono livrachah*, and told him on behalf of three parliamentary groups—the Gahal parties, consisting of Herut and Liberal; the Rafi, which was Ben Gurion's party; and the Mafdal, the Mizrachi party—that we suggest that Ben Gurion become head of a government of national unity, and then I told the Prime Minister that he would be Deputy Prime Minister. Believe me, it is not so easy to say to a prime minister, step down. He did not agree. He likes to speak Yiddish, and he said, *"Dos por folk, vet shoin nit leben tzuzamen."* In other words, That couple, he and Ben Gurion, cannot work together. It happens; it happens in any party. Nevertheless, a government of national unity was formed with Moshe Dayan as Minister of Defense, and myself and Pinchas Sapir, *zichrono livrachah*, as Ministers without Portfolio.

When we returned in the plane from Brussels to Israel with Mr. Ben Gurion, Ben Gurion came over to my wife and, in a fatherly tone, said to her, "My wife Paula was a great friend of your husband and *she knew* people." So, you see, we should never despair about our people. That is our attitude about *Altalena*. Truth will prevail. We fought for democracy from boyhood. We never fought for rule over our people. We fought for the liberation of our people, and since the day when we were liberated, we believe only in the ballot. We believed, we believe, we shall always believe in democracy and the free decision of the people by the ballot.

W.B.: In 1927 and 1928, Vladimir Jabotinsky said, "Don't let your memory be black. Any man can make a mistake or say foolish things. If the good of the people requires that you stretch out your hand to him, forget what must be forgotten and give him your hand." I think that in great measure, Mr. Begin, you have made manifest those words of Zev Jabotinsky.

There is a raging controversy going on, and I'd like to get your opinion about it. It has to do with Soviet Jewry—in particular those Soviet Jews called *noshrim*, or dropouts, who drop out at Vienna while en route to Israel. [*Editor's note*: This was a major problem at the time of this Dialogue.] A joint committee of American Jews and Israelis decided to withhold any assistance to these *noshrim* unless they went to Israel. This resulted in a situation where, for example, Russian Jewish women, because of lack of aid, became streetwalkers, or where Christian missionaries have taken Russian Jews into their church. A debate has been going on concerning this question, and we would be interested in your point of view. What do you think of this situation? Is this a way to encourage Soviet Jews to come to Israel—or is this a move that is divisive and totally lacking in genuine *ahavat Yisrael*, love of Israel?

■ **BEGIN:** Without doubt, the reawakening of our brethren in the Soviet Union is one of the great historic phenomena in our time. Those Jews demonstrating in the streets of Moscow, going to the Supreme Soviet, sitting there under the supervision of the Soviet secret police (K.G.B.), is a real *Kiddush HaShem*. Even the K.G.B. cannot suppress the reawakening. Many of these young people go to prison or to concentration camps, they suffer deprivation, they lose their livelihood, and still they say they want to return home. As they put it in their own language: "We want to return to the stolen homeland of the Jewish people." Today there are more than three million Jews in the Soviet Union. In 1973 we had 34,000 of them coming to *Eretz Yisrael*; in 1974, 20,000; in the last two years [1975–1976] between 10,000 and 12,000 annually. Probably somewhere in the Politburo a decision was made about that quota of between 800 and 1,000 monthly. But it is not enough. We need an *aliyah* from the Soviet Union in the tens of thousands. This is why we must continue with our public campaign for their release.

I was in Strasbourg last year at the session of the Council of Europe and a member of parliament in Sweden, who is now the deputy prime minister, had just returned from the Soviet Union. He brought back a report in which he quoted one of the high Soviet officials as having told him that "now, Western opinion doesn't pay any more attention to this issue, so we can do whatever we want." There is a necessity to prove to the rulers of the Kremlin that Western opinion *does* pay attention. What you have done in New York, with the great mass demonstrations, has done very much to influence the Kremlin to let Jews go. You *should* continue with such demonstrations. I say this as one human being to another, and I say this as a Jew to other Jews. Continue with those mass demonstrations.

w.b.: What do you think accounted for the large number of drop-outs on the way to emigration to Israel?

■ BEGIN: After the Yom Kippur War, some of those who took visas to *Eretz Yisrael* stayed for a while in Vienna and then went to Rome or to the United States or elsewhere and haven't continued on their road to Israel. This is the fact. Why did it happen? We must tell the truth. It is true that ultimately we won the Yom Kippur War. We repelled the enemy on both fronts, going deeply into his territory. We were only 100 kilometers from Cairo and 44 kilometers from Damascus. Yes, we won the war, but it began in a tragic way for us. We were taken by surprise. Indeed, between Rosh Hashanah and Yom Kippur 1973 we had all the information leading to the conclusion that Assad and Sadat would start a war against us. As it happened, that information was evaluated mistakenly, and therefore we were not mobilized or prepared for that attack on Yom Kippur afternoon.

Some of those living behind the Iron Curtain who couldn't know all the facts reached the conclusion that, perhaps as a result of that surprise attack and the heavy casualties we suffered, it may not be so secure to live in Israel. Thus they preferred to go to other countries. This is the trauma of the Yom Kippur War. We have to admit that it even touched part of our own people in Israel, and even our Jewish brethren in the free countries. We are overcoming that trauma. I think that psychologically one of the factors that helped us to overcome that Yom Kippur War trauma was the great humanitarian and national act of salvation at Entebbe. But behind the Iron Curtain, it perhaps did not happen. Another reason for the *noshrim* has been our economic difficulties. We still have them. Suffice it to tell you that we owe billions of dollars. We have already mortgaged the economy of our grandchildren. We have to spend a huge percentage of our gross national product for national defense, and sometimes we even have strikes. These economic difficulties create social problems of all kinds.

Add to this the fact that those still in Russia sometimes get certain kinds of letters from Russians in Israel. Although we cannot prove it, there probably are some among the authorities in the Soviet Union who are interested in proving that not all the Jews do want to go to their "stolen homeland" and so they put on the list people whom they know really don't want to go to Israel. So the letters come. When we combine all these reasons, we can understand what is happening. Still, in my opinion, it should not happen. After all a Jew who leaves his country should go home to Israel. We fought for the land, we liberated it, we sacrificed so much, that if a Jew leaves the land of communist bondage with a visa to the land of Israel, then he should come home to us and live there as a free person.

w.b.:   What about the need for *aliyah* from other countries besides the Soviet Union?

   ■ BEGIN: Of course, when we speak of *aliyah*, we expect *aliyah* not only from the Soviet Union but also from the free countries. To be sure, it is a matter of a free decision to be taken. However, our people should come to the land of Israel to live as Jews. Let us be completely frank. I was in Latin America only two months ago and I heard that more than 50 percent of all marriages taking place there are mixed marriages. My friends, we are all free people. We cannot enforce anything upon our children. We can only try to educate them in the spirit of Jewish tradition and faith and devotion.

   But all of us are a very small minority throughout the world. If *we* don't keep our people, who *will* keep them? After the destruction of six million Jews, how can we watch in our time the disappearance of Jewish children? How can we watch their taking leave of us and going away? When you see it, you have aches and deep pain in your heart. For this is not physical violence done by others. Rather, it is self-disappearance. This is why I think *aliyah* is so important. Yes, we have problems in Israel. I am not going to picture at any time our life as an ideal one. It is not. We have problems, both economic and social. Life is not easy in our country. But it is *Eretz Yisrael*!

We have a wonderful young generation—serious, devoted, serene—always ready to serve in order to save our people. Look at how we rebuilt the ancient Hebrew civilization. Look at how we revived our ancient language. The country is good. It is a beautiful country. Someone once said that perhaps Moses made a mistake—maybe he should have taken us to Switzerland instead of to *Eretz Yisrael*. I don't agree! Let the Swiss live in Switzerland—and we shall continue to live in *Eretz Yisrael*. For despite all the difficulties, it is good to live there.

The anti-Semites used to say that the Jew says, "Where it is good to live, there is my land." We, the Jews and the Zionists, proved the lie of those anti-Semites, for we say, "Where there is our land, there it is good to live," even if it is not always so good.

W.B.: Just to return a moment to the issue of the *noshrim*, the Soviet Jewish dropouts. Just how would you resolve the situation, and what would be your policy?

■ BEGIN: Let me say again that I believe that the Jew who leaves the Soviet Union should go to *Eretz Yisrael*. That is the principle. Nevertheless, there are human problems involved and in my opinion we cannot abruptly cease helping our brethren who do not go to Israel. That we cannot do. We have to give ourselves a certain time, say a year, more or less, as a transition period. And during that transition period we must impress upon our Russian brethren the reality of the situation. We must tell them, "Brothers, don't humiliate your people and don't endanger the *aliyah* from the Soviet Union. You have a visa not to America, not to Switzerland, not to Britain nor to Canada nor to Australia. Your visa is to the

Land of Israel. If you take such a visa, keep faith with your own declaration that you want to go to Israel, and then *go*." And during that transition period help to them must not be stopped because great human problems are involved. If we do all of this, then there is reason to believe that we shall convince the overwhelming majority of them.

Meanwhile we shall perhaps solve some of our own social problems, and eliminate part of our bureaucracy (which is always an obstacle to what is called absorption). If we improve our own ways of absorbing the *olim*, then the wound will be healed and the trauma will disappear. Let us always be optimists. In the years to come tens of thousands, and with God's help hundreds of thousands, will leave Soviet communist bondage and come home to *Eretz Yisrael*.

W.B.: As you have said, since there are so many human problems, to cut off the aid categorically is a very serious mistake, and to some extent may have somewhat of the faint echo of the 1930s and 1940s when total *ahavat Yisrael* was in eclipse. This leads me to a question that is of great concern and, sadly, as contemporary as last night's TV news or this morning's newspaper.

We have been witness to a very frightening phenomenon: the resurgence of Nazism around the world. In South America there is this resurgence. In Frankfurt, Germany, on the anniversary of *Kristalnacht*, there was a "celebration" with Nazi flags and anti-Semitic banners. In England, Nazi parties and literature abound. In Rome and elsewhere, Nazi killers are released with compassion. These are just some of the danger signs in Europe. And here in America, we've seen Archbishop Trifa, a murderer of Jews, whose Bible and collar can never hide his bloody hands, sitting on the board of the National Council of Churches. And he is just one of the former Nazi murderers who live in peace in America. [*Editor's note*: He has since been extradited.]

We've heard how people in Mineola, Long Island, and elsewhere say: "Let's forget the Holocaust." We've seen Nazi parties in Nebraska, Minnesota, Boston, Chicago, Detroit. And we've seen books that attempt to deny and distort the Holocaust. In the 1930s, Vladimir Jabotinsky traveled about to alert Jews to the danger. Mr. Begin, in these days, do you see a sense of danger in the resurgence of Nazism, or do you think it's overrated, overstated, and that these phenomena are merely aberrations?

■ **BEGIN:** Rabbi, I'm very grateful that from time to time when you are asking questions you mention my master and teacher, Vladimir Jabotinsky. That quotation about not having a black memory was most important to me. I really try to do my best about that. And all of us should try our best to heed that advice for the sake of our people's future. To the same extent, we must heed the warnings, the repeated warnings, that among Jews there live people who want to hurt them or even to kill them. You mentioned South America. My wife and I were in Argentina two months ago and we saw Nazi literature being sold openly in the shops. Millions of copies of *Mein Kampf*, authored by that "embodiment of all evil in mankind," as Churchill called him, are being bought. Books of speeches by Goebbels and the writings of Streicher are sold. When I was there, I met with the leaders of the Jewish community and I told them: "Remember, my friends, Nazi literature means one thing—a call to kill the Jew. After the experience of the 1930s and 1940s there is no other interpretation. You cannot tolerate it."

The Argentinians went to the government. However, it is a very difficult situation there with various underground groups killing each other almost every day. Sometimes Jewish youth are among the victims. We hear of Nazis throwing bombs at synagogues and calling to destroy Jewry, using that infamous phrase "Capitalistic Bolshevik Jewry."

Yes, we must always be aware that the danger of resurgent Nazism does exist. Of course, different events make it hard to compare one country with another. Nevertheless, in Argentina as in some of the other Latin American countries, this is now a present danger. I can give only one piece of advice and I give it freely. I say to every Jew and to every Jewish community that the time has passed forever when a bloodthirsty enemy of our people can hurt Jews with impunity. That time has passed *forever*. The Jew has a right to defend himself against such Nazis *wherever* he lives. And it is not only his right—it is his duty to defend himself and to defend the honor and human dignity of the Jewish people. And we in *Eretz Yisrael* do conduct ourselves in this way.

W.B.: Would you say that Operation Entebbe [1976] was an example of the new role the State of Israel has taken in terms of the physical defense of Jews anywhere—something that was missing during the period of the Holocaust?

■ BEGIN: Absolutely. This is what makes Operation Entebbe the great act of national salvation. For Entebbe was connected with the issue of saving Jews and preserving human dignity. During those days, we learned that one of the terrorists was a German. When the people who were captured were brought to Entebbe, we learned that the German had brought them all together and read the list of names and then made a gesture. Some people were to go to one room and others to another room. The citizens of Israel and a few other Jewish names were to go to one side. All the Gentile passengers and some of the Jewish passengers from other countries were to go to the other side. One group went to liberty, life, and freedom, the other group to fear, violence, and death. From afar, one could hear the shout: *Something horrible is happening there!*

Less than forty years after that beast, the so-called "Doctor" Mengele, stood in Auschwitz and made the gesture with his finger—to the right or to the left, to the right to live, to the left to die—was it possible again that a so-called leftist Nazi should stand among people and repeat that gesture—Gentiles to liberty and life, Jew or citizens of Israel to fear and death?

Thus, we resolved to do whatever possible to save them. On that day, on Thursday, we did not yet have a military plan to save them, and so we all decided, government and opposition, in complete national unity and common responsibility, to declare that we were ready to negotiate. Some time later, there were people who surmised that we did it in order to save time. It was not so. We just did not yet have a military plan. Three plans were brought to us by the staff. We had to reject all of them. Why? Because there was only risk involved, with no chance for success. And we will never send our men to suicide. Being surrounded by enemies on all sides and from time to time being hurt or endangered, we sometimes have to take risks, provided that there is a chance for men and women to be saved and for our fighting men to come home safely. However, without such a chance, we cannot take the risks. In those three plans, as suggested to us, there was only risk—and not a chance. We had to reject them and we did.

But then, *Baruch HaShem*, thank God, between Friday and Saturday morning a plan was found with some risk—but also with a chance. We accepted that plan. As we saw, one of our best officers died and there were two other casualties; nevertheless, all the others, the captive passengers and our soldiers, came safely back. Soon thereafter, we said in Parliament that all Nazis, rightist Nazis or leftist Nazis, without exception, must remember that the time has passed when the Jew can be humiliated, persecuted, and ultimately killed. If at any time a human being will say, *Ivri Anochi*, I am a Jew, and because of that he will be humiliated or persecuted or his life will be put in danger, then all our strength in Israel will be behind that human being, that Jew, until we save him and make sure he lives in liberty and in human dignity forever.

W.B.: Your very moving remarks remind me of a story a friend once wrote to me. He told me that he once worshiped in the second oldest synagogue in Europe, which is found in the tiny medieval town of Dubrovnik, on the coast of Yugoslavia. When he went there he found two elderly brothers in charge of the sanctuary, which had been built in the year 1352. They told my friend the story of their community and of their family. During the Holocaust, most of the Jews were deported and few returned. Their own family, which originally came to the town in 1306, had before the war ten brothers and four sisters. But after the hostilities only three of them returned alive from Auschwitz.

And these three decided that they would dedicate the remainder of their lives to preserving this holy synagogue. My friend concluded his letter by telling me that they invited him to the evening Maariv service. When it ended, one of the brothers came to him and asked for a favor: "We are so lonely here, and Israel means so much to us. Would you sing Hatikvah with us?" And then my friend relates: "We stood and sang and as they blended their voices with mine, tears ran down my cheeks. But when I left that synagogue that day, I left with the renewed conviction that no one, no one, can divide or destroy us—as long as we can sing Hatikvah." This is the spirit of the Jewish people, today and tomorrow. And this spirit has been eloquently and movingly conveyed by the Honorable Menachem Begin. For as long as we hope, as long as we sing, as long as we are one—as long as we sing of our hope as one—no one, but no one, will destroy us.

18. ❧ Jerusalem, Capital of the World

Teddy Kollek

W.B.: We are commemorating at this time a very joyous historical event—this is the tenth anniversary of the reunification of the city of Jerusalem. If I were to search for a speaker in any part of the world you all would agree with me that the most appropriate guest for a dialogue dedicated *To Jerusalem with Love* is its distinguished, dedicated, unusual mayor, Teddy Kollek.

Mr. Kollek, from your perspective as the Mayor of Jerusalem, what is it that makes Jerusalem so special to so many? After all, she has no natural resources, she has no port, she really has no great wealth in the accepted sense. Why, then, do so many yearn and fight for *Yerushalayim*?

■ KOLLEK: Of course, it is difficult to imagine today how it all began. But certainly for thousands of years, for almost 3,000 years since David made it the capital of Israel, it was *the* capital of the Jewish people, and much more of a capital to the Jewish people than any capital to any other people. I sometimes think it was even more of a capital to us when we were not there than when we were there. When we were there, it was almost natural and simple; today it's not too natural or too simple because it's still being contested, and we can't be certain that we shall not have great battles to fight—spiritual, or even, God forbid, otherwise—for Jerusalem.

But when we were not there, the very name Jerusalem kept us together. If you want to express the history of the

363

Jewish people for 3,000 years in one word, I think the one word is *Jerusalem*. As for others, there is a certain quality to the city that made Moslems and Christians and thousands and thousands of people over these years risk their lives for Jerusalem. In every way, people—and particularly the Jews—love the city. Still the question remains, why Jerusalem? By now, the origin is not important.

Of course, in terms of the origin, logically you can explain that it was the center of all Jewish tribes; therefore it was the place around which the nation could unite. Or you can explain that in sitting there on the hills, with its mystical light, with its clear air, it gave people a chance to think about things other than only their daily life. Jerusalem has a mystical background in which you can believe, if you are deeply religious; or, if not, you can believe, as I do, in its history and what has happened there during these 3,000 years. No matter what, the fact is that one always comes back to Jerusalem's special quality.

I took a very well-known American journalist around the city not long ago. I showed him the gardens we maintain and the parks and the schools we build, and the kindergartens. He wasn't very interested; he was interested only in political statements. In the end, he said, "Why are you doing all this? Are you certain you will keep it?" I told him that nobody can be certain. Maybe this will sound a little discouraging, but in this sense we may be behaving like ants. As they do, we have built the most beautiful ant-hills for anyone to enjoy, and maybe someone will come one day with a big stick and disturb the ant-hill. So what? We'll build it again, and again, and each time it will be even more beautiful. But one thing remains forever: nothing can or will ever drive us away from Jerusalem.

w.b.: Mr. Mayor, you beautifully and eloquently indicated the relationship of the Jews to Jerusalem. What has been the relationship of the Arab world to Jerusalem, in particular before 1967?

■ KOLLEK: Today it is very unimportant whether or not Muhammed actually came to Jerusalem during his night ride and went from there to Heaven. The fact is that Moslems have believed that for several hundred years. Hence, the Moslems who live there regard it as a holy place, and they regard it as their city. We have in our city administration a fairly high-ranking Arab official whose family came there 800 years ago. They have lived in the same building overlooking Har Ha-Bayit, the Temple Mount, for these 800 years. Certainly in Israel or even in Europe, you can't find many families who have lived in the same building, in the same apartment, or in the same castle, for 800 years.

For the Arab, the attachment is obviously a religious as well as a national one. This, of course, stands in some competition to our Jewish attachment. It is true in a physical sense, particularly, as far as the Temple Mount is concerned. However, we are in a comparatively good position for one reason. According to our tradition, Jews, if they observe all the mitzvot, are not allowed to go on the Temple Mount. Certainly we are not permitted to build a temple. A Temple has already been built; it is in Heaven and is waiting there for the Messiah to arrive. When He does arrive, the Temple will be set in its appropriate place in Jerusalem without much consideration for the building codes or licenses that the city of Jerusalem is issuing.

One way or the other, there's a distinct competition between us and the Arabs vis-à-vis the Temple Mount. The attachment of the Arabs is a long one, and it's a religious one. It is impossible for an observant Moslem to agree that a holy place should not be part of the realm of Islam. We will have to find a solution for ourselves as to how we can live with this, or what to do to alter it, and how Arabs can live with this.

W.B.: Mr. Kollek, as you see it, what is the relationship of the Arab in Jerusalem to the P.L.O.?

■ **KOLLEK:** I think that I can say from close knowledge that the P.L.O. is greatly feared. Even more, it is disliked and hated. That doesn't mean that there aren't numbers of young people, and even older people, who feel that the P.L.O. has given them back their confidence in their history, or their destiny, but the last thing they want is to see the P.L.O. in Jerusalem. And the reasons are manifold.

Number one, many in Jerusalem still remember the spirit and ire of the Grand Mufti of Jerusalem. The Mufti started a rebellion against Zionism, Jews, and the British in the years before World War II. During this revolt between 1936 and 1939, many, many more Arabs than Jews or British were killed by other Arabs in order to create a monolithic political position.

Even later, similar situations occurred in the Arab world. In Algiers (and perhaps this is not a very good example because the Arabs finally drove the French from Algiers) there were people standing up to the French in every city and every village and every hamlet; and finally the French left. The next day, a well-armed group marched in, took over the country, and liquidated all the real freedom fighters, the middle class, and the intellectuals. Nobody knows where the great leaders of that uprising are today. Some say they were killed; some say they were arrested and live in prisons.

In any case, the Arabs in Jerusalem who are on the West Bank know that this is what is going to happen to them if ever the P.L.O. assumes control there, so there is no love lost for them. On the other hand, there is fear. I know a very prominent journalist, the publisher of a well-known Arab paper in Jerusalem, who wrote several articles a few years ago in which he asked, "Why should the people on the outside decide what our fate is? We are a million Arabs on the West Bank and in Gaza. We should decide our own fate and not the few thousands in the terrorist organizations in Lebanon or in Syria, or wherever they are." One night he phoned me to tell me that his new Mercedes was burning. This was on a Friday night. A few of us went to see him on Saturday morning, when one doesn't work but has free time to sit around and chat, and he explained to us that there was really nothing that he could do to protect himself. He was willing perhaps to risk his own life for his opinions, but he wasn't willing to risk the lives of his children for his opinions. And so he stopped writing anti-P.L.O. articles.

The episode didn't make the P.L.O. more acceptable to him or to anybody else, and I could give other examples. The thing to remember is that people are afraid of them, and therefore a great deal of lip-service is paid to them. But when one sits alone with an Arab, he will say, "Well, we would like to be rid of you Jews, and one day we shall get rid of you. Of this we are certain. But if the P.L.O. comes here, we shall not be at all certain if we'll get rid of *them*. So therefore we would like you to stay until the P.L.O. has disappeared, and then we'll see what we can do between you and us."

w.b.: When I was in Jerusalem a year ago, I was out walking at a very early hour and someone said to me, "You see that car? That's the Mayor's automobile. He makes a tour through the city every morning before 5:00." He told me that if Mayor Kollek sees a piece of paper in the street, he stops the car, gets out, picks up the piece of paper, and puts it back into the car in order to have a cleaner Jerusalem. Certainly, we are all very interested in your day. What is it like? What are your responsibilities? What are your headaches? What are your joys? And particularly, what is it like to be mayor of the capital city of the Jewish people?

■ KOLLEK: Well, the story you told before is a vast exaggeration. I pick up paper only when I *walk*; I don't stop the car to pick up paper. And I don't get up at 4:00 in the morning. I get up at 5:00. My day actually begins when I have breakfast with my wife at 5:30. At 6:00, I start on my way to the office, and those are the most productive hours, when one can deal with memoranda and papers and dictation. And I don't ever mind phoning people then, because at least I know I can find them at home at that time.

w.b.: And how do they respond if you call them at 6:00 or 7:00 in the morning?

■ KOLLEK: By now they're accustomed to it. They can't help themselves.

Of course, the rest of the day consists of a variety of things. A great deal of time is taken up by meetings with department heads on problems of education, or finance, or problems of social welfare, or of town planning, and on a variety of other matters. There are meetings of committees, and then there are a great number of visitors of all kinds.

w.b.: You told me a lovely story about the time Walter Cronkite was in Israel.

■ KOLLEK: Walter Cronkite, together with 2,000 other journalists, came to cover the Anwar el-Sadat story in 1977; he's
an old acquaintance of mine. He hadn't been to Jerusalem in
ten years. And so when there was a free hour, I suggested we
walk around the Old City together. We walked through the
Jaffa Gate, and we were met by a large group of American
tourists who recognized Walter Cronkite and were very excited. It was the greatest thing that could have happened to
them. Jerusalem was not important, but Walter Cronkite—
that was *it*! And then we walked on through; I wanted to
show him what we were doing to repair the Old City, to
restore it to some extent to its old form. It had been neglected by subtenants for 2,000 years, and since we, the
owners, have come back we're trying to put it into shape
again. So we walked through the *shuk*, the marketplace, and
we stopped into a lot of Arab shops where people came out
who recognized me and then offered us some coffee and tea.
I explained to Walter Cronkite that the Americans we met
before had been his constituency, and that these Arabs were
my constituency. "But what about security?" he asked. So I
said, "You're right. Tell me how many mayors in the United
States would walk through an area that is regarded at least
by some as dangerous, while protected only by Walter Cronkite!" Well, he couldn't name even one.

But to continue my day. We have a great number of area
committees, mainly of Jewish citizens but also of Arab and
Christian citizens. Practically every day we meet with one of
the area committees to discuss their problems, whatever
they may be—whether it's sewage, or public telephones, or
education, or roads, or whatever the case. And so the day
passes. Sometimes an emergency arises. It may even be that
somewhere an explosive charge is detected. Or a water main
has broken. It may be a complaint that has recurred several
times in a certain area of town. I take fifteen or twenty
minutes to go there and see with my own eyes why people
are complaining.

In the evening there are more meetings, sometimes conferences, or visiting groups from abroad whom I address for a
few moments. Later on there is a lot of paper work that I
take home, or maybe I invite somebody home for a quiet

conversation, the kind of quiet talk about a more serious problem than I can deal with during the hours of the day. So the day goes by.

W.B.: [Former] Prime Minister Menachem Begin has often said that as far as he was concerned, "everything is negotiable." Do you think he was including Jerusalem in that statement as well? Is her status negotiable? And if it is, how? Or to put it another way, will Jerusalem ever be divided?

■ **KOLLEK:** I don't think it will. I don't think that would be an answer to the problems of Jerusalem, and I cannot imagine that this is what Mr. Begin or anybody else who is speaking about Jerusalem means. I believe that lots of things in Jerusalem are negotiable, and we can do many things in Jerusalem that would satisfy the very legitimate needs of others as well as of Jews, or Israelis, but always within the framework of one city, always within the status of the capital of Israel. For instance, if we have permitted Arabs in Jerusalem to remain Jordanian citizens, if they so choose, and therefore have enabled them to travel across the bridges linking Israel and Jordan whenever they like, we have given up a certain right of sovereignty in not forcing those who live in our midst to accept *our* citizenship. Or if we have left the Temple Mount under the administration of the Moslem authorities and not interfered with it, I think we have given up a certain amount of sovereignty, and I think wisely so. For we have not insisted on any rights that are not absolutely necessary to us, but instead have given others a chance to live.

If we had not insisted on turning Jerusalem into a melting pot, we would have then continued the old position of thousands of years that Jerusalem is a mosaic in which Jews live separately and Christians live separately and Moslems live separately. Instead we have chosen to create a united city, and any concessions we have made are for the sake of comparatively reasonable living side by side. I could continue doing this. All these things have been given temporarily. They have not been codified so far; they are not part of Israeli law. Of course, they could be *made* part of Israeli law and by this ensure officially that there will remain rights for minorities.

I believe that in this sense a great number of things in Jerusalem are negotiable in order to make life for others easier within the city. And in *that* sense—and that sense only—I think Jerusalem is negotiable.

W.B.: How do you respond to those who argue that the best and most practical solution to the Jerusalem question is the creation of an international city?

■ **KOLLEK:** That argument is naive. I tell such people that they are damn fools who haven't done their homework. Let me explain. In 1947 the Vatican suggested internationalization of the Holy City. An international committee would have been appointed and it would have been a committee consisting of people who came from countries that had some background connected with monasteries, with religion, and, in a wider sense, with the things for which Jerusalem stood. If today an international committee were to be appointed, it would consist of people from the Third World who, even if they wouldn't choose Idi Amin, are on the whole not very nice people. Some would be Communists from China, or from Russia, or from the Ukraine. Maybe the Christian representative would be a Swede or a Dane who would always vote with the Third World. There certainly wouldn't be a *Christian* majority. Therefore, for some years, the Vatican has not repeated the suggestion of internationalization of Jerusalem. Christians are not interested. We certainly are not interested. Even the Arabs are not interested.

Arabs have a rule: A holy place must be part of the realm of their land. That is their expression for sovereignty, and they express it in two ways. First, in the Friday sermon by the preacher, the name of the Arab ruler of the place should be mentioned. In Jerusalem for the past few years it has not been mentioned because there is no Arab ruler of the place. Second, they have to have the right of coinage. But the main thing is that they cannot be ruled by an infidel. As infidels are defined, Dr. Kurt Waldheim [then Secretary General of the U.N.] is as much an infidel as I am. Therefore, the problem of the Arabs wouldn't be solved by internationalization. Whoever suggests internationalization just repeats a word that came into being several years ago but that has no real meaning and no real substance. It does not solve the needs of the Arabs or the Jews or the Christians. So it is not the solution.

W.B.: Anwar Sadat of Egypt was the only Arab leader to recognize Jerusalem in a *de facto* way as the capital of Israel. Do you think others will ever recognize it as well? Do you think it's time for other nations, in particular one I can think of immediately, to recognize Jerusalem once and for all as the true capital of the State of Israel?

■ **KOLLEK:** Well, I think it's always time, but most nations have not done so. They feel that if they do they might offend some Arabs, particularly Saudi Arabia. Therefore, there is very little hope that they will do so in the near future. President Sadat was *very* careful and made only very ambiguous statements about Jerusalem, much less the statements that he made about the rest of his demands. I think that was partly a result of seeing with his own eyes what was happening in Jerusalem since he was there with an Egyptian fighting unit in 1948, while on the other side. But the recognition of other countries, I think, will not come so soon, and it is mainly their loss.

W.B.: You have gained a world reputation of being the gracious host *par excellence* to international figures. If I'm not mistaken, the best guest—certainly in terms of his unexpectedness—was President Anwar el-Sadat. What was that visit like? What incident stands out most in your mind about it? What was your impression of President Sadat? The American newspapers said that, when he shook hands with you, he said "Shalom, Mr. Jerusalem." What were your impressions of that historic moment in the life of the State of Israel?

■ **KOLLEK:** As you said, it was an unexpected visit, and I think it was his show from the moment he decided to come. From the moment he stepped out of the airplane until the moment he left again, he knew how to carry himself and how to carry off the whole thing. I had a chance to travel with him for about the better part of two hours from the hotel to the mosque through the city, and I felt that I shouldn't impose myself on him. But as I entered his car, I asked him whether he wanted me to sit quietly or whether he wanted me to show him things and comment on what we were seeing while we were passing by. He *wanted* to know and he asked questions all the way there and then back again as we went to the Temple Gate and through the *shuk* and through the various areas we visited and then back again to the hotel. I'm sure you must have noticed on television that he is a deeply emotional and deeply religious person; he means it. He isn't just play-acting when he prays, and he believes in what he does. He is also a better-read and better-tutored man than I would have thought. As we were traveling around and we were passing the Mount of Olives, and Gethsemane, and various other sites, he knew all the connotations and everything that this city has meant for us and for the Christians. As for the future, now we can only be hopeful.

W.B.: In an article in *Foreign Affairs*, you said the following: "I think the history of relations in Jerusalem between Jews, Arabs, and Christians during this decade points to the kind of solution we should eventually evolve for Jerusalem." My questions has two parts: What is that solution? And how do you see the hope for peace in the Middle East in light of recent developments?

■ KOLLEK: First, I would like you to realize that Jerusalem for the last 2,000 years or longer has not been a homogeneous city. Since the days when the Greeks and Alexander conquered Jerusalem in about 300 B.C.E., Greeks lived in Jerusalem, along with Egyptians, Syrians, Romans, Byzantines, and others. It wasn't any more a purely Jewish city. If we walked into the Israel Gate of the Old City 120 years ago when nothing existed around the Old City, but only the Old City within the walls, we would have found a Greek quarter, a Latin quarter, an Armenian quarter, an Abyssinian quarter, a much larger Moslem quarter, and a still larger Jewish quarter. In 1840 the Jews were the majority, and people lived alongside each other. But it never became a melting pot. No Armenian ever wanted to be a Greek, and no Greek ever wanted to be an Arab, and no Arab ever wanted to be a Jew, or the other way around. This principle of not having a melting pot still continues. We are not trying to force people to speak the same language, or eat the same foods, or live together in the same ways. We are a mosaic, and we think that we are avoiding tensions and not adding to the tensions.

Second, you have to know why there is a comparatively good life in Jerusalem. The Arabs want to protect the Arab part of the city. They want to preserve their culture and their civilization there. In order to do that, there must be a comparatively good life. Otherwise, there wouldn't be enough work or enough activity, and many of them would leave. Work is offered all the time to them in nearby countries, so why should they stay in Jerusalem if they can earn a better living elsewhere? From their point of view the Arabs want to protect the Arab character of the city, and that is why they are against terrorism.

From the point of view of the Jews, the majority of Jews in Jerusalem are those who come from Arab countries. While they have no great love for the Arabs, they also want no violence. So from two different points of view—and I could give you a third point of view, the Christian—people are living together without using violence, not because one loves the other, but because of their own self-interests. This self-interest paradoxically creates a situation in which people can live together. Now all we have to do is continue it for the next 200 or 300 years, and it will work well.

W.B.: Mr. Kollek, in your term of office as mayor of a united Jerusalem, you've said that several crucial principles have emerged that will lead toward progress. One is "free access to the holy places." What do you mean by this?

■ **KOLLEK:** As you know, in 1948, when the armistice was signed, we were supposed to have free access to Mount Scopus, to the Hebrew University and Hadassah Hospital there, and free access to the Western Wall. But that did not come about. I will not say it was out of a malicious desire not to carry out the Armistice Agreement. I don't think that any Jordanian government had the guts to do this. It was just that they felt it wouldn't be popular and that all kinds of trouble would come from it. So they didn't permit free access. Since 1967 we have had the policy of free access. We have 150,000 visitors every year who come from Arab coun-

tries, residents of Arab countries who come across the
bridges and can visit their holy places freely, and there will be
another 150,000, 250,000, 300,000. Certainly the Christians
come too, in great numbers, and have free access to their
holy places. This is being carried out fully for the first time
under Israeli rule.

w.b.: The second crucial principle you laid down toward progress is
free reign of Arabs and Christians in their respective sections. How do
you envision this?

■ KOLLEK: I believe that one day we'll run the city divided into
boroughs. To be honest, we have a difference of opinion in
Jerusalem on this. There are Jews who say that if we had
boroughs today this would be the first step toward dividing
the city again. I'm of a different opinion. I think boroughs can
work, because even today you have independent Arab education, independent Armenian education, and independent
Greek education, and the various communities have their
own self-management to a very great extent.

w.b.: What about the principle of equal government, equal municipal
and social services to all areas?

■ KOLLEK: We are still far away from it. We incorporated a
city, East Jerusalem, which was then at a much lower level
technically as far as service is concerned than Jewish Jerusalem, and we haven't caught up yet. For example, all of East
Jerusalem, with the exception of the city within the walls,
had no sewer system. Every house had its individual cesspool. When the cesspool was filled, somebody came and
pumped it out and was paid a fee. As for drinking water
before 1967, 90 percent of the houses did not have any
running water. Today almost all of the houses do. Before
1967, everyone went to the public well. Now hardly anybody
goes to the public well. But we are still working at equalizing
things. We have equalized water but sewage will take us
another three or four years. We have built a great number of
school buildings, but not enough to equalize. Gradually it
will happen, and if we had more money and could do it better
and quicker, it would be good. But so far we don't have it.

w.b.: Mr. Mayor, the final and crucial principle toward progress, one that is most interesting, is the increased contact among the various communities. How do you see this taking place?

■ KOLLEK: As I said, the various communities live very much apart unto themselves. I think there are great advantages in this, even beyond the lack of tension. I believe our low and diminishing juvenile delinquency rate is due in part to the fact that the various communities are strong, autonomous units and that the family unit still means something in most parts of the city. We want the various communities to run their own affairs, and they are doing that already to a great extent. We want to give them independence in running their own affairs, and we are helping them to the extent that they need it. I think this is a good principle to live by. In Jerusalem it is the continuation of a tradition that has existed for a long time and has been proven to work. To break that tradition would not make any sense.

I will, however, add something that I admit will be more controversial. I believe all these principles are right. Everything we have done is correct, and we should have done it, but here and there we might have been a little more generous. Certainly in some cases we could have been less condescending. But again, as long as all these things that we have done—freedom of access, maintenance of nationality, self-autonomy of schools and other things—as long as they are limited to municipal action and are not incorporated into Israeli law but exist as special privileges to an Arab minority, I don't think we will have achieved very much. Because the Arabs can always say to themselves, "You know today we have this, but how do we know we will have it tomorrow?"

w.b.: Mr. Kollek, let us turn for a moment to the realm of personal influence. Who have been those who had the most personal and political influence in your life? Do you consider anyone to be your mentor, someone who has had the most profound effect on your thinking and your outlook?

■ KOLLEK: There is no question that the man who had the greatest influence on me was Mr. David Ben Gurion. I regard him as the greatest Jew in the historical period in which we live, bar none. He saw further than anyone else, and he was the most modest and simple person I've ever met. I couldn't express all I feel and think of him in a few words. But he certainly had the greatest influence on me.

W.B.: The first time we ever visited Jerusalem, my family and I went to the home of a very unusual individual. It so happened that while we were there, you, Mayor Kollek, called on the phone. This gentleman, when told you were on the phone, barked back at his maid, "Tell Teddy Kollek I'm busy." And I was taken aback; after all, the Mayor of Jerusalem was calling! How can you say such a thing? Then I thought to myself that only one man could get away with that. That man was someone who was very beloved, the right-hand to Chaim Weizmann, the unusual Chancellor of the Weizmann Institute, the late Meyer Weisgal. What are your recollections of him?

> ■ **KOLLEK:** He was a most original person: full of good humor, full of great creations and great ideas. He knew how to express himself vividly and originally in all languages, but particularly in Yiddish, and there are few people who were more dearly beloved than he was.

W.B.: Let me turn the clock back. In 1937 or 1938, you met a certain German officer in Europe. Who was he, why did you meet him, and what was your reaction when you saw him twenty years later?

> ■ **KOLLEK:** That German officer was Adolf Eichmann, who became infamous for everything he stood for many years later. At that time, Germans and Nazis were still quite happy to let Jews go if they only had somewhere to go. Those were the years when the Christian world could have saved millions of Jews if they had only taken them in. I was then able to acquire 3,000 immigration visas for young people who had been given agricultural training in Germany, in Austria, and in Czechoslovakia, to go to work in agriculture in England. The man to talk to in Vienna then was an S.S. officer who sat in the old Rothschild chalet. I had been there once or twice in more peaceful times. I was born in Vienna, and my father was a director of Rothschild's, and I had known this building. So I was particularly shocked to see who now occupied it. But I had no particular impression of him aside from his being a little bureaucrat who, in fact, dealt with the problem very speedily.

I got my 3,000 exit permits for the entry permits that I had brought with me from England. So I was perfectly satisfied. It was only later, in 1942 or 1943, that the name of Eichmann, together with the "final solution" and with everything that he organized, became widely known. Of course, it was even more so when he was brought to justice in Jerusalem.

w.B.: You had occasion to meet Henry Kissinger in some of the many trips he made. What is your assessment of Dr. Kissinger?

■ KOLLEK: I met Dr. Kissinger mainly before he became adviser to the President and before he became Secretary of State. He had come to Jerusalem on several occasions either as a lecturer at the university or as a lecturer at the National Defense College, and on several occasions he spent some time at our home. I believe that the Jewish people have done Dr. Kissinger an injustice. We regarded him somehow as with a kind of Queen Esther complex. We felt that he had been chosen to carry out a mission to save the Jewish people, and that as long as he wasn't concentrating only on this job, he was just a no-goodnik. I think this was a parochial attitude, and I can well imagine that the time may still come when we all will respect Dr. Kissinger and his policy.

w.B.: In writing about you, Saul Bellow says, "Teddy Kollek is Israel's most valuable political asset." Particularly, he refers to the wide range of people that you've met and to whom you've been host. In addition to those whom we've discussed, are there any other international visitors to Jerusalem who stand out in your mind and about whom you'd like to comment?

■ KOLLEK: Yes, one—Saul Bellow. As far as I'm concerned, I think you shouldn't take Saul Bellow's book about Jerusalem so seriously. I have great admiration for the writing of Saul Bellow, but on the whole, his great heroes are *shlemiels*. And when he writes about me, I think he writes with tongue in cheek. At least I hope so. So don't take him seriously.

w.B.: Well, I'm sure, Mr. Mayor, that all here will agree that while Saul Bellow may have written about *shlemiels* in the past, in writing about you he wrote about an unusual, great, and noble Israeli of our time.

19. Serving a Nation under Constant Stress

Ariel Sharon

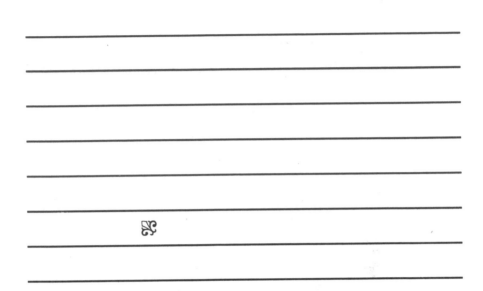

W.B.: The nature of my first meeting with Ariel Sharon tells a great deal about the character of the man. I had invited New York's Senator Daniel Moynihan to participate in my annual Dialogue Forum Series. On the day that he was to appear, I received a call that an emergency had arisen and he would not be able to be present that evening. What was I to do at the last moment? Then I had the idea of calling the Israeli Embassy in Washington to ask whether they had a name to suggest. My call paid off. The Embassy told me that Ariel Sharon was visiting the United States and happened to be in New York City.

I called his hotel, and the General himself answered. I explained my reason for calling and asked whether he would honor us with his presence that night. There was not the usual response, "Let me think about it." His reply was short and to the point: "Yes." I then suggested that I visit his hotel to explain the Dialogue format. His response: "It will be my pleasure to meet you, Rabbi, within the hour."

When I arrived, the door opened and the General, smiling, welcomed me into his suite. The next forty-five minutes remain, for me, unforgettable.

General Sharon's warmth and outgoing manner dispelled any concern I had that he would be a strict military figure—someone who was accustomed to giving orders. In fact, he was the very opposite—a good listener, willing to be guided, kindly, charming, and most charismatic. I explained to him that I never review my questions with my guest, but in light of the circumstances, he might want to share with me any themes he would like me to pose to him for discussion and analysis. He responded that he has two themes that are the leitmotiv of his life: "Israel and the Jewish people. All the rest is commentary. So ask whatever you want."

I was very impressed with his total commitment to Jewish survival and the Jewish people. That evening, as General Sharon and I were facing the door leading to the podium, I asked him to stay behind so that I could first explain to the very large audience that my original guest had cancelled. When I walked out, the crowd realized that something was up. I began by saying that I had walked out alone because the scheduled guest was unavoidably called away to Washington. A groan of disappointment filled the air. When it subsided, I want on to say that at the very last moment I had been able to find a replacement: General Ariel Sharon. At that moment, it was as if the auditorium had been struck by lightning. People began to applaud and to call out "Sharon, Sharon!" When I brought him to the podium, it was nothing less than ecstatic bedlam. As he answered question after question, my awe increased. His responses were very thoughtful. This was not a soldier or a politician speaking. It was a Jew whose love for the Jewish people and Israel radiated passion. All of us were transfixed, for here was a man who tells it as it is. Indeed, not only I but the several thousand people present were swept up by his *ahavat Yisrael*—his love of his fellow Jews.

And now, to our Dialogue.

General Sharon, as you look at the relationship between Israel and the United States, do you feel that the State of Israel has lost its independence? Do you agree with those critics who have stated that because of the armament race and the billions that Israel has been given, Israel has become a vassal of the U.S. government?

> ■ SHARON: I am sorry to say that in many respects Israel *has* lost its independence, although I realize and understand that nowadays it is very hard to be altogether independent. Of course, no nation is completely independent. But the possibility of maneuvering still exists. And when it comes to matters of life and death, even a small country like Israel can be in a position to say "No" when it comes to a most crucial point.

W.B.: Your articles in the Israeli press have shown you to be singularly and uniquely concerned with the inner life in Israel, with Israel's national purpose. You have pondered very deeply about Israel's national purpose and have said: "Israel must become a model state, a worldwide center."

Let's talk about something that we are all aware of, the matter of *yordim*, those people who leave Israel to live elsewhere. I know many American Jews who shun and condemn them. I know many Israelis who are exceedingly critical of them. General Sharon, who are these *yordim*? And why do you think they leave the country?

■ SHARON: To answer your question, I would like to go back
to the Yom Kippur War. As you know, the war took a long
three weeks, and after the war ended our troops were stationed in Egypt for about four months. While we were there,
away from home, we had time to think again and again about
what had happened. One of the main problems that bothered
me then was to try to understand *how* it happened—how
Israel was terribly shocked, shocked in ways from which we
still haven't recovered. All in all, the war was very hard and
very bad, and we suffered thousands of casualties, but the
war was hundreds of kilometers from home. It was not, I
would say, a direct threat to the heart of the country, and yet
it was still a terrible shock.

I try to compare it with the feelings that I had as a very
young officer in the War of Independence in 1948, when we
had in Israel about 750,000 people. We fought for over a year.
Then, too, there were thousands of casualties; we had more
than 7,000 dead and thousands and thousands wounded. It
seemed like an endless war, with no hope; nobody could see
an end to it. And yet we never felt the things that we felt and
thought in the Yom Kippur War.

I have reached the conclusion that in 1948, though the war
was very hard and difficult and dangerous and we suffered,
we looked upon that war as a terrible episode—but still just
an episode. As the war ended, hundreds of thousands of Jews
were in camps in Europe and Cyprus, held by the British. We
were dreaming of a Jewish State. We had a goal; we were
moving from one target to another. When the war was over,
we were going to have a state of our own. By having those
clear national goals, even the Independence War, with so
many casualties, was to us just a terrible episode and no more
than that. We saw it as a natural thing, if one can say that
any war is a natural event.

The Yom Kippur War was different. I think what happened
to us was that Israel became what you could call a normal
country, a normal state. We became like France, Belgium,
Holland. Our goals became normal, became human: to live,
to exist, and so on. For us that is not enough, and that is the
reason why we suffered this terrible shock. It is the reason
why the Yom Kippur War was not just an episode, but rather

something from which we are still suffering. Let me explain further.

Jews are not like other people. I'm not going to say Jews are better or worse. That is not the subject. But what I will say is that Jews are different. Maybe one can symbolically say that as a nation, Jews were not born in a hospital. They were born somewhere on Mount Sinai. And Jews need a reason to live in a hostile world. If the reason to live in Israel is just that life in Tel Aviv is more pleasant than life in Manhattan, then Jews will not live there. You have to understand this. To people who would like to live in Israel just because Israel has become a secure shelter for the Jewish people, I can say that Israel did *not* come into being as a secure shelter for the Jewish people. Of course, we can defend ourselves, and that is something that stands uniquely alone. But in order to live in Israel we must have a clear answer to the question *Why?* Why in Israel? Why not in New York? Why not in London? Why not in Paris? People have to know why.

That brings me to the second half of your question. When you speak about national goals, there are two kinds. One kind should be a physical goal—let's say, doubling the population of Israel. It is not only a goal; it is a necessity. I mean building new towns, new settlements, new industry—these are what I call physical goals. But that is not enough. There must be spiritual and cultural goals. Israel is a modern state, but Israel is also the cultural and spiritual center of the Jewish people. These are two kinds of goals at which we must work in order to achieve a model state. Can we do it? Of course. Jews are strong; Jews can do it very easily.

W.B.: General Sharon, when you spoke about national goals, you touched on the lack of roots and Jewish identity. As you listen to the young people of Israel, do they seem to be skeptical and doubtful? For example, do they have doubts concerning the Jewish right to the State of Israel?

■ SHARON: I would say that Israeli youth are skeptical and have doubts, and I would admit that there are some gaps in their feelings of pride. It is something that will affect us immediately, and we should be worried about it now for two reasons. The first reason is *yeridah* (emigration), which is perhaps the most dangerous problem we have confronting us. The second is that changing those feelings and doubts is a project that will take a generation. That is why we are so seriously concerned with education, for these changes will require education, and I would agree that part of our education must be the study of Jewish history, of the history of the land of Israel, and of relations between Jews in Israel and Jews abroad. There is much ignorance on both sides.

Although we pretend that we know you, and you pretend that you understand all our problems, together we are not equipping our people with enough facts to understand the real situation. That is true in Israel and at the same time it is true in the Diaspora. We are not in contact with the majority of the Jewish people abroad, and that is because the relations that Israel has managed to develop with Jews abroad over the past years have mostly been focused on material contributions and support. Jewish spiritual and cultural life in the Diaspora is in many respects unknown to Israelis in Israel.

w.b.: General Sharon, when you speak about the internal problems of Israel, do you think that the whole process of *mizug galuyot*, absorption and integration of immigrants to Israel from different backgrounds, has succeeded or failed? Where does it stand today?

■ SHARON: I admit to you, I don't think that Israel has managed to solve the problems of integration and absorption. I wrote about this in the Israeli press some years ago and I said that in a way Israel failed in the task of integrating one million of our people into our home. One can say that we were at war, we were engaged in the task of survival between wars, and we had problems. That's true, but we have problems all the time. And yet we still have to admit that we have not managed to solve the problem of integration.

You asked before about the reason for emigration from Israel. During my visits here in the United States I have spent several days with Israeli emigrants. Assuredly, it is one of my reasons for coming here. If I walk in the street, they recognize me, and I can talk to them. I know exactly where to go to see them, and I can have a meeting even without announcements. Yesterday I met Israeli taxi drivers; there are more than a thousand of them in New York alone. It is not something of which to be proud, but it is something of which to take note.

In this new wave of emigration from Israel, you do not find professional people—not doctors, or scientists, or engineers. The vast majority of people are workers coming mostly from Oriental backgrounds. This *yeridah* in particular is one of the most terrible things happening to us now. Naturally, I believe that they must go home to Israel, but I can't force them. And I must admit, I understand their feelings. We've failed them, and I admit we failed. It doesn't make any difference why. What should be emphasized is that efforts must be made at this point to fully integrate these people into Israeli society.

In the last hundred years of modern Zionism, Israel has achieved tremendous accomplishments. What was Zionism? Zionism was a giant revolution that started somewhere in the second half of the last century and proceeded for about eighty or one hundred years, and then it stopped somewhere, let's say thirty or thirty-five years ago. Its revolutionary quality stopped. And so we arrived at a situation of tremendous achievement on the one hand and terrible consequences in other areas on the other—a situation that we have to solve immediately.

W.B.: General Sharon, you have some definite views about Israel's political system, particularly the changes that should be made in it. What reforms do you propose?

■ SHARON: Of course, when it comes to questions of running a state, there are different ideas and different attitudes, whether in matters of the economy, or education, or foreign policy. But you cannot have a political system that makes it impossible to make a decision and to implement those decisions. This is the thing about our political system that should be changed. As a matter of fact, when we talk about all these things that we have to do—*aliyah*, absorption of immigrants, stopping emigration, and making Israel a model state—I don't believe that it can be done unless there is a complete change in the Israeli political system—not for less democracy, but for more.

The first area to be changed must be the system of elections. In the future, we must go into a direct regional system of elections in which the various segments of the population will be represented. In that way, to take just one area, they will also be educated according to their needs. The problem we have is how to provide education that is best suited to the needs of the various populations and groups in Israel, so that we are not giving all the populations the same standard program of formal education. It is very important how this is carried out and who the teachers are. For example, there are some parts of the population that need a long day of study because they come from families with six, seven, or eight children. These children cannot take care of their homework at home, and so they need a longer day at school.

The main thing to remember is that each group is personally represented in government, and they will receive the special kind of education designed to meet their needs. If they are properly educated, then they will integrate into Israeli society. And if they are integrated into society, they will be part of the nation; they won't leave the country to live in the United States. So that is why so much rests upon the very system of education.

Now, of course, when you speak about political systems, the tragedy in Israel is our coalition system. The head of the State, instead of facing the nation and standing with his back to the Knesset, is standing with his back to the nation and looking into the Knesset, trying to form a government dependent upon parties of three and four members. Every decision to be made becomes an endless process, with all kinds of small parties. This observation is not directed to any specific prime minister. It is the way the system operates under any prime minister, and it is ineffective and must be changed.

W.B.: We in the United States and you in Israel have grappled with a troubling question in recent times—namely, do we American Jews have the right to participate in the affairs of Israel? Or is the price we pay for not living there that we can have only a role of financial and moral support?

■ SHARON: In my eyes, Israel is not an Israeli project. Israel is a Jewish project. I don't think that we in Israel would be able to exist without our people abroad—and mostly those here in the United States. And I can also add that Jews all around the world would be unable to exist as Jews without having Israel as an independent, free state. That leads me to the conclusion that to be informed—and I use an even harder word, to *interfere*—is not only your right but your duty.

Many times when I have come here I have tried to convince people that this is what they should do. I know the feeling American Jews have that Israelis are living there, they are fighting, and we are here in the United States, so what can *we* do? But I would try to draw a line. If our people in the United States came to Israel and said, "We don't think that you have to keep that mountain here or that hill there," then I believe Israelis would respond by saying that we are living on that mountain or hill, and if the border were elsewhere, it would create a problem. I would say that we in Israel have to be the ones to decide such direct problems in our day-to-day life. But when it comes to questions concerning the destiny of the Jewish people, the centrality of Israel in the Jewish world, Israel and the Jews, education, economy, immigration to Israel, emigration from Israel, and so on, then it's not only your right—it's your *duty* to be involved! I would add something more: during the past years we've corrupted you and you've corrupted us.

W.B.: General Sharon, you've said that American Jewry must stop buying "Zionist indulgences like Christians in the Middle Ages." You also said, and I paraphrase here, that Zionism has to be more than checkbook Zionism. Would you comment on the fact that stressing the financial aspects demands emphasizing the spiritual and cultural as well?

■ SHARON: My deep belief is that if Israel, in October 1973, did not have three million Jewish inhabitants, but *six* million, the war would not have started. I would go further. If you want Israel to exist, and we spoke about national goals before, the main national goal should be to double the population of Israel by the end of this century. The figures given are that 65,000 North Americans have made *aliyah* over the past four decades. I can tell you that now, North Americans, including the Canadian Jews and their children, number 45,000. After about forty years that is what has happened. My conclusion based on these facts is that the system we use is wrong.

I don't think we should have *shlichim* [emissaries] at all. We don't need them. If the fruit of their tremendous effort is this figure, then we have to send them home. It's not that they are to be blamed; the system is to be blamed. I would very much like it if every American family from Central Park West would beg to live in Kiryat Shmona or Beer Sheva or in Eilat. Maybe in the future that will be the case, but meanwhile it is not exactly the situation. Still, you have to recognize that doubling the population is the most urgent problem we have. But how? I believe the answer to this is to approach American Jews and explain that we need a specific project. Let me give you an example.

We have a problem now in the northern part of the country, in the Galilee. It's a beautiful area. I recommend it, even though I am from the south. The problem in Galilee is that Jews are in a minority there, and Israeli Arabs are the majority population. We must have more towns and cities there.

So I say, take it upon yourselves, come and build a city with an American standard of living, with the American way of life, with the American system of construction—come and do it from beginning to end! From planning to construction, to living, even to making frankfurters and hamburgers for the workers!

Look, Jews nowadays are contributing millions of dollars each year to Israel. I think that you have to come and say, "We are ready to contribute two billion dollars a year, but let us do here what we would like to do." Tell us in Israel what to do and we will do it. I believe that only by bypassing the bureaucracy and changing our approach will we have such new towns—and, of course, thousands and maybe hundreds of thousands of people coming to the country!

W.B.: General, can you tell us, in assessing all that you have so eloquently shared, how you feel as you view the current scene? Do you find you are an optimist or a pessimist?

■ SHARON: Rabbi, generally I am an optimist. Believe me, in my life I've seen many things. I have had in the past some of the most terrible experiences in war and in my personal life, and I must admit I never lost my confidence. But let me tell you one thing: I believe that if we Israelis continue coming to you and saying that everything is in order and that we can solve all the problems and you need merely to support us because we know all the answers, then we all should be very pessimistic.

But if we come to you and you come to us and we both know the situation, then we will recognize the problems together, and we'll fight them together. Let's admit that not all the Jewish genius happens to be in Israel. There are top Jewish people here in the United States in every field of life. Why not confront them and ask them to lend us assistance?

W.B.: General Sharon, no Jew, young or old, will ever forget that Yom Kippur Day in 1973 when news came into every synagogue about the Arab attack on Israel. As you look back on that horrible period, is there any moment or any event that stands out in your mind? If I ask you what you most remember from the Yom Kippur War, what would your answer be?

■ SHARON: There were many, many things to remember. But if I try to emphasize one of the most unforgettable moments, I believe it would be the morning of the 16th of October, the morning after we crossed the Canal. The night before we had been engaged in the most terrible fighting, but it was dark and nobody could really see anything. Suddenly, in the morning, it became so quiet for a while and we looked around and suddenly saw the hundreds of casualities we had.

I think in my division alone we lost that night at least 300 people . . . 300 young men killed. It looked so strange. It was so quiet. Of course, the dead are quiet. But even the Egyptians, I think because of surprise, were also quiet—although for a very short time. It was such a contradiction to see the dead on the one hand and the silence on the other.

W.B.: General Sharon, from your point of view, could a war like the Yom Kippur War ever happen again? Have we learned from it? And more specifically, as you view it, what was the major mistake of that war?

■ SHARON: I think it could happen again. But it depends very much on what we are doing and on what we will do in the future. If Israel is strong—and I mean strong not only militarily but in every aspect—I believe that we can avoid another war like that.

About mistakes? I won't go into the matter of military mistakes here, but I would like to emphasize that I think a major political mistake was made, not by Israel but by then-U.S. Secretary of State Henry Kissinger. Let me explain. I think that at the point when we crossed the canal and were advancing toward Cairo, and when President Sadat was crying and shouting for help, the thing that the Americans could have done was to come to the Egyptians with one sentence: "If you want us to stop the Israelis from entering Cairo, if you want us to see to it that they move back across the canal, then you have to promise here and now that there will be no oil boycott and no oil crisis; that is the only way."

If that had happened, I can assure you there would have been no oil boycott and no oil crisis. That mistake, which I emphasize was not made by us—although, of course, we also made mistakes—was a severe mistake on Kissinger's part. He did not take advantage of the turn of the tide in the war. He had the opportunity to release the free world from the pressure of the Arab sheiks in the desert.

W.B.: Let me conclude, General Sharon, with an observation by a Chasidic rebbe who noted that there are three letters in Hebrew that make up three words. One letter is the *lamed*; another letter is *chet*; and the third letter is *mem*. The *lamed*, the *chet*, and the *mem* make up these words: *lechem*, which is "bread"; *lochem*, which means "to fight"; and *cholem*, which means "to dream." The sage who discovered that these three letters make up these three words said, "Some people fight for bread; some people live to fight; and some people fight for their dreams." And he left the application to each of us. We are an ancient people who have dreamt and fought for enormous dreams. Let us continue to struggle for our dream, especially the dream that Zion will be fully restored, Israel will be at peace, and the Jewish people will be redeemed and renewed.

Our distinguished, brilliant, and dedicated guest has shared with us his own perspective and the unique way in which he has fused his day-to-day actions with courage, valor, and honesty. He truly lives the immortal words of Theodor Herzl: *"Im tirtzu, ein zu agada."* "If you will it, it is no dream." If you and I will it together, if Israel and world Jewry will it together, then yes, it will be no dream.

Avraham Harman

20. ❧ Jewish Interdependence

Avraham Harman

w.b.: What has taken place in Israel has truly been a miracle. The word for miracle in Hebrew is *nes*—and some people see two Hebrew words in it. The *nun*, they say, stands for *neshik*, and the second letter for *sodi*: *neshik sodi*, which means "secret weapon." If, as has been said, the people of Israel possess a secret weapon, that secret weapon has been the determination of its men and women. It has been the dedication and consecration of Israel's leaders, as exemplified by Ambassador Avraham Harman. Ambassador Harman is truly the embodiment of Western culture coupled with a warm, passionate devotion to everything that is Jewish. He is a statesman and speaker who has endeared himself not only in the hearts of Jews, but in the hearts of free people the world over.

It can be asserted without question that the destiny of the State of Israel and of the Jewish people depends on the fullest cooperation between the *Yishuv* in Israel and the people outside of the State. This partnership can be viewed as an economic and cultural partnership. We can look at it as a two-way bridge of information and inspiration. However, one great writer has said that there cannot be a permanent Diaspora once a Jewish homeland has been created. This is a subject of continuing discussion, and we would like to have your point of view on the matter.

■ HARMAN: I have a direct answer to that question. I think that it is written somewhere that since the destruction of the Second Temple, the gift of prophecy in Israel has become the property of fools. I feel that anyone who seeks to prophesy about the future of the Jewish people for all time to come is running a very great risk, and I do not propose to run that risk. I belong to a profession in which there are certain cardinal ground rules. One of them is never to use the word *never*. Because there is now a Jewish State, any statement that there *never* can be a permanent Diaspora is an imprudent approach to the question. I view the relation between the Jewish State and the Jewish people this way: The Jewish State, the State of Israel, was created by the Jewish people. It was brought into existence by the Jewish people for two major purposes. The first was to provide the objective conditions in which Jewish civilization could flourish in conditions of freedom. The second purpose was to have a territory that will always be open to those Jews in need of dignity, citizenship, equality, rootedness, and integration. These are the two purposes. Both of these purposes are of central significance to the Jewish people everywhere in the world, and I think that it was to serve these two purposes that the State of Israel came into existence. I believe that the State of Israel serves these two purposes.

w.b.: Dr. Nahum Goldmann, in the book *Two Generations in Perspective* that was dedicated to Dr. Israel Goldstein on his sixtieth birthday, makes the following observation: "In the disassociation of the young in Israel from the Diaspora, especially the tragedy of Hitler, an attempt to escape the feeling of humiliation and banishing it from consciousness is apparent. An Israeli nation that would strike the Diaspora from its memory would exclude itself from the history of our people and sever Israel from the rest of Jewry." Do you share this sentiment?

■ HARMAN: I do not share the premise of that statement and I do not share its conclusions, if there are any conclusions in it. I think that this statement is based on a fundamental misconception. The youth of Israel is young and the youth of the Jewish community of the United States is young, and therefore they do not look at Jewish history and Jewish experience in the way their elders look at it. I think that this applies both in the United States and in Israel. Take the attitude of our youngsters in Israel to the Nazi period in Jewish history. I have three children, two of whom were born in Israel. The youngest one, who is only 13, was born in Canada, when I was stationed outside Israel. The 13-year-old was born after

Hitler was dead. What does she know about Nazism? She knows from what she reads and from what she hears, but not of her own experience. My son, who is a bit older—he is 18—was born a year before the end of World War II. Fortunately he had no direct experience of the Hitler period and he cannot share my experience of the Hitler period, which equally was not direct. I did not have the experience of living in Nazi Europe, but I lived through the anguish that all Jews who were conscious Jews or conscious human beings at that time experienced as a result of what the Nazis were doing.

It is absurd, I think, to assume that it is possible for me to communicate to my children my experiences of the Nazi period. It is quite impossible, just as it is quite impossible for me to communicate to my children the experience of what it means to create a state, just as it is impossible for a pioneer generation to communicate to its children the meaning of pioneering. This is a universal problem.

The people in your own country who rode the covered wagons out to the West were regarded as boring, when they became grandfathers, for continually reciting to their grandchildren what it meant to travel in covered wagons. There is nothing more boring to a young generation than to be told of the older generation's experiences in the last war. They [the young] are living in the future. They have to go through their own experiences. I cannot understand why anyone should assume that this means that today's young Jewish generation is cut off from the past of the Jewish people. Hopefully, this generation is not going to relive the past of the Jewish people.

There is one thing about our children in Israel. They cannot understand about what happened to the Jews in Nazi Europe because they never experienced anything like that, and one prays to God that they never will. How was it possible for six million people to be slaughtered and not to resist? It has been necessary for us in Israel to correct this misapprehension. It is a distortion of what happened to the Jews in Nazi Europe because there *was* a Jewish resistance movement, a very serious one, and in the most difficult of situations. It is quite impossible for people who live in a free country like the United States to understand what tyranny means, what it means to live under a dictatorship.

Now, I can very well imagine that some youngster who reads this for the first time may ask himself, "Why didn't they do something about it? Why didn't they rise up and revolt?" Rise up and revolt against what? Against the massive power of modern military might that holds people down? I do not know of any country that was suppressed by the Nazis that was liberated without external military intervention. Our children do not understand that. They hear of six million people who were led to slaughter, apparently without resistance, and they are looking for answers. Today there is a new literature being produced in Israel, in Hebrew, about this theme, about the many, many elevating instances we find of Jewish resistance against the Nazis in Europe. This is the thing that we want our children to know. I do not agree that they do not know or are not taught or that they separate themselves from the tragedy of the Jews in Europe. There was a national trial in Israel, as everybody knows. I was not there during the trial, but I know about the impact that this trial had upon our youth and upon the general public in Israel. Therefore, I do not accept the premises or the conclusions of the statement you quoted.

W.B.: Would you want to comment about the specific point that the youth of Israel wish to strike the Diaspora from their memory?

■ HARMAN: I do not agree with that; in fact, I think that the reverse is true. I know of no Jewish community in the world or of no Jewish youth in the world that is confronted more directly with the Diaspora than the youth of Israel. When my kids go to a primary school in Jerusalem, they have the Diaspora in the classroom. You do not have it here in the United States. You have reached the situation in this country that I hope we in Israel will reach in due course: 80 to 90 percent of all American Jews were born in the United States. Therefore, when your children go to school, they go to school mostly with native-born Americans. But my kids go into a class in Jerusalem of thirty to fifty children who come from twenty different countries.

They are much more aware of the Jewish world because of this objective situation than are the Jewish youth in any country in the world. When my boy visits one friend, he hears German spoken by the boy's mother. When he goes to another home, he hears Yiddish spoken; and when he goes to a third home, he may hear Arabic or French. This makes him aware of the breadth and the scope of the Jewish world in a very, very direct kind of way.

You know that we did aim in Israel to build a Jewish State, not to build another Diaspora. That it is a Jewish State and that the vast majority of us there are Jews, we regard as being normal, as being a good state of affairs. We have relations with the Diaspora. I take it that the point of your statement is not that I should teach my son that it would be a good thing for him to settle in Diaspora Israel. I do not think it would be. If I thought so, I myself would not have settled in Israel. I think it is a good thing for him to remain in Israel. Equally, I think it is important and essential, in terms of Israel and in terms of the future of the Jewish people, that he should have rapport with Jews who live outside Israel. This rapport can be developed only within the framework of a common Judaism. I must say that I do not feel that our youth in Israel is cut off from the Jewish world. On the contrary, I believe that our young people very often have the impression that they are right in the middle of the Jewish world. Certainly I receive reports of the Jewish world almost day by day and month by month.

I have a nephew in Israel who is a graduate of the medical faculty of the Hebrew University. About four years ago he came to me in high dudgeon and said that the people in the Jewish Agency, where I was then working, had gone crazy. I said, "What's the matter now?" He said, "I'll tell you what's the matter. The first class of the medical faculty of the Hebrew University has a total enrollment of fifty people. Twenty out of these fifty are immigrant students from a certain country in Europe that I will not mention." He continued, "This is outright discrimination against the Israel-born youth." And it was.

W.B.: Mr. Ambassador, you are familiar with Dr. Moshe Davis. He is teaching at the Hebrew University, where he has established a Contemporary Jewish History Center. He knows American Jewry well, and he writes this regarding the Israel–Diaspora–United States relationship: "Yet it is commonplace that Israelis know far too little of the history, the institutions and aspirations of the American Jewish community. Our melting pot idea has disturbed Israelis." In developing this thesis, he points out the misconceptions that Israelis have about American Jews. One of them is that we are a nation of joiners. Do you feel that Israelis know far too little of American Jewish history and our institutions, and do you feel that they view us merely as a nation of joiners?

■ HARMAN: Behind that statement, with which I would not essentially argue, there is a much deeper question—whether any country whose experience is European or Asian or African is capable of understanding the phenomenon in human history that is called the United States of America. Let us leave Jews out of it for the time being. The United States of America is an absolutely unique creation. I would point out that about half of the people in Israel are of European origin, and the other half are of Oriental origin. There is nothing in the political and social experience of these two groups that could condition them to understand the United States of America. For example, I was born in England, where the Jews are a very tiny minority. I think today about 322,000 out of a total population of some fifty-seven million are Jews. Great Britain is essentially a homogeneous society. It is not a melting pot. There are Englishmen, Scotsmen, Welsh, and Irish, and each of these groups is homogeneous. The Jew, living in any one of these parts of Great Britain, understands that he has to acquire in one or two or three or four generations the language, the outlook, the customs, the habits, the dress, and everything else of the dominant group. This is not the American experience. I do not know whether the United States is a melting pot or not; I am not qualified to say. But it is something unique.

By contrast take the experience of the Jews of the Soviet Union. The Soviet Union, like the United States, is a country made up of many different groups, but with this difference: there is no attempt by philosophy or national purpose to merge these groups into a Soviet nation. There is no such thing as a Soviet nation. There is a Soviet federation of nationalities. In the Soviet Union you are not a Soviet national; you are a Soviet citizen, and then your nationality is Russian or Byelo-Russian or Ukrainian or Uzbek or whatever, or Jewish. Therefore, the Jewish experience in the Soviet Union is utterly different from the Jewish experience in the United States, where the Jews are not a national group and where no philosophical distinction is drawn between citizenship and nationality. In almost the whole of Central and Eastern Europe, there is a philosophical difference, and a very deep one, between citizenship and nationality.

I know Jews in Israel who, whenever they meet a Jew from the United States or anywhere else for that matter, say to him: "Wait! Life is good for you now, but we will see what will happen." This is the experience of the German Jews speaking. Life was very good for the German Jews in the early 1930s—economically, socially, professionally, every other way. Then their world collapsed. It is entirely human for them to assume that this will be the inevitable course of experience for Jewish groups everywhere.

I can give you one instance of this. When I was stationed in New York, a very good friend of mine, a friend whose experience was European, said "Harman, I would like to ask you a very simple question. Can you tell me how a man named Finkelstein could come to my office and tell me that he is 100 percent American?" It was a very good example, because at that time the city treasurer of New York was Jerry Finkelstein, and the mayor was Vincent Impelliteri. I told this friend that if it was possible for Vincent Impelliteri to be 100 percent American, then it was equally possible for Jerry Finkelstein to be 100 percent American. But this was quite outside my friend's experience, just as America is quite outside the experience of the people I know who are of European background.

I think that this is most relevant to the statement by Dr. Davis. It is quite impossible to teach our children in Israel the reality or the problems or the achievements of American Jewry without giving them a thorough understanding of this unique creation that is the United States. That is the essential background for an understanding of the American Jewish community.

I am not sure that these things can be taught out of books. They have to be seen. I welcome the fact that there is a growing tendency among our youth to come to America for brief visits or to study. I think that no person's experience in the twentieth century is complete without a taste of America, and those who get this taste return to Israel with a much deeper understanding of American Jews because they have a much deeper understanding of America.

W.B.: This is a new approach to a matter that we have heard discussed many times along a number of different lines. It is quite obvious that one cannot examine any aspect of life in Israel without taking into account the wellsprings of European Jewish life that have so much influence on the people there.

I am reminded of the story of the man in Tel Aviv who went to his tailor to pick up a suit late one afternoon. The shop was closed, and on the door was a crude sign with four handwritten Hebrew letters: *alef, bais, gimmel, daled*. This made no sense to him, so he waited around for a bit, and finally along came the tailor. After some preliminary expressions of annoyance, the customer asked, "Where have you been? Why did you not leave a message when you had to close in the middle of the day?"

The tailor explained that he had left a message. "There it is on the door: *alef, bais, gimmel, daled*."

"And what is that supposed to mean?" asked the customer. The tailor replied, "*Ich bin gegangen davenen*."

Speaking of *davening*, I would like to discuss religion and the synagogue in Israel. It has been said that the synagogue is emerging as a family institution in the United States, filling cultural and social as well as spiritual needs. In the Diaspora the synagogue is becoming, more and more, a unifying force. Professor Simon Greenberg, Vice Chancellor of the Jewish Theological Seminary of America, wrote: "The synagogue is the only institution that can make an individual identify the sense of unity in space and time, not only with the Jewish people, but with the highest ideals of all mankind. Yet there is a lack in so many of the best Israeli youth of an identification with the totality of the Jewish people of the past and the present. To the Israeli, Hebrew presents a unifying force. Israeli Jews have told me repeatedly that while we in America need the synagogue to identify ourselves as Jews, they in Israel do not require such self-identification, hence they do not need the synagogue. The role of the synagogue, thus interpreted, declares it to be essentially a Diaspora institution, and as such it carries a stigma for many an Israeli."

This is not an uncommon point of view. We have heard it from many sources. What are your feelings on the subject, Mr. Harman? Can you add anything from your own experience in this matter?

■ HARMAN: I would like to say this: I live on a little street in Jerusalem. It is called Disraeli Street. On one corner is a synagogue, and on the next corner is a synagogue. If I stay in bed late on *Shabbat* morning—which happens very often, I am afraid, because it is the only day that I am off—I console myself by the fact that I can hear the services from two directions just by leaving my window open. And when I was sick in bed one Rosh Hashanah, I did not have to listen to the *shofar* on the radio. I think that the two million Jews of Israel have no reason whatsoever to bow our heads to you in terms of synagogue attendance. I make bold to say that this goes for young people as well. But I will say this: we are a mixed bunch in Israel, and on a Saturday morning in Tel Aviv you will find as many people on the beaches as you will in the *shuls*. Tel Aviv has a pretty large population. That means that there is quite a large synagogue attendance on an ordinary *Shabbat* without a bar mitzvah.

What can one gather from this? There is one significant difference. A person in Israel who goes to *shul* goes there to *daven*. He does not have to go there for any other reason. To learn Hebrew, he goes to school. To read a Hebrew book, he sits in his own living room. He does not have to be reminded that he is a Jew. He lives with Jews. He does not have to go to a synagogue dance in order to meet a Jewish girl. If he goes to any café he meets Jewish girls, and in 99 out of 100 cases he will marry a Jewish girl as a natural course of events. This is the challenge to religion in Israel. The synagogue in Israel cannot flourish by social impulse or because it is the fashionable place to go or because it is the place where you meet Jews. You meet Jews everywhere in Israel. You build up synagogues in Israel by attracting people to religion. I happen to believe that you have to attract people to religion, convince them that they should be religious; I believe that you cannot coerce them or force them into being religious.

Therefore, I do not share these views about the role of the synagogue in Israel. We do not have very many beautiful buildings, as synagogues go, in Israel. We regard the synagogue as a place where you pray, and you can pray anywhere as long as you have a *minyan*. I think at the last count in Tel Aviv, where there is probably today a total population of 400,000 people, there are 400 synagogues of different sizes. Some of them are very big and some of them very small. In Jerusalem, when I used to walk to work to the Jewish Agency building or to the Foreign Office, I passed many little synagogues. So the synagogue has struck deep roots in Israel. It is not regarded as a Diaspora institution. It is a Jewish institution.

Because Israel is a Jewish State, there are very many synagogues in Israel, and their number will grow. To populate these synagogues, we will have to teach religion and not organize bingo games or bridge clubs, because for bingo and bridge there are other places of assembly that are Jewish. This is the essential difference. At the same time, I hope that I have not been too sharp. I do not want to denigrate or underestimate the—let us call them the extracurricular activities of synagogues in various countries, where I have had the good fortune to participate in some of these activities. But in Israel, a discussion session like this, of questions and answers on matters of current concern, does not have to be organized in the synagogue. During the winter season in Jerusalem, the Journalists' Association holds a weekly reading called "The Living Newspaper," which is something like "Meet the Press." At these sessions, three or four members of the Journalists' Association interview either an Israeli or a visiting personality. Admission is open to everyone and it is not held in a synagogue but in a public hall. That is the difference.

W.B.: This leads me to something in which I, as a Conservative rabbi, am very keenly interested. Dr. Davis made another statement in discussing religion in Israel. He said, "The choice in religion is between Orthodoxy and secularism." Now, I am very interested in knowing what the hopes are for the growth and development of the Conservative or Reform movements in Israel. As it stands now, if I were to move to Israel, I would be faced with severe limitations on my services as a Conservative rabbi.

What do you think of the possibility of strengthening the Conservative and Reform movements in Israel, which might bring the message of religion to Israeli youth in a more modern and understandable way?

■ HARMAN: Again I am afraid that I do not accept the basic premise inherent in that statement, and I do not believe that it is in accord with the realities of life in Israel. There are many, many segments of life in Israel from the religious point of view. There is a great range, a kaleidoscope of differences. I am persuaded that at this time the average Jew is in the middle and does not want to be confronted by a choice between Orthodoxy and secularism. This has always been the position in Israel since I have been there, which is a very long time. The Israeli Jew likes to ride with his religion. When he goes to *shul*, he likes to go to an Orthodox *shul*, but he does not like to go there three times a day and necessarily every week. When he feels a yearning for religious expression or religious participation, he goes to the kind of Orthodox synagogue that is usually somewhere in the middle. And if he is an immigrant, then of course he goes to the kind of Orthodox synagogue where they sing the same tunes that he heard in his boyhood. Therefore, there is an Italian synagogue in Jerusalem and a Polish and a German, perhaps forty or fifty types of synagogues in Jerusalem.

I would say that the middle-ground people are in the majority in Israel. There is an Orthodox wing and there is a secularist wing, and I believe that the secularist wing is growing, has been growing in the last year or two, not because it is antireligious, but because it is against what they call Orthodox coercion. We have a type of person whom you will recognize very easily, I am sure. There are many different kinds of *nudniks* in the world. One of the most irritating kinds of *nudnik* is the "principle *nudnik*," although it can be argued that without the principle *nudnik* the history of civil liberties and human freedom would be very different from what it has been. I am talking of the kind of fellow who says, "If there were civil marriage in Israel, I would in any case get married before a rabbi, but I do not want to be denied the alternative."

Speaking seriously, this is a tenable position. The secularist movement in Israel must be judged from that point of view— not that it is antireligious or atheistic, but that it believes that the public role of Orthodoxy in Israel is objectionable. It has nothing against religion, and in its ranks there are many people who personally are religious, and even a few who are Orthodox. We have to be very careful in these judgments. I am an average citizen of Israel, and I know the way the people in my circle behave. Nobody could conceive of his boy not being a bar mitzvah.

I say very often that I have noticed one difference between religion in your communities in America and religion in Israel. Many people in America do not even know when they are violating *Shabbat*, because there is no secular evidence of it. On *Shabbat* here, the buses run and the trains run and the businesses are open and the people drive their cars, and life is more or less exactly the same as it is on any other day. Now when I break *Shabbat* in Jerusalem, I know that I am breaking *Shabbat*. The whole town is closed. I am painfully aware of it. I experienced this once very dramatically when I left Israel for a visit to England during *Hol Hamoed* Sukkot, and I spent the first day of Sukkot in Jerusalem and Simchat Torah in London. These are two very different worlds.

As to your specific question—whether these shadings of Judaism that you have produced in the United States would catch on in Israel—I have one question about that. Is everybody so absolutely certain that this trilogy of American Judaism is a set pattern? I do not have this impression. I believe that there is constant change going on, that one group feeds from the experience of another, and that a great deal depends on the personality of the rabbi and the leadership group in the congregation, but I do not believe from my experience of visiting synagogues of various persuasions in the United States that this is a cast-iron division. Maybe there is an ecumenical movement going on in American Judaism. I do not know. This is a question that I would ask because I personally would not like to see the introduction into Israel of a hidebound pattern that in reality is *not* hidebound and that is changing all the time elsewhere.

Several synagogues in Israel are affiliated with the World Union of the United Synagogue (the Conservative movement), and a few synagogues in Israel are affiliated with the Reform movement through the World Union of Progressive Judaism. I believe that there are going to be more of both types. They may be affiliated but I rather suspect that the Reform Jew from Cincinnati who visits one of these Reform services in Jerusalem will find it a trifle Orthodox for his liking, both in terms of the language used for prayer and in terms of the prayers themselves, and of the spirit of the place.

I am not sure that I rightly know what religion is. I personally have not spent a great deal of time on theological reading or research. But I think that I do know the meaning of religious experience—personal religious experience or religious emotion. In the old days, when life in Israel was pretty rough and there weren't even many tablecloths, you could go into many of the so-called secularist kibbutzim on a *Shabbat* eve and there would be sheets on the tables with little bowls of flowers. The older children might be sitting there with their parents, and they would start with a song of Bialik greeting the Sabbath Bride. This was a religious experience. In America, you could institutionalize it and call it Reform Judaism. In Israel, it is called secularist antireligionism.

W.B.: Mr. Ambassador, I would like to make two comments. The first is that you are perhaps the first individual, possibly because statesmen have not often been asked to talk on this subject, who has truly enlightened us on this matter and led us to a deeper understanding. Part of what we are trying to express in this dialogue about bringing the two communities closer is that something very definite and concrete should be done to change this point of view that American Jews have about the religious life in Israel. I think that you have changed it for me as you have changed it for the people here.

My second point leads me to still another question, and that is this: If you were to ask me whether I personally hold the opinion that Conservative Judaism should push itself into the State of Israel, I would be in the camp that says no. If you were to ask me about Reform Judaism pushing itself into the State of Israel, I would say no. I agree wholeheartedly that the growth, the development, the evolution of the religious feeling, pattern, and observance has to be indigenous to the soil, the land, and the people. You are absolutely correct in stating that this tripartite division of Judaism in America is not clear-cut. Someone once described American Jewish life as an architectural monstrosity, where a synagogue downstairs has men and women sitting together and therefore it is, so to speak, left-wing; upstairs it is ultra-Orthodox, where men and women are separate, and that is right-wing. Therefore, the lower level of the building leans to the left, while up one flight it leans to the right. The whole building is thus leaning in various directions.

The Chief Rabbi of the Israeli Army, Rabbi Goren, observed that there should be a Sanhedrin in Israel. Fundamentally, I am completely in accord, but if you were to ask Rabbi Goren if a Conservative rabbi or a Reform rabbi could make a contribution, if there could be some kind of discourse between these groups, he would say no. So he brings down an iron curtain in not allowing the introduction of any new ideas. Because the Orthodox in Israel take this position, the Conservative and Reform movements make an effort to establish themselves in Israel.

Let me ask you to enter the area where angels fear to tread, and to prophesy a little. What do you feel the possibilities are for the establishment of a Sanhedrin in Israel? Do you think that a Sanhedrin, if and when established, could reflect the feelings, opinions, and scholarship of the rabbis of world Jewry? Because some of the finest rabbis in the world are here in America, both in the Conservative and Reform branches of Judaism.

■ HARMAN: I would like to make one or two observations before getting to the question of the Sanhedrin, which I think can wait, because from my point of view it is not going to happen tomorrow. That is a prophecy that can be checked out. There are two differences between American Jewry and the Jewry in Israel. You will forgive me if I speak very frankly. I think that we have in Israel everything that you have in American Jewry, but with this difference. In New York the Jewish community gets on beautifully by the simple process of never meeting. The Rosh Yeshivah of Mire in Brooklyn rarely meets the Rabbi of Temple Emanu-El. They may meet on common Jewish business, but otherwise even a congregant of Temple Emanu-El is unlikely to meet anywhere with an official of the Yeshivah of Mire. In Jerusalem, they meet. Therefore, they sometimes clash. We do not have recourse in Jerusalem to this wonderful modus vivendi that you have, of getting on wonderfully by never meeting or never having to meet. We *have* to meet.

My other observation is this: many American Jews who speak to me about religion in Israel try to convey to me the impression, maybe quite honestly and sincerely, that the whole of United States Jewry, all five and a half million of them, all keep *kashrut* and never break the Sabbath, are all affiliated with synagogues, and all attend synagogue.

As long as I am speaking so very frankly, I'd like to relate one of my first experiences with North American Jewry. It was not in the United States; it was in a city in Canada where I was attending a weekend conference of the Zionist movement in that area. All the delegates were staying at the same hotel. I was there with a colleague who is an Israeli and is not a very Orthodox person and does not come from a very Orthodox home. We met on *Shabbat* morning in the dining room for breakfast at a table for four before going to the synagogue service. I ordered boiled eggs, which is what I liked for breakfast in those days, and he ordered eggs and bacon, which I knew he liked for breakfast. I said to him, "Look, skip the bacon today." He said, "Sure, I understand," and did without the bacon. A couple of minutes later we were joined at the table by two of the principal officers of the convention we were attending—both of them, and I say this most sincerely, outstanding Canadian Jews. They ordered eggs and bacon. After breakfast was over, we all left to go to synagogue and I said, "Well, where is the synagogue?" One Canadian said, "Two or three blocks away," and I said, "Fine, let us walk there." He said, "No, it's winter and it's cold. Get into my car."

Why am I saying this? Because these fellows who had ordered bacon would have been horrified if they had seen an Israeli eating bacon. "It is for this we built Israel that you should eat bacon?"

I want to say, in this connection, that there cannot be two standards. It is very easy for somebody to sit here in New York and criticize my children because they are not Orthodox. But what about his children or his grandchildren? I am more certain about the Jewish identity of my grandchildren than he is of his, but I do not take it for granted. I believe in the process of education. God needs a little bit of help with this. While Conservative rabbis in Israel cannot at this time celebrate marriages, they have every opportunity in the world for religious influence. Many ears will be open to them in many, many parts of the country, including places that are written off as secularist.

I had a discussion once with an Orthodox man who held a position of authority in Jerusalem. I said to him, "I've just come back from America, and they have a wonderful thing there. Children's services are held in the synagogues. Why don't you organize these in Jerusalem? I would be glad to have my children go there." He asked me, "Why don't *you* organize them?"

That's the whole point. I do not feel so strongly about it that I would organize, but I would be a potential client of yours if you would sell me on it. Now, *you* are the impassioned religious person. Why don't you take the initiative and sell me on it? That is why I believe that there is a great need in Israel for the congregational rabbi—Orthodox, Conservative, or Reform, it does not matter.The man who goes out to people will find people. That is how you influence; that is how you educate. You do not wait for people to come to you. And we have attracted some rabbis like that in recent years, and they have done some wonderful things in Israel. I think there is a future for them. There has to be an educational missionary approach.

On this question of the Sanhedrin, I would say this: if there ever is a Sanhedrin, there will be not one but a number of them. I would say to you, Rabbi Berkowitz, that if Rabbi Goren succeeds in organizing a Sanhedrin, you certainly will not be a member of it. But there will be many hundreds of Orthodox rabbis who will pronounce a *herem* on it, and will forbid any rabbi to join it, so that he will be left with only a few people who will join his Sanhedrin.

One of the great beauties of Jewish religious life and Jewish religious history is that we have no hierarchy and that we hold to the principle that there is no vicarious relationship between the individual Jew and God. It is a direct responsibility and a direct relationship. There are certain rabbis who influence us and other rabbis who do not. There have always been schools of rabbis and there always will be schools of rabbis. The Chief Rabbi of Israel has a position in the law of Israel, but he is boycotted by a section of the Orthodoxy in Israel, and always has been and always will be, just as he is not recognized by the Conservative or the Reform people in Israel. I suppose that this situation will also continue.

W.B.: All of us would be interested in your comment regarding the Brother Daniel case and the decision that was rendered by the Israel Supreme Court. [*Editor's note*: This case was current at the time of this Dialogue.]

■ HARMAN: Actually, this matter is so very simple that it has given rise to a great deal of misunderstanding. There are two laws in Israel governing immigration. One is called the "law of return," which applies to Jews; and then there is a general law of immigration, which applies to everyone else. This difference exists because Israel was projected as a Jewish State. Our law-givers enunciated the view that a Jew coming to Israel was, in the deepest historical sense, returning. He was not a new immigrant; rather, he was returning to his ancestral homeland. Therefore, our law provides that a person who is a Jew coming to Israel on an immigrant's visa becomes a citizen of Israel from the moment he lands on the soil of Israel unless he specifically says that he does not want to be one. He is given the right to say that he does not want to be a citizen. That could be a very precarious state of affairs, because if a man asks for an immigrant visa to settle in a country, presumably he wants to be a citizen of that country, but we give him the right to opt out if he wants to.

However, a non-Jew who wants to immigrate to Israel must file an application when he gets his immigrant's visa. He has to be in the country for two years, and then he can apply for citizenship. He is granted citizenship and he becomes a citizen of Israel.

Brother Daniel, whose family name is Rufeisen, and who is settled in Israel, applied for citizenship under the law of return as a Jew, and claimed that he had been born a Jew, that the fact that he had converted to Catholicism did not mean that he had ceased to be a Jew, and that therefore under the law of Israel he was entitled to immediate naturalization as a Jew under the law of return. This was the legal question that our Supreme Court had to decide. The Supreme Court did not try to define who is a Jew. This is a complicated question. But the Court did say that under the civil law of Israel a man who was born a Jew and becomes converted to another religion ceases to be a Jew. This was the decision. The decision was not that because Rufeisen has become a Catholic, he could not become a citizen of Israel. As a matter of fact, Brother Daniel has now *applied* for citizenship in Israel. Although he converted to Catholicism he had a wonderful personal record during the Nazi period. This is a man who with great heroism saved very, very many Jewish lives during the Nazi period and who has a deep devotion to the State of Israel.

I think that his application is being treated very sympathetically. What the Court ruled was that a man who is converted to another religion cannot, under the laws of Israel, be regarded any longer as a Jew. I think this is so obvious that we did not need the learned judges to make this point, but, at any rtate, they did.

W.B.: We feel, to one extent or another, a thrill of pride when we see or hear a reference to the State of Israel, for Israel is the culmination of a long dream for many of us and a dramatic expression of our aspirations as Jews and as human beings. As year follows year, the position of Israel as a democratic force in an undemocratic corner of the world becomes increasingly significant. Avraham Harman, who has all his life been intimately involved with Zionism and with the international Jewish community, has brought the realiy of Israel that much closer to us. All Jews can be proud that the State of Israel has so astute and articulate a representative as Avraham Harman.

PART V

The Next 4,000 Years

ஃ Introduction

There is these days a subculture of social scientists called "futurists." They may be economists, sociologists, or historians—but regardless of their individual fields of study, they apply their knowledge and experience to the conditions of today; they look at the recent past, consider possible trends, and tell us where we are going. Their books and magazine articles are very widely read, and they appear frequently on radio talk shows.

Among Jews, the more serious side of study has always been the question "Where have we been?" rather than "Where are we going?" To help us know more about this, we have the Book of Books that recounts our history as a people, our traditions as a culture, and our beliefs as a religion.

Yet Jews do not and never have lived solely in the past. We have always been very much of the world of today. In other eras, however, we may have been limited to living in the Jewish world. This did not spring from any myopia on our part; it was imposed on us from the outside, which was in great part closed to us. Today, things are different. We are part and parcel of today's United States, today's Europe, today's world.

And of tomorrow's world also. We would be less than human if we did not, at times, wonder about the future of our people. What kind of Judaism will our children's children inherit? How will they change it even further? Which of our traditional concepts will be maintained, which will be cast aside; what will be added? Judaism, as a culture and as a religion, is not static. Even the most rigid Orthodoxy of today is discernibly different from the practices and beliefs of its East European (not to mention Middle Eastern) precedents.

Questions arise: Will there be one unified Jewish religious community, or three, or five? Will differences between Jews and their neighbors continue to become less evident, or will some reaction set in to make us more individual as a people? Will anti-Semitism become more threatening, or less so? Here? In Europe? Will the majority of Jews continue to vote along liberal and democratic lines, or will they swing toward conservatism? Will Israel continue to need massive economic aid from the United States and other Jewish communities? Will some kind of effective peace be achieved in the Middle East?

Futurism is not an exact science, but neither is it merely a pleasant guessing game. We can make no firm predictions, but we can make reasonable judgments as to what the future may hold. Our most important resources are an understanding of the past, a knowledgeable consideration of current situations, and a perceptive awareness of trends.

Basic to these are the points of view expressed by sophisticated observers of and participants in the current scene. Discussions such as those that follow can give us much insight and thereby help us to answer our questions about the future.

21. ❧ A Cure for Pessimism

Dr. Cecil Roth

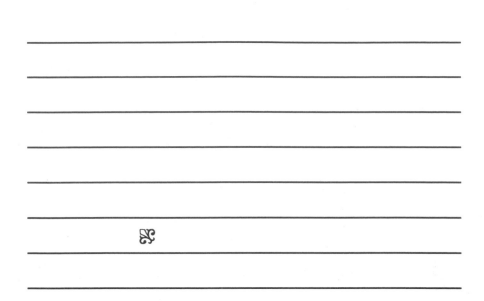

W.B.: Our distinguished guest considers his greatest title of distinction the fact that he was included among those listed as the first five hundred that were to be arrested by the Nazis when and if they succeeded in landing in England. His worldwide reputation as a historian and scholar rests, of course, upon a much more solid basis. The author of more than thirty books and hundreds of articles, Dr. Roth first studied history at Oxford University after his return from service in World War I. His early specialization in Italian history resulted in the publication of *The Last Florentine Republic* in 1925. Since then, Dr. Roth has extended his historical interests and, in particular, has written about various aspects of Jewish history. He is known for his *History of the Jews in Italy, History of the Marranos, Jewish Contribution to Civilization, History of the Jews in England, Life of Manasseh Ben Israel, Life of the Duke of Naxos,* and *Short History of the Jewish People,* among others.

Dr. Roth has been actively involved in Jewish Studies at the University of Oxford, for many years beginning in 1939. He has lectured extensively in Europe, Africa, and America, and is now a resident of Israel.

Professor Roth, inasmuch as it is more than four decades since your first visit to America, I thought it would be interesting if we spent some of the time on your views and your opinions about Jewish life in America as you have observed it during that time.

We know that American Judaism is divided into three branches. In fact, I would say that American Judaism is even further divided—into four or five or six branches. Do you believe that some day, perhaps in the far distant future, the three groups will merge into *Am Yisroel Echod*—into one peoplehood of Israel, religiously speaking?

■ ROTH: In fact, I do not. There is, unfortunately, a halachic difference among these various groups—let us say a difference on the point of Jewish law. I remember years ago that Professor Israel Davidson said that there was a future for Judaism in America; he meant Conservative Judaism. Of course, there *is* a future for Judaism in America and probably, I would say, for "Judaisms." One of the troubles that I see the Jewish world faced with today is the very fact that in marital matters we are becoming divided into more than one people.

The trouble is that Halachah, Jewish law, cannot be modified. In certain respects Jewish law could not be modified, even by a rabbinical assembly or *beit din*. And when the Jewish marital laws are completely neglected by a large element of Jewry, you will have very, very serious difficulties in the future. I remember that years ago I spoke to Rabbi Leo Baeck when he was at the Hebrew Union College in Cincinnati, and I wish that what he told me there had been recorded in its totality because I think it is of such importance. Leo Baeck, as you know, is almost the "patron saint" of Reform Judaism, a truly venerated figure. Reform Judaism has had many important figures, but I have a vague idea that it does not have many venerated figures. He said to me that there are some things to which all Jews must adhere if we are to remain Jews. He cited circumcision as one example. He said, "I don't know why. Rationally I cannot explain it, but if we give up the *brit milah*, we are finished as a people." He said that we must control our marriage laws in accordance with the *Shulchan Aruch*, the traditional code of Jewish law. He said that Reform Jews would interpret it more liberally and the Orthodox would interpret it more strictly, but unless all Jews hold to it, by and large they will be divided into different peoples and different groups.

I am afraid that this is what is happening. When a young couple comes to be married, they have to produce not merely their own birth certificates but the *ketubot* of their parents and their parents' parents for a number of generations back. Israel manages it, surprisingly enough, a shade more liberally. But unfortunately we are getting to a stage where in all the countries of the world we are going to have a group of people whose immediate ancestors control their marriages in accordance with the traditional Jewish religious code, and another group whose parents were careless of such things as marriage with a woman who has not received a Jewish religious divorce—a *get*; or marriage of a *Kohen* and a widow, and similar things. It may be highly regrettable, but the first group is already beginning to refuse to intermarry with the second group. I am afraid that American Judaism in the not very distant future is going to be divided between these two groups, who, if they do not intermarry with one another, will not be able to mix with one another in a normal fashion.

W.B.: To what extent, beyond the question of Halachah, would you say that the tripartite division of Judaism in the United States is continued because of institutional rivalry. We live in a society in which we must advance, we must be the biggest, the greatest. We have three institutions, Yeshiva University, the Jewish Theological Seminary, the Hebrew Union College. We have three synagogue associations. Institutions are headed by boards of directors composed of very human people. I am not trying to step on any toes, but I would like to know whether you can see American Jewry achieving unity in light of the institutional rivalry of the three groups.

■ **ROTH:** In a community as enormous as the American community, I do not think that this rivalry can do anything but good. In England we are in a different position, with a very small community that can barely keep up one rabbinical seminary; we now have two or three, which I think is most regrettable. But here there is plenty of room for all of them. I do not see any reason why they should not continue.

W.B.: I would like to quote a few sentences from your essay "Proselytes of Righteousness." You write: "The indication that proselytizing was a recognized institution in Jewish life however much it may have been concealed was fact." Then you say: "The blood of some proselyte, more remote or less, must course in the veins of every Jew in the world today." I wonder whether you think that Judaism will begin to seek actively to convert non-Jews, and whether, in the next few years, there will be a more aggressive mission to the Christian community.

■ **ROTH:** Of course. It must be obvious that the blood of converts courses in all of our veins. It has been calculated that we all had a million ancestors in the year 1066. We all have had two parents, and four grandparents; if you go back in geometric progression, you get to about a million in 1066. It is certain that among those million names there must be some non-Jews; it cannot possibly be otherwise. There cannot be such a thing as a Jew whose blood is absolutely pure. You must remember that there have been periods in Jewish history when the amount of conversion to Judaism was quite considerable. It was so at the time of the Second Temple; it was so in the Roman Empire; I think it was so at the beginning of the period of Jewish settlement in Europe; it was so in the period of the Khazars; it was so in Russia in the Czarist period.

However, in the course of the Middle Ages it became almost second nature to the Jews to refuse to encourage proselytes. It became almost a tenet of Judaism that proselytes must be rebuffed, and admitted only with difficulty. I think we continue to have that as part of our nature today. We receive proselytes, but we barely welcome them, and we certainly do not encourage them. I do not think that we are ever likely to change this. It has become second nature. You know that there is a movement for *giyur* in Israel today that is beginning a certain propaganda for conversion to Judaism. It has not had any remarkable success and has not received any outstanding support. I do not think that Judaism is going to become a proselytizing religion.

W.B.: I recall a leading rabbi observing that before there could be an aggressive mission to the Christian community, there should be one to the Jewish community. He made the very perceptive comment that the Jewish people have enough *goyim* in their midst, and, therefore, they should first convert the Jews themselves. This, I think, is a very telling observation.

On the subject of Jewish ancestry, you wrote a fascinating essay called "Who was Columbus?" I have discussed it from the pulpit, as others have. You say, regarding the stories about Columbus being of Jewish ancestry, that "these inquiries convinced me, not that the theory was true, but that it must be taken seriously—that Columbus was a Spaniard and a Jew." Would you briefly care to discuss this?

■ ROTH: You know that the question of the ancestry of Columbus has been discussed for many years. There is not too much doubt that he was born in Genoa, though I myself have visited no less than three of his "birthplaces." The Spaniards wanted to claim him as a Spaniard, and the only method by which they were able to do it was by trying to demonstrate that he had Jewish ancestry. Only yesterday I saw, in a bibliography of articles published in Italy during the war in 1942, when Italy was still on the German side, an article titled "The Jewish Conspiracy to Deprive Genoa of the Honor of Being the Birthplace of Columbus."

A great deal has been written about Columbus. There was an old gentleman in New York who noticed that on the right-hand side on the top of some of Columbus's letters there was a little squiggle, and he remembered that his father used to write *Baruch HaShem* at the top right-hand corner of all his letters. He tried to read these marks as *B'ezras HaShem* and thus to show that Columbus tried to reveal his Judaism by putting two Hebrew letters at the top of every letter he wrote. He wasted quite a considerable fortune on this rather pathetic and ludicrous attempt. But there was very much more to it than this. Just before the last war, when my book on the Marranos had just appeared, I was approached by some people who were writing on Columbus and wanted to know what I thought about his Marrano ancestry. I must say that I did not think very much of it. However, I have read one or two things that I found remarkable and inexplicable. In his mystical signature, which he told his heirs always to use, Columbus used the three letters *AAA*, which was the Marrano abbreviation for *Adonoi*. In all Marrano literature, when they wanted to use the name of God there was always an *A* with a full stop before and after, in the same way that Columbus used it in his signature.

Then there was another curious point. It is difficult to tell anything about Columbus because he was certainly a most uncontrollable liar. One cannot believe a word he said, and he obviously had something to conceal. But sometimes, something comes out of his concealment. We know that he sailed from Spain on the third of August, early in the morning, 1492. And no one was ever able to understand why he postponed his departure until the third of August, when the tides were favorable and everything was ready on the second. But the second of August that year was Tisha B'Av and there is a rabbinical dictum: "If anybody does any work on Tisha B'Av, he never has any blessing from that work."

That is probably only a coincidence, but one other thing is almost unanswerable. In one passage Columbus says: "Up to the present year, which is the year of our Lord 1468, there have elapsed 1,400 years since the destruction of the Second House, *La Secunda Casa.*" *La Secunda Casa* is *Bayit Sheinee*, which is the Second House or Second Temple, which is essentially a Jewish phrase. I cannot understand how a non-Jew could have used it. "There had elapsed since the destruction of the Second House 1,400 years." Now that means, since he was writing in 1468, that he regarded the Second Temple in Jerusalem as having been destroyed in the year 68. In fact, it was destroyed in the year 70. However, according to the ancient and completely erroneous Jewish tradition, the destruction of Jerusalem was in the year 68, and not in the year 70.

So here is Columbus using a Jewish phrase and a Jewish calculation, and I really cannot imagine how a non-Jew could have done it. I must say that there is really a very great and increasing weight of evidence about the hypothesis of Columbus's Jewish birth. Since the publication of my book, further evidence has been accumulated which seems to suggest that Christofo Colón was a *chuta* of Majorca. That name was found among the archives of the island of Majorca. While I cannot be positive about it, I think the probability is that he *was* of Marrano birth.

W.B.: Whenever the name of Columbus comes up I recall the story of the Jewish immigrant who appeared before the examiner and was exceedingly nervous. After he gave his name and address, the next question was about when he had arrived in America. Instead of saying 1941, he said 1491. The examiner turned to him and said, "Why didn't you wait another year; you could have come with Columbus."

You have made two very interesting comments on the unassimilable Jew. You say: "Thus, what with the non-Jewish strain among the Jews, and the Jewish strain among the non-Jews, the Jew and his neighbor have had far more common ancestry in these centuries than is generally imagined." In the same essay you say: "Far from being unassimilable, then, the Jews are—from the Jewish point of view—only too assimilable. That, however, is their own problem." It has been said that the American climate of acceptance is hostile to our survival in this society as Jews. Why should a society as free as ours be detrimental to Jewish survival—or is it?

■ ROTH: You must realize that the essays included in this volume were partly journalistic and partly written in response to the requirements of the period. That particular essay was written during the period of the rise of the Nazis and the constant charge that "Jews and Semites" and "Aryans" belonged to two completely different parts of the human race. One was said to be distinctly inferior to the other, and the Jews had shown themselves throughout history to be completely unassimilable. This was an essay in which I tried to demonstrate that this charge was untrue. Jews have been assimilable, and the Jews have assimilated as totally as they could almost throughout history.

According to some people, during the peak of the Roman Empire there were ten million Jews in the world. Now if these ten million Jews had continued to propagate in a way one might normally have imagined, today there would have been I do not know how many hundreds or thousands of millions of Jews in the world. But the fact remains that the vast proportion of the Jewry of that period became assimilated in one way or the other among their neighbors.

The same happened at other periods. One can think of the number of Jews who existed in the world at other periods. This erosion continued; the number of Jews did not maintain itself and even decreased considerably. In the Middle Ages, according to Salo Baron, the number of Jews wavered between a million and a half and a million, and I believe he suggests that in the seventeenth century there were even fewer than a million. What happened to the rest? Some of them simply died out; some of them were, I suppose, massacred; but some of them simply became merged with their neighbors. In every country of the world, along with occasional Christian conversions to Judaism, you find massive Jewish conversions to Christianity. In England, at the time of the Expulsion of 1290, there were 120 former Jews in the home for converted Jews in London. The house of converted Jews in Rome always harbored its converts. If you look at the Jewish communities of the past, small Jewish communities here and there, you find that they have disappeared. In part it may have been by what you might call racial suicide—that is, failure to maintain their numbers—but to some extent it was simply by merging with their neighbors. You can pinpoint dozens of communities where that has been true. The Jews of China disappeared. The Jews of Avignon nearly disappeared. The resettlement community in England almost disappeared. I know English Jewry intimately, and I know of only one family who can trace its descent authentically from a seventeenth-century family. In this city [New York] there is, I believe, only one family that can authentically trace its descent back to the settlers of 1654. What happened to the rest? A large majority of them simply became merged with the majority population.

Now of course in the case of England we are speaking of a small minority; and in the case of Italy, a small minority subject to considerable outside pressure, both cultural and physical, who were unable to maintain their identity. In the case of the great communities of the Western world today, merging into the majority is quite out of the question. When people speak to me about what they consider to be the problematical future of American Jewry, I tell them I do not know what is going to happen to the smaller communities but that it is a physical impossibility for New York Jewry to become assimilated in the forseeable future, because marriage within the community, and the preservation of some degree of Jewish culture, are absolutely certain, are inevitable.

W.B.: Then do I take it that you believe intermarriage is less of a problem today than it was in the past? Many statistical studies have been made to indicate that it is quite rampant. What is your view as you look at America?

■ ROTH: Of course, intermarriage is rampant here and is rampant in all countries—in some countries so much so that it constitutes an absolute menace. For example, in Italy it is, in Scandinavia it is, and in Germany in the pre-Hitler period it was. Here in the United States it has an unfortunate degree of prominence, and, I suppose, in the smaller communities it is a serious problem. However, I have a vague idea that when I first came to the United States a couple of generations ago, the intermarriage rate on the West Coast was something fantastic, up to 60 percent or something like that—far, far higher than it is today. I believe it has been stemmed to a great extent during the last generation and has not increased. That is the impression I have.

On the other hand, when you come to the New York community you can use a computer to calculate the probabilities of intermarriage on the part of the average New York boy or girl. After all, young people live generally in physical propinquity, they work, generally, in much the same trades or occupations, and so the probability for a New York Jew to marry out of the faith is quite high.

W.B.: You have taught on a number of college campuses. What about the commitment, the quality, the intensity of Jewish life among our collegians today? This seems to be a very serious problem. We are concerned by the fact that Jewish education for the average child stops at the age of 13, and then he moves ahead into the world and is not equipped vis-à-vis his Jewish heritage. What about Jewish life on the campus today, in comparison with twenty years ago?

■ ROTH: You must realize that I do not see those who have gotten away. I see only those who stay. You must also realize that the numbers involved in this country are vast. I have occasionally aroused mirth at a lecture but never so much as I did once in a lecture in Johannesburg, when I spoke on university conditions in England and said that the number of Jewish undergraduates at Oxford had become something enormous; probably there were as many as three hundred. The roar of laughter with which I was greeted could be heard all the way to Cairo, because there were some two thousand Jews where I was lecturing. I have an idea that there are colleges and universities in the United States where the Jewish registration runs well up into five figures. But among those five figures there is a minority of persons who are very considerably interested in their Judaism, and it is those, I suppose, whom I normally meet.

I believe that the situation now is better than it was a generation or two ago. My impression when I first came to America was that the younger generation was running away from Judaism as fast as it could go. That is certainly no longer true. On the other hand, what one is faced with—even on the part of the well-informed—is in some cases a most extraordinary and deplorable and tragic ignorance. In recent lectures I found one young man who did not know what I meant when I spoke of the Second Temple. Another young man did not know what was meant by the Messiah; I do not mean that he did not know what the idea meant philosophically or religiously, but simply that the word *Messiah* was entirely alien to him. He had spent some time in coming to a Jewish lecture and he obviously had some inner urge, but what sort of Jews can we have in the future who are not familiar with even the basic idea that has kept us Jews going for two thousand years?

W.B.: There is a classic illustration of this. A few years ago a Christian professor at one of the universities, who had the responsibility of instructing Jewish students in Jewish matters, always gave them a little test. He would list about ten or fifteen names and ask the students to identify them. The first was Hillel, and I think that of the fifty boys and girls who took the test, about forty-five identified Hillel as an organization on American college campuses sponsored by B'nai B'rith. Some thirty of the fifty said that *menorah* was a journal. Most of them said that Daniel was a lion tamer. This lack of knowledge and its implications for the quality of adult Jewish life in the next generation is a perfect bridge to my next question. What changes, if any, have you seen in the education of adults? What changes, if any, have you seen in synagogue life in America through almost half a century?

■ **ROTH:** I was not in very close contact with adult education when I was first here, but I do not believe that it was very well organized. In those days it was said that there was only one civilized Orthodox synagogue in New York. I suppose there was some truth in it, for only since then has the modern Orthodox synagogue with which most of us are familiar come into being.

I suppose that adult education, such as it was, was confined to the old talmudic classes. Adult education since then has become, if you like, secularized, has become vernacularized and has become extended so that the Torah we learn is no longer the Torah contained in the folios of the Talmud. To my not inconsiderable personal advantage, it has become extended to such subjects as history.

W.B.: What do you think of the rise and growth of the day school movement? What effect will this have on Jewish survival in America?

■ **ROTH:** If the education is effective, it is going to have a very great influence. One trouble is, I think, that in some of the day schools they play around the edges of Judaism without getting down to the essentials.

W.B.: In your view, is there a real renaissance of religious life in America today, or is it superficial and lacking in depth and content?

■ **ROTH:** I always say that of the five million Jews in America, about 10 percent are the dregs of the earth, 10 percent are the salt of the earth, and the other 80 percent are somewhere in between. But you must remember that the 10 percent who are the salt of the earth—10 percent of five million—is half a million, 500,000. Five hundred thousand is far more than the number of the total of European Jewry in the year 1100, the time of the Crusades. The Jewish world of Europe was far smaller than the totality of New York Jewry today.

The half million who today are really devoted to Jewish values and to Jewish life and to Jewish culture here are as many as made Jewish culture in the past. And this 10 percent is really capable of developing a very great Jewish civilization comparable to the civilization of the past. I always say that in the past our communities were not dependent on numbers. But here you have not only the desire but also the numbers for development of a really strong Jewish life. And you know that one finds here an interest, an enthusiasm, and a devotion that one finds in few other places of the world. You ask me about the future of Jewry in America, and I say that half a million American Jews are capable of evolving a really great Jewish culture.

And if you take note of those around you, the bibliophiles, the students, the venerators of study, the supporters of study, the people who go out of their way to be friendly with scholars, the people who are building up collections of Jewish books, or collections of Jewish art in their homes, you are amazed at the concentration in this area of a high degree of culture such as one will find in very few other places in the world.

w.b.: Dr. Roth, one final question on the subject of commitment and involvement. The statement has been made that the community that maintained the laws of *kashrut* survived; the community that did not maintain the laws of *kashrut* died as a Jewish community. Do you find in your travels throughout America that *kashrut* is dying out, or is it being observed?

■ ROTH: What you say about communities dying or surviving is very likely true, but it is not because communities observed the law of *kashrut* that they survived. Because their Jewish outlook included the law of *kashrut* they survived. That is to say, the fact that they had the comprehensive Jewish outlook that regarded the maintenance of the Jewish home as important, is what gave them the strength for survival. I think that *kashrut* is more widely observed by the American-born Jew now than it was thirty or forty years ago. After all, Jewish public functions now tend to be kosher. Public functions twenty or thirty years ago tended not to be kosher. I remember speaking in Boston at a Jewish professional club where I was the only person in the room who had not been born in an Eastern European ghetto, yet I was the only person in the room who did not eat *trefe*. I do not think you will find that today.

w.b.: The Jews have been for the past two thousand years essentially a literary and an educated people. The Jew was from early times book-conscious. It was a sheer necessity of life. Today we have such men as Malamud, Singer, Mailer, Bellow, Samuel, Shaw, Wouk, to mention a few American Jewish writers who have achieved prominence. Could you give your views on their work, with some explanation for this kind of literary Jewish renaissance among the general reading public in the United States?

■ ROTH: It is a very curious phenomenon that on both sides of the Atlantic the Jewish novel has been so very popular and fashionable. Another curious thing is that most of the novelists in question are ghetto-born, and the Judaism and the Jew that they depict are still to a large extent ghetto-rooted.

There is something that I miss in this. It is the warmth and sympathy and even the knowledge that a man like Israel Zangwill showed. Israel Zangwill began this idea of the Jewish genre novel, using ghetto life as the mine for depicting a warm and interesting life. But today I think that our writers have ignored his standards, and I am not quite so keen on the Jewish novelists today as I was on the Jewish novelists of my youth. Herman Wouk is an exception from that point of view, although I must say that I preferred his writing—his fictional writing—when he was not dealing with the Jewish scene.

w.b.: We often speak about the state of American Jewish leadership, and I have here a very perceptive comment: "There is a feeling today that the Jewish leaders of the past in America were giants compared to the leaders of today. Modern Jews no longer need leaders with new ideas; they do not have to be led. They want mechanisms through which they can give expression, and there has been a shift today in terms of the outlook of American Jewish leadership from the man to the organization man."

■ ROTH: Of course, one always looks back on the characters of the past and thinks them giants. And one is very likely right. When I think of the Jewish leaders on both sides of the Atlantic in my youth, I think that they were cut of a stronger metal and on a more gigantic scale than those of today. And perhaps that is so although it may only be because of the way in which we always look back to the pygmies of long ago and make them giants.

On the other hand, the other point that you mentioned is, I think, a very serious one. There are so many Jewish organizations today in all countries and so many people are living off them that it has become an economic necessity for a very large number of people to have these organizations continue. There may be, for example, an organization of lodge tailors in New York that started as a mutual assistance society and in due course acquired a secretary. Now there are no more lodge tailors in New York; they have acquired considerable fortunes, they no longer need any mutual benefits. But if the society folds up, the secretary will be left without a job and his wife will be left without a fur coat. So the secretary inevitably has to try to keep this organization alive, and even to make it expand and possibly to divert its purposes to something else—perhaps an organization for the support of the Falashas or Jewish orphans. A very large number of organizations today, in England as well as here, are kept going for the benefit of the Jewish civil service.

The Jewish civil service today has become enormous, and enormously lucrative. I would say that sixty years ago the total travel budget of all Jewish organizations throughout the world for a single year was perhaps a thousand British pounds. That may be an overestimate. Today I would think it must run into millions of American dollars. And in every other way this civil service has become organized and possibly tends to dominate our lives, sometimes to our benefit but sometimes possibly not entirely to our benefit. I think it is a matter that we ought to take into consideration.

W.B.: In the course of the forty-one years that you have been coming back and forth to America, have you discovered any deepening sense of unity in the American Jewish community, or is there now a trend toward division? Which way do you think we are headed?

■ ROTH: I think that there was a tendency for unification twenty years ago that now has become negated. Up to twenty years ago, the increasing tendency was toward unification of America Jewry, but now there is a greater and greater tendency, I am afraid, toward division within the community.

W.B.: What brought you to the world of Jewish scholarship rather than the world of general scholarship?

■ ROTH: There were two factors. One is that I was brought up in a bookish household by a father who was devoted to Jewish studies and Jewish values, a household that was book-lined and where I was encouraged to make use of the books. The other factor was absolutely accidental. In 1924, when I was living in Florence and I had just completed my first book on the last Florentine Republic—an extremely *goyishe* work— a tragedy happened and I escorted a girl whose sister had died to her relatives in the far north of Italy. I came back with an introduction to her cousin, the Rabbi of Verona. I told him that I was interested in books, and asked if he could help me get some. Through him I acquired a sort of *genizah*, the miscellany of rubbish left in the loft of the rabbinical family.

It consisted mainly of the letters and notebooks and poems of an Italian rabbi of the eighteenth century. While I was waiting for the publication of my *goyishe* book, I started putting these papers in some sort of order, and I wrote my first Jewish historical essay.

W.B.: Professor, in any library, one of the classic books is the *Jewish Encyclopedia*, published in 1902 or thereabouts. In more recent years there appeared the *Universal Jewish Encyclopedia*. Now I understand that you were involved in producing a new Jewish encyclopedia. Why?

■ ROTH: This encyclopedia, of some ten million words divided into some twenty volumes, is the *Encyclopaedia Judaica*. The reason for this one is that the old Jewish works of reference have lost their validity. The *Universal Jewish Encyclopedia* is a praiseworthy work but not a great work. On the other hand, the old *Jewish Encyclopedia*, which was produced eighty-five years ago, was an amazing achievement. It was produced at a time when there could not have been more than perhaps two hundred thousand English-speaking Jews, and it was superb. It is still the standard work of reference. Some of the articles are of great importance and perfection, but on the other hand it reflects the period in which it was produced. An encyclopedia cannot stand still. There is always additional research that must be embodied if an encyclopedia is to remain valid. In the case of the *Jewish Encyclopedia* this is all the more important because at the time the old *Jewish Encyclopedia* was published, almost all the modern writing on Jewish studies was in German, and German is inaccessible to the average American reader today. And there has been a vast amount of research since those days, largely in the English language. So the encyclopedia must not only be brought up to date but it must be given an Anglo-American slant from the point of view of the literature.

Apart from the normal advance of learning, there have been three revolutionary changes in Jewish studies. One was the discovery of the Cairo Genizah, which the old *Jewish Encyclopedia* could take only into partial account. There has been the discovery of the Dead Sea Scrolls, which revolutionized our ideas of Jewish life and of biblical antiquities at the beginning of the Christian Era. And then there has been the discovery and investigation of medieval art, a whole new area of Jewish art which barely existed as a subject in 1900. Today it is a great subject.

In addition to this, American Jewry has emerged since 1900. As I say, the number of English-speaking Jews in the world then was probably about 200,000. Today it is something aproaching six million. North American Jewry has emerged and in association with it the Spanish-speaking Jewry of South America. So there is a New World to cope with and a New World to describe. And alas, the Old World has had its appalling tragic changes, with the annihilation of Eastern European Jewry and Central European Jewry, the loss of the great centers of the former Jewish scholarship and of the Jewish masses, the virtual disappearance of Russian Jewry. A Jewish encyclopedia, if it is to reflect the world of today, must take into account this appalling tragedy, although it cannot allow this tragedy to overwhelm it. The old *Jewish Encyclopedia*, if it spoke of Warsaw or Moscow or St. Petersburg, reflected an entirely different world from the world that an encyclopedia today must reflect.

And then there has been the amazing resurgence of the State of Israel. Clearly our new encyclopedia devotes a very great deal of space and attention to the State of Israel, in quite another manner than Palestine was treated in the old *Jewish Encyclopedia*.

The old *Jewish Encyclopedia* was a superb mirror of Jewish learning and Jewish life and the Jewish world as it was in 1900. But the Jewish world has radically changed since 1900. The average reader wants to have the world of today reflected in his works of reference. That is why a new Jewish encyclopedia became necessary.

W.B.: You have recently moved to Israel. Will you share with us your views of life in *Medinat Yisrael*.

■ ROTH: Life in *Medinat Yisrael* is extremely pleasant, especially for one who, like myself, lived for a quarter of a century in the very nearly total Gentile environment of Oxford. One does not find quite the same contrast in New York. In fact, the other day I was passing an apartment here and I noticed shelves of books visible from the street level and I thought how like Jerusalem that was.

Israel is losing a good deal of its former picturesqueness and color. However, the land is becoming more fertile, intellectual life is becoming more active, and the inhabitants are becoming more self-confident. If you feel at all pessimistic about the future of the State of Israel, go there and you will immediately lose your pessimism. As Queen Victoria said, "In this house the idea of defeat does not exist." And in Israel the idea of defeat or failure does not exist.

w.b.: For four thousand years the Jewish people have made the book their companion. We live by the book only because individuals in each generation, great and learned men, took the book, interpreted it, reinterpreted it, added to it, and made each of us feel the worthwhileness and the dignity and the meaning of being a Jew. Unquestionably, Professor Cecil Roth is one who has accepted the book that our ancestors received on Mount Sinai and is carrying it aloft in England, in Israel, in Italy, in France, and in America. By virtue of his mind, his personality, and his pen, he is making us proud to say: "Who is like unto the people of Israel, one nation on earth."

22. ❧ All Humanity on Trial

Dr. Henry Kissinger

W.B.: Few men or women have had the experience of influencing world history in a period of critical world events. It would not be overstating the case to assert that Dr. Henry Kissinger is one of those people. He has been in "the eye of the storm" when world leaders made pivotal decisions that resulted in international headlines. He has also been deeply involved in the slow and silent turning of the wheels of diplomacy behind the scenes. Dr. Kissinger was Secretary of State from 1973 to 1977, and National Security Advisor to the President from 1969 to 1975. He has since been a confidant and advisor on international affairs to presidents and other key political figures.

Dr. Kissinger offers great insights on world affairs based on his experience in crucial Middle East negotiations, the Strategic Arms Limitations Talks, the Persian Gulf crisis, the world role of the President of the United States, and the relationships between the U.S. and Israel. He wears both the hat of political philosopher and that of political activist. There is no contradiction here, if the proper material is selected and the designer is skilled. With great analytical ability, patience, and insight, Dr. Kissinger brought academic theory beyond the ivy-covered walls of the university into the arena of world affairs.

The Jewish origins of Dr. Kissinger are well known. Everyone is familiar with the story of the boy who fled Germany in 1938 with his parents to escape the Nazi terror—and went on to become a noted academic on the faculty of Harvard University, and later the second or third most important person in his country's leadership.

Whenever Jews learn that a person in high public position is Jewish, the discussion frequently takes a particular tack: The parochial viewpoint, "Is he good for the Jews?" may be expressed; and also possibly, "If he does anything wrong, we *all* will be blamed." Neither of these reactions is true to Jewish tradition or teaching. While we must be concerned with Jewish survival, it is important that we go beyond a merely parochial outlook. As Jews we have the awesome responsibility of completing Creation—and we also have the knowledge that the peace, justice, and security that will then come to the world will benefit *all* peoples.

Dr. Kissinger, one of the major questions on our minds and in our hearts these days is the matter of the American hostages in Iran. [*Editor's note*: This Dialogue took place shortly before the Carter–Reagan presidential election.] Do you feel that the imprisonment of these innocent individuals has become politicized in this election year?

■ KISSINGER: The hostages in Iran turned into a great human tragedy for the people involved and for their families. Against their wishes they have become a symbol of America's role in the world, and have been caught up in the last stages of an election campaign. I do not suggest that this was planned by the Carter administration. I do believe, however, that it was planned by the Iranian authorities and that in this sense it is their final insult to the United States to believe that they can affect the American election by particular proposals. I want to stress that the President is right in exploring what has been put before him. My own view, in general, is that in hostage situations, one does not negotiate. If this were last November, for example, I would be strongly opposed to any negotiations. I agree with the Israeli method, which is not to negotiate. If the captors learn that there is a price, one then moves from the issue of principle to the issue of the specific price to be paid and one is then in an endless process.

Since this position was not taken eleven months ago, we now find ourselves confronted by four specific demands. I have serious questions about them. I have serious questions about the staged release of the hostages in relation to the demands, because it creates the impression that each group is being held hostage for the fulfillment of another demand and therefore violates the concept that hostages should not be for sale. That is why I think all the hostages must be released together. I find unacceptable the proposition that if we do not meet these demands, these hostages will then be tried. *That*, I believe, must be firmly rejected. Then, there seems to be an idea that the United States has to pay off the Iranian debts in the United States. On this I have the most serious questions because that seems to me to be a disguised form of ransom. Last, I have consistently opposed the introduction of large quantities of military equipment in a war in which the national interest of the United States is so uncertain, and no less on behalf of a government that has systematically humiliated us for a year, and that will attempt to achieve a fanatical hegemony in the Persian Gulf area if it prevails. That particular aspect of the exchange causes me serious doubts.

On the other hand, I do think the Carter administration is correct in exploring whether it is possible to reduce the terms as they are now stated to conditions that are compatible with our honor and with our laws and with our integrity. So, I do not criticize the process of negotiation, but I do want to indicate those aspects of the outcome that would give me grave difficulty.

w.b.: In a broader sense, Dr. Kissinger, beyond even the immediate resolution of the hostage situation, what insights can our foreign policy makers gain from the entire event, from the way we dealt with our ally Iran and how we related to the Shah? What is your assessment of the lessons we can learn from the entire Iran situation?

■ KISSINGER: It is important to understand the nature of the relationship that existed between the Shah and eight U.S. presidents of both political parties. This was never a partisan issue. It was the policy of Democratic and Republican presidents alike. Allow me to provide some background to the situation. Iran is the most populous country in the area. It has frontiers with the Soviet Union, with Iraq, and with Pakistan. In 1972 the Soviet Union introduced large quantities of modern weapons first into Syria, then into Iraq. That was followed by a friendship treaty between Iraq and the Soviet Union, which usually means that the foreign policies of the two countries are made very closely compatible with each other. Simultaneously, the British withdrew their forces from the Persian Gulf. So, therefore, the practical problem was that there be some counterweight to the Soviet armed radical regime in Iraq; otherwise it would achieve domination of the Persian Gulf and radicalize the entire area. This was the reasoning that led us to approve the sale of arms to the Shah of Iran, as a means of counterbalancing the Soviet arms in Iraq. We did not do this as a favor to the Shah. This sale is often presented as some sort of act of personal friendship, for example, between the Shah and me. But to the Shah, the Secretary of State was about four levels below him—unbelievable as this may seem—and while he treated me with great correctness and politeness, it was not on the basis of personality or personal friendship but on the basis of similar national interests.

As for the collapse of the pro-American government in Iran, that was a sheer political tragedy. Whether it could have been averted, we will never know. But what we do know is what Ambassador Sullivan, who was our last ambassador to Iran, published: there were three incompatible policies being pursued simultaneously by the United States Government, the practical result of which had to be to complete the demoralization of the existing structure and to create a vacuum in the Middle East and in the Persian Gulf—of which we now see the consequences. The second lesson from this is the illusion that our natural friends are radicals, that we can somehow appeal to the radicals in that area and elsewhere. This is a tendency that led us sometimes to Libya, sometimes to flirtations with the P.L.O., and sometimes to flirtations with Khomeini. The purpose of the taking of the hostages seems to me to have been twofold: One, to radicalize the government of Iran, and move it as far away from the United States as it is possible to be; and second, to create such an impression of American impotence and American unreliability that no element of Iran would any more rely on the United States.

Both those objectives seem to me to have been achieved, and the haggling that is now going on about the hostages is to culminate the process and is, therefore, a matter of profound worry. Moreover, the whole situation in the Middle East has shaken the confidence of moderate governments in the United States. When the King of Jordan takes a trip to Baghdad at the beginning of a war, we're in a new environment, because five years ago he would have taken a trip to Washington. This indicates that the moderates have lost their confidence and are trying to appease the radicals. And now we are caught in a situation in which two governments are fighting a war. As I said rather flippantly a few weeks ago—and I repeat it here—my only regret in the war between Iran and Iraq is that only one of them can lose.

W.B.:   You've worked at one time or another in different capacities for a variety of American presidents. As you see it, what are the qualities that make for a great president? And what are the qualities that lead to a flawed presidency?

■ **KISSINGER:**   The most important task of a national leader, and especially of a president as the only national elected leader who has executive authority, is to take our country from where it is to where it has not been. That is, he must have a vision of the future. And this presents a dilemma because when his scope for *action* is greatest, the knowledge on which to base such an action is very often at a minimum. However, by the time the *knowledge* is greatest, the scope for action has often disappeared. For example, in 1936, one French division could have stopped the Germans, the Nazis, when they reoccupied the Rhineland. And I'm sure the world would still be arguing today whether Hitler was a maniac or a misunderstood nationalist. Doctoral theses would be written on that subject. The fact is that the French and British leaders did not have the courage to act upon their intuition, or maybe they did not have the intuition. They waited until they were sure, and waiting cost twenty million lives.

The same problem exists at every moment, and especially in the contemporary period, which is characterized by upheavals in technology, in the social structures of states, and in the relations among states. That is why the most important task of a president, of a national leader, is to have a vision of what it is that one wants to build. I believe the most important quality of a leader is vision and courage. One can hire all the analysis one needs, but what one cannot hire is courage and some view of the future. Therefore, every national leader, every president, must have some of the attributes of a prophet. But at the same time, he cannot get too far out of touch with the people, because if he does, then they cannot follow him. And if he confines his activities only to public opinion polls, he will always be a prisoner of events, and the public does not forgive its leaders for catastrophes, even if the catastrophes reflect what they thought they wanted. So these are the two extremes between which a president must navigate and on which a president will be historically judged.

W.B.: In recent days, because of the presidential campaign, the issue of presidential decision-making has emerged once again. As the public understands it, a president is surrounded by advisors who present him with various options, policies, and possibilities; but it is at this point that public confusion abounds. What happens after a president is offered the options? How does the act of decision occur? Is the president, for example, a captive of his advisors? Do his advisors argue it out in a collegial style before the president? Does a president, for example, reject all the advice he might get and then follow his own course? On what basis is a presidential decision made and does the president himself need to be a first-rate intellect or statesman in order to come to the right decision?

■ KISSINGER: That is a very important and difficult question. There is no simple answer because it depends so importantly on the personality of the president. Actually, there are two aspects to the decision-making process. There is always a formal decision-making process, and then there's the *real* decision-making process. The formal decision-making process is expressed in the Cabinet, in the National Security Council, and in a whole host of committees that have either legal or other authority to address a problem. However, it is safe to say that I know of no administration in which the Cabinet made any decisions. The Cabinet is composed of too many disparate elements for that. The Cabinet sessions that I have attended or of which I have heard debriefing sessions, in which various cabinet members reported to their colleagues what they were doing, have not been distinguished by excessive precision or revelation of the most intimate details. Frankly, almost everything you tell in a Cabinet meeting leaks. Therefore, major issues are brought to smaller committees, such as the National Security Council for foreign policy or the Council for Economic Policy for economic policy. I'm most familiar with the National Security

Council process. Theoretically, the president is supposed to be presented with options, and every new president who comes into office claims that that is what he wants, and that is indeed what he thinks he wants. But the fact of the matter is that individuals in the government very often have very strong opinions. And if you ask them to present three options, they usually give you two absurd ones and one realistic one. I used to say, when I was in the State Department, that if I asked for three options, even if I didn't know anything about the subject and even if the options were written in Swahili, if I had picked the second option out of the three, I would have been in accord with the bureaucracy 90 percent of the time. You see, the middle option is usually the one they want. So the first thing you have to distinguish between is the real options and the phony options.

The second thing is that you generally do not become the president unless you have a very strong will. And an advisor generally does not go into government unless he wants the job. And so there is a subtle psychological interplay between the president and his advisors in which one has to resist the temptation of becoming a courtier and telling the president what he wants to hear. And there *is* a great bias in the deliberations toward what the president is presumed to want. President Kennedy in 1962, during the deliberations of the Bay of Pigs, wisely absented himself from the meetings of the executive committee that was dealing with these matters until they had reached some sort of a consensus, and *then* he joined them so that his actions or presence would not intentionally influence their deliberations. I think this was a very good procedure.

In general, though, I have to repeat that the decision-making process depends on the president. As a general proposition I have seen that the degree of preparation of the president in a subject determines how active a role he will play and is the case as his administration goes on. This is true of almost every president that I have seen. Moreover, he has to keep in mind not only the intrinsic merit of the subject but the attitudes of the people around him. He has to consider the morale of his associates. One of the hardest things for a president to achieve is to get really objective advice. And one of the hardest things for him to do is to take a decision that removes himself from the conflicts of the various Cabinet members and advisors who at one and the same time are men of strong convictions and men whose success or failure determines the relative pecking order in the organization.

W.B.: You personally experienced in your own lifetime the ugly and violent presence of fascism and Nazism. In recent months we have been witness to a dramatic surge of fascism and neo-Nazism around the world—in Italy, Belgium, France, England, even in the United States. What do you think this signifies about our world?

■ KISSINGER: I think it is no accident that historically Jews have been in the forefront of the struggles for justice, for liberty, and for equality. This has been the case because they know from their own experience that when these principles are violated by people, they themselves become early victims.

We are living now in a world in which the use of force in the settlement of international disputes and in the settlement of domestic disputes is becoming more and more prevalent. We are also living in a world in which there are organizations—like, for example, the P.L.O.—that have a vested interest in organizing distrust of the Jewish communities around the world. Then there is the oil problem, which is gradually bringing about a change in the economic and social structure of all industrial democracies. Before OPEC imposed the oil problem in 1973, the political issue for most countries was how to divide an increasing costly share of the gross national product. Now they have to divide a constant and in some cases a shrinking share of the gross national product. For all these reasons, plus the encouragement of groups with vested interests, a situation has developed in the public mind in which certain problems, like the West Bank negotiations, have become a cop-out and a surrogate for everything else. People then like to believe that "If only it were not for Israel and for Jewish pressures, there would be no oil problem." And this in violation of all experience that all these underdeveloped countries have developed their own radicalism! I think indeed we are facing a very serious problem. In addition, I think the problem of anti-Semitism is inseparable from the problem of justice in the world in general. The problem of anti-Semitism is not a purely Jewish problem because in a world in which anti-Semitism is tolerated, oppression becomes the tool of the strongest against everybody who is weak and everybody who is defenseless.

W.B.: Dr. Kissinger, what role do you see human rights playing in a concrete fashion within American foreign policy?

■ KISSINGER: I think, Rabbi Berkowitz, that this is a very difficult question to answer. Philosophically, the United States has to stand for human rights on a global basis. However, then it faces two concrete questions: What does that mean in terms of foreign policy? What methods are most appropriate to achieve these objectives? When I was in office I believed—and perhaps excessively—that the best method in dealing with totalitarian systems was not to use a direct, visible means of confrontation but to use quiet diplomacy. By these methods we managed to increase immigration of Jews from the Soviet Union from some 400 in 1969 to some 35,000 in 1973. I would say in retrospect that more public statements might well have been a useful adjunct to that policy.

Our successors adopted a very challenging human rights policy and abandoned it as far as the totalitarian states were concerned—that is, as far as the Communist states were concerned—after about six months. They did that because they found it interfered too much with other objectives. And so they then concentrated on allies. But that is and was a big undertaking. If the United States makes as its task to bring about democratic institutions in all friendly countries, then I would say that we have an obligation not simply to overthrow or undermine governments with which we disagree but to fight for—at least ideologically and politically—governments with which we agree. Otherwise we will turn the world over to radicals. The practical consequence of assaulting pro-American governments that are not democratic is to turn the countries over to totalitarian governments that are no more free, and on top of it violently anti-American. This is what has happened in Central America. It also was one of the reasons that led to the collapse of the Shah of Iran. And it has affected our policies elsewhere. So indeed, you have raised a very complicated issue. We have to stand for human rights. We have to insist that the rights of minorities be protected. But we *also* have to know what the best methods are to achieve practical results and we also have to know that if we take the first step, we must be prepared to take the next step. Otherwise we're simply engaging in public relations exercises.

W.B.:   In a statement at NATO headquarters in Brussels some years ago you said, "I believe that the relationship between morality and foreign policy is not a simple one. I agree that it is necessary to have strong moral convictions, but it is also necessary to bring into relationships the realities of the situation with moral purposes. I believe foreign policy without moral convictions lacks a sense of direction." Dr. Kissinger, could you amplify on what you see as the relationship between foreign policy and morality? How do the two realms differ, and how does one attain moral purpose in foreign policy while avoiding moralism on the one hand and cynicism on the other?

■ KISSINGER: This is the most difficult question of statesmanship. For the philosopher there are no gradations of morality. A thing is either good or evil. For the statesman, on the other hand, there are rarely absolutes. The philosopher needs a clear perception of his goals. The statesman needs that also, but he is doomed to approaching his goals in stages. The statesman lives in a world in which today there are 150 sovereign states, meaning 150 independent wills. And so the art of the statesman is to keep in mind his objective while approaching it in steps, each of which is imperfect. Hopefully, each will be a moral improvement over its predecessor. But by definition it has an element of immorality and even an element of amorality. Thus, the morality of the statesman is expressed in his willingness to persevere toward distant goals that indeed *have* to be moral, through stages that are very frequently, and indeed usually, imperfect.

It is not always easy to tell the difference between a charlatan and a truly moral man, between a moralist and a man of great moral convictions. Yet, paradoxically, the pure pragmatists become prisoners of events. They are adrift on the sea of circumstance. But it requires faith to build something of substance. For example, I have often believed, as I've often said, that the State of Israel was a dream before it became a reality. And if it hadn't been a dream, it would never have become a reality, and realists would never have gone there to build a state. So, one must ask how to have dreams that are not purely fanaticism, and yet be willing to operate by stages in a complex environment. This is our deepest challenge. And it is not easy to give a pat answer for how to solve it.

W.B.: Dr. Kissinger, in an address before the World Jewish Congress you said the following: "One cannot separate the destiny of Israel and the destiny of the Jewish people from the destiny of mankind." What did you mean by linking these destinies?

■ **KISSINGER:** I would say that a world in which Israel could become a purely expedient object for the power politics of other nations, and a world in which the Jewish people would be treated as a minority defined only by its own strength, would be a world without justice. It would be a world without deeper purpose, a world without human rights, and a world that would have committed such an offense to humanity that it would no longer be recognized. For this reason the fate of Israel is more than simply the fate of a national state, but is a test of the conscience and of the principles of liberty and freedom for all of mankind. And Israel can never be assessed simply in terms of power politics, but has to be assessed in terms of the deeper purposes of human motivation.

W.B.: A major issue in recent years has been the relationship of the United States to Israel. One school of thought asserts that Israel is a definite strategic ally of and asset to the United States and thus should be supported. Another school of thought declares that Israel has moral value and historical significance and shares common values with the United States, and warns that commitments based on strategic assets and *realpolitik* are dangerous, since they are essentially amoral and capable of changing. Dr. Kissinger, what is your view? How should the United States view the State of Israel—as strategic asset, moral commitment, or both?

■ **KISSINGER:** The United States has to view Israel as *both*. There is a moral commitment to Israel that does not derive from the fact that it is a strategic asset even though it *is also* a strategic asset. When all is said and done, it is the one country that we can be sure will never change its friendship for the United States, and that in a foreseeable crisis represents a relationship of fundamental strategic importance. Nevertheless, I would not rest the relationship on that strategic importance alone.

W.B.: In recent months we have seen an attempt by the United States to become close to the P.L.O. What are your thoughts on the position that the United States should take? Should there be recognition of or negotiation with the P.L.O.?

■ KISSINGER: This is a subject on which I have been expressing myself since 1973, and therefore you are all able to see that I'm not saying now what is expedient for this moment. I do not believe that the P.L.O. is a negotiating partner for the United States. I even go further than the official position: *I do not think that the P.L.O. is a partner for the United States even if it accepts Resolution 242.* The last thing we need in the Middle East from an American point of view—and I'm not speaking now from an Israeli point of view—is another radical state armed by the Soviet Union, with its leadership trained by the Soviet Union, and wedged between Jordan and Israel and a menace to both of them. Therefore I have consistently opposed the idea of a Palestinian state and the idea of the P.L.O., and I think the negotiation of the West Bank should be conducted between Jordan and Israel. Everything else is an illusion.

W.B.: Dr. Kissinger, what is your overall assessment of America's Middle East policy? How *should* the policy of the next president, no matter who, differ? And finally, American friends of Israel have been concerned that if Ronald Reagan were to win the election he would appoint individuals to his cabinet who would bow to the Saudi and oil company interests. How do you respond to these genuine concerns?

■ KISSINGER: When President Carter came into office, I was hoping for a two-term administration, having gone through the experiences of the Vietnam conflict and of Watergate. I thought that America, which has not had a two-term presidency since the 1950s and therefore has a young generation that has never seen a presidency without catastrophe, required a successful two-term presidency. However, I have become progressively more critical of the Carter administration, and I have strongly supported Ronald Reagan because I have been convinced that the policies of the current administration are crisis-prone, that there is a bias toward radical movements and states, that there is an inadequate appreciation of the balance of power and of regional balances, and that the cumulative effect of this will be such an undermining of the international order that there is a risk, a constant risk abroad and a constant threat to friendly countries.

Now to reply specifically to the Middle East policy: I was extremely critical at the beginning of the administration of the attempt to arrange a Geneva conference with Soviet support or Soviet participation that would include the P.L.O. and would attempt to settle all issues in the Middle East simultaneously in one great conference. I thought this would lead to the isolation of our friends, to the isolation of the moderate governments of the Middle East, and to a high risk of an explosion. Obviously, President Sadat shared the same assessment and took his heroic initiative in going to Jerusalem, which was answered by the government of Israel with an equally heroic, though less dramatic, response in its willingness to give up the tangible security guarantees of the possession of the entire Sinai for the intangible assurances of peaceful intentions, and one *has* to give credit to this tremendous act on the part of the Israeli government. I believe that the Camp David agreement was a major step forward, and I've always supported it. But since then, I feel that our policy has started to disintegrate. There has been an unstated premise that the autonomy negotiations could be pushed in a direction that would be tantamount to creating a Palestinian state in the guise of a Palestinian entity or some other form.

In addition, in terms of the Carter Middle East policy, there has been the passivity in the face of the collapse of the era of the pro-American government in Iran, which in turn has given such tremendous impetus to the radical elements in the Middle East that those states that used to rely on us in the Arab world and that we required for a compromise solution have become much more cautious and much less willing to follow our lead. I believe that a Reagan administration would differ from the Carter administration in understanding first of all that the West Bank is just one small part of a big problem in the area that has several components.

First, there must be a military balance between East and West in that area or nothing can succeed. Second, the United States must support the moderate against the radical element. Therefore, it is inconceivable to me that a Reagan administration would ever find itself tacitly or in any other way playing up to Libya or the P.L.O. or to similar organizations. Third, I believe that there would be a coherent design in which it is understood that one cannot yield political objectives to economic blackmail because if that process is started once, we would find ourselves in the same position as with the hostages in that the demands escalate constantly.

Let me add that I am speaking to you in my private capacity. I have supported Ronald Reagan out of a profound conviction. But I am not a member of his staff. Therefore, I cannot answer you about whom he will appoint to what cabinet position. But I *have* had many talks with him and precisely because I am independent, precisely because I owe him nothing and precisely because I want nothing from him, I can say with complete sincerity that his presidency would be better for the national security of free people and for the future of our country and of Israel.

W.B.: Dr. Kissinger, since we're discussing Ronald Reagan, let me ask you about the attempts to call him a war-monger, a belligerent man who is trigger-happy, someone who is dangerous. You have said that you've spent a good deal of time with him; you understand his views and his approaches. How do you assess the characterization of Ronald Reagan as a war-monger, or as trigger-happy? Would a Reagan administration jump into war at the drop of a hat? What seems to be Reagan's understanding of the world?

■ KISSINGER: I have concluded, concerning my judgment of Ronald Reagan, that he is a prudent man who would make deliberate and thoughtful decisions. I believe, even more importantly, that the risk of war is not the rash action of a president. Once you are president and you know what modern weapons can do, reality forces you to be prudent. Rather, the risk of war is an international environment that grows so out of control that sooner or later vital American and free world interests are threatened, and then a war becomes unavoidable. Who would have thought it possible four years ago that the Straits of Hormuz would be threatened on both sides by potentially hostile regimes? Who would have thought it possible that 10 million barrels of oil could suddenly disappear as the result of a war between Iran and Iraq? We have had since 1977 two invasions from Communist territory in Zaire. We've had Cuban troops in Ethiopia. A Communist coup in South Yemen. Soviet occupation of Afghanistan. Vietnamese occupation in Cambodia. The collapse of Iran. The Iran–Iraq war. That process, if it continues, promises a great likelihood that something will get out of control of the statesmen.

Therefore, I think the obligation of a president is to *avert* crises from happening. I have seen a campaign commercial for President Carter that says that he's confronted twelve war-like situations and has managed to keep America out of all of them. I would like to see a commercial that we've had a president who prevented twelve war-like situations from *arising*. I do not think a Reagan administration would go to war at the drop of a hat, but I also must tell you in all candor that an administration that says it will *never* go to war may *invite* war, because it is only the readiness to defend your fundamental principles that makes aggressors desist from their course. And it's easy enough to make statements about peace, but if we want to have both peace and justice we have to be prepared to defend them seriously. No one should pretend that he can forego the readiness to defend his fundamental values.

Finally, as far as Ronald Reagan's understanding of the world, I think that what he wants is to return American policies to some fundamental principles and to create a predictable American foreign policy so that allies and adversaries both know what they can expect. I think he has healthy instincts in these respects and from what I have seen I think he will surround himself with responsible and thoughtful advisors.

w.b.: Let me turn to a very crucial area that affects us all: the future of U.S.–Soviet relations. In recent days, we have heard a great national discussion on the entire matter of SALT and the issue of strategic superiority. Dr. Kissinger, in a nuclear age, does nuclear superiority make sense? Does it have strategic value? Does it have political impact?

■ KISSINGER: That is again an extraordinarily complicated question, because we are dealing here with weapons of extraordinary destructiveness, whose impact is almost theoretical in the sense that nobody really knows what would happen if they were used in a systematic manner. We enjoyed a meaningful nuclear superiority for about twenty-five years. By meaningful, I mean that we were in a position to offset the Soviet conventional superiority, geographic advantage, and capacity to intervene in contiguous areas by having a significantly larger number of nuclear weapons. We had at least a theoretical advantage to do to the Soviet retaliatory forces what Israel did to the Egyptian air force in 1967—that is, to reduce their counterblows to acceptable levels. In 1962, during the Cuban missile crisis, the United States had something like 3,500 warheads, and the Soviet Union had about 70. In 1973, at the end of the Middle East War, when we went on nuclear alert, we had about 8,000 warheads, and the Soviet Union had 700. Now, that was already very uncomfortable, because of the enormous destructiveness of the weapons. But still, if you are an old-time Russian general looking at the superiority against you and see it is 12 to 1, you decide that you are going to have the confrontation some other day. And therefore, in the middle of Watergate, while we were being assailed from all sides, the Soviets quit that confrontation after about twenty-four hours.

Today the numbers are so large on both sides that it is very hard to answer your question of who is superior. And it also becomes very complicated to argue whether it is indeed possible to achieve superiority—which, however, does not mean that you can stand still, because to maintain parity you have to make certain efforts. But one of the consequences of nuclear parity is that the conventional balance, the regional balance of power, becomes of greater and greater importance, and that is why we therefore must have the capability of intervening in trouble spots. If, for example, we had a 1973–type situation again in the Middle East, the Soviets might not quit in twenty-four hours, and then the ability to reinforce locally would be of the most decisive importance. And so *that* is particularly the problem we have today, not the question of nuclear superiority in the abstract.

W.B.: I would be remiss if I didn't ask one more geopolitical question. During the course of this year we've seen a number of events, such as the Russian combat forces in Cuba, the Soviet intervention in the Horn of Africa, the invasion of Afghanistan, to cite just a few. Do you see such Soviet military boldness as a result of a premeditated plan, or simply the action of an aggressive power, flaunting its military superiority? Furthermore, do you see the United States in a second-rate position in terms of our standing with the Soviets, and in the world? Do you see us, as some have charged, in global retreat, which could lead to a situation in which war or surrender are the only courses that we have before us? If this is so, how do you suggest that we go about reversing this frightening trend, especially in light of the advisability of maintaining some form of détente?

■ KISSINGER: Rabbi Berkowitz, if we were to take a map of the world in 1970 and compare it with a map of the world in 1980, we could only conclude that there has been a systematic Soviet expansion. If you look at Cuban troops in Ethiopia, and Soviet troops in Afghanistan, you see two prongs of a pincers that are taking the Middle East between them and are gradually squeezing it. If you add to it that Communist-armed guerrillas from Libya are invading the territories of Morocco, and if Morocco should then suffer the same fate as Iran, you would see the whole northern coast of Africa—with the exception of Egypt—in hostile hands. Whether that is a Soviet geopolitical design, or a show of its military potential, makes no difference to us.

If you add to that the turmoil in Central America, partly caused by us, you can at least say that there is no trouble spot in the world where the Soviet Union exercises a soothing influence. There is no terrorist movement that the Soviet Union does not directly or indirectly support, train, and use. There's no embarrassment to the Western world that the Soviet Union does not encourage. As long as this continues, true peace is impossible, and détente is going to be just a series of palliatives. In the long term this is not even in the Soviet interest, because the United States will not be defeated without noticing it, and when we notice it, we'll resist. And this is the ultimate danger of war. And it's to prevent that situation from arising that you describe as either a collapse or going to war that statesmanship consists of.

You ask me what should we do. It is extremely difficult to elaborate a blueprint within the limits of our discussion. Let me make, nevertheless, a few headings of what needs to be done. First, we need to rebuild our military capacity, and we need to rebuild it not only by throwing money at it but by dealing with the conceptual problem that I described earlier: What is American security in a world of more or less nuclear parity, and therefore in greater danger of conventional and local aggression? Second, we must rebuild our alliances and bring home to our allies that there has to be a certain homogeneity in political as well as in military outlooks. The United States cannot forever supply the defensive areas to countries that conduct essentially neutralist policies in the Middle East, and in East–West relations. I think our European allies will have to choose between the two. There cannot be military integration and totally separate political policies. The third goal has to do with the developing countries. We have suffered from the nostalgia that we can win over the radicals to our side. But our normal allies in the developing world are the moderate governments that do not base their policies on anti-Americanism, that do not foment every disturbance, that do not appeal to every slogan. We have to make a distinction between moderates and radicals.

There has to be a benefit to being America's friend, and a penalty in being America's adversary. If you watch the resolutions of the nonaligned movement, they have become progressively more insolent and hostile to the United States as we have attempted to approach them. I said to a leader of the nonaligned world last year, after the Havana Conference, that it is statistically not possible that we are *always wrong*. Just by accident, we've got to do something right, *sometimes*. But if they insist on hostility as their organizing principle, then they cannot demand our support, and that is a choice we must impose on them. With respect to the Soviet Union, as I said earlier, it is in keeping with the Soviet interest that they learn a sense of their limits. We have to bring an end to the Soviet geopolitical offensive that you have described earlier. It is not possible for them to preach coexistence and at the same time engage in aggression in every part of the world. On the other hand, if they are prepared for genuine coexistence, we must be prepared for genuine negotiations and not make confrontation a principle of our policy for its own sake. So we must be prepared to negotiate, but the Soviet Union must be prepared to accept some principles of international conduct. And finally, this leads me to a fundamental issue that can best be illustrated by the current Iranian situation: How do you encourage moderation? Do you encourage moderation by giving in to the demands of radicals and hoping that they then become moderates, or do you encourage moderation by thwarting the demands of radicals and showing that only the moderate course can prevail? I believe in the second course.

W.B.: The Talmud, in a splendid discussion of history and its forces, discusses whether it is the time, or the locale or situation, or the *person*, that is the primary determinant of events. Whatever one's perspective on this issue might be, you, Dr. Kissinger, certainly have known the leading figures of our time. I would be most curious to know your recollection and assessment of three leading figures who, sad to say, are no longer with us. The three that I bring back to mind with great reverence, affection, love, and regard, are Hans Morgenthau, Nelson Rockefeller, and Golda Meir.

■ KISSINGER: Hans Morgenthau was my teacher and my friend, occasionally my intellectual adversary, and always a man I respected and admired. He lived in the world of ideas and was never given an opportunity to put them to the test in practice. He was scrupulously honest, and he believed that it was important to free the United States from the sentimental oscillations between excessive commitment and excessive withdrawals. He therefore had the courage to develop a political theory based on the national interest, which in his sense had a moral quality, because he included, and attributed in his view of the national interest, the moral convictions and purposes of a society. He and I differed about how to end the war in Vietnam, without either of us being comfortable with our allies. He was not a protestor by nature, and I was not a warrior by nature. Still, we had reached different conclusions as to how to extricate the United States from the morass of Indo-China. While we differed here, afterwards our paths converged again. And throughout, I admired his integrity, and I liked his understated sense of humor. He was one of the seminal figures of thought and someone without whom life is a great deal emptier.

Now Nelson Rockefeller, on the other hand, was a completely different personality. He was a man of action, and he was an artist. His great strength was an intuitive perception of the right course. He was an aristocrat in a society that doesn't have a formal aristocracy, and therefore he felt that he owed to this society national service for all the advantages he had inherited. Above all, he had a very touching faith in the power of reason. He was constantly assembling panels of experts, which I as a professor, knowing how Ph.D.s are acquired, valued somewhat less, perhaps, than he did. I was his associate in three presidential campaigns, which failed in part because he had a very naive belief that you get to be nominated president because you have the best program, and he spent an inordinate amount of time and money on developing programs that others later implemented. To me, Nelson Rockefeller had a quintessentially American quality: extremely optimistic, a little inarticulate, idealistic, hopeful, and a great sense of obligation toward the oppressed, the disadvantaged, and the threatened. I thought he was a great man, and I thought it was an enormous tragedy that he never became president.

Golda Meir, as you must also have experienced her, Rabbi Berkowitz, was an original. I dealt with her as a friend, and occasionally as an adversary, but always with enormous affection. She treated me like a favorite nephew who, if he happened to stray from the family line, would be the subject of a particular outburst of displeasure. She once told me that somebody came to her and said, "What I can't stand about Kissinger is that he is first an American, then he's Secretary of State, and then he is finally, and thirdly, a Jew." And she said, "That's OK with me, because you see, I read from right to left anyway!" I remember that after we had gone through the controversies in front of her advisors that our positions imposed on us, we always went out into the kitchen and had a little private talk, and I'm proud to say we never failed to come to an agreement. Once Golda had made an agreement, she had the courage of a lioness in fighting it through a cabinet not known for its excessive reticence.

For Golda, Israel was not a country; it was part of her being. The boys who were killed or wounded in wars were not citizens; they were part of her family. I never saw her show any emotion in the conduct of official business, except once when I brought a list that we had finally gotten of the prisoners from Syria. I had brought it back from Damascus, and I gave her the list, and she handed it to the chief of staff, and both of these rather hardboiled characters turned their backs on me and started weeping for a few moments. It was that combination of sentimentality, courage, dedication, and faith that not only was what made Golda and Israel, but it's what mankind needs for survival and for hope.

w.b.: Dr. Kissinger, in studying your writings and speeches, the inevitable conclusion seems to be that they are pervaded by a sense of pessimism and even of tragedy. Do you regard your thought as being essentially tragic? In the role of statesman or historian, do you feel yourself to be an optimist or a pessimist?

■ **KISSINGER:** May I recall a comment that a British reviewer made on my book? He said, "I don't know if Mr. Kissinger is a great writer, but anyone finishing this book is a great reader." I think that Rabbi Berkowitz has proved that he is a great reader. Now, to answer your question, I would have to say it is the duty of a statesman, insofar as he can, to be neither an optimist nor a pessimist, but to be a realist, to make as accurate an assessment as he can of the real forces as he finds them. Under contemporary conditions, these show very grave dangers and very grave complexities.

Let me also respond to the second aspect of your question, which asks not only whether I am a pessimist or an optimist, but also whether I have a sense of tragedy. In a way I am not *only* a historian or *only* a statesman. As a historian, you cannot avoid a sense of tragedy. No society in history has ever been permanent. Everything built by humans has sooner or later collapsed. If you look at the varieties of nations and societies in the kaleidoscope of history, you would be arrogant to believe that any one statesman or maybe even any one nation is more than a speck of dust in an infinity of time. On the other hand, as a statesman, you have no right to act this way. As a statesman, you must act *as if* you could build for eternity, and you must act to ensure continuity and hope and progress to the people whom you represent and hopefully to the people of the world, even though deep down you know that there may be a greater design of which you are only an infinitesimal part.

W.B.: And finally, Dr. Kissinger, are you hopeful about the future of America?

■ KISSINGER: Well, I would say this. For the next five to six years, we face a period of enormous danger. There is a great Soviet military capacity. There is turmoil in the Persian Gulf, in East Asia, in Central America; we have never before faced so many crises simultaneously, and therefore for the next five to six years, even under the best of management, it will require enormous discipline, enormous dedication, and enormous wisdom. On the other hand, if I look at the problem of our principal adversary, the Soviet Union, I would conclude that the only thing I could really add is the accumulation of military power. After all, they have a political system that has not solved the problem of succession. They have an economic system that is inherently stagnating because you cannot run a modern economy by a system of total planning. They have huge bureaucracies that are in constant conflict with each other. And when you look at China, which is a simpler society, and the fantastic problems *they* have in restructuring it and in escaping some of the tendencies that are inherent in communism, you can see what lies ahead for the Soviet Union when they turn to their problems of domestic reform. Now, unfortunately, there is a grave danger that they will try to escape their domestic problems by foreign adventures. *That* is the challenge of the next five to six years.

And, if we get through these next five to six years, then I am quite optimistic about the next fifteen years. And I *do* think that we have an opportunity to get through the next five years. It will be difficult, but I believe that we will in fact reach a turning point toward a stabler and more hopeful future. And that I consider to be the biggest issue of the moment.

W.B.: Many years ago, a young scholar wrote, "Men become myths, not by what they know, or even by what they achieve, but by the tasks they set themselves." Little did the author of these words realize that they could one day be applied to his own life. For the author of those words, Dr. Henry Kissinger, has become a legend in his own time for the paramount tasks he has set for himself: the building of a structure of peace, of a stable world order in the midst of chaos, confusion, and disarray. Indeed, throughout these years, his work has continually reminded us that if the democratic nations fail, it will be because of the faulty strategy of idealists with too many illusions, facing the cynical realists with too little conscience. Hence what is needed is both idealism and realism. And so whether we share his unique blend of idealism and realism or not, whether we agree or disagree with him, is secondary, for no one can disregard his talents, his efforts, his achievements, his dedication, and his devotion.

Dr. Sol Liptzin

and C. Bezalel Sherman

23. ❧ Judaism in the Year 2090

Dr. Sol Liptzin

C. Bezalel Sherman

W.B.: For a discussion of this most interesting subject, we are indeed fortunate to have two most outstanding persons. Actually, I imagine we should have a crystal ball because we are going to look into the future in an attempt to determine what American Jewish life will be like in the years ahead.

The Talmud makes the observation that after the destruction of the Temple, those who engaged in prophecy were either babes or fools. Although neither these two men nor I myself are in the first category, and we trust that we are not in the second, our intention here is to try to forecast for the year 2090 on the basis of what we now know.

First, I will introduce our two distinguished panelists. Professor Sol Liptzin was Professor of Germanic Languages and Literature at the City College of New York. He is a very warm, friendly, and down-to-earth human being. He has made great contributions to Jewish letters, and has served as president of the Jewish Book Council of America. Our other panelist is a noted sociologist and an eloquent speaker and writer. He was the director of Cultural and Community Affairs for the Labor Zionist Organization of America—Mr. C. Bezalel Sherman.

We have decided that we will begin this session with an opening statement by each gentleman, and so before I turn to my questioning, I would like to call on Mr. Sherman to present his views in general about American Jewish life in the year 2090.

> ■ SHERMAN: One would have to be a bold prophet indeed to predict the development of the American Jewish community in these revolutionary times of rapid change. All one can do is to try to assess the present-day Jewish situation in the

United States in the light of the history of the American
Jewish community and to state that, given certain circumstances and conditions, we have reason to expect that the
American Jewish community will take on certain particular
shapes.

The Jewish community in the United States has developed
as a result of an interplay of negative and positive forces that
have marked Jewish history throughout the ages. Some of
these forces have existed at other times and other places, and
some are unique to American Jewish life.

A unique feature in American Jewish life and a unique
contribution of American Jewry to Jewish historical experience is the fact that, for the first time in Jewish history, we
have a voluntary community based neither on governmental
nor on state prerogatives nor on compelling religious authority. Ours is a voluntary community that the Jews have
evolved themselves in response to pressures from within and
from without. It has not been planned. It has not been fash-
ioned on the basis of any kind of blueprint but has evolved as
a result of developments in American Jewish life to which
American Jews have had to react. It is also important to
remember that we live in a country in which there is no state
religion, and that this has left its impress upon the march of
Jewish events in the United States. As far as the state is
concerned, the Jews have attained a degree of integration the
like of which is not to be found in any Jewish community in
history. Full equality is our lot in this country. It has come to
us as a right and not as a sufferance. We were born to it. We
never had to struggle for emancipation. This is very important because we did not have to pay a special price for enjoying the privileges of citizenship that other citizens of this
country enjoy.

At the same time we must draw a line between state and
society. While we live in a country in which the state has no
recognized religion, no recognized church, as far as society is
concerned, America is Christian, predominantly and over-
whelmingly. In a democratic land it is society that is sometimes more important and more determining than state, because the state is the servant of society, unlike the situation
in totalitarian lands, where the state is imposed upon society.

Since our society is Christian in its overwhelming majority, the Jew faces a situation in this country in which he has to adjust and accommodate himself to conditions shaped by non-Jews.

The unique contribution of American Jewry to Jewish historical experience consists precisely of this: we have demonstrated our ability to adjust to American conditions without losing our identity. This is a remarkable achievement not only in terms of Jewish history but also in terms of American development. No other white ethnic group has been able to maintain its integrity as a community for as long a period as we have. This we have done in spite of the fact that we have moved economically and culturally in the same direction as has the whole country. Economically, as a matter of fact, while moving in the same direction as the country, we have been at times ahead of others. We became a middle-class community long before America itself became a middle-class country.

We have been exceptional in that we have made economic progress ahead of others but in the same direction as others. Now we are reaching a point in our development in this country where we will probably no longer be the exception to the general rule, insofar as the country as a whole is moving in the same direction, insofar as the United States as a nation is becoming more and more middle-class. The economic distinctiveness that characterized our position in this country will probably be lost in 2090. We will take on, economically, the shape of all other citizens, and we will probably act increasingly in accordance with the economic status we will have achieved as a result of losing our distinctiveness.

The same thing is true of our cultural development. We have been exceptional in that we have been ahead of others in our general educational achievements in this country. We brought with us the tradition of learning that stood us in good stead. But here, too, we are losing our distinctiveness and are no longer the exception to the rule. America is moving in the same direction. College education is becoming the standard for everybody. As a result, we find very little today to differentiate the Jewish student from the non-Jewish student, in appearance, in the choice of profession, in general outlook and in approach to social problems.

As we are woven into the fabric of American society and as we take on the coloration of and become more adapted to the mores and folkways of this country as a whole, and to that extent lose our distinctiveness, we will, as time goes on, lose some of the vitality that has sustained us for so many years. We have never been culturally self-sufficient in this country. We have always drawn upon the older Jewish communities, religiously and culturally. We have never developed sufficient strength in American Jewish life to sustain us without the support from the older communities.

The question that American Jewry will face in the next few decades, if conditions continue as they are at the present time, will be this: Is it possible for Jews to enter deeper into the fabric of American social and cultural processes and still maintain their identity as they have maintained it throughout the three centuries of Jewish sojourn in this country? My own prediction is that we will not be able to do so. As time goes on we will lose our ability to buck the tide and to retain our own individuality. The only thing that will help us will be the creativity of the State of Israel, which will be all that we will have to draw upon to make up for at least part of the deficit that will be created in the course of growing deeper into the processes of American life.

I feel that there will be a Jewish community in this country also because of pressure from without. Whether this community will maintain itself as a result of its own will to live, and as a result of its determination to survive out of a realization that it has something to survive for, or whether it will maintain itself because of reaction from without, will be the basic issue facing American Jews within the next century.

If the American Jew is determined to survive, as a Jew and as an American, I think he will find ample opportunity in American life to maintain his identity, but only on condition that he become more closely integrated into the historical, cultural, and religious processes of the Jewish people as a whole. American Jewry will not maintain itself as a tribe. It will maintain itself as an integral part of the Jewish people centered about the national homeland in Israel.

W.B.: This very fine opening statement has given us background for our questions. Now we turn to Dr. Liptzin for his presentation.

■ LIPTZIN: I agree completely with the facts and the analysis presented by Mr. Sherman. I do not agree with his conclusions, however, because I am not as much a determinist as he is, since I believe in freedom of will. The question before us is, What will American Jews be like in the year 2090? My answer is that they will be what we American Jews today want them to be. And if we do *not* want them to be, then they will not be, and the Jewish people will have to carry on their millennial existence without the American branch. If we American Jews of today prefer to assimilate, integrate, melt into the majority group, then our children, grandchildren, and great-grandchildren will be well on the way toward this by the year 2000, and certainly long before 2090. If, on the other hand, we prefer a golden era of Jewish creativity, we can bring it about by then if we take the necessary steps now in our generation, which I call the "generation of decision."

For this discussion we are asked to garb ourselves in the togas of prophets and to forecast the future. There are two kinds of prophets. I call the one type Hellenic and the other type the Hebraic. According to the Greeks, a prophet is a person who can foresee the future but who cannot change it. Greek prophets and prophetesses could foresee the future accurately, but what good did it do them or their people if this future was ordained in the stars and could not be altered under any circumstances? On the other hand, according to the Jews, a prophet is a person who foresees possibilities, good and bad, tragic and exhilarating, and who directs attention to the possibility that will best further the creative survival and efflorescence of the group. He points to the steps that must be taken now, in the present, so that this possibility becomes a reality in the future. He warns, he adjures, he inspires, he mobilizes a people's energy toward the envisaged goal. When the goal is then reached, the people look back and call him a true prophet and erect a monument upon his grave.

Now, the three of us are Americans and Jews. We live in American space and Jewish time. We participate in that reality known as Americanism and in that other reality known as Jewishness. We are still bicultural. The question before us is, What will be the relationship a century hence of these two realities now operating upon us and within us? Will the present unstable condition of dualism have yielded by then to a more stable and less perilous monistic existence? Will we have given up most of the unique traits that still separate us from our neighbors of non-Jewish origin? I do not think so, even though I agree that the American environment is inhospitable to Jewish survival. American *friendliness* to Jews, not American anti-Semitism, imperils Jewish individuality. It was the American friendliness to Jews that dissolved pre-Revolutionary Jewry, so that despite Jewish immigration, their number half a century after the Revolution was still the same as before the Revolution, about 3,000. I once said that if we had attempted to call together the descendants of Colonial Jewry to celebrate our tercentenary in 1954, we would have had an assembly of the finest Christian families of America.

What saved the American Jewish communities from extinction in the mid-nineteenth century was the influx of tens of thousands of German Jews. Their immigrant generation up to 1880 formed an enclave in America. Their second generation from 1880 to 1914 was tricultural: German, Jewish, and American. Their third generation between the two World Wars consisted of Americans of German–Jewish origin. Their fourth generation has now reached the same point of dissolution as that of the pre–Civil War Jews—in which there are probably more descendants outside of the Jewish fold than within it.

What saved the American Jewish communities from extinction by the mid-twentieth century was the immigration by the hundreds of thousands of Eastern European Jews since the 1880s. Their first generation, from 1881 to 1914, formed a Yiddish-speaking enclave in the large cities of the Eastern seaboard, especially New York. Their second generation, from 1914 to the founding of Israel, was bicultural but engaged in flights from Jewishness, which it associated far too frequently with slums and childhood poverty. Many of us here today came to maturity in those years. Their third generation, from 1950 on, consists of Americans of Jewish origin. Their fourth generation, which will be dominant by about the year 2000, should therefore be in a state of dissolution and complete cultural assimilation, except that some of these American Jews may be attending a synagogue on Sunday instead of a cathedral.

So argue some historians—Jacob Marcus, Oscar Handlin, and others—who project past tendencies onto the future; so argue most determinists. So I do *not* argue, because I hold that history is a guide to group conduct. It is not the dead hand of the past compelling us on to an inevitable future. It is the accumulated wisdom of the past, the records of errors, achievements, frustrations, and successes. It helps us to avoid pitfalls. It does not condemn us to repeat mistakes.

Now, I agree that our environmental forces in America drive us to decay and disintegration as a distinct Jewish group. If these were the only forces impelling our group, then pessimism would indeed be justified. But as I look about me I also see forces of regeneration and rejuvenation persisting among us. These have their source in the will of millions of us to live on as Jews, to live on as a distinct group, no matter the price that may have to be paid for our uniqueness. We are today five million Americans whose Jewishness ranges from close to zero at one extreme to close to 100 percent at the other extreme. Those who are close to zero we shall have lost by the next century as the overfriendly American environment nibbles away at them. The greater our inertia, the greater will be the drift toward zero—toward assimilation, intermarriage, conversion.

Yet, although we may lose millions, our saving remnants, still amounting to millions, will remain. If we strengthen Jewish education and keep synagogues the center of our community, the drift will be toward the 100 percent direction, and even those who intermarry will prefer to affiliate with us, and our numbers may even increase. Those who remain with us in the coming decades will be basically what we are today, still divided into a rich variety of secular and religious organizations, still arguing about the meaning of Jewishness in those reconstituted ghettos that we today call Jewish suburbia and that a century hence will be megasubur-

bia. Millions of us will still exist in the year 2090 by continuing our more difficult but also more zestful existence
in American space and Jewish time. Many of us will still
want to adhere to that world-people whose heart is in
Israel, whose lungs are in America, and whose limbs extend to all continents. Millions of us will still want to
share with kinsmen in a glorious past, in an exciting present, and in visions of a Messianic future that we can help to
bring about.

When American Jews meet, several decades from now, at
the centennial of Israel's rebirth—which was but the first
chapter in the contemporary Jewish rebirth—then the second
chapter should be nearing its climax: the rejuvenation of the
Jewish people in America and throughout the Diaspora. Our
prophets will be setting their sights on centuries to come and
preparing for the third chapter, the moral regeneration of the
world under the inspiring example of the rejuvenated Jewish
people.

What will American Jewish life be like in the year 2090? My
answer is this: It will be what we want it to be. A golden era
of American Jewishness is one of several possibilities before
us. Let us work to make it a reality. Let us unleash the
creative effort of our group and not stifle it with nihilistic,
paralyzing cynicism. Let us intensify Jewish education, and
we can arrest assimilation to non-Jewish ways. Let us keep
the vital energies of our people alive and healthy. Let us carry
on the golden chain of Jewish tradition and hand it on to our
heirs in the century to come. Let this be our unfaltering will,
our joyous purpose, our faith and our hope, now and in the
days to come, until our destiny shall have been fulfilled and
the purpose of our group survival, since the dawn of history,
shall have been achieved; and the Messianic Age of peace,
unity, and good will shall reign throughout the realms of this
lovely, lovely world of ours.

w.B.: Mr. Sherman, do you believe that Reform and Conservative
Judaism will have merged into one denomination by the year 2090?

■ SHERMAN: I believe that we are witnessing at the present
time a *rapprochement* between those two groups, and I would

say that the Orthodox group and the Neo-Orthodox groups are not far behind. I believe that theologically the various Jewish denominations are getting closer to each other, so that the differences between them are not as pronounced as has been the case throughout the last three or four generations. I am concerned that while they are getting closer to each other theologically, they are drifting apart institutionally. If this process that has been in motion for the past twenty-five or thirty years continues, it is conceivable that we will see the emergence of a Jewish religion in the United States which will be made up of three components—Orthodoxy, Conservatism, and Reform—and which will probably be unlike any Jewish religious trend outside the United States. That is another reason why I feel that, if prevailing conditions continue, there will be a tendency for the Jews of America to drift away from the Jews in other lands, unless it is Israel that binds them together.

w.b.: In other words, you envision the possibility that Conservatism and Reform might merge into one denomination. Dr. Liptzin, would you say that Conservative and *Orthodox* Judaism will merge into one group?

■ LIPTZIN: As a Jew who is Orthodox, Conservative, *and* Reform, my answer is no, they will not merge. And I will give you my reasons for this. Insofar as Jewishness is meaningful to us, insofar as it is a living organism, I envisage it as a sort of tree, with Orthodoxy as the strong, gnarled trunk whose roots are deep in the earth. It may have excrescences, it may have ugliness about it, but it is strong indeed. I envisage Conservatism as the branches that come out of this trunk. And I envisage Reform Judaism as the beautiful leaves, flowers, and fruits at the end of it. All three are necessary for the health of the tree of Judaism.

w.b.: In the year 2090, Mr. Sherman, do you think that Judaism will be seeking actively to convert non-Jews?

■ SHERMAN: That is a very difficult question to answer. My inclination, and I have no basis in fact for this answer, would be to reply in the negative.

W.B.: That it will not?

■ SHERMAN: That it will not. I would like to share Professor Liptzin's optimism, and as far as his wishes are concerned, I certainly share those, for I would like to see Jewish life take on the will to live. But I am not so sure that conditions in the United States are conducive to strengthening our will to live. On the contrary, it seems to me that conditions are more conducive to weakening the will to live. I cannot agree that it is only up to us. I do not feel that the Jews in the United States will have the inclination or the desire to convert the country. Now the Catholics, for instance, have never given up the ambition of becoming the majority religion, the dominating religion in the United States. Jews have never been seized by that kind of desire. It seems to me that Jews have learned from sad experience that conversion has created more problems than it solved. It is inconceivable to me that much attention will be paid to converting or proselytizing.

W.B.: Dr. Liptzin?

■ LIPTZIN: I believe that by 2090 there could be mass conversions to Judaism. If we build quality Jewishness, and if our way of life is morally superior to that which surrounds us, then I see no reason why the best elements among all people should not be converted to us. That is why I am an assimilationist—because I believe that ultimately all peoples will be assimilated to us, or to our emphasis on the moral way of life.

■ SHERMAN: Under those conditions I can agree.

W.B.: I turn now to a question in another area. Mr. Sherman, do you feel that Jews will be practicing their religion openly in the Soviet Union in 2090? [*Editor's note*: This Dialogue took place before Russian policy granting greater religious freedoms took effect in the late 1980s.]

■ SHERMAN: That would depend upon qualifying conditions. If the present conditions obtain, my answer would be definitely no. I doubt very much that there would be enough Jews left who would care to practice their religion even if they were given an opportunity to do so. I think that Jewish life in the Soviet Union is being pulverized to such an extent that if this were to continue for another generation, there would not be enough vitality left to restore Jewish life. If, on the other hand, conditions were to change, then there is no reason why Soviet Jews should not only practice their religion but also become an integral part of the Jewish people and establish relations with the Jewish communities throughout the world, particularly with the Jews of the State of Israel.

W.B.: Do you have any comment, Dr. Liptzin?

■ **LIPTZIN:** I agree completely that if conditions do not change, things will happen as Mr. Sherman has said. But I do believe that naught is changeless but change, naught is permanent but impermanence, and that, therefore, the Soviet Union in the year 2090 will not be what it is today.

W.B.: Mr. Sherman, do you envision that the Reform movement will sponsor Jewish parochial schools by 2090?

■ **SHERMAN:** I would say yes to that. My answer is based on what I said before. I can see that there is a *rapprochement* among the Jewish religious denominations in the United States. The interesting part of it is that Reform is becoming more and more traditional. If Reform really wants to sustain Jewish life, it will realize that Jewish education is the mainstay of survival and that the best Jewish education we can give to children is in a Jewish day school. I do not like the term *parochial school*. I would rather use the term *day school*.

W.B.: Day school it is, then. But why do you feel that Jewish day schools can be the primary instrument of Jewish survival in the coming one hundred years?

■ **SHERMAN:** I did not say that *only* through the day school can we preserve Judaism. I said that the best Jewish education we can give our children today, in a country like the United States, is a day-school education. I am also aware of the fact that the day school will not be the predominant trend in Jewish education. It will be the supplementary school. Now, the Orthodox day schools have taken the lead in this direction, and more power to them. I am very happy to see that Conservative Jewry is making headway, rapid headway, along the same road. The question that the Rabbi asked was whether I believed that the Reform movement will have day schools in the year 2090, and I have answered in the affirmative.

■ LIPTZIN: I believe that Sunday School education is better than no Jewish education at all and that supplementary afternoon schools are preferable to Sunday schools. I believe in day schools for the elite out of which will come the future leaders, lay and religious, of American Jewry. The Orthodox have already begun, the Conservatives have already begun, and, if Reform Jewry is to survive, it will have to follow suit and train a percentage of its congregants in Reform day schools.

W.B.: I would like to add my own comment on this. Certain segments of our Jewish people have held a negative attitude toward the Hebrew day school. This has stemmed, in part, from the fact that the day schools did not represent the norm in American education—that they seemed to be a bit unworldly in their approach. This is changing, and the day schools are beginning to keep pace with the best that other institutions have to offer, from biology to baseball, from social studies to social clubs—with the added benefit of a good Jewish education.

Now, Dr. Liptzin, in your opening presentation you said that American friendliness is hostile to our survival in the society as Jews. Would you care to expand on that somewhat? Why should a society as free as ours be detrimental to Jewish survival?

■ LIPTZIN: I did not say detrimental, I said inhospitable: American overfriendliness is inhospitable to Jewish survival. I have no doubt that we will survive as human beings, as Americans. What I am fighting for is that we survive as quality Jews in America.

America permits one to develop one's own way and one's own culture in freedom and democracy. Every other group that has come here has preferred not to accept this offer of America and has grafted itself onto the Anglo-American tree because it came here to escape from an old way of life. We Jews, on the other hand, came here in order to live our Jewishness because we were not permitted to live it undisturbed in Russia, Germany, Rumania, Poland, and other countries. Therefore, while all other groups, as minority groups, will inevitably disappear, I believe that the American environment permits us, allows us, to retain our Jewish minority-group status and is indeed happy if we do so. It is entirely up to us. If we do not want to, I say we will dissolve. America offers us the possibility of building Jewishness. Do we want to take that offer? No other country has offered such freedom to develop Jewishness.

w.b.: Thank you for your explanation. Now I would like you to continue with a forecast, Dr. Liptzin. What major changes will take place in American Jewish life, in the education of children and adults, in the forms of worship by the year 2090?

■ LIPTZIN: The chief change will be that people will be praying meaningful prayers; people will be praying in the language that they understand.

w.b.: What does that mean, "meaningful prayers"?

■ LIPTZIN: I assume that by 2090, Jewish education will have reached the point where every Jewish child will understand Hebrew, so that these prayers will be meaningful. Beyond that, since our prayers look forward to our homecoming to Zion, and since a good portion of our people will have returned to Zion, the fulfillment of these prayers must lead us to assume that our other prayers will also be answered. Therefore, when we pray we shall find heightened meaning in what we pray, and our prayers will then be a more significant part of our lives.

■ SHERMAN: It seems to me that this would largely depend upon the rabbinate and upon the religious institutions in the United States and particularly on the synagogue. If the synagogue continues along the same lines that it has been proceeding for the past twenty-five years, the synagogue will become the center of secularism in Jewish life rather than religion in Jewish life. It is becoming a secularized institution, in that membership in a synagogue is not translated into mitzvot, and despite the growth of religious affiliation in American Jewish life, religious observance has not increased correspondingly. If, on the other hand, the synagogue devotes itself to its main objective—that of being the center of the Jewish faith—then, of course, the whole mood and the whole atmosphere about it will change, and this will have a profound effect upon the worshipers and the members of the synagogue.

W.B.: I would like to make a comment and step out of my role as moderator. There is a rabbinic dictum, "While at the outset one may not be motivated for its own sake, if he continues he will be moved to do so for its own sake." I take issue with your statement, Mr. Sherman, that the synagogues of today are secular institutions. The people who go to the synagogues may come for secular reasons, but the institution is such, and the leadership it offers is such, that it certainly is not secular in character. We are trying to bring about a deeper and more qualitative renaissance of Jewish religion and Jewish meaning for our young people and adults.

But let me ask another question. Mr. Sherman: In the year 2090 will there be a unified American Jewish community?

■ SHERMAN: I believe there will be. On this I can speak with some authority. I think that the whole trend in American Jewish life is toward unification of effort. I think we have a more consolidated Jewish community, and this is really a remarkable achievement. Moreover, it is unique in American experience. We have a more consolidated Jewish community today than we have ever had before, and interestingly enough the consolidation grows in proportion to the so-called Americanization of American Jews. The further removed we are from the immigrant generation, the more unity there is in Jewish life. All divisions based on place of origin and on economic classifications are now being obliterated. We live in the age of the third generation, and the third generation does not care too much about the place of origin of the grandparents. The fact is that we live within the same American environment. I feel that as time goes on we will have a more unified Jewish community and, I would add, a more democratic Jewish community than we have in the present.

W.B.: Professor Liptzin, speaking of the unified community, will there be a United Jewish Appeal in 2090?

■ LIPTZIN: I think that there will, but it will not necessarily be called U.J.A. It depends on the cycles. There were times when we had to rush in to help the Jews of Russia. There were times when we had to rush in to help the Jews of Germany. There were times when we had to rush in to help the Jews of Israel. There may be hours of peril when the Jews of the world may have to come in and help us, because I do agree with our friend Mr. Sherman that there always is unity among Jews in hours of peril. At other times we can afford the luxury of disunity and differences of opinion, but in an hour of peril we will come to help the Jews of the world and in an hour of peril they will come to help us.

W.B.: Will there be a Zionist Organization of America?

■ LIPTZIN: The Zionist movement was a dream of 1897. It was fulfilled with the establishment of the State of Israel. We are now in a generation beyond Zionism, the generation of the rebirth of the Jewish people in all lands. In 2090 there will be no Z.O.A.

W.B.: Will there be a Hadassah?

■ LIPTZIN: There will always be the union of Jewish women to help in the type of work that Hadassah does, although many of the functions of Hadassah will have been taken over by the State of Israel.

W.B.: Mr. Sherman, will you comment?

■ SHERMAN: My comment is that Jewish life in the United States in the past, and I am sure in the future, has revolved and will revolve around three pivotal points. One is the synagogue, or religion. Another is institutional life, the network of social service and philanthropic institutions that we have built up and that play a tremendous role in consolidating and maintaining the Jewish community. The third is the concern of the American Jew with the fate of Jews outside the United States and of the Jewish people as a whole. If the Jewish community is to survive, and I am sure it will survive in this country, it will still revolve around these three pivotal points. Whether there will be a Z.O.A. or there will not be a Z.O.A., the concern will be here. It would really be a sad day for the Jews of America if they were to lose that concern, and if they were to lose some concrete way of expressing that concern in terms of practical and specific action. Whether it is through the Z.O.A. or U.J.A. is not important.

W.B.: Mr. Sherman, will there be English-Jewish newspapers in 2090?

■ SHERMAN: My answer is no. First, I cannot see a very great need for them. Second, I cannot see that they will have the financial resources. And third, I cannot see that there will be a profound interest in them. What we need is not special newspapers. We need publications that will present the Jewish point of view as far as news is concerned. The *New York Times* is perfectly satisfactory to me, and the Yiddish press will also serve its purpose.

W.B.: That leads me to the next question. I am going to put it in two parts, Dr. Liptzin. Will the Yiddish press survive to the year 2090?

■ LIPTZIN: There will be a language that will be the successor of what we today speak of as Yiddish, just as there is a language today that is the successor of Chaucerian and Shakespearean English, which very few of us understand. I do believe that its base will probably be Hebrew, and it will be enriched by the Yiddish that was and by the English that was. If we were able to put our thinking and feeling into the German language in the course of a few hundred years and make it a Jewish language, we can do the same with English. A few hundred years from now English might be the Jewish medium of expression, and we will have our Jewish newspapers in English.

W.B.: In other words, the language of American Jews in 2090 will be what?

■ LIPTZIN: The successors of the languages spoken today by Jews—Hebrew, Yiddish, and English. Today we are still trilingual.

W.B.: Now, Mr. Sherman, will kosher restaurants and butcher shops exist in the year 2090?

> ■ SHERMAN: In answering this question, I would like to make this observation. I do a lot of traveling, and one of the disheartening things to a person like myself, who is not very strict in his observance, is that there are huge Jewish communities with few if any kosher restaurants. Cities like Los Angeles, and in Argentina the city of Buenos Aires, although there are nearly 400,000 Jews living there. I would say, then, to answer your question, *no*, merely on the basis of facts as I see them and as I interpret them. But the need for kosher restaurants will exist, and I hope that the Jews will surmount these difficulties and maintain kosher restaurants and butcher shops.

W.B.: Professor Liptzin, you are a noted author and deeply involved in the field of literature. Would a book on a Jewish theme have won the Pulitzer Prize by 2090?

> ■ LIPTZIN: If it is of good literary quality, why not?

W.B.: Good enough. Mr. Sherman, will a Jew have run for president or vice-president, and if so, will he have been elected president or vice-president by the year 2090?

> ■ SHERMAN: Theoretically, I can see no reason that this could not come to pass. As I said, we have become thoroughly integrated into the political processes of the United States, enjoying equality in the fullest sense of the word. I believe America is moving forward, becoming more liberal, and thus there is no reason why there could not be a Jewish candidate for president, and why one could not be elected. If you were to ask whether I could get along without a Jewish president, my answer would also be yes.

W.B.: Dr. Liptzin, will there be more anti-Semitism in America than there is today?

> ■ LIPTZIN: If the standard of living of the Jewish segment of the American population should rise at a faster pace than that of the general population in periods of prosperity, or fall

at a slower pace than that of the general population in periods of depression, then anti-Semitism would increase. Otherwise, it could decrease.

W.B.: Will there be more anti-Semitism in other countries? And if yes, which country?

■ LIPTZIN: I think there will be less anti-Semitism throughout the world as the pressure of excessive Jewish talent upon other countries is relieved by the migration of Jews to Israel.

W.B.: Mr. Sherman, will there be a peace treaty between Israel and the Arabs by the year 2090?

■ SHERMAN: Oh yes, of that I am quite convinced. It is the one thing that I can answer unequivocally in the affirmative. There will be a peace treaty. I think harmonious relations will exist between the State of Israel and the Arab countries. *Halevai!* It is inconceivable to me that this present situation will last for longer than another decade or so. There is every reason in the world that there should be peace between them, and I am sure that peace will be achieved.

■ LIPTZIN: There I agree completely. I have no doubt that we are heading toward peace now between Israel and the Arabs.

W.B.: Now we turn to another category. Dr. Liptzin, will religion be taught in American public schools?

■ LIPTZIN: No. I think that the separation of church and state is one of the fundamental principles of the way of life that we call American.

W.B.: Mr. Sherman, will the religious revival continue in America?

■ SHERMAN: Well, now, the question is whether we are truly experiencing a religious revival. We see an increase of congregational membership and affiliation. Are you relating this to the Jewish community?

W.B.: No, I am just speaking generally. We are going into the general scene a bit. Will the religious revival, assuming that there is one, continue in America?

■ **SHERMAN:** I would say yes. And I am not so sure that it is not going to penetrate the public school system.

W.B.: In other words, you feel that religion may be taught in the American public schools?

■ **SHERMAN:** It will make itself increasingly felt, if religion is really taken seriously by American society. As I said, in a democratic country, society is the determining factor. I am not so sure that it will be kept out of the school system altogether. Whether or not it will be officially taught is another matter.

W.B.: Dr. Liptzin, do you think there will be a closer understanding between the three major religious faiths in America in the year 2090?

■ **LIPTZIN:** To me, the three major religious faiths teach ethical conduct and the good life, and I believe they will each still retain their basic theology.

■ **SHERMAN:** I feel that this will depend upon the development of those religious faiths. I think that they will simply find a way of living with each other. There may be more cooperation, but unless they change their theologies and whole scheme of religious faith, I would not say that there can be any real unanimity.

W.B.: Will intermarriage increase?

■ **SHERMAN:** Intermarriage is on the increase in the United States today among all religious groups, including Jews. Jews still intermarry less, and in the United States we have the lowest rate of intermarriage in the Western world. But it is on the increase, and there is every indication that it will continue to increase.

■ **LIPTZIN:** I would agree that the rate of intermarriage will increase from decade to decade. However, I also believe that a greater proportion of those who will intermarry will join our faith than is the case at present.

W.B.:   Dr. Liptzin, it is your turn for another question. Will the religion of candidates still influence the American voter in the year 2090?

> ■ LIPTZIN: Just as much as the looks of the candidate and the age of the candidate or other factors. It is one of the factors that will influence the opinions of people.

W.B.:   And the final question in this category is for Mr. Sherman. What changes will have occurred in religious life and practice as the result of such twentieth-century media as television, radio, and motion pictures?

> ■ SHERMAN: These are not the only media of change. It seems to me that we are living, in this atomic age, in a time of insecurity—an age in which the individual has lost the ground from under his feet, and he is looking to heaven for a hold on life. Unless we have a more stabilized society than we have at the present time, it seems to me that people will increasingly turn to religion to find that sense of security which society has not provided.

W.B.:   Let us turn now to the final category—world affairs. I think that we should end on a universal note, and "World Affairs in the Year 2090" is most appropriate. Dr. Liptzin, do you think that the human species will survive to that time?

> ■ LIPTZIN: As Jews, we believe—it is one of the cardinal articles of our faith—that there is purpose to existence, that there is meaning to existence. And if there is meaning to life, then there is meaning for us as individuals. There is meaning to our group existence, and we will survive.

W.B.:   Your comment, Mr. Sherman?

> ■ SHERMAN: Well, it will take more than meaning. If the contending forces somehow find a way of coexistence, for lack of a better term, humans can survive. In other words, if we do not have a third World War, which will be an atomic war,

then humankind will survive. On the other hand, if we have another war, it will probably destroy the world and humankind with it.

W.B.: Will the United Nations be a world government, Mr. Sherman?

■ SHERMAN: I can only express a wish. I would like to see some supergovernment supersede nationalistic governments, because it seems to me that here lies the only hope for humankind to survive. If humankind is divided along nationalistic lines, we are going to have wars, and war at the present time means destruction and ruin. I would therefore like to see the United Nations assume greater responsibility for maintaining the peace of the world. We would, of course, have to invest it with greater authority than it enjoys at the present time.

■ LIPTZIN: I do not believe that we will have one world by the year 2090, but I do believe that centuries hence we probably will. I do believe that we are now passing beyond the state of nationalism to an age of supernationalism, or "cultural continents." One such cultural continent is our Occident, which extends from the Elbe to the Golden Gate. Another is the Slavic cultural continent, which extends from the Elbe to the Yalu. A third is the Islamic, a fourth is the Chinese, a fifth is the Indian, and so on.

This is the world we are now entering, and the United Nations can provide a forum in which the differences between these vast aggregations of power are ironed out. I do believe that when we come to the twenty-second or twenty-third century, the time will be ripe for the cultural continents of the world to unite into one world. By that time we shall have, in Israel, an effective bridge between the cultural continents. There will be people of experience, with the wisdom of Europe and the adventurous spirit of America, who have gone through the collective disillusion of the Slavic East, who live in Islamic surroundings, and understand Oriental thinking and the feeling of an awakening Asia and Africa. So finally from Zion and Jerusalem will come forth the Law of

God and the unity of man. The *Shema*, which is the basic article of our faith, ends in the word "oneness." Thus will our faith in our religion have been justified.

■ SHERMAN: I would like to say amen to that.

W.B.:   I would like to say amen to that as well. It provides a high note on which to end our discussion, and I would like to conclude with a story that has a lesson.

A little boy walking down the road was stopped by a stranger who asked him, "How long will it take me to get to the next town?"

"I'm sorry, sir," said the boy, "I really cannot tell you." The stranger walked on, and a few moments later he felt somebody pulling at his coattail. Turning around, he saw the little boy. The little boy said, "You have about a half hour's walk to the next town."

The stranger said, "Thank you, but I'd like you to tell me something. A few minutes ago I asked you and you said you didn't know. Now you tell me I have a half hour's walk."

"Well," replied the little boy, "I watched you as you left me and I saw your steps. Based on your steps, I figured you have a half hour's walk."

I think the lesson that we will take away in terms of Judaism in the year 2090 is the fact that it all depends upon the steps we take. I think the present time is indeed fortunate to have two men of the caliber that we have had for this discussion, to help make these steps firm so that Jewish life, please God, will continue to be dynamic and vibrant, and will indeed flourish in the years to come.

Rabbi David Max Eichhorn
and Rabbi Immanuel Jakobovits

24. &c Shall Jews Missionize?

Rabbi David Max Eichhorn

Rabbi Immanuel Jakobovits

W.B.: The theme we are to discuss is a current question in American Jewish life: Shall we have Jewish missionaries? Some people would give an unqualified yes to this question, but some feel otherwise and would say no. Perhaps, as we discuss this, we may find that there is no clear-cut yes or no answer. It is not a matter of black or white; perhaps it is gray. There are many sides to the subject, and we have chosen to explore two different points of view, with perhaps my own inserted from time to time as a third. To give you two disparate aspects of the subject of Jewish missionary activity, we have selected two rabbis who have had close relationships with the questions involved.

One of our authorities is Rabbi David Max Eichhorn. Dr. Eichhorn was the director of field operations of the Commision on Jewish Chaplaincy, National Jewish Welfare Board (J.W.B.). Before taking this post, he was a pulpit rabbi, and immediately before coming to the J.W.B. he served as a Jewish Army chaplain in Europe during World War II. He is a theologian and philosopher who is deeply versed in the subject of proselytism; he is a noted lecturer, and the author of several books.

The other authority has had a rich and colorful rabbinic career both here and abroad, having served as Rabbi of the Great Synagogue of London and as the Chief Rabbi of Ireland. He is a prolific writer on Jewish law and has lectured extensively throughout the United States. He was the Rabbi of the Fifth Avenue Synagogue in New York City, and is now Chief Rabbi of the British Commonwealth—Rabbi Immanuel Jakobovits.

I would like to open our discussion with our usual procedure, giving an opportunity to each speaker to develop his particular point of view. The first problem is, I think, to establish a frame of reference, to set the background.

Rabbi Eichhorn, can you tell us the history of the development of missionary work in Judaism? Has Judaism traditionally been a proselytizing religion?

■ EICHHORN: The answer to that direct question, Rabbi Berkowitz, is an unqualified yes. The average Jewish person has a completely mixed-up picture of the attitude of Judaism toward proselytism, of the attitude of Judaism toward the convert, and of the historical picture in this whole field. Part of the difficulty is the fact that in Hebrew there is no word for *convert*. The word *convert* is a completely Christian term. It derives from the Latin *conversus*, which means *to change*. The Christian concept is that a person who becomes a Christian changes over from something else. He has a certain religious point of view one day. Then he has a great vision, or sees a great dream, or hears a great sermon, or he goes down on his knees and hits the sawdust trail. Yesterday, as the old story goes, he was a fish, and today he is a chicken; yesterday he was an unbeliever, and now he is a Christian. This miracle, this phenomenon that converts an individual from one religion to another, is completely absent in Judaism.

The Hebrew word that we use for convert—because we have to go along with the language of the country in which we reside—is *gair*. The Hebrew word *gair* comes from the root *goor*, which means "to live with," and when a non-Jew becomes a Jew he does not change over from one religious point of view to another. He approaches, he becomes part of, he comes to live with a group of people and becomes a member of a religious fellowship with whose point of view he has agreed for a long time, sometimes consciously, sometimes unconsciously. He has found a group of people whom he considers very worthwhile. Here is a theology and philosophy he wants to espouse, and so he comes into the group.

In the Bible this is very clear; the word for *sojourner*, the word for *stranger*, the word for *convert* are all in this word *gair*. In the Bible there are a number of types of *gairim* depicted. There is the type of *gair* who simply comes to live with the group, and there is another type of *gair* who comes not only to live with the group but also to become completely part of it. When, in the Book of Esther, the expression "to Judaize"—to become part of the Jewish people—is first used in the Bible, we have in this one verse in which this word is used something akin to the process of complete proselytism.

With the single exception of the Book of Ezra and Nehemiah (for these are really one book), the consistent attitude of the Bible is that we welcome those who wish to affiliate with us. Outside of this book, in which Jews who had married non-Jewish women were forced to divorce their wives and to put aside the children of these wives, the Bible maintains that we welcome others not only as fellow members of our group but as partners in a job that God has given to us. God has chosen us from among all peoples to teach His Law to the nations, to become, as the Bible says, very specifically, "a light unto the nations and unto all the peoples." So we are a people who wish to have additional adherents. We are a people that has a message to give to the world. This is stated hundreds of times in the Bible and in the Talmud.

w.b.: Dr. Eichhorn, I would like to interrupt. Now that we have established the premise, may I point out that this theme of missionary activity is appropriate to the *Sidra* that speaks of Abraham and Sarah, who went out to win new souls. My basic question to you is this: What has been our history from Abraham until, let us say, the present time? Has Judaism been a proselytizing religion?

■ EICHHORN: In the sense of sending out professional missionaries, in the sense of giving people food, clothing, medical help, and bribes in order to persuade them to adopt our religion, we have never been a missionary religion, and, please God, we never will be. We do not hold out any sort of inducement to anybody to enter our religious fold except that of finding a way of life that for him is better than the way of life that he has. I would categorically say that in Jewish history, professional people have never been employed for this purpose, but I would also say categorically that in Jewish history, from time immemorial, every Jew was destined and every Jew was bidden to be a missionary. The Bible tells us we are a kingdom of priests and a holy people. What is the Bible trying to tell us but that as individuals and as a people we should be setting an example to the rest of the world, an example that we should be seeking to have the world follow.

What sort of people would we be and what sort of individuals would we be if we said to those who followed our example, "So far, no further. You can only come up to the door, but you cannot come in." This would be absolutely unthinkable. As I said before, there was no parallel in biblical times to what we today call a convert. The early Talmud period and the pre-Christian centuries contained synagogues that were filled with non-Jews who were interested in hearing sermons and attending services. There are numerous references in the Talmud to these people, especially women, because one of our problems was that we were very insistent on circumcision. This was a very dangerous and painful operation for a male to go through, especially in those early days of which we are speaking. So actual converts seemed to have been much more prevalent among females than among males.

The Christian Testament states that the Pharisees would cross land and sea to make one convert. This is somewhat of an exaggeration, of course, but among the Pharisees, among the Essenes, certainly among the Rabbis of the Talmud, we find again and again many evidences that there were people who did everything within their power to try to persuade non-Jews to become Jews. We have a famous story that has been authenticated by many historical proofs, that a whole kingdom, the Kingdom of Adiabene, lying between the Roman and Parthian Empires, converted to Judaism. A Jewish traveling merchant from Palestine had come to the court of the King of Adiabene and, while selling silks to the King's daughter, interested her in Judaism so that she, her father, and her mother eventually converted. When the war broke out between the Romans and the Jews in the year 66, a whole regiment, a whole troop, from Adiabene fought alongside the Jews against the Romans. They perished to the last man, including two or three princes of the royal household. This country remained Jewish until it was overrun by the Parthians in about the year 100. This is just one among many instances.

W.B.: So we could say that, up to a point in Jewish history, the answer—for want of a better term—was that there was a more or less aggressive mission to non-Jews. Now, in which period of Jewish history did the attitude change to a "no" attitude?

■ EICHHORN: When the Christians entered the picture, the attitude became "no." When Constantine the Great made Christianity the official religion of the Holy Roman Empire, and when the Code of Justinian was instituted, one of the features of that code of law was that any Jew who tried to convert a Christian to Judaism would be put to death, and that any Christian who became converted to Judaism would likewise be put to death. This put a rather sharp and quick end to Jewish proselytizing efforts. Later on, when the Moslems came into that part of the world and instituted the Code of Omar, this code had exactly the same provision. By about the seventh century it was practically impossible for a Jew to try to convert either a Christian or a Moslem, and it was almost impossible for a Christian or a Moslem to become a Jew. As this situation continued on into the Middle Ages, the Jews began to adopt what we might call a sour-grapes attitude, or what is sometimes referred to as a religious inferiority complex. They thought, "If we cannot have them, then we do not want them." Later on, certain Jews became converts to Christianity and Islam in order to feather their own nests, and some of these not-so-nice people turned on their fellow Jews and became even more bitter oppressors than the Christians or Moslems. The Jewish attitude "If we cannot have them, then we do not want them" developed into suspicion and then into hatred. Because of the medieval experience with Jews who converted to other religions in order to benefit themselves, we turned that same suspicion, and sometimes even that same hatred, on those who tried to become Jews. A typical reaction of many Jews today toward people who want to adopt Judaism is, "What is in it for him; what does he expect to gain by it?" Or "She is looking for a rich husband," or "She knows that Jews make better husbands than non-Jews." This is the typical, unfair reaction.

w.b.: Would you say that this attitude is very prevalent today toward the non-Jew? Would you say it is characteristic? What is the Jewish attitude of the Jew toward the non-Jew?

■ EICHHORN: Well, I am not going to try to give a dissertation on the attitude of the Jew toward the non-Jew, but certainly with reference to some well-known non-Jews who converted to Judaism, there is a suspicion, on the part of many that one talks to, that these converts may be insincere. If you mention that a movie star is keeping a kosher home, someone points to last night's headline and says that she is getting a divorce. Well, a lot of Jewish-born women get divorces from Jewish husbands, too. The question that may be asked is, "How much of the conversion was dependent upon a real belief in the principles of Judaism and how much upon convenience?" We have an example in Norma Shearer, who converted to Judaism when she married the late Irving Thalberg. She became the president of the sisterhood of Rabbi Magnin's synagogue in Los Angeles. Then her next husband was a Catholic, and she converted to Roman Catholicism when she married him. So we certainly cannot claim Norma Shearer as a very sincere convert.

w.b.: Dr. Eichhorn, I note that the Reform rabbinate in 1950 organized a Committee for the Unaffiliated. I believe that this is vital to our issue under discussion. What does it mean? What does it do?

■ EICHHORN: That committee was formed after a very heated discussion at the 1950 convention of the Reform rabbinate, and the motion to form the committee squeaked through by a very narrow margin, just a little more than half. The committee was set up to explore ways and means of increasing the influence or acceptability of the Jewish religion.

It was a very innocuous kind of motion, but everybody knew what it meant. It meant the study of the possibility of going out into the non-Jewish world with some sort of a program of attracting unaffiliated non-Jews to Judaism. The idea of even studying this was so fearsome to even the most liberal Jewish groups of this country—at least those who consider themselves the most liberal—that this resolution had a hard time getting through. This committee, of which I had the honor to be chairman, met very regularly and studied the subject. In 1957, after many months of investigation, our committee came to the Reform rabbinate with the following recommendations: that to give as much information as possible on Judaism to the non-Jew is not only a right, but an obligation and a responsibility; that we should make the non-Jew aware of the fact that we would welcome him warmly if he were to come to us voluntarily and state that he wishes to become a member of our religious group, agrees fully with our religious tenets, and wants to help promote them throughout the world.

W.B.: And after he is welcomed? Once he comes, what happens? Do you give him a course of study?

■ EICHHORN: Oh, yes. First, I would like to make one or two further points with regard to the program that this committee proposed. They proposed that texts be printed and distributed in hotels, in airports and railroad depots, and so on. There should be preaching missions at which non-Jews will be invited to listen to the teachings of Judaism, and there should be radio and television programs specifically devoted to the idea of disseminating knowledge of Judaism and letting non-Jews know that we would welcome them. This proposal, this proposed program on the part of the committee, was passed by something like three hundred members of the Central Conference of American Rabbis without a dissenting vote.

As far as the Reform rabbinate is concerned, I am glad to say there is a whole change of heart. I also have first-hand indications that some members of the Conservative and Orthodox rabbinates are rethinking this whole matter. We are going back to first principles. We are sweeping out some of the cobwebs that grew in the minds of some of us during our dark days in the ghettos during the Middle Ages.

W.B.: May I ask this question? When you mention putting signs in depots or inviting non-Jews to lectures and activities of this kind, would you not call this an aggressive mission to the Christian community? If not, how do you term this?

■ EICHHORN: No, I do not call this an aggressive mission to the Christian community. The texts, the missions, the radio and television programs will do one thing and one thing only: they will set forth positively and without apology exactly what Jews believe.

W.B.: What *is* an aggressive mission to the Christians?

■ EICHHORN: An aggressive mission to the Christians would be, as far as I am concerned, saying on that television program, "We've got the true religion. All other religions are false. Come to us and be saved." This is what the Christians say when they preach their religion, and we have no intention of doing this.

W.B.: What *will* you say when you get on television?

■ EICHHORN: We will say that for us Judaism is the religion that best meets our needs and best fits our desires. Those who share this feeling with us may, if they wish, come and join us. We will be very happy to have them. I hope that neither I nor anyone else will ever be guilty of saying that we have the only true religion, or that our religion is better than anybody else's religion. Nobody knows who has the true religion, and nobody knows who has the best religion.

W.B.: A few minutes ago, you mentioned "removing the cobwebs from our minds," of removing the ghetto thinking of the Dark Ages, and this point of view, you said, was shared by some Conservative and Orthodox Jews. I know of a questionnaire concerning this that you sent out in 1954. I think some of the statistics from that would be most interesting.

■ EICHHORN: First, approximately 2,500 non-Jews are being converted to Judaism every year in the United States. Second, about five out of six of these are women. Let me put it this way: in the Conservative movement, five out of six are females, and in the Reform movement, four out of five are females. Why Reform does a little better with the males is traceable to the fact that Reform Judaism does not demand circumcision of the male convert, while Conservative Judaism does. Of the converts who are now coming in, fourteen out of fifteen are coming in because of an impending or an existing marriage. I wish we could develop the reasoning that I think is behind that. I hope that some day a student of this field will study this phenomenon. I think he will find that what attracts non-Jews to Jews is far more than just physical attraction and far more than just the feeling that one partner—the non-Jew—is going to better himself. I have had a great deal of experience with mixed marriages and with conversion, and it is questionable in my mind who is the more fortunate member of the couple in many of these marriages. Sometimes the Jew is getting much the better of it, and I do not think we ought to pat ourselves on the back too hard.

Ninety-one percent of the Reform rabbis and 68 percent of the Conservative rabbis answered this questionnaire. Any of us who knows anything about questionnaires knows that this response is phenomenal. It means that rabbis are really deeply interested in this problem. These rabbis were asked to rate the converts who are members of their congregations as being low-average, average, or above-average Jews—comparing these with the born Jews in the congregation. A heavy majority of the Conservative and Reform rabbis stated that, on the average, the convert is a better member of the congregation than the born Jew. This also, I am sure, will come as a bit of a surprise to some who think that converts are not as good as other Jews.

W.B.: Now we turn to our second guest, Rabbi Jakobovits. Naturally, Rabbi Jakobovits's point of view might be different from Rabbi Eichhorn's. We will try to determine that difference. The first question, Rabbi Jakobovits, is, What is the attitude, not only of Jewish history but of Jewish law, toward proselytizing?

■ JAKOBOVITS: I agree in principle with a great deal of what has been said. I also say that we welcome proselytes with open arms, and that we make them feel not only at home but as equals in our midst. Where I differ is on the conditions under which we are to accept proselytes. While I will proceed to show that our conditions are extremely rigid and therefore will allow for the admission of only a tiny percentage of those who apply, the Reform attitude as presented here by Rabbi Eichhorn is that the net ought to be cast considerably wider. That is one difference. Second, I want to make it quite clear that I do not propose to give here what may appear to be my personal attitude on the matter. I will try as well as I can, and as objectively as I can, to give the attitude of Jewish law, as I find it, toward this question.

Now, concerning the specific question as to the Jewish attitude, I can put it quite simply: if the would-be convert is agreeable to the conditions that Jewish law lays down for his conversion, then we place no obstacle whatever in his way. In fact, we give every assistance to him and then, upon conversion, welcome him with open arms. I think that would sum up the answer.

W.B.: Now the question is the "if." What does "if they meet the requirements" mean? Can you define what the requirements are? And how would you determine sincerity?

■ JAKOBOVITS: Well, here we come to the heart of the problem. As far as Dr. Eichhorn's historic presentation is concerned, I must take issue with one item, and that is his allegation that the present-day lukewarm or rather hesitant attitude toward the acceptance of proselytes is the result of the sour-grapes attitude developed in the Middle Ages, when the hostile attitude of the Church toward allowing the Jew to convert others colored our own attitude. I think that this is an extremely arbitrary reading of history. All I know is that the Jewish law that governs today's attitude to conversion was laid down in the Talmud very expressly 2,000 years ago, long before there were any Middle Ages. This attitude has, by and large, remained constant in all authentic rabbinic writings on the subject. If at one time we did have larger proselytizing movements than at another, it was due simply to the exigencies of the times; at certain times people felt more attracted by the rigid conditions that Judaism placed before them, and at other times less so. So much about the historical element. As a matter of fact, you could cite the conversion to Judaism in the Middle Ages of the whole Khazar Kingdom in Russia as evidence of the fact that when the ground was fertile for such proselytizing, it could be done on a massive scale even in the Middle Ages.

Our attitude on this matter is governed by two principal considerations, which I want to spell out as well as I possibly can. First, we do not believe that God meant all humans to be Jewish and to perform the duties that Judaism imposes upon us in order to find favor in His eyes. In this respect, we differ radically from the Christians. We do not say that a non-Jew, in order to be perfect in God's eyes, in order to be saintly, or in order to fulfill his destiny as a human being, must eventually be a Jew and conform to Jewish law. We believe, on the contrary, that so long as the non-Jews observe the fundamental laws of Noah, as we call them, the certain basic cardinal laws of humanity, which include the basic moral law, then they are just as virtuous and just as meritorious in the eyes of God as the Jew who fulfills the entire rigid discipline of Jewish life.

Therefore, it was not anticipated by our prophets that the distinctions between religions will be obliterated even in the perfect days, when there will be universal peace, and when "the knowledge of God will cover the earth as the waters cover the sea." We do not believe that there will come a time when everyone will have to embrace the Jewish faith, as the Christians believe that in order to be saved one must be baptized and must embrace the Christian faith. This basic premise of Judaism, incidentally, means that Judaism is bound to be far more tolerant of other faiths than probably any other religion, certainly any other monotheistic religion.

Following from this premise comes my second one. Why then were we chosen to have our own religion—you might almost call it our own national religion—identified with our people, and to retain this limitation? We believe that we were chosen to be pioneers in this world. We were chosen to accept a mission in this world that only the few can carry out. The demands, the sacrifices, the privations, the discipline that are required of the advance guard of an army are far greater than those of the ordinary soldier. We were placed into this world so that we might make the initial breaches in the walls of paganism or immorality, as they existed in the past. Once we have broken through, as a small advance guard, the area can then be broadened, and the masses—the infantry, as it were—can follow and mop up.

w.b.: Does that mean, if we follow this to its logical conclusion, that the Jewish people are therefore a superior people?

■ JAKOBOVITS: No, it does not mean anything of the sort. It depends upon how you measure inferiority and superiority. We believe that every nation is sent into this world to fulfill a specific role. We believe that the Romans were here to teach us, possibly, the arts of government and warfare. The Greeks were here for art, for science, and for philosophy. We believe the Jews are in this world to be the pioneers of monotheism, the pioneers of religion and social justice, the pioneers of a people that will live on a higher level, so that ultimately the time will come when God will be sovereign of the whole world, yet without Judaism ruling the whole world.

The Bible itself is very specific on this matter. The Bible tells us, the Torah tells us, that we Jews are chosen people because we were the smallest of all peoples. With a small group you can achieve more, you can demand more, than with a big mass. Had we, in the days of the rise of Christianity, competed with the Church at that time, the chances are that today we would be a mass religion, counting hundreds of millions of people all over the world. We did not go in for this. We did not compete with the missionaries of the Church at that time, because we felt that we would then lose the ability to remain what we were and do what we were meant to do—that is, to live on a supreme level of self-discipline and self-sacrifice, which cannot be asked of the masses. Since it is in the smallness of our numbers that our strength lies, the overall attitude has been one of the greatest caution in admitting those who we were not convinced would carry the historic responsibility that we believe destiny and Providence have placed upon us.

These are the two basic considerations that, to my mind, govern the Jewish religious attitude toward conversion. Now, to complete the answer to the question that has been posed, What does Jewish law demand? Under what conditions do we accept converts? Let me give you some statistics. In this country we have no overall statistics of applicants and admissions. In England, where virtually all would-be converts apply to the London Beit Din, the central religious agency to which the majority of English Jewry owes allegiance, there are something like 400 to 500 applicants for conversion each year. Out of these, hardly more than 1 percent are admitted. One percent of all the applicants! And we ask, Why is this? I think Dr. Eichhorn has given the answer. He said that [in the U.S.] fourteen out of fifteen people are admitted *not* because they fall in love with Judaism but because they fall in love with a Jewish person. And this is precisely where I take issue. We say that if the motive for joining Judaism is not an appreciation of what Judaism as such stands for, if a person is unwilling to impose upon himself or herself all the rigors of Jewish law without exception, if the motive is the convenience of a marriage that might otherwise not be successful, or the bringing up of children who might otherwise have to grow up in a spiritual or religious no-man's land rejected by Jews and by Christians alike, if a party has fallen in love with a Jew instead of with Judaism—if all this is so—then we believe that such a person will not be able to join our ranks to the extent required by our law.

W.B.: There is a talmudic statement, which I have quoted frequently but which comes to mind again: *M'toch shelo l'shmuh buh l'shmuh*, that is, When someone does not *come* for its own sake, he nevertheless will end up doing it *l'shmuh, for* its own sake. Statistics tell of women who convert because of marriage and who then go on to lead full and fruitful Jewish lives. In the face of these statements, and in terms of experience, why would your position still be as it is?

■ JAKOBOVITS: The whole question here is what in fact constitutes *l'shmuh,* "for its own sake"? On this, of course, we may differ. Let us say that a person tells us that he or she will adopt the entire range of Jewish law, will keep a kosher home, will observe the moral and ethical requirements of Judaism, the business relations, the Sabbath; but that he or she cannot subscribe to, takes exception to, and cannot fulfill one law. We will reject this applicant. You may say very logically that such a person will be a far better Jew than most of those who were born Jewish; therefore, why should we turn down a person who, out of all the 613 laws, rejects one? Let me give you the answer. If you have a child of your own, then good, bad, or indifferent, he remains your child and you cannot disown him. If that child turns out to be bad, he is still your own child, because you have given birth to that child, and you share, as it were, in the fortunes and misfortunes of this child. But if you adopt a child, take a child in and make it your own by adoption, the matter is different. There you can choose. You can say, "The child who is going to prove an asset, I am going to adopt. One who I know has had a bad history, or comes from a family with a proclivity to crime or ill health," you will say, "I do not want to adopt." After all, you are making an open, free choice. That is our attitude here. If Jews are born as Jews and they ignore Jewish law, reject Jewish law, may not even remember that they are Jews, we still recognize them as Jews. We say, "*Yisrael af al pi shechata Yisrael hu.*" A Jew, even though he sins, even though he is a renegade, even though he may be baptized, is still looked upon as a Jew. He is our child. He is born into our people. You cannot escape from Judaism. If, however, we are to adopt a Jew, if we are to invite one who is not born Jewish to assume these responsibilities and make him into one of ourselves, we can ask to be assured that he will be an asset to us. If he will be a liability, if he becomes a law-breaker, why should we impose the burden on him?

If I apply for American citizenship, I will appear before a judge and be asked to take an oath of loyalty to this country, and I will be told that I will have to swear that I will abide by the Constitution of this country and by all its laws and regulations. Now, imagine that I tell this judge that I am quite ready to fulfill all the clauses of your Constitution except one, which I do not like. I am not going to abide by one clause in your Constitution or one law that your Congress has passed because I have a conscientious objection against it. He will say, Go home and retain the passport that you had before. I will then ask the judge, Why are you stricter with me than with your own Americans? You have many Americans who are traitors and who are law-breakers and who are in prisons, and they are still Americans. You have not taken away their nationality. I come to you, I want to fulfill 99.9 percent of all your laws, I make a little exception, and you reject me. He will answer, quite rightly, that I am being naturalized. I am being accepted as an American citizen and he will not allow me to make exceptions, though he may have to allow people who were born Americans to be exceptions. If we naturalize a non-Jew to become a Jew, we adopt precisely the same perfectly logical attitude. I would not argue with that judge, any more than I would like a would-be convert to argue with me, were I to give him the same answer.

There is another aspect of this problem on which I want to lay great emphasis. It is often suggested, and this is part of my answer to your question, that Orthodox rabbis who see these would-be converts and who reject them or who at least do not make it very easy for them, are callous, and perhaps ignore the human duties that they owe their fellow human beings when they come for help. It is this aspect that I would like to put in its proper perspective. If I had a part as a rabbi in converting a non-Jewish woman to Judaism, then, first of all, I must realize that I do not convert only her; I automatically convert her children and her children's children for all future generations. My act is converting them as well. Therefore, the decision I have to make is a crushing responsibility, purely from this point of view. Next, if this woman, before she was converted, worked on the Sabbath, she did nothing wrong in the eyes of God. She was perfectly honest, law-abiding, religious, and devout, in the eyes of God. The Sabbath was not given to her in our sense. If *after* I convert her she works on the Sabbath, thereby desecrating it, I am aiding and abetting her in the desecration of Jewish law.

w.b.: I would like to bring some of these things into perspective. You state that if you were to convert this woman, you realize that this is a crushing responsibility because you also convert her children and children's children. On the other hand, if you do not convert this woman, and she marries a Jew and has a home that is non-Jewish, what about *that* crushing responsibility?

■ JAKOBOVITS: It is the same crushing responsibility. If I reject the woman who potentially could have fulfilled the conditions of Jewish law and become converted, then I face at least the same responsibility by this withholding of what we call the Wings of the Divine Presence from the person who should rightfully enjoy that protection of Jewish law. There-fore, the responsibility works both ways. The crushing re-sponsibility to say yes as well as no. But I want to explain that it is not callous of a rabbi if he conscientiously feels, after having explored the case, that he must come to a negative decision in the matter.

Let me just develop this idea of responsibility. I was saying that I will have a share in every religious offense that she commits, because through my conversion of her she becomes a law-breaker. Through my converting, through my act, laws may be broken that will be on my shoulders to an extent that I could have foreseen. We are all only human. We are only expected to be human. But we should be at least human, and we should genuinely explore and examine the case, possibly through years of trial, in the same way that America keeps me waiting for five years until I can apply for naturalization.

We believe that a change of religion is rather a more se-rious matter than a change of national allegiance. It is not just a change of passport, it is a change of heart. I always tell people who apply to me that I do not convert them; they convert themselves. If the change has occurred in their hearts, they will feel as a Jew feels: when Jews are suffering anywhere in the world their hearts will bleed as Jewish hearts; if they see Jewish triumphs, their hearts will rejoice as Jews; if they see Jewish law being broken, they will grieve, and in them there will be a pain at the violation of Jewish law. If it came to the point that the supreme sacrifice were de-manded of them, a supreme act of heroism, martyrdom, these people would say, "I will lay down my life for my faith." If this is their attitude, then we will adopt them.

Ruth, the most famous convert of all times, said to her mother-in-law, *"El asher telchi elech,"* "Where you go, I will go." But she went on, *"uva'asher tolini olin,"* "and where you spend the night, I will spend the night": Even in the darkness when there is persecution, I will share that darkness with you. I will feel as a Jew in whatever circumstances may come to me.

I cannot help fearing what is happening today, when large-scale conversions are being performed. We have had the figure of 2,500 in this country alone. Each year 2,500 are converted. Do not forget these conversions are not all recognized by many Conservative rabbis, and none by the Orthodox rabbis. This is creating a situation in which we are raising generations of people whom one Jew will call a Jew and another Jew will call a non-Jew. You can imagine the havoc that this has wrought in Jewish ranks. I know of it. I have been Chief Rabbi in a country [Ireland] where every such case had to come to me, and have seen the agony, the misery, the suffering that has been inflicted as a result of the make-believe that has taken place, where one has stamped someone into a Jew, and somebody else, following his law, cannot recognize this conversion. It has led to untold misery and suffering and often to the infliction of the sins of the parents on innocent children.

A sense of responsibility is necessary here to a degree that is required in perhaps no other rabbinic decision. We decide on an issue that affects the very deepest and innermost feelings of a person's heart. And we do not have spiritual X-ray eyes that can look into the heart. But at least one thing we can do is to try, and—by living with that person, sharing experiences with that person, and by showing that person what a Jewish life is— to be able to judge after two or three years whether his heart is in fact now a Jewish heart, 100 percent and not 99 percent.

W.B.: Would you, for example, accept someone as a candidate, work with him for two or three years, and then at the end of that period determine whether you would convert him, or would you immediately reject a candidate when he or she comes to your study? Are you not then setting yourself up in authority as a judge to determine who is really sincere and who is not sincere in terms of your particular point of view?

■ JAKOBOVITS: The point I am making is this: when you apply for citizenship the judge is not going to question you in detail. He will ask whether you accept the Constitution. You will say yes or you will say no.

You raised the point that if the convert violates one of the 613 laws, we reject him; it then becomes not only a quantitative but also a qualitative matter. If you say, after having worked with the person for two or three years, that you feel the person is not ready, fine. But can you say at the very outset that you do not believe him to be a fit candidate?

I can give you a very categorical answer to this. I have

myself participated in a number of conversions, and I can assure you that those people I have converted have remained true Jews. I can assure you that to this day, they and their children are, so far as I know of them and have remained in contact with them, an asset rather than a liability.

Now you ask, how can we set ourselves up as judges? I am afraid that a rabbi, in making 101 decisions every day, has to be a judge. If he has to advise people, he has to be a judge, to show them what is the right course. I do not believe that when I reject a candidate for conversion I do that person any harm. I think, on the contrary, that in rejecting a person who is not in fact converted at heart, I do that person a favor. And I believe that ultimately that person will come back to me and thank me for it.

w.b.: Providing that you are right. You are operating on the premise that you are right. When someone comes to my study to discuss something with me, I then try to guide him. I never tell him to do this or not to do that. I speak for Rabbi Eichhorn and I speak for myself when I say we have not been reckless in our conversions, and I can cite examples of people who have been equally devoted and equally sincere. Who am I to sit in judgment and say to Miss X, who comes for conversion because of marriage, that it will never work out? Who are you, with all due deference and respect, to say that if Miss X comes for conversion because of marriage, or Miss Y comes for some other reason, it will work out or it will not? This categorical yes or no makes for a problem.

■ JAKOBOVITS: I do not think the problem actually exists. This is quite simple. You say I am operating on the assumption that I am right. I presume that you do the same. If you thought you were wrong you would act differently. Again, I did not suggest that if someone comes who is married to a Jewish party and therefore wants to be converted, that I necessarily reject him. But I have to find out the primary motive, the innermost motive. Does this person want to live a Jewish life? Is that person fascinated and enamoured with Judaism, or is it merely a matter of using Judaism as a cloak for an easier marriage relationship? This I must explore, and I explore it as honestly as I can. I spend hours with every applicant. And even if I form my own impression the first moment that the young people walk in, I still spend a few hours with them, if only to explain what our attitude is. I do not want them to walk out of my office without feeling that whatever judgment I have given them is a justified judgment, a rational, logical judgment. I can say that, as a rule, if they cannot share my views they at least respect them. They feel that there is here an attitude of law that is perfectly consistent.

Dr. Eichhorn mentioned the celebrity conversions that have taken place. One is getting married, another is getting a divorce, and the third is very sick. I can only say that this is precisely why we want to be strict. We do not want Judaism to be used for the glamour of Hollywood. We do not want our religion to be dragged down to a point at which a woman is going to have as many religions in her life as she is going to have husbands. To me, this is sickening. I believe in drawing the line somewhere by laying down the basic conditions that we want these people to accept, not this, that, and the other law in detail but the totality of Jewish law, just as I am expected to accept the totality of the Constitution of the United States. If I say that I will not accept that totality, that I will make an exception, I will be rejected as an American citizen. If anyone comes to me and says that he cannot accept the totality of the Jewish law—the Jewish constitution of life—then I must say, for precisely the same reason, that I cannot assume the responsibility for converting him.

W.B.: It cannot be stated more clearly than it has been stated here. We have heard two differing attitudes toward the acceptance of converts to Judaism, yet a central ideal, it seems to me, is common to the presentations made by both of the speakers: Judaism welcomes sincere converts to our faith. Such differences as have been expressed seem to lie mainly in the definition of sincerity and devotion to our Law, and this definition is colored by the backgrounds of the speakers.

I conclude with this point. I believe that it cannot be denied that there is a burning need for Jewish missionaries today. However, I also believe that our generation requires Jewish missionaries to the Jews, for there are too many Jews who are ours in name only. And likewise, many thoughtful Christians recognize the need for Christian missionaries to the Christians. The task of such consecrated spirits must be to win those who are Jews or Christians merely by accident of birth to a fervent and enlightened loyalty toward their ancestral religions. A religion that demands nothing is worth nothing. Like everything else that is worthwhile, true religion must begin at home.

❧ Index

Aaron of Karlin, 71, 74
Abraham (prophet), 215–216, 221
Abstraction, Reconstructionism and, 38
Acheson, Dean, 286
Agnon, Yosef, 192
Agudas Yisrael, 37
Aleichem, Sholom, 172, 199, 204, 263–264
Alexander the Great, 88–89, 372
Alexandria, Platonic school and, 97
Algiers, France and, 366
Allegorism
  defined, 96
  manifestations of, 96–98
  traces of, in present, 98
Altalena incident, Begin, Menachem on, 347–352
America. *See* Canada; United States
American Jewish Committee, American Jewish Congress and, 287–288
Amin, Idi, 370
Anti-Semitism. *See also* Ethnic prejudice
  Begin, Menachem on, 357–358

Eichmann Trial and, 242–247
future predictions for, 481–482
Goldmann, Nahum on, 178–179
Holocaust and, 326
Jewish history and, 212, 248
Kissinger, Henry on, 446–447
neo-Nazi movement and, 229–230
separatism and, 175
United Nations and, 329
United States and, 274
Anti-Zionism, as anti-Semitism, 329
Antonescu, Ion, 282
Apostasy, intellectualism and, 92
Arabic philosophy, rationalism and, 94
Arabs. *See also* Islam
  Begin, Menachem on, 345
  Israel's creation and, 332
  Israel's future relations with, 482
  Jerusalem and, 364–365, 369
  Wiesel, Elie on, 309–310
Arafat, Yassir, 332
Argentina
  Eichmann and, 237
  Jewish population in, 180–181
  neo-fascism in, 358

Aristotle, 12, 94, 95
Armenians, Turkey and, 273
Assad, Hafaz el-, 354
Assimilation. See also Integration;
    Separatism
  conversions and, 425-426
  cultural pluralism and, 155
  Jewish populations and, 425
  Judaists and, 160
Assyrian civilization, 214
Attitude, Chasidism and, 80
Austria, 229
Authenticity issue,
    Reconstructionism and, 38-39
Authoritarianism, education and,
    150

Baale teshuvah movement, Steinsaltz,
    Adin on, 59-60
Baal Shem Tov, 67, 69, 70, 75
Babylonian civilization, 214
Babylonian exile, 89, 209, 215
Baeck, Leo, 420
Baron, Salo, 425
Bay of Pigs invasion, 445
Bea, Augustine Cardinal, 184, 185
Beard, Charles, 147
Beauty, Chasidism and, 75-76
Begin, Menachem, 323-360, 369
Bellow, Saul, 191, 377, 430
Benderly, Samson, 41
Ben Gurion, David, 235, 258, 346,
    348, 352, 375-376
Berkowitz, William, 7-9, 11, 13, 14-
    17, 18, 19, 20, 21, 22, 23, 24, 25,
    29-30
Beth El Synagogue (New Rochelle,
    New York), 9
Biafra, 292
Bible
  extremism and, 345
  God and, 97
  Hebrew language and, 33
  proselytism and, 490-491
  United States history and, 155
  written tradition and, 91
Biddle, Anthony Drexel, 279

Blau, Joseph L., 87-102. See also
    Intellectualism
Boringness, Steinsaltz, Adin on, 54-
    55, 58
Bourguiba, Habib, 172
Brand, Joel, 257, 258, 259, 284-285
Brandeis, Louis D., 99, 147, 148,
    149, 153-154, 176
Brandeis University, 251, 266
Brazil, 181
Brezhnev, Leonid, 304
Brickner, Barnett, 18
Britain. See United Kingdom
Brother Daniel, 410-411
Buber, Martin, 78-79, 80, 95, 98,
    322, 325
Bulgaria, 275

Cabalists and Cabalism, 69
  Creation and, 98
  Jewish history and, 220-223
  Spanish expulsion and, 324
Calendar, radical reformers and,
    15
Camp David agreement, Egypt and,
    451
Canada
  Jewish history and, 396
  Sabbath observance in, 408-409
Cantor, Eddie, 291-292
Carter, Jimmy, 440, 441, 450, 451,
    452, 453
Castro, Fidel, 181
Catholicism, 494. See also Christianity
  Christian-Jewish relationships,
    184-186
  indifference of, during Holocaust,
    274-275
  modernity and, 90
Celebration, patriotism and, 132-134
Ceremony, Reform Judaism and, 12,
    13. See also Ritual
Chamberlain, Neville, 330
Change, Conservative Judaism and,
    16
Character disorder, 110, 111-112
Charity. See Social responsibility

Chasidism, 12. *See also*
    Denominationalism
  allegorism and, 96, 98
  attitude and, 80
  cultural pluralism and, 153–154
  denominationalism and, 81–82
  differences among, 77
  esthetics in, 75–76
  Hebrew language and, 79–80
  historical précis of, 66–68
  interpersonal relationships and,
    80–81
  joy and, 73–74
  kavonoh (intention) in, 74–75
  love and, 74
  Lubavitch Chasidism, 77–78
  Neo-Chasidism, 78
  rebbe relationship in, 69–72
  social status and, 8
  song and, 76–77
  theology and, 81
  tzadik's role in, 68–69
  Wiesel, Elie and, 314–315
  women and, 72–73
  Yiddish and, 79
  youth and, 80, 81–83
Children. *See* Youth
China, Kissinger, Henry on, 460
Chmelnitzki period, 327
"Chosen people"
  Jewish survival and, 176
  Reconstructionism and, 42–43
Christianity. *See also* Catholicism
  critical times and, 89
  Enlightenment challenges to, 35
  God and, 326–327
  Jerusalem and, 369
  Jewish-Christian relationships,
    184–186
  Jewish conversion to, 493
  Jewish history and, 221, 225
  modernity and, 90
  proselytism and, 58–59, 421–422,
    425, 490, 492, 495–496
  rationalism and, 95
  Reform Judaism and, 17
  world and, 176

Churchill, Winston, 276, 358
Church/state division, Orthodox
    Judaism and, 22
City College of New York, 465
Civil War (U.S.), cultural pluralism
    and, 156
Code of Omar, 493
Cohen, Hermann, 95
Columbia University, 101, 102
Columbus, Christopher, 422–424
Committee for the Unaffiliated, 494–
    495
Communal confession, psychiatry
    and, 115–116
Communism
  Judaism and, 303–305
  Kissinger, Henry on, 453
  Soviet military adventures and,
    455–457
Community
  Reconstructionism and, 41
  synagogue role in Diaspora, 402
  United States and, 432
Compromise, Orthodox Judaism and,
    10
Concentration camps, Jewish history
    and, 226. *See also* Holocaust
Confession, therapy/religion
    contrasted, 115–116
Conformism
  Holocaust and, 245–246
  Jewish survival and, 177–178
Conscience, Reconstructionism and,
    45
Conservatism, Reform Judaism and,
    17
Conservative Judaism. *See also*
    Denominationalism
  ceremony and, 13
  challenges facing, 25
  Chasidism and, 81–82
  cultural pluralism and, 153–154
  foundational issues and, 36
  future predictions for, 472–473
  historical précis of, 14–17
  intellectualism and, 93–94
  Israel and, 56–57, 404–407

Conservative Judaism *(continued)*
  law and, 25
  Neo-Orthodox Judaism and,
    35-36
  origins of, 3, 7-8
  proselytism and, 496-497
  Reconstructionist views of, 37
  reexamination by, 34
  Reform Judaism and, 24
  social status and, 8
Constantine the Great (of Rome),
    212, 493
Constitution. *See* United States
    Constitution
Conversion requirements, described,
    498-499. *See also* Proselytism
Cosmology, Platonic school, 97-98
Cosmopolitanism, Reconstructionism
    and, 43-44
Creation, Philo and, 97-98
Crisis, critical times and, 88
Critical times definition,
    intellectualism and, 88-90
Cronkite, Walter, 367-369
Crusades, 328
Cuba
  African adventures of, 453
  Bay of Pigs invasion, 445
  missile crisis and, 454
Cults, Steinsaltz, Adin on, 53
Culture
  cults and, 53
  integration and, 34-35
  Israel and, 23
  Israeli cultural absorption and
    integration *(mizug galuyot)*, 385-
    386
  Jewish history and, 213-214, 219
  Jewish literature and, 198
  Judaists and, 160
  pluralism and, 25, 147, 151-154
  rationalism and, 94-95
  Reconstructionism and, 39-42
  Reform Judaism and, 17
  segregation and, 34
  United States, 429
  women and, 44

Czechoslovakia, Jewish resistance
    and, 254, 258

Dante Alighieri, 238
Davidson, Israel, 33, 420
Davis, Moshe, 399-402
Dayan, Moshe, 352
Day school movement
  future predictions for, 475-476
  Jewish education and, 429
Dead Sea Scrolls, 12
Declaration of Independence,
    cultural pluralism and, 152-153
Delitzsch, Franz, 33
Dembitz, Louis, 149
Democracy
  church/state division and, 22
  education and, 151
  Israel and, 352, 387
  pluralism and, 25
  separatism/assimilation issue and,
    173
Denmark, Jewish resistance in, 267
Denominationalism. *See also*
    Chasidism; Conservative
    Judaism; Neo-Orthodox Judaism;
    Orthodox Judaism; Reform
    Judaism
  cultural pluralism and, 153-154
  future predictions for, 472-473
  ignorance concerning distinctions
    among, 8, 11
  institutional rivalry and, 421
  intellectualism and, 93-94
  Israel and, 404-407
  Judaists and, 159
  law and, 420
  proselytism and, 496-497
  rationalism and, 94-95
Depression
  guilt and, 114-115
  Job and, 114
Desegregation, Reconstructionism
    and, 39-42
Dewey, John, 147, 148, 150-151
Dexter, Robert, 284
Diamond, Malcolm, 101

Diaspora
  Israel and, 224–225, 395–402
  Jewish history and, 219, 221, 224
  Sanhedrin reconstitution and, 23
  synagogue role in, 402–404
Dies, Martin, 280
Dimont, Max I., 207–226
Discipline, Orthodox Judaism and, 10
Disorder, education and, 150
Dogma, Conservative Judaism and, 15
Dostoyevski, Feodor, 193, 194, 195
Doubt, Chasidism and, 71
Dov Baer (Maggid of Mezerich), 71
Dulles, John Foster, 331
Dybois, Josiah E., Jr., 283

Ecumenical Council, Christian–Jewish relationships, 184–186
Education. *See also* Jewish education
  Dewey, John and, 150–151
  politics and, 151
  social responsibility and, 135–137
Egypt
  Camp David agreement and, 451
  culture of, 214
  exodus from, critical times, 89
  Jerusalem recognized as capital by, 371
  Yom Kippur War and, 391
Ehrlich, Arnold B., 33
Eichhorn, David Max, 489–507
Eichmann, Adolf, 256–258, 284–285, 376–377
Eichmann Trial, 233–248
  anti-Semitism issue and, 242–247
  defense in, 241–242
  emotional reactions to, 238–239
  ex post facto issue and, 235–236
  Holocaust responsibility and, 247–248
  Israel's statehood issue and, 236–237
  kidnapping issue and, 237–238
  remorse and, 240–241
  sympathy in, 239–240

Einstein, Albert, 154
Eleazar Askari, 76
Eliezer, Aryeh Ben, 350
Elimelech of Lizhensk, 68, 73
Emancipation Proclamation, cultural pluralism and, 156
Emigration and immigration
  Conservative Judaism and, 15
  from Israel, 382–384
  to Israel, 353–357
  Israeli policies of, 410–412
  Soviet Jewish emigration to Israel, 184
  United States and, during Holocaust, 264–265, 273, 277, 281, 288–290
  Yom Kippur War (1973) and, 354
Emotion
  Chasidism and, 77, 82
  Eichmann Trial and, 238–240
  rationalism and, 96
England. *See* United Kingdom
English United Synagogue, 93
Enlightenment, Reconstructionism and, 35
Entebbe raid, 354, 358–360
Equality
  cultural pluralism and, 152–153
  separatism/assimilation issue and, 173
Eshkol, Levi, 350, 352
Essenes, 12
Esthetics, Chasidism and, 75–76
Ethics, Reform Judaism and, 12
Ethnicity, Israeli religious diversity and, 405
Ethnic prejudice, United States, 234–235. *See also* Anti-Semitism
Evil
  Chasidism and, 77
  psychiatric/religious views contrasted, 117–118
Existentialism
  Chasidism and, 80
  Jewish history and, 222
Extremism, Begin, Menachem on, 343–344, 345

Fackenheim, Emil L., 319–335
Family
  Chasidism and, 70
  kashrut and, 44–46
  Reconstructionism and, 44
  role models and, 141–143
  sensation and, 140–141
  social responsibility and, 135–137
Fanaticism, Steinsaltz, Adin on, 55–56
Fascism, 90. *See also* Holocaust; Nazism; Neo-Fascism; Neo-Nazism
Finkelstein, Jerry, 401
Flaubert, Gustave, 195
Fleischman, Gisi, 258–259
Flinker, Moshe, 264
Foreign policy, morality and, 448–449. *See also entries under names of countries*
France
  Algiers and, 366
  Altalena incident and, 350
  Libya and, 303
  Wiesel, Elie on, 311
  World War II and, 443
Frank, Anne, 264
Frankel, Zechariah, 3, 7–8, 14, 15
Frankfurter, Felix, 181
Freedom, Chasidism and, 71
French Revolution, 7, 13, 169
  radical reformers and, 15
  Reform Judaism and, 17
  terrorism and, 346
Freud, Sigmund, 110, 111, 119, 120, 122
Funk, Walther, 245
Futurism, Berkowitz, William on, 415–416

Galili, Israel, 350
Geiger, Abraham, 3, 7, 95
Genocide, United Nations Genocide Convention, 292–293. *See also* Holocaust
Germany. *See also* Nazism
  Conservative Judaism and, 15

Eichmann and, 237
Fackenheim, Emil L. on, 319–321
neo-Nazi movement and, 229–230
rationalism and, 95
Reform Judaism and, 7, 13–14
United States compared, 401
World War II and, 443
Gersonides, 95
Ghetto
  French Revolution and, 13
  Jewish world and, 7
  separatism/assimilation issue and, 173, 174
God
  Christianity and, 326–327
  Holocaust and, 324–327
  Jewish history and, 212–213, 221–223, 321–324
  Jewish literature and, 193–194
  Jewish survival and, 176
  Orthodox Judaism and, 10, 20
  Philo and, 97
  Reconstructionism and, 42–43, 44
  Reform Judaism and, 13, 17
  sexuality and, 216
  Steinsaltz, Adin on, 54
Goebbels, Joseph, 248, 358
Goering, Hermann, 244, 248
Gogol, Nikolai, 204
Golden, Harry, 191
Goldmann, Nahum, 169–186, 277, 283, 396
Goldstein, Israel, 22, 396
Golovensky, David, 9–10, 12, 20, 22–23, 24–25
Gordon, Aharon D., 163
Goren, Shlomo, 407, 410
Graetz, Heinrich, 209–210
Great Britain. *See* United Kingdom
Great Depression, the, 280
Greenberg, Simon, 402
Group identity, individual and, 8
Guilt
  mental illness and, 116
  psychiatry and, 113–114, 116–117
  religion and, 114–115
Gypsies, extermination of, 326

Hadassah, future in United States, 479–480

Haganah, 346, 347, 348, 350

Halachah. *See* Law (Halachah)

Halevi, Yehuda, 95

Happiness, Reconstructionism and, 43–44

Harman, Avraham, 395–412

Harriman, Averell, 285

Hausner, Gideon, 233

Hayes, Carlton, 284

Hebraism, pluralism and, 154–157

Hebrew language
  Bible and, 33
  Chasidism and, 79–80
  future of, 480
  Israel and, 202–203
  proselytism and, 490
  Reform Judaism and, 14
  unifying force of, in Israel, 402
  Yiddish and, 199–200

Hebrew Union College (Cincinnati, Ohio), 202, 420

Hebrew University, 151, 399

Hecht, Ben, 347

Hegel, G. W. F., 13, 95, 171, 304

Hellenism, 89
  God and, 321–322
  Palestine and, 91
  slavery and, 156

Hermeneutics, intellectualism and, 98–100

Hersch, Samuel, 95

Herzl, Theodor, 18, 392

Heschel, Abraham J., 80, 98

Hillel, 99, 428

Hirsch, Samson Raphael, 3, 8, 95

Hirschmann, Ira, 274–275, 283, 284, 285

History. *See* Jewish history

Hitler, Adolf, 171, 175, 224, 241, 247–248, 253, 259, 260, 273, 275, 289, 358, 396, 397, 443

Hitlerism. *See* Nazism

Holiness, Jewish literature and, 190

Holocaust. *See also* Jewish survival

Eichmann Trial and, 238–239. *See also* Eichmann Trial
  forgetfulness and, 298–299
  God and, 324–327
  international indifference and, 271–293. *See also* International indifference
  Israel and, 334–335
  Jewish history and, 226
  Jewish survival and, 175
  meaning of, 229–230
  precedents of, 327–329
  repetition, possibility of, 301–302, 329–331
  responsibility for, 247–248
  trivialization of, 299–300

Hostage crisis (Iranian), Kissinger, Henry on, 440–441

Hull, Cordell, 277–278, 279

Humanism, Reconstructionism and, 43–44

Human rights, United States policy and, 447–448

Human survival, future predictions for, 484–485. *See also* Jewish survival

Humor
  language translation and, 204
  strength and, 137–138
  Yiddish and, 200–201

Identity. *See* Jewish identity

Ideology, Christian–Jewish relationships, 185–186. *See also* Denominationalism

Immigration. *See* Emigration and immigration

Immortality
  Chasidism and, 81
  Reform Judaism and, 17

Indifference. *See* International indifference

Individual
  cultural pluralism and, 152
  group identity and, 8
  psychiatry/religion contrasted, 121–122

Indoctrination, Jewish education and, 157–158
Infinity, Steinsaltz, Adin on, 54
Inner-directedness, Reconstructionism and, 31
Innovation
  allegorism and, 96–98
  hermeneutics and, 98–100
Institutional rivalry, denominationalism and, 421
Integration. *See* Assimilation; Separatism
Integration, culture and, 34–35
Intellectualism, 87–102
  allegorism and, 96–98
  apostasy and, 92
  Conservative Judaism and, 93–94
  critical times definition and, 88–90
  cultural pluralism and, 154
  hermeneutics and, 98–100
  Jewish history and, 214–216
  Jewish survival and, 331–334
  literalism and, 91–92
  Lubavitch Chasidism and, 77–78
  Orthodox Judaism and, 92–93
  rationalism and, 94–96
  Reconstructionism and, 37–38
  Roth, Cecil on, 432–433
  youth and, 100–102
  Zionism and, 149
Intention (*kavonoh*), Chasidism and, 74–75
Intermarriage. *See also* Marriage laws
  Begin, Menachem on, 355
  future predictions for, 483–484
  proselytism and, 494, 497
  Reconstructionist view of, 40–41
  Roth, Cecil on, 426–427
International indifference, 271–293
  documentation of, 272
  Hull, Cordell and, 277–278
  Pope Pius XII and, 274–275
  United Kingdom, 286–287
  United States, 273–274, 275, 277–293
  War Crimes Commission and, 275–277

  War Refugee Board and, 283–284
Interpersonal relationships, Chasidism and, 80–81
Intimacy, Chasidism and, 79
Iran hostage crisis, Kissinger, Henry on, 440–441
Iran, United States relations with, 441–443
Irgun
  Altalena incident and, 348, 350
  Begin, Menachem on, 345–347
Irrationality, psychiatry and, 119
Islam. *See also* Arabs
  critical times and, 89
  Jewish conversion to, 493
  rationalism and, 94
Israel
  American Jewry and, 387–388, 408
  Berkowitz, William on, 339–340
  Conservative Judaism and, 36–37
  creation of, 332
  cultural absorption and integration in, 385–386
  denominationalism in, 404–407
  Diaspora and, 224–225, 395–402
  Eichmann Trial and, 236–237
  emigration from 382–384
  Entebbe raid and, 358–360
  fascism and, 90
  future predictions for Arab relations with, 482
  Holocaust and, 334–335
  immigration policies of, 410–412
  immigration to, 353–357
  international relations and, 302–303
  Jewish history and, 223–224
  Jewish survival and, 171–173, 330, 345
  Kallen, Horace M. on, 163–165
  Kissinger, Henry on, 449
  Neo-Orthodox Judaism and, 37
  Neturei Karta and, 159, 160
  Orthodox Judaism and, 93
  political reforms in, 386–387
  population issues and, 388–389
  Reconstructionist view of, 40

religious freedom in, 162–163
religious life in, 56–57, 402–412
Roth, Cecil on, 434–435
Sanhedrin reconstitution
    possibility in, 21–23, 408–410
Singer, Isaac Bashevis on, 202–203
Soviet Jewish emigration to, 184
Soviet Jewry and, 307
Steinsaltz, Adin on, 56, 57
synagogue role and, 402–404
United States and, 310–311, 382,
    449–450
war likelihood and, 390–391
Wiesel, Elie on, 307–309, 310
Yiddish language and, 202–203
youth and, 384–385
Istanbul office, Jewish resistance
    and, 253–254
Italy, 278–279

Jabotinsky, Vladimir, 348, 353, 357
Jakobovits, Immanuel, 93, 489–507
James, William, 147, 148, 149–150
Jerusalem, 363–377
    Arabs and, 364–365
    equality principle in, 374
    free access principle and, 373–374
    intergroup contacts in, 375
    international city status and, 370–
        371
    as model for political solution,
        372–373
    negotiable status of, 369–370
    neighborhood rule and, 374
    Palestine Liberation Organization
        and, 365–367
    recognition as capital, 371
    security in, 368
    specialness of, 363–364
Jewish education. *See also* Education;
    Youth
    adults and, 428
    day school movement and, 429
    future predictions for, 475–476,
        477–478
    indoctrination and, 157–158
    Israel and, 164

Jewish encyclopedia and, 433–434
Jewish survival and, 178–181
Judaists and, 158–161
Orthodox Judaism and, 24–25
Reconstructionism and, 33
Roth, Cecil on, 427–428
Wiesel, Elie on, 313
Jewish history, 207–226
    attitudes toward, 225–226
    Cabalists and, 220–223
    conversions and, 425–426
    Diaspora and, 224
    Dimont's writing technique and,
        210–211
    God and, 212–213, 321–324
    Graetz, Heinrich and, 209–210
    historiography and, 217–218
    ideas and, 214–216
    internationalism and, 333
    Israel and, 223–224
    Israeli youth and, 396–402
    Jerusalem and, 363–364, 372
    Jewish encyclopedia and,
        433–434
    Jewish populations and, 429
    Jewish survival and, 218–220
    language problems and, 211–212
    main events in, 214
    persecution and, 248
    proselytism and, 421–422, 490–
        494, 497–498
    Roth, Cecil and, 432–434
    specialness issue and, 208–209,
        213–214
    Wiesel, Elie on, 312–313
Jewish identity, confusion in, 41–42,
    105–106
Jewish law. *See* Law
Jewish leadership
    in United Kingdom, 432
    in United States, 431–432
Jewish literature, 189–204. *See also*
    Literalism
    commentary and, 197–198
    future of, 481
    God and, 193–194
    holiness and, 190

Jewish literature (*continued*)
  Jewish reader's desires and, 189–190
  maximum/minimum Jew and, 196–197
  positive/negative issue in, 194–195
  remuneration and, 192–193
  saleability and, 191
  special quality of Jews and, 195–196
  translation and, 203–204
  United States and, 430–431
  women and, 190–191
  writers and, 191–192, 193
  Yiddish and, 198–202
Jewish populations
  Argentina, 180–181
  assimilation and, 425
  Israeli security issues and, 388–389
  Tel Aviv, 403–404
  United States, 429
Jewish resistance, 251–267
  Begin, Menachem on, 343–344
  Eastern Europe, 266–267
  Eichmann negotiations and, 256–258, 284–285
  Fleischman negotiations and, 258–259
  international refusal to assist in, 259–260, 271–293. *See also* International indifference
  Istanbul office and, 253–254
  Nazis and, 251–252, 398
  Palestine and, 252–253
  Soviet Union and, 254–255
  United States and, 255–256
  Warsaw Ghetto, 260–266
  Western Europe, 267
Jewish survival, 169–186. *See also* Holocaust
  Begin, Menachem on, 344
  Christian-Jewish relationships, 184–186
  conformism and, 177–178
  Entebbe raid and, 358–360
  future for human survival, 484–485
  future in United States, 476–477, 478, 479–480
  intellectuals and, 331–334
  international perspective on, 170–171
  Israel and, 171–173, 224, 330, 345
  Jewish education and, 178–181
  Jewish history and, 218–220
  laws of *kashrut* and, 430
  optimism and, 169–170
  separatism and, 173–175
  Soviet Jewry and, 181–184
  stubbornness/nonconformism, 175–177
  United States and, 424–426
Jewish Theological Seminary (New York City), 15, 33, 41, 123–124, 402
John XXIII (Pope), 274–275
Joseph, Jacob, 32
Joy
  Chasidism and, 73–74
  song and, 76–77
  strength and, 137–138
Judaists, Jewish education and, 158–161
Justice, Kissinger, Henry on, 446–447

Kallen, Horace M., 147–165
Kant, Immanuel, 95
Kaplan, Mordecai Menachem, 29–46, 100, 160. *See also* Reconstructionism
Karaite movement, literal tradition and, 91–92
Karo, Joseph, 16, 222–223
Kashrut laws. *See also* Law (Halachah)
  future of, 481
  Jewish survival and, 430
  Reconstructionism and, 44–46
  Steinsaltz, Adin on, 57–58
Katz, Label A., 185
Katz, Shmuel, 347, 349, 350
Kavonoh (intention), Chasidism and, 74–75
Kehillah, Reconstructionist view of, 41

Keitel, Wilhelm, 244
Kennedy, John F., 445
Kertzer, Morris, 137
Khomeini (Ayatollah), 55, 56, 442
Khrushchev, Nikita, 182, 304
Kibbutzim, 163–164, 407
Kidnapping issue, Eichmann Trial
    and, 237–238
King, Martin Luther, Jr., 327
Kingship, Jewish history and, 216
Kishinev massacre, 273
Kissinger, Henry, 377, 391, 439–461
Klein, Edward E., 9, 11–14, 17–18,
    19, 21–22, 23–24
Kohler, Kaufmann, 17
Kollek, Teddy, 363–377
Korzybski, Alfred, 79–80
Kovner, Abba, 334–335
Kristalnacht, 288, 297, 357
Krochmal, Nachman, 13
Ku Klux Klan, 230

Labor, sacred/profane time and, 131–
    132
Labor Zionist Organization of
    America, 465
Lang, Daniel, 125
Language problems, Jewish history
    and, 211–212
Law (Halachah). *See also Kashrut* laws;
    Marriage laws
  Alexandrian Jewish community
      and, 97
  Conservative Judaism and, 16, 25,
      37
  denominationalism and, 420
  hermeneutics and, 99
  Jewish history and, 221
  Jewish survival and, 430
  Orthodox Judaism and, 10, 20–21
  proselytism and, 497–498
  Reform Judaism and, 19
  Steinsaltz, Adin on, 58
  women and, 58
  Zion and, 23
Lechi, 346, 347, 348
Lecky, William Edward, 220

Leeser, Isaac, 15
Lehman, Herbert, 278
Levenson, Sam, 131–143
Leviticus, 80
Levi Yitzchak of Berditchev, 60–61,
    68, 314
Lewin, Kurt, 151
Libya, 303, 442, 452
Lincoln, Abraham, 344–345
Liptzin, Sol, 465–486
Literalism. *See also* Jewish literature
  intellectualism and, 91–92
  Orthodox Judaism and, 92–93
  responsibility of, 139–140
  Roth, Cecil and, 433–434
Literature. *See* Jewish literature
Long, Breckinridge, 278–279
Love, Chasidism and, 74
Luria, Isaac, 69, 220

Maccabees, 91
Magnes, Judah L., 41
Maimonides, Moses, 12, 23, 25, 39,
    95, 134, 156, 222
Malamud, Bernard, 430
Marriage laws. *See also* Intermarriage;
    Law (Halachah)
  denominationalism and, 420–421
  Roth, Cecil on, 426–427
Marx, Karl, 177, 304
Marxism, 217, 264
Maupassant, Guy de, 194, 195
Mayer, Saly, 285, 290
McClelland, Roswell, 284, 290
Meir, Golda, 267, 457, 458–459
Mendel of Kotsk, 66
Mendelssohn, Moses, 90, 95
Mengele, Josef, 359
Menorah Society, 156
Mental illness
  defined, 111
  guilt and, 116
  psychiatric/religious views
      contrasted, 112–113
  psychiatry and, 110
Messianism
  Conservative Judaism and, 19

Messianism (*continued*)
  Jewish history and, 221
  Reform Judaism and, 18
  spirituality and, 138–139
  Wiesel, Elie on, 307
Middle Ages
  ghetto mentality and, 7
  Jewish populations in, 425
  proselytism and, 422
  rationalism and, 94–95
Minyan
  education and, 150
  Israel and, 403
Mishnah, literal tradition and, 92
Mitnagdim, 12
Mizrachi movement, 31
Modernity
  Catholicism and, 90
  critical times and, 90
Monotheism, Jewish history and,
  215–216, 221
Montessori Method, 151
Morais, Sabato, 15
Morality
  foreign policy and, 448–449
  psychiatric/religious views
    contrasted, 117–118
  social responsibility and, 134–137
Mordechai of Chernoble, 68
Morgenthau, Hans, 457–458
Morgenthau, Henry, 278, 281–283
Morse, Arthur, 271–293
Moses, 215, 219, 308
Moshavim, 163, 350
Moyne, Lord, 285
Muhammed (prophet), 364
Music, Reform Judaism and, 17
Musmanno, Michael A., 233–248
Mussolini, Benito, 279
Mystery, Steinsaltz, Adin on, 54

Nachman of Bratzlav, 70
National ancestry, group
  identification and, 8
National Council of Churches, 357
Nationalism
  critical times and, 90

dangers of, 171
Israel and, 223–224
patriotism and, 132–134
Reconstructionism and, 43–44
Reform Judaism and, 18
separatism/assimilation issue and,
  173–174
Steinsaltz, Adin on, 55–56
violence and, 172
Nazi and Nazi Collaborators Law
  (Israel), 235
Nazism. *See also* Germany
  Jewish persecution and, 243
  Jewish resistance and, 251–252,
    253–254, 398
  modern Jewish youth and, 396–
    397
  revivalism and, 8
  United States reaction to, 279
  War Crimes Commission and, 276
Neo-Chasidism, described, 78. *See also*
  Chasidism
Neo-Fascism
  Begin, Menachem on, 357–358
  dangers of, 292
Neo-Nazism
  anti-Semitism and, 229–230
  Kissinger, Henry on, 446–447
  Wiesel, Elie on, 297–298
Neo-Orthodox Judaism. *See also*
  Denominationalism; Orthodox
  Judaism
  Conservative Judaism and, 35–36
  future of, 472–473
  Orthodox Judaism distinguished
    from, 92–93
  Reconstructionist views of, 37
  Reform Judaism and, 35
Netherlands, Jewish resistance, 267
Neturei Karta, Israel and, 159, 160
Neurosis
  concept introduced, 110
  defined, 111–112
  religion as, 120–121
Neusner, Jacob, 101
New School (New York City), 148
Nigeria, 292

Nobel Prize in Literature, 189
Nonconformism, Jewish survival and, 175–177
Nuclear armaments
  psychiatry, 124–126
  United States/Soviet Union and, 454–455
Nuremberg Trials, 235, 243–247

Obedience, Holocaust and, 245–246
Obsessional neurosis, religion as, 120–121
Oil embargo
  Kissinger, Henry on, 446, 453
  Yom Kippur War and, 391
OPEC, oil embargo of, 446
Optimism/pessimism continuum
  Jewish survival and, 169–170
  Kissinger, Henry on, 459–460
  Sharon, Ariel on, 389–390
  Wiesel, Elie on, 313–314
Oral tradition, written tradition and, 91
Orthodox Judaism. *See also* Denominationalism
  challenges facing, 24–25
  Conservative Judaism and, 15, 16
  cultural pluralism and, 153–154
  Halachah (law) and, 20–21
  historical précis of, 9–10
  Israel and, 56–57, 162–163, 223, 404–407
  Jewish education and, 24–25
  literal tradition and, 92–93
  predictions for, 472–473
  Reform Judaism and, 17
  resurgence of, 3–4
  Sanhedrin reconstitution and, 22–23
  social status and, 8
Ostow, Mortimer, 109–127
Oxford University, 419, 434

Paganism, monotheism and, 216
Pakarski, Moshe, 75
Palestine
  Hellinistic influences and, 91
  Israel's creation and, 332
  Jewish resistance and, 252–253, 255
Palestine Liberation Organization (P.L.O.), 332, 450, 452
  Begin, Menachem on, 347
  Jerusalem and, 365–367
  Kissinger, Henry on, 446
  United States and, 442, 450, 452
Palestinian Arabs, Wiesel, Elie on, 309–310. *See also* Arabs; Islam
Paradox, religion and, 87–88
Patriotism
  celebration and, 132–134
  radical reformers and, 15
  social responsibility and, 134–137
Paul, Randolph, 283
Pehle, John, 283
Pell, Herbert C., 276
People
  identificational confusion among, 41–42, 105–106
  Reconstructionism and, 34
  Reform Judaism and, 19
Peretz, Isaac L., 199
Persecution, Jewish history and, 248
Persian civilization, 214
Personal encounter, Steinsaltz, Adin on, 53
Pessimism. *See* Optimism/pessimism continuum
Pharisees, 12
Philo, 12, 94, 96–97, 156
Phylacteries, allegorism and, 96
Pinsky, David, 192
Pittsburgh Platform (1885), 15, 93
Pius XII (pope), 274–275
Plato, 12, 95, 97
Platonism, 95, 97
Pluralism, 147–165
  Conservative Judaism and, 25
  cultural pluralism definition, 151–154
  Hebraism definition and, 154–157
  Israeli religious freedom and, 162–163

Pluralism (*continued*)
  Jewish life and, 161–162
  pragmatism and, 149–150
  Reform Judaism and, 11, 21–22
  teaching and, 148
Podhoretz, Norman, 333
Pogroms, United States reaction to, 273
Poland, 254. *See also* Warsaw Ghetto
Politics
  Argentina, 181
  Brandeis, Louis D. and, 149
  conformism and, 177–178
  education and, 151
  Israeli, 352, 386–387
  Israeli religious freedom and, 162–163
  Jewish history and, 216
  presidential qualities, 443–444
  psychiatry and, 124–126
  terrorism and, 346
  United States decision-making process, 444–446
  United States indifference and, 280–281, 287–288
  United States–Iranian relations and, 441
  War Crimes Commission and, 276
  World War II and, 257–258
Pompidou, Georges, 303
Positive historical school, Frankel, Zechariah and, 7
Poverty, spirituality and, 138–139
Pragmatism, pluralism and, 149–150
Prayer, Reform Judaism and, 17
Prejudice. *See* Anti-Semitism; Ethnic prejudice
Presidency (United States)
  decision-making process and, 444–446
  Kissinger, Henry on, 443–444
  prediction for Jewish president, 481
Progressive education, Dewey, John and, 150–151
Progressivism, Orthodox Judaism and, 20

Prophecy, Talmud and, 465
Prophets, radical reformers and, 15
Proselytism, 489–507
  Christianity and, 495–496
  conversion requirements, 498–499
  future of, 473–474
  Jewish history and, 490–494
  Jewish law and, 497–498
  judgments and, 506–507
  Reform Judaism and, 494–495
  Roth, Cecil on, 421–422
  sincerity and, 494, 505–506
  statistics on, 496–497
  Steinsaltz, Adin on, 58–59
  superiority issue in, 500–501
  Talmud and, 501–503
Psychiatry, 109–127
  communal confession concept and, 115–116
  definitions in, 111–112
  guilt and, 113–114
  guilt treatment and, 116–117
  individual/social distinction and, 121–122
  morality and, 117–118
  political power and, 124–126
  psychoanalysis in field of, 109–111
  rationality and, 122–123
  religion as obsessional neurosis, 120–121
  religious education and, 123–124
  religious view of mental health contrasted, 112–113
  ritual and, 119
Psychoanalysis, psychiatry and, 109–111
Psychosis, 111–113

Qaddafi, Muammar al-, 303
Quakers, 290

Racism, Zionism and, 301–302
Raddock, Charles, 73
Radical reform
  Conservative Judaism and, 15
  tradition and, 93
Raeder, Erich, 244

Rationalism
  dangers of, 95–96
  intellectualism and, 94–95
Rationality, psychiatry and, 122–123
Reagan, Ronald, 450, 451, 452–453
Reams, Robert Borden, 278, 279
Rebbe relationship
  in Chasidism, 69–72
  in Neo-Chasidism, 78
  youth and, 83
Reconstructionism, 29–46
  abstraction and, 38
  authenticity issue and, 38–39
  "chosen people" and, 42–43
  Conservative and Reform Judaism
    and, 24
  desegregation and, 39–42
  foundational issues in, 36–37
  hermeneutics and, 99–100
  humanism and, 43–44
  inner-directedness and, 31
  intellectualism and, 37–38
  Jewish education and, 33
  kashrut and, 44–45
  planning and, 34–36
  women and, 44
Reform Judaism. *See also*
  Denominationalism
  Baeck, Leo and, 420
  challenges facing, 23–24
  Chasidism and, 81–82
  Conservative Judaism and, 24
  cultural pluralism and, 153–154
  Enlightenment and, 35
  future of, 472–473, 475
  historical précis of, 11–14
  Israel and, 56–57, 163, 404–407
  law and, 19
  origins of, 3, 7
  proselytism and, 494–495, 496–497
  Reconstructionist views of, 36–37
  ritual and, 17–18
  Sanhedrin reconstitution and, 21–
    22
  social status and, 8
Reform Pittsburgh Platform of 1885,
  15, 93

Reines, Yitzhak, 31
Religion
  critical times and, 89
  group identification and, 8
  guilt and, 114–115
  individual/social distinction and,
    121–122
  Israel and, 223, 402–407
  paradox and, 87–88
  psychiatry and, 109–127. *See also*
    Psychiatry
  rationalism and, 95–96
  Reform Judaism and, 12
  therapy contrasted, 115–116
Religious education, psychiatry and,
  123–124. *See also* Jewish
  education
Renaissance, rationalism and, 95
Resistance. *See* Jewish resistance
Responsa, Reform Judaism and, 16, 18
Revelation, Reform Judaism and, 19
Revivalism, United States, 8
Revolution, conformism and, 177
Reynolds, Robert, 280
Ribbentrop, Joachim von, 244
Richter, Conrad, 201
Riencourt, Amaury de, 219
Riesman, David, 31
Ringelblum, Emanuel, 262, 263–264
Ritual
  Judaists and, 159
  psychiatry and, 119
  Reform Judaism and, 12, 13, 17, 18
Rockefeller, Nelson, 458
Role models, family and, 141–143
Rome
  anti-Semitism and, 212
  Jewish history and, 221
  proselytism and, 422
Roncalli, Angelo, 274–275
Roosevelt, Eleanor, 277, 280–281
Roosevelt, Franklin D., 257, 276,
  278, 279, 280–281, 283, 287, 291
Roosevelt, Theodore, 273
Rosen, Ben, 158
Roth, Cecil, 419–435
Roth, Henry, 192

Rubenstein, Richard, 324–325, 329
Rublee, George, 286
Ruchel, Chanah, 73
Rumania, 282, 284
Russell, Bertrand, 183
Russia. *See* Soviet Jewry; Soviet
    Union
Russia (Czarist)
    proselytism and, 422
    terrorism and, 346
    United States and, 273

Sabbath. *See Shabbat* (Sabbath)
Sadat, Anwar el-, 354, 368, 371–372,
    391, 451
Sadducees, 12, 91
SALT talks, Kissinger, Henry on,
    454–455
Salvation, Reconstructionism and,
    43–44
Samuel, Maurice, 199, 203, 430
Sanhedrin reconstitution
    Israel and, 21–23, 145–146, 408
    Orthodox Judaism and, 22–23
    Reform Judaism and, 21–22
Sanity, cults and, 53
Sapir, Pinchas, 352
Sartre, Jean-Paul, 222
Saudi Arabia, Jerusalem and, 371
Schacht, Hjalmar, 286, 287
Schachter-Shalomi, Zalman, 65–84.
    See also Chasidism
Schechter, Solomon, 15, 16, 17, 37
Schmidt, Helmut, 299
Scholarship. *See* Intellectualism
Scholem, Gershom, 324
Schwarzenberg (prince of Austria),
    290
Second Temple, written tradition
    and, 91
Secularist movement, in Israel, 404–
    407
Segregation, Jewish culture and, 34
Self-fulfillment, Reconstructionism
    and, 43–44
Senesh, Hannah, 252, 256–257
Sensation, values and, 140–141

Separatism. *See also* Assimilation;
    Integration
    Jewish survival and, 173–175
    Soviet Union and, 183
Sermon
    Conservative Judaism and, 17
    Orthodox Judaism and, 17
    Reform Judaism and, 17–18
Servatius, Robert, 243
Settlements issue, Steinsaltz, Adin
    on, 56
Sexuality, God and, 216
S'forim, Mendele Mocher, 199
Shabbat (Sabbath)
    in Canada, 408–409
    Chasidism and, 75
    in Israel, 406, 407
    meaning of, 132
    Orthodox Judaism and, 21
    Reform Judaism and, 19, 20
    in United States, 406, 407, 408
Shah of Iran, Kissinger, Henry on,
    441
Sharett, Moshe, 285
Sharon, Ariel, 381–392
Shaw, Irwin, 430
Sherman, C. Bezalel, 465–486
Shevirat ha-keilim, Jewish history and,
    221–223
Shulchan Aruch, literal tradition and, 92
Siebert, Willi, 245
Silver, Abba Hillel, 18
Sin, guilt and, 114
Singer, Isaac Bashevis, 189–204, 430
Singer, Israel J., 197–199
Six-Day War (1967), 311, 320, 352
Slavery, cultural pluralism and, 156
Social conditions, Reconstructionism
    and, 44
Social responsibility, patriotism and,
    134–137
Social status, Jewish group
    identification and, 8
Society
    cultural pluralism and, 151–154
    psychiatry/religion contrasted,
    121–122

Song, Chasidism and, 76-77
Soul, Chasidism and, 81
Soviet Jewry, 172
  Begin, Menachem on, 353-357
  emigration and, 184
  future of, 474-475
  Israel and, 307
  Jewish survival and, 181-184
  United Jewish Appeal and, 479
  Wiesel, Elie on, 303-307
Soviet Union. *See also* Russia (Czarist)
  human rights and, 447
  Jewish resistance and, 254-255
  Kissinger, Henry on, 460
  Middle Eastern relations and, 441-
    442
  military adventures of, 455-457
  United States and, 454-455
  United States compared, 400-401
  World War II and, 257-258, 285
Spain, Jews expelled from, 324
Spanish Inquisition, 307
Spengler, Oswald, 218, 219, 225
Sperber, Manes, 304
Spiegel, Sholom, 114
Spirituality
  omnipresence of, 138-139
  Steinsaltz, Adin on, 54
Stalin, Joseph, 182
Steinberg, Milton, 319
Steinheim, Salomon, 95
Steinsaltz, Adin, 49-61
  biography of, 50-51, 52
  on boringness, 54-55
  contributions of, 49-50
  on cults, 53
  on Israeli religious life, 56-57
  on kosher-centered Judaism, 57-58
  on nationalism, 55-56
  on personal encounter, 53
  on proselytism, 58-59
  on settlements issue, 56
  Shefa Institute and, 51-52
  on spirituality, 54
  Talmud and, 51, 55
  on women, 58
  on youth, 52-53, 59-60

Stephen Wise Free Synagogue (New
    York City), 9
Sterility, rationalism and, 95
Streicher, Julius, 358
Strochlitz, Sigmund, 309
Stubbornness, Jewish survival and,
    175-177
Sullivan, William, 442
Sumerian-Akkadian civilizations,
    214
Supernaturalism, Reconstructionism
    and, 42-43
Survival. *See* Human survival; Jewish
    survival
Sweden, efforts of, in World War II,
    290-291
Symbolism
  cultural pluralism and, 154
  psychiatry and, 119
Synagogue
  adult education and, 428
  Reconstructionism and, 44
  role in Diaspora, 402-404
  role in Israel, 402-404
Syrkin, Marie, 251-267
Syrkin, Nachman, 251

Talmud
  Hebrew and, 33
  literal tradition and, 92
  Orthodox Judaism and, 10
  prophecy and, 465
  proselytism and, 491, 501-503
  radical reformers and, 15
  Reform Judaism and, 11, 14
  Steinsaltz, Adin and, 51, 55. *See also*
    Steinsaltz, Adin
Taylor, Myron, 274
Teaching
  Kallen, Horace M. on, 148
  pluralism and, 148
Tel Aviv, population of, 403-404
Temple Mount, Arabs and, 365
Terrorism, Begin, Menachem on,
    345-347
Thalberg, Irving, 494
Theology, Chasidism and, 81

Therapy, religion contrasted, 115–
116
Tikkun, Jewish history and, 221–223
Time, sacred/profane, 131–132
Torah
  Conservative Judaism and, 14, 16
  Jewish history and, 215, 216, 222
  Orthodox Judaism and, 9–10, 20
  Reconstructionism and, 44
  Reform Judaism and, 13–14
  Sanhedrin reconstitution and, 22
Toynbee, Arnold, 174, 213, 218–219,
  303–305, 329
Tradition
  allegorism and, 96–98
  Conservative Judaism and, 14, 16
  hermeneutics and, 98–100
  Orthodox Judaism and, 21
  radical reform and, 93
  remembrance and, 319
Trifa, Valerian, 357
Truman, Harry S., 235, 292–293
Tunisia, 172
Turkey, Armenians and, 273
Tzadikim role, Chasidism and,
  68–69
Tzimtzum, Jewish history and, 221–
223

Union Theological Seminary, 79
Uniqueness, Jewish survival and,
  175–177
United Jewish Appeal, future
  predictions for, 478–479
United Kingdom
  Begin, Menachem on, 344
  Brand, Joel imprisoned by, 284
  Eichmann, Adolf and, 237
  Grand Mufti and, 366
  Irgun and, 346
  Jewish leadership in, 432
  Middle Eastern relations and, 441
  neo-fascism in, 357
  United States compared, 400
  War Crimes Commission and,
  275–276
  World War II and, 286–287, 443

United Nations
  Altalena incident and, 350
  anti-Semitism and, 329
  Eichmann, Adolf and, 237
  future predictions for, 485–486
  Israeli establishment and, 332
  Wiesel, Elie on, 301–302
United Nations Genocide
  Convention, 292–293
United States
  adult education in, 428
  Conservative Judaism and, 15
  day school movement in, 429
  decision-making process in, 444–
  446
  division of Jewish philosophy and,
  9
  Eichmann, Adolf and, 237
  ethnic prejudice in, 234–235
  future of, 465–472
  future of anti-Semitism in, 481–
  482
  future of politics in, 484
  future of religious revival in, 482–
  483
  human rights policy and, 447–448
  indifference of, during Holocaust,
  273–274, 275, 277–293
  intermarriage and, 426–427, 497
  Iran and, 440–443
  Israel and, 302–303, 310–311, 382,
  387–388, 449–450
  Jewish education in, 427–428
  Jewish history and, 396
  Jewish immigration and, 264–265,
  273, 277, 281, 288–290
  Jewish leadership in, 431–432
  Jewish literature and, 430–431
  Jewish populations in, 429
  Jewish president prediction, 481
  Jewish resistance and, 255–256
  Jewish survival and, 424–426, 476–
  477
  Kissinger, Henry on, 460–461
  Middle Eastern foreign policy of,
  450–452
  moral foreign policy and, 448–449

neo-Nazism in, 230, 298, 357
Orthodox Judaism and, 20–21
Palestine Liberation Organization
    (P.L.O.) and, 450, 452
presidential qualities and, 443–444
radical reformers and, 15–16
Reagan policies and, 452–453
religious revival in, 8, 429
Sabbath in, 406, 407, 408
Soviet Jewry and, 305–307
Soviet military adventures and,
    455–457
Soviet Union and, 454–455
unique conditions of, 400–402
unity in, 432
Wiesel, Elie on, 310–311
United States Constitution,
    hermeneutics and, 99
Unity, Reform Judaism and, 11
Universalism, Reform Judaism and,
    18
Universal Jewish Encyclopedia, 433
Uris, Leon, 191
Utopian idealism, Reform Judaism
    and, 18

Values, sensation and, 140–141
Vatican, indifference of, 274–275
Victoria (queen of England), 435
Violence, nationalism and, 172
Vishinsky, Andrei, 285

Waldheim, Kurt, 229, 370
Wallenberg, Raoul, 290–291
War Crimes Commission, United
    States and, 275–277
War Refugee Board
    actions of, 283–284
    German negotiations and, 285
    work of, 288
Warsaw Ghetto, 230, 254, 260–266,
    323, 334
Weisgal, Meyer, 376
Weizmann, Chaim, 376
Welles, Sumner, 275, 281
Wendell, Barrett, 155
Wiesel, Elie, 297–315

Winterton, Lord, 287
Wise, Stephen Samuel, 18, 275
Wislitzeni, Willy von, 258
Women
    Chasidism and, 72–73, 76
    Jewish literature and, 190–191
    proselytism and, 496–497, 503–504
    Reconstructionism and, 44
    Reform Judaism and, 13–14
    Steinsaltz, Adin on, 58
World Jewish Congress, 169
World Union of the United
    Synagogue, 406
World War I, 149
World War II, 257–258. *See also*
    Holocaust; Nazism
World Zionist Organization, 169
Wouk, Herman, 430
Written tradition. *See* Literalism

Yad Mordecai, Kibbutz, 334
Yeshiva University (N.Y.C.), 32
Yeshivot, Steinsaltz, Adin on, 59–60
Yiddish language
    Chasidism and, 79
    Israel and, 202–203
    Jewish literature and, 198–202
    predictions on future survival of,
        480
    translation and, 203–204
    youth and, 201–202
Yom Kippur, guilt and, 115
Yom Kippur War (1973)
    immigration and, 354
    Sharon, Ariel on, 383–384, 390
    Wiesel, Elie on, 307–309, 311
Yordim, Sharon, Ariel on, 382–384
Youth. *See also* Jewish education
    Chasidism and, 80, 81–83
    intellectualism and, 100–102
    Israel and, 384–385, 395–402
    Orthodox Judaism and, 3–4
    proselytism and, 503–504
    Roth, Cecil on, 427–428
    Sharon, Ariel on, 384–385
    Steinsaltz, Adin on, 52–53, 59–60
    Yiddish and, 201–202

Zangwill, Israel, 430–431
Zionism
  Altalena incident and, 347–352
  anti-Zionism as anti-Semitism, 329
  Brandeis, Louis D. and, 149
  future in United States, 479
  Jewish resistance and, 256
  Jewish survival and, 345
  Kallen, Horace M. and, 147
  law and, 23

  Neo-Orthodox Judaism and, 37
  partition and, 171–172
  radical reformers and, 15
  Reconstructionist view of, 40
  Reform Judaism and, 18
  Sharon, Ariel on, 386, 388
  United Nations and, 301–302
Zohar, Creation and, 98
Zunz, Leopold, 18

About the Editor

Rabbi William Berkowitz is a leading member of the American rabbinate and of the New York Jewish community. Concerned with adult Jewish education as a major aspect of his calling, he designed the Dialogue Forum Series in 1951, which has been the model for similar adult programs throughout the world.

A graduate of the Jewish Theological Seminary, Rabbi Berkowitz was President of the New York Board of Rabbis. He has been National President of B'nai Zion, National President of the Jewish National Fund, Member of the Presidium of Histadrut Ivrit, and President of the American Jewish Heritage Committee. He has also served on numerous national and international agencies.

Rabbi Berkowitz received the honorary degree of D.H.L. from Spertus College of Judaica in Chicago for his contributions to the field of adult education in the Jewish community. He is the author of six books, including *I Believe—The Faith of a Jew* and *Let Us Reason Together*, as well as many monographs and articles.

Photo Credits

p. 28   John H. Popper

p. 48   Gary Eisenberg

p. 86   Robert C. Frampton

p. 108 Fred Marcus

p. 130 Diana Bryant

p. 270 Ann Zane Shanks

p. 296 Philippe Halsman

p. 380 Alexander Archer

p. 438 Bern Schwartz

p. 488 Godfrey Argent